SPOKEN LIKE A WOMAN

SPOKEN LIKE A WOMAN

SPEECH AND GENDER IN ATHENIAN DRAMA

Laura McClure

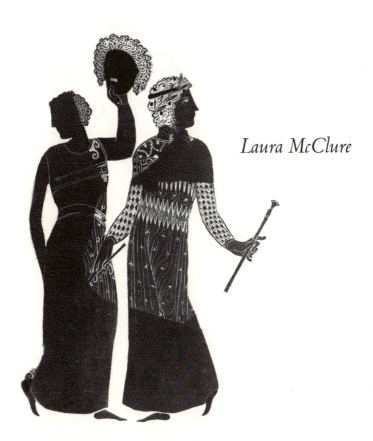

PRINCETON UNIVERSITY PRESS · PRINCETON, NEW JERSEY

Copyright © 1999 by Princeton University Press
Published by Princeton University Press, 41 William Street, Princeton, New Jersey 08540
In the United Kingdom: Princeton University Press, Chichester, West Sussex

McClure, Laura, 1959–
Spoken like a woman : speech and gender in Athenian drama / Laura McClure.
p. cm.
Includes bibliographical references and index.
ISBN 0-691-01730-1 (cloth : alk. paper)
1. Greek drama—History and criticism.   2. Women and literature—Greece—
Athens—History.   3. Greek language—Sex differences.
4. Gender identity in literature.   5. Greek language—Spoken Greek.
6. Sex role in literature.   7. Speech in literature.   I. Title.
PA3136.M39   1999
882′.0109352042—dc21   98-55157 CIP

This book has been composed in Galliard

The paper used in this publication meets the minimum requirements of ANSI/NISO
Z39.48-1992 (R1997) (*Permanence of Paper*)

http://pup.princeton.edu

Printed in the United States of America

10 9 8 7 6 5 4 3 2 1

For Richard

CONIUGI OPTIMO

CONTENTS

ACKNOWLEDGMENTS

I AM GRATEFUL to the following individuals for offering to read part or all of this book: Helene Foley, Laura Slatkin, Seth Schein, Charles Segal, Lillian Doherty, Christopher Faraone, Edith Hall, Barbara Goff, and André Lardinois. I have profited immensely from their considerable knowledge and generous help; to them can be attributed all that is good in this book. Thanks are also owed to my colleagues, past and present, especially Denis Feeney for his support in the early stages; Patricia Rosenmeyer for her detailed reading of the entire manuscript; Jim McKeown for his impeccable philological skills; and Nick Cahill for help with the cover illustration. Norma Maynard in the Classics Department office at the University of Wisconsin–Madison deserves recognition for providing much-needed humor and wisdom, as well as more tangible forms of support, over the last few years. The Graduate School at the University of Wisconsin–Madison furnished very generous financial support for this project over the course of several summers. Thanks also to my indefatigable research assistant, Holly Sypniewski, for saving me from more than one mistake, and to Sherry Wert, my Princeton copyeditor, for her careful preparation of the final manuscript.

Thanks are owed to my parents, Charles McClure and Miriam Selby, for their love and support, and to my children, Nikolas and Jakob Heinemann, for growing into such wonderful boys even as this book was being completed; their lively presence has continually given me a fresh perspective. I would also like to acknowledge their child-care providers, Ruth Harding Weaver, Darann Morgan, and Denise Mirkin; without their work, my own work would not have been possible. Finally, I owe more than I can say to my husband, Richard Heinemann, who has humored and believed in me—and read all my work—from the early years of graduate school to the final stages of this book.

NOTE ON ABBREVIATIONS

NAMES OF AUTHORS and titles of texts are abbreviated in accordance with the list in *The Oxford Classical Dictionary*, 3d ed. (1996), pp. xxix–liv. Greek and Latin citations refer to the Oxford Classical Texts unless otherwise specified; passages from elegiac and iambic verse are taken from M. L. West, *Iambi et Elegi Graeci* (= *IEG*). All translations are my own except those attributed to others.

NOTE ON ABBREVIATIONS

NAMES OF AUTHORS and titles of texts are abbreviated in accordance with the list in *The Oxford Classical Dictionary*, 3d ed. (1996), pp. xxix–liv. Greek and Latin citations refer to the Oxford Classical Texts unless otherwise specified; passages from elegiac and iambic verse are taken from M. L. West, *Iambi et Elegi Graeci* (= *IEG*). All translations are my own except those attributed to others.

SPOKEN LIKE A WOMAN

Chapter One

THE CITY OF WORDS: SPEECH
IN THE ATHENIAN POLIS

I N A HIGHLY metatheatrical moment from Aristophanes' *Thesmopho-riazusae*, the tragic poet Euripides instructs his kinsman to disguise himself as a woman in order to spy on the female participants of the Thesmophoria, a women-only religious festival, in which the poet is to be put on trial for slandering women. The Relative equips himself with a prostitute's yellow gown and a woman's veil, breast-band, and slippers, and even submits to shaving and the female practice of pubic depilation. After completing his physical transformation, he is instructed to speak like a woman: "When you talk, see to it that you speak cleverly and persuasively like a real woman" (267–68). But in Aristophanes' play, speaking like a woman entails several adjustments, many of which are grammatical, since the ancient Greek language marks the gender of the speaker more strongly than English. And yet as the play progresses, the Relative repeatedly under-cuts his feminine self-presentation with his masculine use of obscenity. The incongruity of gender and genres denoted by the Relative's continual shifting from masculine to feminine speech not only makes for good com-edy, it also affords insight into the role of speech in constructing dramatic characters on the fifth-century Athenian stage.

The Relative's performance reminds us that female parts were played by male actors who rendered plausible impersonations of women primarily through their speech and gestures, and that there was a set of speaking conventions for portraying women that may or may not have corresponded to the practices of actual spoken language in ancient Greece. These conven-tions were flexible and could be freely deployed by the poet for dramatic effect. In the *Agamemnon*, for example, Clytemnestra is repeatedly charac-terized as speaking like a man, while Blepyrus, in a moment of comic pathos, calls upon a quintessentially feminine deity, Eileithyia, as he strives for a birth of quite another sort in Aristophanes' *Ecclesiazusae*. Although of central importance in constructing character, speaking conventions in classical drama also have a broader social and political significance, par-ticularly given the role of free speech (*parrhēsia*) in the Athenian democ-racy. The aims of this book are to identify the verbal genres associated with men and women in the ancient Greek literary tradition, especially in fifth-century drama; to explore their contexts; and to consider how a few plays deploy male and female discursive practices as a vehicle for exploring the function and status of the speech of adult citizen males in the democratic *polis* ("city-state") during the second half of the fifth century B.C.E.

The importance of gender for understanding political identity and symbolic structures in ancient Greece, what Vernant has termed the "mental world" of the Greeks, has already been elucidated by many classical scholars.[1] Whereas the earliest scholarship on women in antiquity focused on the status of women and the *realia* of their lives,[2] the awareness that male-authored texts always mediate ancient views of gender and that the experience of ancient women could not thus be fully recovered compelled many feminist classical scholars to consider the conceptual foundations that inform the literary and mythical representation of women and how they intersect with social and political institutions. Central to this project has been the study of women and gender in Attic drama, a genre that offers a rich array of complex female characters. Two important essays in the early 1980s can be said to have inaugurated this study: Foley's "The Concept of Women in Athenian Drama," and Zeitlin's "Playing the Other: Theater, Theatricality, and the Feminine in Greek Drama."[3] Both pieces shifted the focus from recovering women's historical reality to understanding the conceptual framework behind their literary and mythic representation and relating it to the social and ideological context of democratic Athens.

At the same time, the increased attention to dramatic performance as a social institution, initiated by Goldhill's essay on the City Dionysia, along with the structuralist and anthropological readings of the French school, including scholars such as Vernant, Vidal-Naquet, Detienne, and Loraux, have radically altered how contemporary critics think about the meanings and functions of fifth-century Athenian drama. For these critics, Attic drama continually engaged in a dialogue with the other discursive spaces of the city.[4] In addition, the work of Foucault, whose *History of Sexuality* is based in part on Dover's research on homosexuality in ancient Greece, has had a major impact on the study of women in antiquity, shifting the focus away from women exclusively to the idea of gender as a vehicle for negotiating power.[5] The concept of gender as a social category that deter-

---

[1] Vernant 1988: 30.

[2] Blok 1987 provides a very useful historiographic survey of the study of women in antiquity.

[3] Foley 1981b; Zeitlin 1985a (= 1996: 341–74).

[4] An important collection of essays edited by Winkler and Zeitlin in 1990 heralded the new focus in the United States on the social context of Greek drama and was strongly influenced by the earlier work of Vernant, especially his 1972 volume, *Mythe et tragédie en Grèce ancienne* (Vernant and Vidal-Naquet 1972).

[5] Foucault (1988, originally published in French in 1979) bases the second part of his *History of Sexuality*, the volume that focuses on classical antiquity, on the work of Dover

mines how power is distributed among various members of society further illuminates the link between literary representation and social institutions.

The privileging of speech as the sign of citizen status and the concomitant strictures placed on women's nonreligious public speech in democratic Athens, on the one hand, and the presence of a complex array of speaking female characters in Attic drama, on the other, suggest a dialectical relation between the two discursive spheres. Because adult male citizens were the exclusive possessors of political power in the classical polis, fifth-century Athenian drama, produced by men and for men, may be regarded, in the words of Case, "as allies in the project of suppressing real women and replacing them with masks of patriarchal production."[6] In the same way, literary representations of women may be viewed as male constructs appropriated by men for the purpose of speaking about male concerns rather than as simple reflections of social reality, as Zeitlin, Halperin, and others have argued.[7] Thus the constructed women of Attic drama may serve as figures of substitution that convey social and political issues important to men, particularly the complicated problem of speech and its status in the democratic polis. As Halperin observes, "Greek men effectively silenced women by speaking for them on those occasions when men chose to address significant words to one another in public, and they required the silence of women in public in order to be able to employ this mode of displaced speech—in order to impersonate women—without impediment."[8] But Attic drama should not be understood simply as a univocal, hegemonic discourse in service of civic ideology; it is a complex, polyvocal, and polysemous genre that alternately subverts and reinforces the dominant agenda. Even social and legal discourses, genres traditionally considered less ambiguous and more reflective of social reality than drama, do not adequately describe the conflict, anxiety, and ambivalence that normally characterize the regulation of social norms, in Athens as elsewhere.[9]

Recent scholarship on the representation of women in fifth-century Athenian drama has tended to be more optimistic and, not coincidentally, more sympathetic to the possibility that citizen women actually attended the dramatic festivals.[10] This strand of scholarship has suggested that the

---

(1989, originally published in 1978). Richlin's 1991 critique notwithstanding, I agree with Foxhall and others that Foucault's general analysis of power and its transmission through discursive practices is an invaluable tool for feminist classicists and nonclassicists alike; see also Cohen 1992; Foxhall 1994; Skinner 1996.

[6] Case 1985: 7.

[7] Zeitlin 1985a (= 1996: 341–74); Padel 1983; Foley 1988a: 1301–2; Halperin 1990b. Most recently, Stehle 1997 discusses how archaic lyric poetry deploys female voices to convey a male political idea.

[8] Halperin 1990b: 290.

[9] Cohen 1991: 170.

[10] Recent scholarship on Greek drama has tended to assume that women attended the city Dionysia, e.g., Winkler 1990b: 39n.58; Csapo and Slater 1995: 286–87; Henderson 1996:

fictive unreality of Athenian drama embodies and extends the democratic ideal to all individuals through its dialogic form. The diversity and complexity of female roles displayed in Attic drama, as well as those of slaves and barbarians, disclose "an implicit egalitarian vision whose implementation in the actual society which produced it was absolutely inconceivable."[11] The affiliation between drama and democracy as an art form is exemplified, although not very positively, by the character of Euripides in Aristophanes' *Frogs*, who describes his tragedy as *dēmokratikon*, "democratic," because it allows all types of individuals to speak—the matron, the slave, the master, the maiden, and the aging widow (Ar. *Ran.* 949–52). Echoing Euripides' character, Henderson has similarly argued that the tragic and comic stage brought the concerns of Athenian women out of the house, providing "a vicarious public voice for the one class of citizens otherwise debarred from public expression, thus (in good Dionysiac fashion) exposing the artificiality of, and in effect inverting, the public and 'official' pattern of authority."[12] Given the preponderance of negative opinions voiced about women in the plays and their generally unflattering portrayal, it is hard to see tragic and comic plays as exemplars either of social realism or of "art's 'utopian tendency.' "[13] Whereas some plays may represent women as speaking positively and authoritatively on behalf of the city or family, like Iphigeneia in Euripides' *Iphigeneia in Aulis*, or Aethra in *Suppliants*, Attic drama more commonly depicts women's speech, even when it takes a ritual form, as disruptive and subversive of social stability. Nonetheless, the very presence of women in tragic drama (and it is noteworthy that only one extant tragedy, Sophocles' *Philoctetes*, contains no female characters), and to a lesser extent, comedy, indicates how necessary was the part they played in the democratic equation, since through them male identity and social hierarchy was negotiated.

This book considers how Attic drama represents the speech of women and seeks to understand its social and political function across genres and

---

16. Goldhill 1994 and 1997a: 62–66 offer a refreshing reassessment of this trend. Drawing parallels between the discursive space of the theater and other political arenas from which women were excluded, like the law courts and the Assembly, Goldhill concludes that women most likely did not attend the dramatic festivals. The fact that this question cannot now be securely answered provides a major stumbling block for our understanding of the representation of women in Attic drama. But I do think we can safely assume that the poets at the very least addressed themselves to a "notional audience of men"; for this view, see Henderson 1991b. For further discussion, see Ehrenberg 1951: 27n.2; Dover 1972: 16–17; Podlecki 1990; Pickard-Cambridge 1991: 263–264.

[11] Hall 1997: 125.

[12] Henderson 1996: 26–28, esp. 27. It is tempting to see in this debate between optimists and pessimists the age-old quarrel originating in Aristophanes about whether Euripides was a feminist or a misogynist.

[13] Hall 1997: 125.

from the perspective of multiple authors.[14] The verbal genres associated with women in the Greek literary tradition have been largely neglected by scholars, with the notable exception of ritual lamentation, a type of speech strongly identified with women throughout ancient Greek civilization. Much of this research has posited that the restrictions placed on women's ritual lamentation, beginning in the early sixth century B.C.E., reflect a growing concern on the part of the polis with regulating women's voices, even their religious utterance, a genre traditionally considered integral to the well-being of the community.[15] Loraux argues that this suppression culminates in the rise of the *epitaphios*, the collective funeral oration composed and delivered by men in a civic context in celebration of military and political values. This type of speech supplants and erases the more traditional laments sung by women at the tomb from the earliest times.[16] As the prerogative of public speech became the tangible symbol of citizen status in democratic Athens, it appears that women's voices became increasingly excluded from public life.

This book focuses on five plays that involve a similar strategy of containment—Aeschylus' *Agamemnon*, Euripides' *Hippolytus* and *Andromache*, and Aristophanes' *Thesmophoriazusae* and *Ecclesiazusae*. These plays show how women's uncontrolled speech disrupts the male-governed household and city unless it is suppressed or transmuted into a ritual form. This feminine verbal license works in tandem with a common plot type in tragedy in which the male head-of-household or husband is temporarily or permanently away from the home, thus leaving the women to their own devices; in the case of the comedies, however, the freedom to speak is sanctioned by a ritual context in which the women gather alone, away from their husbands. The freedom entailed by the absence of men leads to verbal transgression: in all these plays, the women show an unusual rhetorical proficiency normally associated with men and the tangible sign of their power in the polis.

Produced in the changing political environment of Athens in the years spanning 458–392 B.C.E., these plays, through their speaking female characters, engage in a dialogue about the place and function of rhetorical and persuasive speech in the democracy. It is no coincidence, therefore, that

---

[14] Interest in speech and gender has been confined to a few important tragedies: for the *Oresteia*, see Goldhill 1984b; for Euripides' *Hippolytus*, see Zeitlin 1985b; Rabinowitz 1987; Goff 1990; Segal 1993; on female speech in Aristophanes generally, see Taaffe 1993. A handful of brief articles consider linguistic distinctions between male and female speakers in literary sources: see Gilleland 1980; Adams 1984; Bain 1984; McClure 1995; and Sommerstein 1995. For the association of women's speech with deception in archaic literature, see Bergren 1983.

[15] See especially Foley 1993; Loraux 1987; Holst-Warhaft 1992.

[16] Loraux 1986: 42–50.

the democratizing of Greek tragedy associated with Euripides in the *Frogs* corresponds to the increasingly important role played by rhetoric in the democratic polis. At the same time, Euripidean drama in the 420s increasingly deploys rhetorical structures, terms, and arguments, even in its portrayal of women. Aeschylus in the mid-fifth century set the stage for a kind of self-conscious, collective reflection on political discourse partly through the medium of Clytemnestra and Athena in his *Oresteia* trilogy; after the death of Pericles, interest in this issue intensified in the drama of Euripides and Aristophanes, some of whose female characters provide a metadiscourse on the problem of persuasion in the polis. Thus the plays not only illustrate the dangers entailed by the intrusion of women's voices into the public sphere, where male civic identity is consolidated through speech, but they also deploy the problematic speech of women as a means of conveying the complex issue of speech and rhetoric in the democratic polis. In order to understand more fully the political climate in which these plays were produced, it is necessary to consider the role of speech in constructing citizenship in the democratic polis during the period from 450–400 B.C.E., a time of intense political and social change in classical Athens.

SPEECH AND THE CONSTRUCTION OF CIVIC IDENTITY

Athens and the Athenians were famous in antiquity for their love of speech. Plato in the *Gorgias* has Socrates claim that Athens allows greater freedom of speech than any other city (Pl. *Grg.* 461e2), and Diodorus refers to the Athenians simply as *philologoi*, "lovers of speeches" (Diod. sic. 12.53.3). Speech in its many forms played a critical role in constructing civic identity in the democratic Athenian polis. To be a citizen was an act of speech, since to be a citizen meant to participate actively in the speech of the city, whether in the courts, the Council, the Assembly, or the agora.[17] In classical Athens, the right to speak in public was confined to adult citizen males; women, foreigners, and slaves were denied this privilege. Ober has stressed the importance of exclusivity as a means of coalescing political identity in the classical polis: as a group, the citizen body distinguished itself from the vast crowd of others, including foreigners, metics, women, and slaves, through its elite practices.[18] Although freedom of speech by the second half of the fifth century perhaps served as the defining feature of Athenian democracy, this privilege may have existed as early as the time of Cleisthenes. Though Cleisthenes' revolution in 508 extended power to the people by founding the *Boulē* (Council), in the early fifth century B.C.E. political power at Athens still remained in the hands of a few aristocratic

---

[17] Goldhill 1986: 66.
[18] Ober 1989: 5–6.

families who were represented by leaders such as Cimon.[19] Toward the middle of the fifth century, however, Ephialtes' democratic reforms began the process of eroding the boundary between aristocrats and the lower classes by stripping the Areopagus of its traditional powers, restricting its jurisdiction to intentional homicide cases, and redistributing the power of adjudication to the popular courts, the Assembly, and the Council. These reforms further guaranteed to all citizens the prerogative of *isēgoria*, "right of all citizens to speak on matters of state importance in the Assembly."[20] The rhetorical formula customary in the opening of the Assembly, "Who wishes to speak" (τίς ἀγορεύειν βούλεται), exemplifies the idea that such public political speech was open to all citizens.[21]

By the second half of the fifth century, the concept of *isēgoria* was expanded to include the more general idea of *parrhēsia*, a concept that stressed "the necessity and validity of individual freedom of thought," rather than simply a shared access to public speech.[22] After Pericles' reform of 451/50, which made citizenship possible only for a male born from an Attic mother as well as from a citizen father, Athenian women played a central, if indirect, role in legitimating *parrhēsia* in their male offspring.[23] Greek tragedies performed in the years following the reform echo this ideology. For example, Euripides' Ion flatly asserts that *parrhēsia* comes from the mother: "May the woman who bore me be Athenian, since free speech derives from the mother" (ἐκ τῶν Ἀθηνῶν μ' ἡ τεκοῦσ' εἴη γυνή, | ὥς μοι γένηται μητρόθεν παρρησία, Eur. *Ion* 671–72). Although a foreigner, Phaedra in the *Hippolytus* similarly emphasizes the role of the mother and her unsullied reputation in imparting political legitimacy to her sons: "But may my sons dwell as free men in the famous city of Athens, thriving by means of their free speech, held in high esteem because of their mother" (ἀλλ' ἐλεύθεροι | παρρησίᾳ θάλλοντες οἰκοῖεν πόλιν | κλεινῶν Ἀθηνῶν, μητρὸς οὕνεκ' εὐκλεεῖς, Eur. *Hipp.* 421–23). The right to speak publicly in classical Athens was so essential to political identity that one of the primary results of *atimia*, "loss of civic rights," was the denial of speech; thus Demosthenes describes how Meidias, in successfully disenfranchising Strato, prevented him from speaking in public.[24] From

---

[19] Until the time of Pericles, political disputes in Athens tended to consist of rivalries within traditional families, with small factions based on personal ties; see Sinclair 1988: 36.

[20] Ober 1989: 74. Although most scholars believe Ephialtes was responsible for *isēgoria*, Ostwald (1986: 203 and n. 17) argues that this principle may have been a feature of the Athenian polis as early as the time of Cleisthenes.

[21] For the standard formula for opening an Assembly debate, cf. Aesch. 1.27; Dem. 18.170; Ar. *Ach.* 45, *Thesm.* 379; and *Eccl.* 130; for a discussion of the formula, see Ober 1989: 296.

[22] Ober 1989: 296; see also Loraux 1986: 210–11; Momigliano 1971.

[23] The law actually states ἐξ ἀμφοῖν ἀστοῖν; see Arist. [*Ath. Pol.*] 26.4; see Loraux 1993: 119.

[24] Dem. 21.92–95.

Demosthenes and Aeschines we also learn that men who had prostituted themselves could not address the Assembly or enter temples.[25]

As a consequence of *isēgoria* and *parrhēsia*, the art of rhetoric became increasingly important for any citizen anxious to gain influence over his peers in the law courts and the Assembly. The principle of limited terms for offices and frequent rotation, combined with the increasing wealth amassed by Athens through the tributes of allied city-states and other interests, meant that more individuals were needed to fill these offices.[26] Several hundred officials served the Athenian government each year; in the case of the courts, a cohort of 500–1,000 men had to be recruited to serve as jurors for a single trial. Pericles, the famous Athenian statesman whom the citizens reelected to the office of general for fifteen consecutive terms, played a direct role in shaping the new political environment and making it accessible to more members of the polis. Although of an aristocratic background similar to that of Cimon, as the grand-nephew of Cleisthenes and a descendant of the Alcmeonids through his mother, Pericles saw the need to take the *dēmos* seriously, and he recognized the importance of rhetorical skill in persuading the masses.[27] Although the context is unclear, a comic fragment by Eupolis describes the enchanting effects of his persuasive eloquence: "A kind of *peithō* sat on his lips. That is how he, alone among the orators, bewitched and left a sting in the ears of his audience."[28] In order to recruit more jurors for the popular courts, Pericles introduced jury pay, a change that both expanded his political base and allowed a broader spectrum of the Athenian populace to participate. In the years that followed, officials received pay for administering the business of the polis; at the very end of the century, citizens were even compensated for attending the Assembly.[29]

Given the importance of the art of rhetoric for Pericles, it is not surprising to find that he seems to have played a critical role in facilitating the activities of the sophists at Athens and that he included in his circle the sophists Protagoras and Anaxagoras. Although the Athenians attached paramount

[25] *Dem.* 21.74; Arist. *Rhet.* 1378b29; Aesch. 1.46. See also Dover 1989: 104n.89; Winkler 1990a: 54–64; Halperin 1990a: 94–98; Cohen 1991: 73, 175–76; Hunter 1994: 104. As Halperin (1990a) observes, inviolability of one's body was the physical correlate of *parrhēsia* in the democratic polis.

[26] Sinclair (1988: 9–11) attributes Athens' growing wealth in the fifth century not only to taxation, but also to the slave trade and increased industrial activity, such as shipbuilding. On Athenian offices, see ibid: 68–69.

[27] Although the term *dēmos* technically refers to all citizens, it often signified the common people or lower classes, as opposed to aristocrats, particularly by the end of the fifth century. Sinclair (1988: 15) observes: "*Dēmos* could, and did, unmistakably carry the sense of the common people or the lower classes."

[28] Eupolis fr. 102 KA. Translation adapted from Rothwell 1990: x, who discusses this fragment in detail and relates it to Aristophanes.

[29] Sinclair 1988: 67.

significance to the role of speech in shaping public opinion in their political institutions, as well as in representing social conflict in dramatic poetry, they nonetheless exhibited a deep-seated ambivalence toward the art of rhetoric, particularly when it became the means for nonaristocratic members of the polis to have access to political power and to manipulate the lower classes.[30] Thus, Aristophanes has the "Just Argument" in the *Clouds* maintain that the best form of education for the city's youth should consist of learning traditional songs, not the art of rhetoric (Ar. *Nub.* 964–68). Much of the suspicion attached to the sophists, a group of itinerant teachers who instructed wealthy youths in the art of speaking on both sides of the question for the purpose of gaining control in the Assembly and the courts. All sophists taught rhetoric, and many subscribed to a kind of cultural relativism, viewing all laws, customs, and religious beliefs as the product of social convention.[31] As a group, sophists were normally foreigners, neither Athenian leaders nor citizens, but "provincials" from minor cities.[32] Their public performances often took place in the private residences of wealthy citizens, as well as at festivals like those of Olympia, a context that they used to link themselves to the Homeric rhapsodes, even going so far as to don their distinctive purple robes. With Pericles as their patron, the sophists rapidly made inroads into Athenian social and political life.[33] By the time of Aristophanes, the term *sophistēs*, although originally neutral, is pejorative, implying deceit and quackery, a standard view that was not seriously challenged until Kerferd in 1981.[34]

---

[30] Ober (1989: 189) sums this problem up as follows: "On the one hand, education in the arts of persuasion is dangerous to the state, since it threatens to undermine the validity of democratic institutions by destroying the ability of mass Assemblies and juries to come to the right decisions. This in turn threatens the fabric of society, since the decisions of the Assembly and courts, along with the laws, served a normative function. . . . On the other hand, the Athenians recognized that skilled orators could be useful." Isocrates (*Antid.* 249) also describes the ambivalent attitude the Athenians held toward the art of persuasion; on the passage, see Buxton 1982: 34.

[31] Guthrie 1971: 48. This position has been somewhat complicated by the recent publication of P. Oxy. 3647, a fragment attributed to Antiphon, in which he appears to condemn cultural relativism; see Funghi 1984. But the meaning of this passage is far from clear: Antiphon appears to criticize *nomos* but does not necessarily champion *phusis*; for a discussion, see Ostwald 1990: 303.

[32] Guthrie 1971: 40.

[33] Kerferd 1981: 15.

[34] Kerferd (ibid.: 8–10) argues that the contemporary view of the sophists as charlatans and imposters largely derives from George Grote's nineteenth-century depiction in *History of Greece* by showing the important role they played in the intellectual movement of Athens during the last half of the fifth-century; for the more traditional view, see Guthrie 1971: 33. According to Ostwald (1986: 242–45), Protagoras was the only person known to have identified himself as a *sophistēs*. Certainly the term assumes a negative connotation by the time of Plato, an obviously hostile source, but it is unclear when exactly it became derogatory. For example, Barrett (1964: 339–40) asserts that σοφιστής at Eur. *Hipp.* 921 is a neutral

The teachings of the sophists concentrated on political advancement through persuasive speech. By making such skills accessible to wealthy but nonaristocratic families for a fee, the sophists aroused the resentment of the upper classes who in the first part of the century had monopolized public discourse simply by virtue of birth. In the Platonic dialogues, Socrates condemns the sophists for accepting pay on the grounds that this practice compromised the objective pursuit of truth; his use of trade metaphors in connection with them, most notably in the *Sophist*, identifies them with the merchant and manufacturing classes (Pl. *Soph.* 224a1–225a1). What the elite really seem to have objected to, however, was that the sophists offered their services to everyone, without discrimination, thereby eroding traditional boundaries between aristocrats and the mass.[35] Their claim, that aristocratic virtue, *aretē*, could be taught, meant that anyone could move into the world of politics, even those of low birth. Because the sophists allowed for a new kind of social mobility, the conservative elite considered them a dangerous source of political subversion.

A distinct political climate in late fifth-century Athens created a demand for the skills taught by the sophists. W. R. Connor has argued that personal ties between citizens were gradually replaced by loyalty to the city, a shift reflected in a new political terminology, which included terms like *dēmagōgos*, "politician," and *rhētōr*, "orator": "The new terminology brought with it a new style and a new technique. It made possible . . . a rapid rise to power based on the power of hitherto ill-organized segments of the citizenry."[36] Rhetorical skill thus became instrumental in forging political alliances among disparate citizens and in opening the avenues of power to the lower classes. The decline in the importance of generalship and the increasing political prominence of aspiring young men in the post-Periclean age attests to the newfound prominence of rhetoric in the polis.[37] As Thucydides explains it, Pericles was able to check private individual ambition and greed and promote the interests of the group because of his political expertise and incorruptibility (Thuc. 2.65.7–8). Advising his citizens to be "lovers of the polis" (Thuc. 2.43.1), he found a way to transfer the personal feeling and private interests of his constituents to the polis.

Although Thucydides probably exaggerates the differences between Pericles and his successors, it is clear that the political atmosphere in Athens changed after his death.[38] Though Alcibiades shared Pericles' aristocratic credentials, others did not. Instead, we find expanded political opportunities for members of the lower classes, particularly those of the manufactur-

---

term, but I think even in this passage its negative associations are patent, a point that I discuss more fully in Chapter 4.

[35] Kerferd 1981: 26.

[36] Connor 1971: 118; on the *dēmagōgos*, see p. 111, and on the rhētōr, see p. 116.

[37] Ibid.: 135.

[38] Sinclair 1988: 40.

ing and merchant classes, and a decline in prestige of the older families.[39] Nicias, for example, had acquired wealth through mining interests, while Cleon's father owned a profitable leather factory.[40] Although of low birth, these men had the economic resources necessary, then as now, to finance ambitious political careers. But because their wealth came from manufacturing or trade, they were reviled by the landed aristocracy, whose views are represented by conservatives like Aristophanes and Thucydides, our main sources for their activities.[41] These new politicians appealed directly to the *dēmos*: the fact that most of them did not hold any official political office meant that they were not accountable in any way for the consequences of their proposals. Cleon, the politician much abused by Aristophanes and deemed the most persuasive speaker in the *dēmos* by Thucydides (πιθανώτατος, Thuc. 3.36.6), embodies the spirit of this new age, since he achieved political success through his demagoguery, only becoming a general much later in his career.

Though demagogues exerted their influence in the Assembly, their favorite venue was the courts, a realm populated by a broad spectrum of society and heavily controlled by popular sentiment. Even though Ephialtes had laid the groundwork for the popular courts, the demagogues were directly responsible for their growth, particularly in the 420s.[42] The jury system was the hallmark of democratic process at Athens: Thucydides repeatedly remarks on the Athenians' love of litigation (φιλοδικεῖν, Thuc. 1.77.1; cf. 1.86.3), whereas Strepsiades in Aristophanes' *Clouds* refuses to believe that what he sees upon looking at a map is Athens because he finds no law courts (Ar. *Nub.* 206–8). In *Wasps*, the elderly Philocleon, addicted to jury duty, remarks that the Athenians are so litigious that they will eventually hear cases in their own homes (Ar. *Vesp.* 801). In Aristotle's view, jury pay, while not substantial, greatly increased opportunities for lower-class citizens to participate in the democratic process.[43] Thus the popular courts might be said to incarnate the principle of equality on which the Athenian democracy was founded, since they invested a socially diverse audience with the power to make judgments about its peers. Indeed, Thucydides held the belief in equality responsible for the excessive litigiousness of the Athenians, arguing that people are more likely to take legal action in a democracy because they consider themselves on an equal footing with their fellow citizens (Thuc. 1.77.4).

[39] Ibid.: 41.

[40] Connor 1971: 151.

[41] Ostwald 1986: 202–3; see also Sinclair 1988: 45.

[42] Ostwald 1986: 209.

[43] Arist. [*Ath. Pol.*] 1274a5, 1293a5–7. Following Aristotle, Sinclair (1988: 127) asserts, "There is little reason to doubt that poorer citizens were in general prominent in the Dikasteria." Drawing on Aristophanes, Ostwald (1986: 82–83) describes Athenian jurors as idle old men who eagerly looked forward to earning a wage while listening to "juicy gossip."

Although many of the sources discussed thus far focus on the dangers posed by the demagogues and the art of persuasion learned through the sophists, they place almost equal emphasis on the vulnerability of the Athenians to rhetorical manipulation. In the Mytilenian debate, a deliberative context in which Cleon deliberately exaggerates the negative characteristics of his peers in the service of his own rhetoric, the Athenians are rebuked for their passivity and the pleasure they derive from listening to clever and novel arguments; even the aristocrats, Cleon asserts, are easily deceived by an innovative speech (Thuc. 3.38.4–5). He further describes them as spectators who sit at the feet of sophists and who put pleasure in listening above all else (Thuc. 3.38.7). Although the context of this speech partly explains Cleon's strong rhetoric and recourse to name-calling, nonetheless the topos of the passive spectator must have been a familiar one to his audience. For example, Aristophanes in the *Wasps* portrays Cleon, through the dream of the slave Sosias, as haranguing an audience of sheep (Ar. *Vesp.* 34). In contrast to Thucydides, however, Aristophanes' target is not the *aristoi*, but commoners, those who were likely to serve as jurists and whom he portrays as governed by pleasure and therefore easily duped.[44] The lassitude of the forensic audience depicted in the *Wasps* resonates with a passage in Aristotle's *Athenian Constitution*, in which the system of jury pay is blamed for making people "idle, cowardly, garrulous, and greedy," characteristics frequently associated with women.[45]

As democratic reforms gradually widened the sphere of political influence to nonaristocratic Athenians, parity and its consequences became a central preoccupation of late fifth- and early fourth-century writers. Thucydides has Pericles observe in his funeral oration that the equality of all citizens distinguishes Athens from other city-states (πᾶσι τὸ ἴσον, Thuc. 2.37.1), and yet, a few chapters later, he attributes the failure of leadership after the statesman's death to this very principle (Thuc. 2.65.10). In the fourth century, Plato argues that radical democracy, by espousing political equality, *isonomia*, abolishes the "natural" social hierarchies of father over son, men over women, or slave over master (Pl. *Rep.* 562e7–563a1). Threatened by the increased power of the mob, Athenian traditionalists increasingly viewed the idea of equality as "responsible for licentious self-indulgence and the degeneration of social order as every man, whatever his background, education or character, could seek to realize his desire."[46]

---

[44] The elderly Philocleon describes his longing for the courts as a form of sexual desire (ἐρᾷ, 89; ἔραμαι, 751); words for pleasure receive emphasis (ἥδιστον, 604; ἡδόμενος λέγοντι, 641).

[45] Socrates states that Pericles, by introducing jury pay, made Athenians "idle, cowardly, garrulous, and greedy" (ἀργοὺς καὶ δειλοὺς καὶ λάλους καὶ φιλαργύρους, Pl. *Grg.* 515e). See Sinclair 1988: 20; for a similar description of the effect of jury pay on jurors, see Arist. [*Ath. Pol.*] 27.4.

[46] Farrar 1988: 122–23.

In this light, it is difficult not to view Euripides' democratized tragedy as one literary expression of this political phenomenon. The two oligarchic coups, in 411 and in 403/2, were clearly a response to the destruction wreaked on the polis by demagogues such as Cleon. According to Xenophon, the Thirty banned the teaching of the art of rhetoric.[47] However, the aristocrats blamed not only the demagogues, but also their teachers, the sophists, who privileged education over birthright, for providing the theoretical foundations for this social collapse. Some scholars have even suggested that one of the questions debated by the sophists, and one consistent with their emphasis on social convention, was the position and status of women.[48] In the same way, Aristophanes extends this principle of equality to women and then stages its comic consequences in his *Ecclesiazusae*.

SPEECH IN THE THEATER OF DIONYSUS

All Athenian citizens engaged in the contest of words either as actors or as spectators not only in the Assembly and the courts but also in the dramatic and poetic competitions of the city Dionysia. In all arenas of public life, the Athenians were "spectators of speeches" (θεαταὶ μὲν τῶν λόγων, Thuc. 3.38.4). Orators repeatedly made reference to tragic drama in their speeches just as the tragic poet implicitly "reminded the audience that the theater of Dionysos was in many ways analogous to the Pnyx or *dikasterion* or *bouleuterion*."[49] In this way, the theater of Dionysus taught the orator's audience how to listen to speeches in the courts and in the

[47] Xenophon (*Mem*. 1.2.31) describes the ban on rhetoric with the phrase λόγων τέχνην μὴ διδάσκειν; see Buxton 1982: 16.

[48] Kerferd (1981: 159–62) argues that fourth-century texts that posit a new role for women, such as Aristophanes' *Ecclesiazusae* and Plato's *Republic*, may point to earlier sophistic discussions about their position in society: "So it is not surprising that the new thinking of the sophistic movement should lead to the posing of questions concerning the rights and position of women in Greek societies, though there is no evidence that this led to any actual movement for the improvement of their position" (159). This idea seems to have originated with Wilamowitz ([1900] 1962: 126) and Nestle (1901: 266–67); see also Bruns 1901. Henderson (1996: 144) describes how Aristophanes' *Ecclesiazusae* reflects "actual contemporary discussions, both popular and philosophical, about the wisdom of women's traditional exclusion from participation in male (executive) culture, and about the virtues and potential civic value of women." In support of women's equality, he cites Pl. *Rep*. 5 and Xen. *Symp*. 2.9, but provides no concrete external evidence of such a debate. I discuss in Chapter 5 how Eur. *Andr*. may make reference to this debate.

[49] Ober and Strauss 1990: 248. Dover (1974: 32–33) points out that Attic Old Comedy and oratory made use of similar types of vilification by maligning an individual's parents as foreign-born or engaging in menial trades, or suggesting that an opponent or his relatives may have served as prostitutes.

Assembly.[50] A passage from Aristophanes' *Wasps* further suggests how closely linked the performative realms of the courts and the theater were in the Athenian imagination: after describing the various types of entertainment offered jurors by desperate defendants (Ar. *Vesp.* 562–72), Philocleon wishes someone would take legal action against the tragic actor Oeagrus so that he might perform one of his Niobe speeches for the jury (Ar. *Vesp.* 580). Moreover, the structure of the dramatic festival also resembled the courts in that poets competed before a mass audience for prizes awarded by judges, while the theater itself served as the site of a special postfestival assembly where various offenses committed during the course of the festival, particularly disorderly conduct, were discussed, and other public business was transacted.[51]

On a formal level, drama, particularly that of Euripides, borrowed from the popular courts the agon, a structured, highly rhetorical debate in which competing speakers argue on opposite sides of a question.[52] It also shared rhetorical elements, such as arrangement of speeches, types of argument, and a specialized terminology, with the courts.[53] The two types of contest made use of fictions organized around the same topic, miscreants and their punishment.[54] Some of the plays even included trial scenes, with the most famous example being the establishment of the homicide court, the Areopagus, in Aeschylus' *Eumenides*; the lost Danaids tetralogy also apparently included a trial at Argos. The courts and the plays made use of the same kind of rhetorical proof, since the *anagnōrisis* or recognition scene in tragedy hinged on the presence of signs, a type of inartificial proof discussed in Aristotle's *Rhetoric*.[55] Similarly, the litigant at trial delivered a lengthy *rhēsis* before a jury just as the tragic actor declaimed his speech before the chorus and the festival audience. The fact that a literary form could derive so directly from a political structure further supports a close association between the theater of Dionysus and contemporary civic institutions.[56]

[50] Ober (1989: 152) observes: "The experience of the Athenian demos in the theater had much to do with its experience as an audience of oratory. . . . In each case, the mass audience faced, listened to, and actively responded to individual speakers. In all cases, cooperation, both between individual and mass audience and between the members of the audience, was necessary."

[51] Dem. 21.8–10; Pickard-Cambridge 1991: 64 and 68. On the formal similarity between dramatic contests and trials, see also Hall 1995: 39.

[52] It is also possible that sophistic speech contests, λόγων ἀγῶνες, first introduced by Protagoras, may have influenced the tragic agon; cf. Diog. Laert. 9.52 = DK 80A1; Kerferd 1981: 29; in Euripidean tragedy, Nestle 1901: 36–37. On the tragic agon and its relation to judicial contests, see Reinhart 1960: 232; Garner 1987: 96–97; and Lloyd 1992: 13–14.

[53] Bers 1994: 177–78 discusses the role of rhetoric in Greek drama and relates it to Attic oratory; see also Goldhill 1997b: 132–33.

[54] On the content of plays and trials, see Eden 1986: 3; Hall 1995: 39–40.

[55] Eden 1986: 11–12 discusses the relation of artificial, *entechnos*, and inartificial, *atechnos*, proofs in Aristotle's rhetoric and relates them to tragic *anagnōrisis*.

[56] Hall 1995: 40.

From a performative standpoint, both tragic and comic drama were inextricably bound to the city by virtue of their inclusion at the state festivals, especially at the greater Dionysia. In Aristophanes' view, as voiced by the character of Aeschylus in the *Frogs*, it was the responsibility of the dramatic poet, as the *didaskalos* or teacher of the polis, to create good citizens by inculcating civic ideology and aristocratic values.[57] The city Dionysia itself, as Pickard-Cambridge and, most recently, Goldhill have shown, also served an undeniable political function: held at the end of March, and open to the entire Hellenic world, the festival became an occasion for displaying the power and wealth of Athens.[58] The opening ceremonies of the festival further strengthened the link between the dramatic plays and the state; four events are of particular significance: the pouring of libations by the generals who were to serve as judges of the plays, the distribution of awards to the city's benefactors, the parade of the orphaned ephebes across the stage in full armor, and, after the founding of the Delian league, the display of tributes paid to Athens by subject-allies.[59]

The festival also entailed the suspension of legal proceedings, such as the taking of security for debt, and the release of prisoners to attend the plays. According to Goldhill, these events stressed not only the authority of the polis, but also the responsibilities of the individual to the city.[60] The official and public nature of the festival is further reflected in the composition of the audience: it is almost certain that slaves were not allowed to attend, and few women, if any, probably would have been present; in any case, fifth-century Athenian drama clearly addressed itself to a conceptual audience of male citizens. Lead tokens that appear to have been theater tickets also reveal that spectators were probably seated by tribes in the theater, an arrangement that may have resembled seating in the Pnyx, where the Athenian Assembly convened four times a month.[61] The festival audience therefore replicated the political composition of the city both in its seating arrangement and in its exclusion of noncitizens, particularly slaves and women.

[57] On the concept of the poet as teacher of the city, see the parabasis in Ar. *Ach.* 626ff., esp. 658; cf. Ar. *Ran.* 1007–10. See also Goldhill 1986: 58–76.

[58] Pickard-Cambridge 1991: 58; Goldhill 1990.

[59] Goldhill 1986; Pickard-Cambridge 1991: 58–59; Winkler 1990b.

[60] Goldhill 1990: 126.

[61] Pickard-Cambridge 1991: 271; Winkler 1990b: 38–42; Ober 1989: 132–33; Ober and Strauss 1990: 238. Interestingly, the scant and contradictory evidence supporting the presence of women in the theater of Dionysus indicates that their seats would have been at the very edges of the audience, separate from the men, in an arrangement that coincidentally would have replicated their actual political position in democratic Athens, if they attended. See Pickard-Cambridge 1991: 269–70; Winkler 1990b: 39 and n. 58. On the similarity of the layout of the Pnyx to that of the theater of Dionysus, see Arist. [*Ath. Pol.*] 42.4; Ober 1989: 132; Arnott 1989: 75.

The dialectical relation of the theater of Dionysus to other civic institutions is also evidenced by the fact that actors and orators apparently employed similar delivery techniques. Because Attic drama relied on the convention of wearing masks, thereby rendering facial expressions unalterable in dramatic productions, the voice became an important tool for conveying character. According to Aristotle, the skills required for delivery in oration resembled those of actors; both required strong voices capable of expertly modulating volume, pitch, and rhythm.[62] The actor Hegelochus's famous mistake while delivering a line from Euripides' *Orestes*, one that earned him incessant ridicule from the comic poets, illustrates the vocal precision involved in dramatic delivery. His breathless delivery of γαλῆν instead of γαλήν' changed the intended meaning of the sentence from "I see the *calm* after the storm" to "I see the *skunk* after the storm."[63] It is unfortunate that next to nothing is known about how the male actor manipulated these features when impersonating women. Although dealing mostly with gesture and not voice, Aristotle does provide one clue in his censure of the tragic poet and actor Callipides for excessive restless movements in portraying lower-class women (Arist. *Poet.* 1462a9–10). In fact, his penchant for overacting earned Callipides the nickname "the Ape" (Arist. *Poet.* 1461b34). Although not always reliable, anecdotal evidence attributing the training of orators in vocal technique to that of tragic actors further shows how linked tragic and rhetorical performance were in the Athenian imagination; Aeschines, the *euphōnos*, apparently left professional acting for politics in 343 B.C.E., not unlike the former U.S. president Ronald Reagan. Other orators, like Demosthenes and Archias of Thurii, are said to have learned public speaking from famous actors.[64] Finally, orators frequently quoted speeches from Greek tragedy in court, the most famous example being Praxithea's speech in Euripides' *Erechtheus* quoted at length by the late fourth-century orator, Lycurgus (*Leoc.* 98–100; fr. 50A 350 TGF).[65]

While these examples suggest that Attic drama engaged dialectically with the other discursive spheres of the city, providing an alternative discourse that commented on contemporary political concerns, dramatic poetry obvi-

---

[62] Arist. *Rh.* 1403b20–1404a1; cf. 1413b20–25; see also Eden 1986: 4–5; Pickard-Cambridge 1991: 167–68. Hall (1995: 41) rightly observes that Aristotle downplays the performative aspects of public speaking in his *Rhetoric*.

[63] Cf. Eur. *Or.* 279; Ar. *Ran.* 303–4; Strattis, frs. 1 and 60 KA; and Sannyrion, fr. 8 KA.

[64] Accounts vary as to which particular tragic actor taught Demosthenes his art; see Ober (1989: 154), who mentions Satyrus, and Arnott (1989: 51), who identifies Andronicus and Polos.

[65] No one has as yet suggested the possibility that this tragic fragment, which survives only as an exemplum in a rhetorical speech (Lycurg. *Leoc.* 100), may have received its rhetorical polish from the orator himself; both the linguistic and rhetorical texture of this speech are remarkably unlike those of any other extant Euripidean rhēsis, as Austin (1967: 17) observes: "Mais il faut dire que le morceau est assez décevant et indigne du meilleur Euripide; la rhétorique en est sèche et désinvolte et les lieux communs abondent."

ously functioned differently from judicial and forensic discourse. Positioned both inside and outside the civic discourse of the democratic polis, it could explore and exploit the cultural anxieties and conflicting values policed, however imperfectly, by social and political ideology.[66] Communal rituals as well as stage drama are inherently self-reflexive; by creating a frame or liminal space, the theater allows a culture to look at itself.[67] By reconstituting the discourses of the city in the imaginary world of the theater, the city Dionysia allowed its audience in a self-reflexive gesture to see itself through the other:[68]

> Tragedy is not only an art form; it is also a social institution that the city, by establishing competitions in tragedies, set up alongside its political and legal institutions. The city established under the authority of the eponymous archon, in the same urban space and in accordance with the same institutional norms as the popular assemblies or courts, a spectacle open to all the citizens, directed, acted, and judged by the qualified representatives of the various tribes. In this way it turned itself into a theater. Its subject, in a sense, was itself and it acted itself out before its public.[69]

Attic Old Comedy quite literally assimilates the space of the theater to that of the Assembly in a reflexive, metatheatrical gesture. The opening of Aristophanes' *Acharnians* provides a clear example of this dialectical process: sitting in an imaginary Pnyx, Dicaeopolis describes and addresses the *prutaneis*, the men who presided over the Assembly, while looking and gesturing at the audience.[70] Tragic drama, with its love of staged debates and trial scenes, also makes use of the dialectical relation established between theatrical spectatorship and participation in the civic institutions of the democratic polis, although not as directly as comedy. Thus fifth-century Athenian drama reconstructed the discursive spaces of the city as a literary fiction that both assimilated and transformed the social processes of everyday life. As one of many overlapping and interconnected discursive spheres in fifth-century Athens, the dramatic festivals offered a continual commentary on the other discursive practices of the polis, and mobilized some of its female characters in service of this task.

THE SILENCE OF ATHENIAN WOMEN

The rights of *parrhēsia* and *isēgoria* that democratic reforms extended to adult citizen males in the Athenian polis, distinguishing them from the mass of noncitizens, did not apply to citizen women. Instead, both Athenian and

---

[66] Ober and Strauss 1990: 238; Vernant 1988: 29–48.
[67] Turner 1995: 35.
[68] Goldhill 1986: 61.
[69] Vernant 1988: 32–33.
[70] Dover 1972: 82.

non-Athenian literary texts universally praise female silence and verbal submission while equating women's talk with promiscuity and adultery. In Semonides' iambic invective against women, out of the ten types of women discussed, only the silent bee woman receives commendation because she sits apart and does not gossip about sex with other women (Semon. fr. 7.91). We find a similar sentiment in the fifth-century Athenian adage, "Silence brings adornment to women," first expressed by Sophocles and reiterated by several later authors.[71] The public silence required of women in the literary sources was perhaps even enforced by law: an anecdote attributed to Plutarch about the *hetaera* or courtesan Aspasia, the wife of Pericles, recounts that it was illegal for women to speak in the law courts in classical Athens. Responding to accusations made against her by the Athenians, Aspasia composed a speech and instructed a man to read it for her in the courts: "If the law allowed women to speak in the courts, I would defend myself, but now, one of you, lend me your voice and read this speech, adding or omitting nothing."[72]

Not only did literary texts portray the respectable woman as silent, they also promoted silence about women in the public sphere. In a much-discussed passage from Thucydides, Pericles enjoins widows in his funeral oration not to be talked about whether for praise or blame:

εἰ δέ με δεῖ καὶ γυναικείας τι ἀρετῆς, ὅσαι νῦν ἐν χηρείᾳ ἔσονται, μνησθῆναι, βραχείᾳ παραινέσει ἅπαν σημανῶ. τῆς τε γὰρ ὑπαρχούσης φύσεως μὴ χείροσι γενέσθαι ὑμῖν μεγάλη ἡ δόξα καὶ ἧς ἂν ἐπ' ἐλάχιστον ἀρετῆς πέρι ἢ ψόγου ἐν τοῖς ἄρσεσι κλέος ᾖ. (Thuc. 2.45.2)

If it is necessary for me to mention the virtue of wives, with respect to those of you who will now be widows, I will make all of my advice brief. Your great reputation is not to become worse than your original nature. For your glory is not to be talked about for good or evil among men.

What exactly Pericles, or Thucydides, means by this passage has been the subject of some considerable debate: on the one hand, it implicates women as noisy and disruptive, like the mob; on the other, it may represent an attempt to curb their excessive lamentation over the slain soldiers.[73] Kerferd

[71] Soph. *Aj.* 293; Arist. *Pol.* 1260a30–31 and 1277b20–23; Democr. fr. 274 DK; Plaut. *Aulularia* 123–126 and *Rud.* 1114; cf. 1 Cor. 14:35 and 1 Tim. 2:11.12.

[72] I am paraphrasing Ehlers' German translation of a Syriac text; see Ehlers 1966: 77n.158; Lagarde 1967: 182. Thanks are owed to Professor Michael Fox of the Department of Semitic Studies, University of Wisconsin-Madison, for his help in translating the original Syriac. Stehle (1997: 114–18) discusses women's inscriptions in Attica as a form of authoritative public speech. She further notes (73n.7) that even though women in the Roman empire were allowed to hold public offices, they seldom held positions requiring them to speak.

[73] For general commentary on this passage, see Hornblower 1991: 1. 314. Plutarch (*Mor.* 242E) understands Thucydides to refer to the necessity of secluding women. Lacey (1964)

has also suggested that Pericles is made to respond in this part of his speech to a famous saying of the sophist Gorgias: "Not the looks of a woman, but her good reputation should be known to many."[74] The idea that women should not be the subject of conversation is carried over to the courts, where orators employed elaborate periphrases to avoid uttering the names of respectable women.[75] Similarly, citizen women were not allowed to serve as witnesses in trials, since their testimony was deemed unreliable, nor were they permitted to appear in court at all, unless foreigners. As both Hunter and Cohen have demonstrated, the marketplace gossip of men reiterated in the courts played a critical role in policing women's behavior in classical Athens.[76] The polis seems to have conspired in the silence about women from birth, since the names of female infants were not inscribed anywhere on the lists of citizens, in contrast to their male counterparts, and it is questionable whether the birth of a female child was even recorded in the phratry.[77]

Women's lack of access to the political sphere was also reflected in their legal status: they could not hold office, own or dispose of property valued at above one *medimnos* (about a day's ration of grain), or vote; in short, they were excluded from those speech acts which conferred upon males economic power and civic identity. Debarred from public speech in the democratic institutions that governed the polis, an Athenian woman had to rely on her *kurios*, "legal guardian," usually a father or husband, to speak publicly on her behalf; thus women had no public voice or presence except through men.[78] The kurios' function was primarily economic: he ensured that his ward was properly betrothed and married; he managed her dowry and acted on her behalf in any financial transaction above one *medimnos*. But he was also responsible for any public representation required by his wife or daughter: in an anonymous dramatic fragment, the speech of a young girl suggests how the kurios might have functioned as the vehicle for a woman's public and authoritative speech:

---

was the first to suggest that Pericles refers not to women generally, but to widows, arguing that the passage aims at restricting their excessive lamentation. For the association of women with *thorubos*, "disruption," see Loraux 1985: 21. More recently, Hardwick (1993) has argued that this advice must be understood in the larger political context of the oration: Pericles attempts to thwart the gossip about women that might lead to rivalries between men and to promote civic unity by suppressing disagreement and discord.

[74] Gorg. 22 DK; see Kerferd 1981: 160 for further discussion.

[75] Schaps 1977; a similar convention apparently governed the naming of women in Greek comedy, for which see Sommerstein 1980.

[76] Cohen 1989; Hunter 1994.

[77] Hunter 1994: 112. It is unclear whether girls at birth were formally introduced into the phratries or not: for opposing views, see Gould (1980: 40–42), who argues against the practice, and Golden (1985), who argues for it.

[78] Hunter 1994: 53.

ὦ πάτερ, ἐχρῆν μὲν οὓς ἐγὼ λόγους λέγω,
τούτους λέγειν σέ· καὶ γὰρ ἁρμόζει φρονεῖν
σὲ μᾶλλον ἢ ἐμὲ καὶ λέγειν ὅπου τι δεῖ.   (P. Didot 1.1–3)[79]

Father, you should make the speech which
I am now making. For it is fitting for you,
rather than for me, to think and speak where necessary.

The term that designates a woman of citizen status, *attikē*, further underscores the different relation women had to the Athenian polis, since it
denotes an inherited, familial connection rather than a political affiliation.[80]
In contrast, the adjective *Athenaios*, normally used of the male citizen,
refers to an official or a "member of the politically sovereign body," and
as such implies a relation to political speech.[81]

Of course, it is a mistake to attempt to understand something as complex
as gender identity solely in terms of a conceptual dichotomy. The silence
of women in classical Athens was neither monolithic nor absolute. It has
been well established that women played an important religious role in
the polis, participating in civic festivals like the Panathenaia in honor of
Athena, and in other religious festivals reserved for women only, like the
Skira and Thesmophoria, as well as performing other duties, including
funerary rituals.[82] In fact, much of the speech that is represented as socially
sanctioned for women in Attic drama revolves around these religious activities, as will be discussed in subsequent chapters. Maternity also conferred
upon women a measure of prestige in the polis: they bore sons who would
fight for the city, and, after 451/50, they imparted citizen status to them.
Indeed, female characters in Aristophanic comedy frequently use their
standing as mothers to argue for the authority of their proposals.[83] Older
women, past the childbearing years and often widowed, apparently enjoyed
a measure of independence and freedom not accorded to younger wives.
And although the legal process excluded women, recent work on fourth-
century Attic oratory suggests that women played an important role behind
the scenes, generating disputes between men and encouraging husbands
and sons to take legal action; moreover, their legal status was critical "in
creating the political status of their households."[84] And although women

---

[79] P. Didot 1 = Ps.-Eur. fr. 953.1–3 *TGF*; see also Sandbach 1979: 328.

[80] Patterson 1987: 50. Chantraine notes that words ending in -*ikos* tend to refer to slaves
or people of the lower classes; see Chantraine 1956: 110–11; Loraux 1993: 116–23; Goldhill
1986: 59.

[81] Patterson 1987: 53.

[82] Foley 1981b: 131.

[83] Ar. *Eccl.* 233–34 and 635–44; cf. *Thesm.* 832–45; see also Ober and Strauss 1990:
267–68.

[84] On women as a source of male conflict, see Foxhall 1996: 140; cf. [Dem.] 45; Dem.
41; [Dem.] 55.23–25, 27; on their legal status in the courts, Foxhall 1996: 140–41.

were debarred from testifying in a trial, oaths may have served as a means of inserting the testimony of women into a court case.[85]

A final divergence from the model of silence and seclusion promulgated by scholars in the past are courtesans and prostitutes, who appear to have been exempt from many of the strictures that governed the lives of respectable women in classical Athens.[86] The most famous example is probably the hetaera Neaera, whose physical presence at her own trial is repeatedly signaled by Apollodorus' use of deictic pronouns ([Dem.] 59.44, 50, 64, 115). A fanciful anecdote recorded by Athenaeus further illustrates that persons of liminal status, such as courtesans, could breach discursive and ideological boundaries. In an unusual legal maneuver, the orator Hyperides ripped the clothes off his client, the courtesan Phryne, and bared her breasts to the jury while simultaneously delivering a piteous closing argument, all in order to avert a guilty verdict. Although Phryne herself does not speak, but rather her body "speaks," her public display in the courtroom corroborates the special status accorded courtesans (Ath. 13. 590e). Because they had more interaction with men, they engaged in a larger variety of verbal contexts, if only as a requirement of the job, as evidenced by the courtesan Alce in a speech of Isaeus (Isae. 6.17.19–21). In fact, they were frequently portrayed as outspoken and even rhetorically skilled. The courtesan Aspasia was famous throughout antiquity for her rhetorical ability. Not surprisingly, the tradition links her rhetorical ability to her sexual status.[87] In the *Menexenus*, Socrates attributes to her an extraordinary talent for composing political speeches (Pl. *Menex.* 235e5) and then identifies her as the author of the *epitaphios* he is about to pronounce. The negative emphasis on the *epitaphios* as the supreme genre of the rhetoricians and its associations with magic and trickery (ποικίλλοντες and γοητεύουσιν, 235a), perhaps serves as a means of discrediting this type of speech.[88] The persuasive hetaera, seductive in both speech and body, embodied the strong association between erotic and political persuasion in the Greek imagination. For Aristophanes and Plato, the courtesan who speaks serves as a metaphor for political corruption and social disorder, a metaphor found as early as Alcaeus, who compares the ship of state to a worn-out prostitute.[89] And just as the literary tradition

---

[85] Foxhall 1996: 143; see also Gagarin (forthcoming), on how the orators put to use the words of women to support their arguments. On the absence of women in the law courts, see Goldhill 1994: 357–59; Foxhall 1996.

[86] Gagarin (forthcoming) distinguishes between foreign women, such as Neaera, who was most certainly present during her trial, and citizen women.

[87] Henry 1995: 35.

[88] Loraux 1986: 223.

[89] For the ship of state metaphor in Alcaeus, see fr. 306 ii.6–15 Voigt. Henry (1995: 35) observes that in Aristophanic comedy, "politicians . . . speak with the mouths of whores"; cf. Ar. *Thesm.* 805, where the politician Cleophon and the courtesan Salabaccho are equated;

depicts prostitutes as outspoken and rhetorically gifted, in the same way, it repeatedly equates women's public speech and presence before men as a sign of sexual license. According to Theophrastus, a late fourth-century author, a woman who appears at the house door, calls to passersby, or speaks to men was considered a courtesan.[90] Although women were largely excluded from the discursive realms in which male civic identity was consolidated in classical Athens, their silence and seclusion have to be understood partly as the fictional constructs of men: women did speak, to their husbands, their sons, to one another; they found a public voice through ritual, whereas noncitizen and lower-class women frequently moved through the public world of men.

WOMEN AS SPEAKERS IN ATHENIAN DRAMA

Tragedy, in its capacity as an "official" discourse, also reinforced the ideology of silence and seclusion for women promulgated by other texts even as it represented speaking female characters engaged in a diverse array of roles. Many of the plays feature silent women, from Cassandra in Aeschylus' *Agamemnon*, to Tecmessa in Sophocles' *Ajax* and Alcestis in Euripides' play of the same name. However, the orthodoxy of women's silence presented the dramatic poets with a representational problem, since most of the extant plays situate the action at the house door, a realm that is both a private domestic context and a public platform, where women's presence was considered a potentially disruptive and dangerous intrusion into public space.[91] For this reason, tragedy tirelessly enumerates the importance of remaining within the house for both women and girls.[92] Even a nontrans-

---

cf. also *Vesp.* 1015–35; *Pax* 739–59. Demetrius (285 Innes), relating an assertion of Demades, an Athenian politician and orator of the later fourth century, implies a similar equation: "The city, not the naval power of our ancestors, but an old woman, wearing slippers and gulping down barley water" (πόλιν, οὐ τὴν ἐπὶ προγόνων τὴν ναυμάχον, ἀλλὰ γραῦν, σανδάλια ὑποδεδεμένην καὶ πτισάνην ῥοφῶσαν). The noun is possibly obscene, referring to the receding of the foreskin on erection; see Henderson 1991a: 184–85.

[90] Theophr. *Char.* 28.3 Edmonds; on the inadvisability of being seen at the house door, Lycurg. *Leocr.* 40; on noble women ashamed to be seen by male relatives, see Lys. 3.6–7; Cohen 1991: 148; cf. Ar. *Eccl.* 877ff., where crones styled as courtesans confront a prospective lover at the house door.

[91] In one of the first articles to deal with this issue, Shaw (1975: 256) asserts, "By the very act of being in a drama, which always occurs outside the house, they are doing what women should not do." Foley (1982) offers an important qualification of this position by arguing that house and city should not be viewed as so rigidly polarized and that women as ritual agents served an important public function in the polis. See also Easterling 1987.

[92] Tragic drama contains numerous examples of girls and women being rebuked for appearing outside the house, particularly when they might encounter men: cf. Soph. *El.* 518; Eur. *El.* 343–44; *Or.* 108; *Phoen.* 1276; *Andr.* 877–79. A fragment from Euripides best sums up the view: "A woman, remaining indoors, must be noble, since she is worthless outside"

gressive departure from the house requires justification, as the character of Macaria illustrates in Euripides' *Children of Heracles*, who leaves her suppliant's seat in the temple to declare her willingness to die for her brothers:

ξένοι, θράσος μοι μηδὲν ἐξόδοις ἐμαῖς
προσθῆτε· πρῶτον γὰρ τόδ' ἐξαιτήσομαι·
γυναικὶ γὰρ σιγή τε καὶ τὸ σωφρονεῖν
κάλλιστον εἴσω θ' ἥσυχον μένειν δόμων.   (Eur. *Heracl.* 474–77)

Strangers, do not think me bold for coming outside.
For first I will beg this thing from you.
For a woman, silence and chastity
are fairest of all, and remaining quietly inside the house.

Macaria's speech functions ambiguously: it simultaneously proclaims the moral authority entailed by her voluntary act of sacrifice and disavows the authority of her speech. Because she confronts an exclusively male internal audience, she must justify her presence outside, an inappropriate context that might unfairly prejudice her interlocutors. Her excuse for speaking outwardly resembles techniques familiar from forensic oratory, while the content, that a woman should not appear in public, is strictly feminine. Defending herself against a charge of impudence (θράσος), Macaria touches upon the three cardinal virtues prescribed for females in classical drama: silence (σιγή), sexual self-control (τὸ σωφρονεῖν), and that virtue which encompasses the other two, remaining passively within the house. But because Macaria speaks on behalf of her brothers and her natal house, and because of her virgin status, her speech is not considered dangerous, especially since the Greek imagination strongly associated virgins with truthful speech. She is represented as reinforcing Athenian gender ideology regarding speech even as she publicly makes her case before men.[93]

More often, however, fifth-century Athenian drama portrays women, particularly wives, as masterful and persuasive speakers whose words get the better of men. Ancient critics complained, about Euripides in particular, that the tragic poets created women who were too heroic and brave (Arist. *Poet.* 1454a23–24), too rhetorical (Plut. *Mor.* 28A), or too philosophical (Origen C. *Cels.* 7.36.34–36). At the same time, a woman skilled at

---

(ἔνδον μένουσαν τὴν γυναῖκ' εἶναι χρεὼν | ἐσθλήν, θύρασι δ' ἀξίαν τοῦ μηδενός, Eur. fr. 521 *TGF*). The impropriety of females speaking to men is illustrated by a passage in *Iphigenia in Aulis*, where Euripides portrays Clytemnestra, in an ironic reversal of her Aeschylean counterpart, as ashamed to find that she is speaking to a man to whom she is not in fact related; cf. Eur. *IA* 830–54.

[93] Zeitlin (1990: 85) observes that women who speak for themselves rather than for the group or the family in tragedy are seen as dangerous. I would add that social status also plays an important role: the speech of married women always causes trouble, whereas the speech of girls is normally represented as benign.

manipulating male political discourse strains the limits of dramatic verisimilitude; in Aristophanes, both Lysistrata and Praxagora are made to explain how they learned the art of persuasion. Given a few verses from Euripides' *Melanippe the Wise*, Lysistrata claims, "By listening often to my father's words and those of the old men, I have not been badly educated" (τοὺς δ' ἐκ πατρός τε καὶ γεραιτέρων λόγους | πολλοὺς ἀκούσασ' οὐ μεμούσωμαι κακῶς, Ar. *Lys.* 1126–27). Praxagora, on the other hand, declares that she learned her art directly from listening to politicians declaiming in the Pnyx, "As a refugee, I lived with my husband in the Pnyx. Then I learned from hearing the *rhētores*" (ἐν ταῖς φυγαῖς μετὰ τἀνδρὸς ᾤκησ' ἐν πυκνί· | ἔπειτ' ἀκούουσ' ἐξέμαθον τῶν ῥητόρων, Ar. *Eccl.* 243–44). Although a rhetorically skilled female could use her gift to save the city (the case of Praxagora is less clear cut), typically her persuasiveness involves trickery and deception to challenge or subvert the status quo. The dramatic poets also frequently made use of the traditional equation between women's speech and promiscuity in depicting wives. We are never far from this idea with Aeschylus' characterization of Clytemnestra, since her speech at several points is inextricably bound with her adultery, as Goldhill has shown.[94] In the case of Phaedra in Euripides' *Hippolytus*, the association is even stronger, because her speech is depicted as arising directly from her uncontrolled *erōs*.[95] Similarly, Hermione's brash speech in Euripides' *Andromache* betrays her inability to control her lust, a genetic liability inherited from her mother and dramatized at the end of the play by her elopement with Orestes.

The tradition joining women to deceitful speech originates in Hesiod's depiction of Pandora, the first woman, as false and cunning (Hes. *Op.* 78–80), a figure popularized in the fifth century by Sophocles in his satyr play *Pandora*.[96] In an influential article, Bergren argues for the "double nature of female discourse," asserting that women are represented as capable of two contradictory speaking modes, that of prophecy and that of deception.[97] She locates this ambiguity in women's sign-making activity par excellence, weaving, an art that serves as a metaphor for cunning, trickery, and deception throughout Greek literature.[98] Winkler offers an-

[94] Goldhill 1984b; see also Zeitlin 1990: 80.

[95] Rabinowitz 1987.

[96] This subject is discussed in more detail in Chapter 2. On the topos of women's untrustworthy oaths, cf. Soph. fr. 811 Radt (ὅρκους ἐγὼ γυναικὸς εἰς ὕδωρ γράφω); cf. also Catull. 70; Prop. 2.28.7–8; Ov. *Am.* 2.16.45–56. For commonplaces about women's verbal treachery in Euripides, cf. Eur. *Hipp.* 638–50; on their untrustworthiness, cf. *Hipp.* 480–81; *Or.* 1103; *IT* 1298; *Med.* 408–9; fr. 463, 464, 671 *TGF.* Consider also Aristotle's description of the female sex as fond of raillery (φιλολοίδορον), shameless (ἀναιδέστερον), and deceitful (ψευδέστερον, *Hist. an.* 608b3–609b18). For Sophocles' *Pandora*, cf. fr. 482 Radt; on satyr drama as an expression of "masculine, homosocial consciousness," see Hall 1998.

[97] Bergren 1983: 70.

[98] Ibid.: 71–75.

other way of conceptualizing the paradox along sociopolitical lines: in his study of Sappho, he concludes that Greek women had an expanded or double "consciousness" because they experienced not only their own segregated culture, but that of men as well.[99] Women, as a muted group, must learn the dominant discourse in order to speak and yet, at the same time, they generate specific, alternate codes that they may use among themselves. As a result, women can be considered "bilingual" in that they understand both their own discursive strategies and those of the dominant group, engaging in " 'code-switching' in order to function in societies where they are subordinated."[100]

A similar discursive dynamic occurs in Attic drama where outsiders, particularly women and slaves, are represented as particularly skillful at manipulating the dominant discourse of men while simultaneously maintaining a separate discursive sphere of their own. The tragic and comic plays are full of female characters who deceive their male interlocutors through their persuasive speech. Clytemnestra plays the part of a faithful wife before the male chorus, the messenger, and ultimately her husband, but abandons this disguise once she has successfully carried out her plan. Whereas female characters in Attic drama are often portrayed as dissimulating before men, they typically speak candidly to other women as a means of enlisting their support. Phaedra in the *Hippolytus* confides her illicit love to the Nurse and the female chorus, and yet concocts a different story for men. Even more illustrative are Medea's alternating confessions to the female chorus and dissimulations in the presence of men; in fact, she manages to dupe all the male principals in the play. A similar dynamic is comically deployed in Aristophanes' *Ecclesiazusae*, where Praxagora conspires with the female chorus in the first part of the play and then skillfully deceives the male citizens gathered in the Pnyx, as well as her husband.

The continuous association of women with deceptive speech throughout the Greek literary tradition prompts the question, "Why should a certain power of language be thought of in terms of gender at all?"[101] One answer may be found in male anxieties about women's reproductive power: because men can never know the true paternity of their children, they are forever plagued by uncertainty, while women alone know the truth and therefore are capable of falsehood.[102] In the fifth century, especially after the citizenship laws of 451/50 and the frequent absences required of men

[99] Winkler (1990a: 174–175) argues that "women in a male-prominent society are thus like a linguistic minority in a culture whose public actions are all conducted in the majority language. To participate even passively in the public arena the minority must be bilingual; the majority feels no such need to learn the minority's language."

[100] Cameron 1985: 105; see also Kramarae 1981: 4; for the idea of women as a muted group, see S. Ardener 1975: xii.

[101] Bergren 1983: 71.

[102] Ibid.: 75.

during the Peloponnesian war, this concern may have been uppermost in the minds of Athenian spectators. And yet the new role of persuasion in the polis and the shifting class lines entailed by the reforms of Ephialtes and Pericles as well as by the teachings of the sophists suggest that tragedy negotiated an even larger issue than reproductive control through its false and persuasive women. By representing rhetorically proficient women who use their skills to subvert male social hierarchy, the plays examined in this study deploy their female characters as a means of expressing anxiety about the transmission and consolidation of power among the political elite in the democratic polis through the control of speech. By depicting women as employing persuasion out of self-interest and in the pursuit of *erōs*, fifth-century Athenian drama further affiliates them with a principle of self-interest later derided by Thucydides and others as destructive of the polis.

For Aristophanes, the destructive potential of both rhetoric and tragic drama resides in their ability to seduce and deceive the unwitting masses, who are portrayed as self-serving pleasure seekers. Persuasive rhetoric therefore becomes a powerful and dangerous tool in the hands of demagogues, many of whom moved beyond their low birth to positions of political influence in the courts and the Assembly in the late fifth century. Aristophanes and Thucydides pinned the demise of the democratic city on such figures, who sacrificed the interests of the polis in favor of personal advancement. As a consequence, Aristophanes consistently identifies the corrupting rhetorical skills of the politicians with the sexual charms of young boys and women, particularly prostitutes, adept at wooing clients for a profit. Although these figures frequently serve as targets of comic invective, Aristophanes' critique goes deeper than comic name-calling. Skillful rhetoricians are portrayed in Attic Old Comedy and elsewhere as possessing a powerful means of subverting the normative social order and blurring class lines: thus speakers of low birth may gain power over aristocrats, thereby jeopardizing, from the standpoint of the elite, the stability of political and social hierarchy. Women, because they stand largely outside the discursive spheres controlled by men in classical Athens, and because of their long-standing association with deception in the literary tradition, provide the perfect vehicle for conveying this contemporary political crisis.

One might argue that the equation between women and the subversive potential of the art of persuasion is confined to Aristophanic comedy because it is a genre that self-consciously engages with contemporary social and political issues. But given the dialectical relation between the theater of Dionysus and the other discursive spheres of the city outlined in the first part of this chapter and the absence of real women from all civic spaces except ritual, it is conceivable that the fictional construction of dangerously persuasive women on the tragic stage could have served as a means of representing the problems of discourse within the democratic polis. In my view, Aristophanes merely brings to the fore the issue of the status and function of speech in the polis initiated by Aeschylus in the *Oresteia* and later reexamined in the plays of Euripides. This book considers the issue of speech and gender in seven plays by three different authors: five tragedies, including a trilogy, and two comedies. These plays, which span a period of over sixty years, intersect with the rise of democracy in Athens and the attendant interest in rhetoric necessitated by democratic reforms and promoted by the sophists. All of the plays considered in this book involve a similar dynamic: they begin by depicting women's speech as operating outside the bounds of masculine control and conclude with its successful containment. All of them establish separate discursive spheres for men and women and then show how female speech permeates and infiltrates the male world, particularly through deception and seductive persuasion. Given the dialectical relation between the theater of Dionysus and Athenian civic institutions, this movement indirectly comments on the status of male speech in the polis, reflecting on the one hand the principle of exclusivity by which the citizen elite distinguished themselves from noncitizen others, and on the other, the growing ambivalence about rhetoric and its potential for undermining the power of the aristocratic elite.

SUMMARY OF CHAPTERS

Although Athenian women during the classical period were denied access to public, political speech, the Greek literary tradition provides a wealth of information about the other kinds of speech associated with them. Chapter 2 examines some of the ways in which male and female discursive practices were delineated as background for the subsequent analysis of plays. These sources typically, although not exclusively, identify speech genres such as gossip, seductive persuasion, lamentation, and other forms of ritual speech as feminine. Women's collective and socially sanctioned speech genres, particularly in a ritual context, are viewed as productive of social ideology and communal stability. In contrast, genres like gossip and seductive persuasion of individual women are represented as potentially subversive of social hierarchy. The literary tradition thus suggests that although men sometimes viewed women's speech as belonging to a separate women's culture apart from men's, it nonetheless played an important role in the larger community.

Chapter 3 examines how the *Oresteia*, a trilogy that allegorizes the rise of democratic Athens and the place of speech within the polis, conceptualizes the role of speech in the democratic polis by means of gendered discourses. The trilogy depicts a movement from the feminine, figurative, and false speech of Clytemnestra in the *Agamemnon* to the masculine and divinely sanctioned speech of the courts in the *Eumenides*, illustrating how feminine verbal guile can destabilize the social order. The final play integrates the figurative and deceptive speech of women and the masculine discourses of the polis through the androgynous figure of Athena, whose enchanting persuasion benefits rather than harms the city. Athena converts the androgynously dangerous speech of Clytemnestra into the divinely sanctioned and "truthful" speech of the courts. And yet, paradoxically, since she, too, is an androgyne, her speech in the Areopagus reinscribes gender roles and resolves the category crisis of the first two plays by rendering the female invisible. The trilogy thus problematizes the role of female speech in the polis as potentially subversive of the normative social categories that the civic discourse of the law courts seeks to produce and maintain.

Chapters 4 and 5 consider the destructive effects of women's uncontrolled speech on the household in Euripides' *Hippolytus* and *Andromache*. Chapter 4 reexamines the much-discussed issue of speech and gender in the *Hippolytus* in terms of the increasingly important role played by the politics of reputation in the democratic polis. Phaedra's slander of Hippolytus can be viewed as corresponding to the role played by gossip, particularly that relating to the conduct of a man's female kin, in the popular courts. While the play first establishes women's speech as operating outside the boundaries of masculine control, although it belongs to the domestic sphere, the second part of the play, particularly the agon, shows its potential to infiltrate and subvert the public, juridical discourse of men. Theseus' inability to uncover the truth combined with his vulnerability to deception is suggestive of the mass audience who filled the courts and the Assembly in the democratic polis. Finally, by converting Phaedra's destructive and erotic speech into the ritual song of girls, the play assigns a partial public voice to women, but one that reinforces gender ideology by teaching wives to be chaste.

Chapter 5 turns to the *Andromache*, a play frequently overlooked in Euripidean criticism and fundamentally preoccupied with many of the same issues of speech and gender raised by the *Hippolytus*. Structured around an antithesis between Hermione, the Spartan princess, and Andromache, a Trojan slave, the play impugns women's speech as the source of political and social instability, showing how women's gossip disrupts and subverts the relatively stable institution of marriage. Hermione's self-proclaimed access to the free speech of men contrasts with Andromache's imprecations of silence; her garrulity and lack of restraint hint at her sexual preoccupations, which lead to adultery. But the play offers a corrective to the destructive effects of female speech by instructing women how to speak like men: Andromache utters the traditional *psogos gunaikōn*, "rebuke against women," associated with Hippolytus and the Hesiodic tradition, as she reviles Hermione for her lack of sexual self-control. By the end of the play, Hermione also adopts this genre as she censures other women for their corrupting power of gossip. Conversely, the play correlates the cunning and treacherous speech of women with the unscrupulous and corrupt speech of men in the political sphere.

Chapter 6 focuses on obscenity and social status in Aristophanes' *Thesmophoriazusae* and *Ecclesiazusae*. In contrast to the tragedies, Attic Old Comedy makes a fundamental distinction in how it represents the speech of male and female characters: male comic obscenity typically consists of scatological and pathic (or sexually submissive male) humor, while female obscenity, when it occurs, tends not to take this form. The language of comedy, in fact, can be characterized as masculine, because its most striking linguistic feature, that of obscenity, is traditionally associated with men. The comic poet deploys these gendered speech conventions for dramatic effect: in the *Thesmophoriazusae* an effeminate male speaker, Agathon, uses euphemisms, as a woman might, rather than more masculine primary obscenities. At the other end of the spectrum is the speech of older women, like the three crones in the *Ecclesiazusae*, who use obscenities like men. The second part of the chapter explores how various characters, particularly the Relative in the *Thesmophoriazusae* and Praxagora in the *Ecclesiazusae*, transgress linguistic norms. The disjunctions between gender and speech genres in these plays reflect a larger social disturbance entailed by gender inversion. These plays locate the source of this disorder in the seductive and corrupting speech practices of the politicians, embodied by pathics and women. But in both of these plays, comic obscenity, a speech genre identified as emphatically masculine, affirms and restores traditional gender roles.

Chapter Two

GENDER AND VERBAL GENRES IN

ANCIENT GREECE

ALTHOUGH women were debarred from the discursive spheres that consolidated masculine political identity in classical Athens, as discussed in the preceding chapter, their speech was not altogether erased from the polis; in fact, certain women's speech genres, particularly those connected with ritual, were deemed indispensable for ensuring the well-being of the community. While the last chapter discussed the discursive practices identified with men and women's exclusion from the public sphere in the democratic polis, this chapter explores the types of speech associated with women in dramatic and nondramatic literary texts and their intersection with political and social institutions. Although representational structures are naturally infused by everyday life, my purpose is not to recover actual women's voices, or to suggest an exact correspondence between historical women and their literary depiction, but to understand how women's voices were conceptualized by male-authored texts produced both in Athens and elsewhere over a broad span of time. This chapter thus provides a general overview of women's linguistic practices and speech genres in the Greek literary tradition and discusses their social significance in order to establish a foundation for the subsequent chapters on fifth-century Athenian drama.

The study of women's language and verbal genres can be traced to a few stereotypical remarks made by the linguist Otto Jesperson in his chapter "The Woman," in *Language, Its Nature, Development and Origin*, originally published in 1922. Influenced by folklinguistics, Jesperson associated a refined, euphemistic, and hyperbolic discursive style with women and identified linguistic innovation, slang usage, and a preference for the vernacular with men, a model that has prevailed even in more recent feminist analyses of gender-based linguistic differences. The contemporary study of women's speech has been influenced by three main approaches: sociolinguistics, which examines the formal properties of speech and relates them to social context and social roles; discourse analysis; and comparative ethnographic studies that focus on verbal genres.[1] The sociolinguist Robin Lakoff pioneered the study of women's speech as an academic subfield in

---

[1] For sociolinguistic approaches, see Henley and Thorne 1975; Philips, Steele, and Tanz 1987; for women's speech genres in other cultures, see Keenan 1974; Gal 1991; Raheja 1996.

the early 1970s with her book *Language and Woman's Place*. She discovered a range of feminine linguistic characteristics, particularly special vocabularies, like color terms, related to women's social roles, intensification ("so" and "such"), restriction of negative emotion, avoidance of obscenity, diminutives, tag questions, and hedging.[2] Lakoff speculated that these features conveyed greater uncertainty and deference and, as a sociolinguist, correlated them to the marginality and powerlessness experienced by women in contemporary American society. This pattern of verbal deference reflects traditional expectations about women's speech; from medieval and Renaissance advice manuals and etiquette books to contemporary teen magazines, females are cautioned to avoid gossip and loud, aggressive and sexually suggestive language.[3]

Although contemporary research on women's language has generally concurred that gender-based linguistic differences exist, the ways in which men's and women's speech diverge as well as their social meanings have provoked much debate.[4] One theory holds that divergent paths of socialization engender distinct linguistic styles in men and women. Coates has argued in her analysis of male and female discursive practices in the workplace that women's speech tends to be more cooperative and collaborative, while men's speech is more competitive and adversarial, a difference that stems from the split between public and private spheres.[5] Women have not traditionally been accepted as public speakers before men, although they may speak before a group of women, and therefore have not been considered fluent in public speech genres until recently.[6] Other studies have indicated that women's speech is linguistically conservative, tending toward prestige forms, a feature also remarked upon by the ancients, notably Plato and Cicero.[7] Conversely, some recent British studies have suggested that divergence from standard forms and linguistic innovation

[2] Lakoff 1973, 1975, and 1978; see also Coates 1986: 103–9. It is striking how closely some feminist observations resemble the views of Jesperson (1922: 237–54); see Cameron 1985: 35–44.

[3] Bornstein 1978: 132 discusses the repeated injunction for women to be "lytill of langage" in fourteenth- and fifteenth-century European courtesy books, one of which, written by the Ménagier of Paris for his fifteen-year-old bride, provides an interesting parallel to Xenophon's *Oeconomicus*.

[4] Recent debate has centered on whether sociolinguists promulgate a dominance or a difference model; see Johnson in Johnson and Meinhof 1997: 9–10 for a discussion. The dominance model views gender-based language differentials as the product of power dynamics, a view supported by Lakoff 1973; Henley and Thorne 1975; Henley, Kramarae, and Thorne 1983; West and Zimmerman 1983. The difference model views women's linguistic behavior as the product of socialization, represented by Coates 1986 and Tannen 1996.

[5] Coates 1995: 13; see also 1986: 11.

[6] Kramarae 1981: xiv and 72–73.

[7] For a discussion of women's linguistic conservatism, see Baron 1986: 2. Coates (1986: 43 and 64) argues that linguistic conservatism tends to occur among muted groups whose

are viewed as markers of masculinity, particularly by working-class men.[8] Related to the masculine preference for the vernacular is the long-standing association between male speech and obscenity, a verbal genre taboo to women in many cultures.[9] Instead of specific linguistic features, other research on women's language has emphasized the analysis of discursive strategies and verbal genres in specific social contexts rather than lexical or morphological features. This work has revealed the ambiguities and complexities involved in interpreting stylistic elements of conversation; silence, for example, may express dominance and disapproval, or it may indicate submission.[10] Similarly, interruptions can show conversational control, or the active participation and enthusiasm of the listener.[11]

---

status consciousness leads to a preference for prestige forms. In Cicero's *De oratore*, the interlocutor L. Licinius Crassus also remarks upon the conservative nature of female speech when he describes listening to his mother-in-law's speech:

> Equidam cum audio socrum meam Laeliam—facilius enim mulieres incorruptam antiquitatem conseruant, quod multorum sermonis expertes ea tenent semper, quae prima didicerunt—sed eam sic audio, ut Plautum mihi aut Naevium videar audire, sono ipso vocis ita recto et simplici est, ut nihil ostentationis aut imitationis adferre videatur; ex quo sic locutum esse eius patrem iudico, sic maiores.   (Cic. *De or.* 3.12.45)

> Easily indeed do women preserve the old pronunciation unspoiled, because they do not converse with a number of people and so always retain what they first learned. When I hear my mother-in-law Laelia speak, I feel like I am hearing the speech of Plautus or Naevius, her voice is so unaffected and natural that she seems to bring no trace of display or affectation; and I consequently infer that that was how her father and her ancestors used to speak.

Cicero represents women's speech not only as more archaic, but also as more colloquial, more natural, and less artificial or affected.

[8] In four British studies discussed by Coates (1986: 76–77) working-class women's speech tended to be hypercorrect, whereas the men's speech showed a marked divergence from standard forms. Coates (1986: 94) further speculates that women's adherence to more standard linguistic forms is due to the fact that they are not exposed as frequently to vernacular speech.

[9] Several recent studies have reinforced Jesperson's view (1922: 245–47) that avoidance of obscenity is a characteristic of women's speech; see Bornstein 1987: 135; Henley 1977: 147; Coates 1986: 108–9, on aggressive speech and gestures; Lakoff (1973: 50) describes obscenity as masculine and argues that women tend to use weaker expletives, such as "oh dear." De Klerk (1997: 152) associates this verbal genre with a dominating discursive style. She concludes from her study of obscenity among adolescents in South Africa that "males generally used words which scored higher in terms of shock value."

[10] Gal (1995: 171–73) shows how silence can have a range of cultural meanings; see also Tannen 1996: 36–37.

[11] On the ambiguity of linguistic strategies, see Tannen 1996: 20–21; on interruption, 35–36. Coates 1986: 99–100 discusses one study of mixed group conversation in which men initiated forty-six of the forty-eight interruptions. West and Zimmerman (1983: 102–3) correlate interruptions with a dominant discursive style that sustains status differences; they cite in support of their position studies of parent-child interaction in which parents are far more likely to interrupt a child than the other way around.

The concept of the verbal or speech genre used by anthropologists and, to a lesser extent, by literary critics has proven very useful to this study. Verbal genres correspond to and accompany activities and social practices; they are the "culturally recognized, routinized, and sometimes though not necessarily overtly marked and formalized forms and categories of discourse in use in particular communities and societies."[12] Thus a diverse array of speech genres, from the personal letter to the legal brief, from scientific tracts and literary texts to military commands, are encountered in everyday life and deployed in literary texts. These speech genres conform to a relatively fixed set of stylistic criteria with the result that "even in the most free, the most unconstrained conversation, we cast our speech in definite generic forms, sometimes rigid and trite ones, sometimes more flexible, plastic and creative ones."[13] Because men and women inhabit distinct social spheres in many societies, particularly in ancient Greece, the speech genres associated with them tend to differ.

Most ethnographic studies of linguistic practices in communities that show strong gender segregation have noted a distinction between public and private speech genres. While men and women participate in both spheres, in most cultures women's involvement in the speech practices and discourses of public life is attenuated. Gal observes, for example, that among the Kuna Indians of Central America, public verbal genres, particularly ritual and traditional forms of speech, are the province of men, while women, who spend most of their time in the home, are responsible for "the more privately performed genres of lullabies and tuneful mourning."[14] Among the Araucanians of Chile, men are trained to be good orators, and conversationalists from boyhood, and their speech is viewed as promoting group solidarity; only they may serve as leaders, public orators and messengers. On the other hand, the ideal Araucanian woman should be silent and submissive, as illustrated by the following cultural practice: "A woman, on first arriving in her husband's home, is expected to sit silent and face the wall, not looking anyone in the household directly in the face."[15] Nonetheless, the women participate in ritual, public forms of speech in a type of curing ceremony and in their role as mourners. The Laymi women in Bolivia control and create genres of publicly performed song and music essential to courting rituals, and yet only the men have authority over speaking in the local political assembly.[16] Among the Malagasy of Madagascar, men avoid the speech practices associated with women, such as market haggling, gossip, and accusations, while women are excluded from the

[12] Sherzer 1987: 98.

[13] Bakhtin 1986: 78; Sherzer (1987: 98) also emphasizes that speech genres are not always formal or literary forms of discourse, but include casual and everyday forms.

[14] Gal 1991: 182; see also Sherzer 1987: 99.

[15] Sherzer 1987: 100.

[16] Gal 1991: 182.

major speech genre of oratory required in political events.[17] Similarly, women's perceived lack of verbal self-control in modern rural Greece diminishes their public authority.[18] Although women participate in public life through ritual songs and language, in all these instances their access to public speech is often more restricted than that of men, who normally control this discursive sphere. Moreover, women's verbal performances, whether lullabies, laments, or storytelling, normally occur in a nonpublic setting, such as in the home. In the case of women's speech in ancient Greece, a similar model obtains: the literary tradition rarely represents women as public speakers in a political context, as orators or messengers, except in comedy, a genre that frequently inverts gender roles and linguistic genres for comic effect. But the literary sources do frequently portray women as engaging in a quasi-public, ritual speech, albeit in a context that often excluded men. Ritual lamentation, for example, remained a socially sanctioned, authoritative speech genre for female characters in all phases of Greek literature.

Several ethnographic studies have revealed that women's speech genres must be viewed not simply as a marker of social status, but also as a discursive strategy strongly affected by the gender of the interlocutor. Gal observes that ethnographers working among the Kwaio of the Solomon Islands in the South Pacific received very different responses from their female subjects depending on their gender. Although silent in the presence of a male ethnographer, the Kwaio women later engaged in lengthy conversations when interviewed by a woman. This research prompted Gal to conclude, "If speech enacts a discourse strategy and is not simply a reflex or signal of social identity, then attention must be paid not only to the gender identity of the speaker but also to the gender of the audience."[19] The ancient Greek literary tradition similarly portrays women's speech communities as separate from those of men and represents women as speaking differently among themselves than they do before men. Recent scholarship on Sappho, one of the few female literary voices available to us from the ancient world, has suggested that the poet at least conceptualized herself differently from her male counterparts, both in her erotic sensibility and in her poetic discourse, a difference that may have in part been influenced by her female audience.[20] Similarly, Skinner has shown in her analysis

---

[17] Ibid.: 179; Keenan 1974: 137–39.

[18] Gal 1991: 180. Herzfeld (1991: 80) complicates the traditional view of women in modern Greece as unable to speak rationally and coherently by showing how through this behavior they "perform a submission that ridicules."

[19] Gal 1991: 181.

[20] Stehle (1981 and 1997: 262–318) argues that Sappho's poetry represents an alternative women's song tradition performed for a speech community separate from men, one consisting of adult women rather than *parthenoi*. For a similar view, see also Winkler 1990a: 162–87; Skinner 1993; and Greene 1994; but *pace* Lardinois (1994). Rayor (1993) similarly argues

of an epigram by the female Hellenistic poet Nossis that women may have addressed one another differently, by their mother's name rather than by that of their husband or father, when alone.[21] In tragedy, female characters are often represented as speaking one way when alone with other women and another way when men are present, as will be explored in subsequent chapters. Participation in women-only festivals like the Thesmophoria in honor of Demeter was strictly prohibited to men, thereby reinforcing the idea of a separate women's culture with its own exclusionary speech practices, like *aischrologia*, "ritual obscenity."

One of the questions raised by these comparative ethnographic studies, as well as by sociolinguists, is whether women's expressive genres reinforce or subvert the dominant discourse. Even women's silence may denote a form of resistance rather than passive submission: "Women's special verbal skills are often strategic responses to positions of relative powerlessness."[22] Raheja, working on women's ritual songs and proverbial speech in rural North India, remarks that women's ritual speech, while viewed as "auspicious and necessary," is frequently monitored or restricted in some way.[23] Similarly, Caraveli has observed that women's ritual laments in contemporary rural Greece may function as a vehicle for social protest, a strategy that can perhaps be seen even in the character of Antigone, as Foley has argued.[24] Although it is not known whether women's speech genres in fact functioned subversively in ancient Greece, many of the literary sources, particularly tragedy, depict both women's ritual and nonritual speech as dangerous because of the pervasive equation between speech and power in classical Athens.

It may seem paradoxical to look for signs of women's oral culture in male-authored literary texts. But although the conversations that took place among the women of ancient Greece, their songs, and the ritual forms they uttered are now lost to us, literary sources may provide a partial view of their discursive practices. As Sherzer observes, literary models are found in everyday verbal reality and yet create stereotypes that in turn inform everyday life, a process that reflects "the complex sociological matrix in which speech occurs and from which culturally symbolic interpretations are derived."[25] This chapter will examine speech acts and verbal performances associated predominantly, although not exclusively, with women

---

that Corinna reworks traditional male narratives for an audience of women. Williamson (1995: 81) argues that the poetry of Sappho, which she compares to that of a male counterpart, Anacreon, shows a continual shifting of subject positions in which the boundaries between self and other are "elided" but not dissolved.

[21] Skinner 1987.

[22] Gal 1991: 182.

[23] Raheja 1996: 151.

[24] Caraveli 1980 and 1986; Foley 1993: 111–13.

[25] Sherzer 1987: 109.

in the Greek literary tradition from the archaic through classical periods, including ritual lamentation, ritual obscenity or *aischrologia*, women's ritual cries, like the *ololugē*, female choruses, gossip, and seductive persuasion.

ANCIENT OBSERVATIONS ABOUT WOMEN'S SPEECH

In recent years, classical scholars have attempted to reconstruct the speech of ancient women primarily by using a sociolinguistic model; these studies have focused on comedy because of its mixture of paratragic and colloquial language. This task is complicated by the fact that almost all literary representations of female speech and all descriptive evidence for its sound and diction come from male writers. Nonetheless, several linguistic features that may have characterized the talk of women in everyday life have been identified in the literary sources: exclamations, polite modifiers, forms of oaths, imperatives, forms of address, and self-reflexive adjectives.[26] Denniston even speculates that particle usage might vary according to a speaker's gender: "Perhaps women, on the principle that τὸ θῆλυ μᾶλλον οἰκτρὸν ἀρσένος ['the female is more emotional than the male'], were peculiarly addicted to the use of particles, just as women to-day are fond of underlining words in their letters."[27] Some of these markers of female speech, especially those connected with ritual lament, can also be found in the highly formalized language of tragedy, although to a lesser extent than in comedy: the exclamation οἲ 'γώ, for example, signals lament and is employed only by female speakers in extant Euripidean drama.[28] Female speakers in Aristophanes use primary obscenities far less frequently than do their male counterparts, a point I explore more fully in Chapter 6.[29] And more recently, it has been suggested that differences in elevation of diction may have distinguished masculine from feminine speech in satyr drama.[30]

Several ancient sources suggest that the sound, diction, and content of women's speech were considered different from those of men. Aristotle asserts that the females of all species in general tend to have higher, weaker voices than do the males (λεπτοφωνότερα, ὀξυφωνότερα, *Hist. an.* 538b12–15) and contrasts female with male voices, which he deems more noble because of their depth of tone (καὶ δοκεῖ γενναιοτέρας εἶναι φύσεως

---

[26] Gilleland 1980; Bain 1984; Adams 1984; Dickey 1995 and 1996.

[27] Denniston (1959: xxiii) bases this conclusion on the suggestion "that γε denotes 'feminine underlining' in the Plathane scene in the *Frogs*." Denniston and others were no doubt influenced by Jesperson (1922: 243), who identifies "the excessive use of intensive words and the exaggeration of stress and tone-accent to mark emphasis" as a characteristic of women's speech in Japanese, French, and English.

[28] McClure 1995.

[29] Sommerstein 1995.

[30] Hall 1998.

ἡ βαρυφωνία, *Gen. an.* 786b35–787a1).[31] According to Herodotus, the mythical Amazons, separatists in every way, spoke a language that could not be learned by men: "The men could not learn the women's language, but the women learned the speech of men" (τὴν δὲ φωνὴν τὴν μὲν τῶν γυναικῶν οἱ ἄνδρες οὐκ ἐδυνέατο μαθεῖν, τὴν δὲ τῶν ἀνδρῶν αἱ γυναῖκες συνέλαβον, Hdt. 4.114.1–2).[32] Plato remarks in the *Cratylus* that women's speech tends to be linguistically conservative, retaining the features of an older, more archaic language (αἱ γυναῖκες . . . μάλιστα τὴν ἀρχαίαν φωνὴν σῴζουσι, 418c).[33] Other sources indicate that certain forms of address were associated with women.[34] Herodotus, in his description of the Carians, asserts that the wives never address their husbands by name, nor do they share their tables (Hdt. 1.146). Two scholia on Plato comment that the forms of address ὦ τάλαν, ὦ τάν, ὦ μέλε, and ὦ οὗτος are gender-specific features of women's speech, even though they were once used interchangeably by both sexes (as found in Attic Old Comedy).[35]

In addition to differences of address or diction, later writers attributed specific types of song or musical genre to women; Plutarch, for example, quotes the words of a work song, possibly obscene, apparently sung by a woman while grinding: "Grind, mill, grind; for even Pittacus ground when he ruled the great people of Mytilene" (ἄλει, μύλα ἄλει· | καὶ γὰρ Πιττακὸς ἄλει | μεγάλας Μυτιλήνας βασιλεύων, 869 *PMG*).[36] Athenaeus also attributes several types of song to women: the *ioulos* or spinning song, songs of lament such as the *olophurmos*, *goos*, *thrēnos*, and *ialemos*, the Linus song, the *humenaios* or wedding song, and the *katabaukalēsis* or lullaby,

---

[31] Aristotle (*Gen. an.* 787a29–30) remarks that females and the young usually have high-pitched voices (ὀξύφωνα). Aristotle also correlates bodily potency to the sound of the voice, observing that older men often have shrill voices (Arist. *Hist. an.* 787a28–29), as do the castrated males of any species (Arist. *Gen. an.* 787b20ff; *Hist. an.* 632a1). High pitch has also been traditionally viewed as a negative phonological characteristic of women's speech; see Kramarae 1981: 96; Baron 1986: 62 and 67.

[32] How and Wells (1967: 341) could not resist the urge to comment on the scholarly talents of the mythical Amazons: "The greater aptness of the Amazons is a delightful touch of nature; but they were inaccurate [in their use of the Scythian dialect] (cf. σολοικίζοντες c. 117), as lady linguists often are."

[33] The full sentence at Pl. *Cra.* 418c reads as follows: "You are aware that our forefathers very much enjoyed using the sounds ι and δ, especially the women, who in particular preserve the ancient way of speaking" (οἶσθα ὅτι οἱ παλαιοὶ οἱ ἡμέτεροι τῷ ἰῶτα καὶ τῷ δέλτα εὖ μάλα ἐχρῶντο, καὶ οὐχ ἥκιστα αἱ γυναῖκες, αἵπερ μάλιστα τὴν ἀρχαίαν φωνὴν σῴζουσι). Identifying *iōta* and *delta* as features of the Boeotian dialect corresponding to Attic *epsilon* and *zēta* respectively, Sommerstein (1995: 82–83) argues that this passage indicates that women's linguistic practices were actually innovative rather than conservative.

[34] Dickey (1996: 246), after exhaustively surveying the data, concludes that there is not enough evidence to support the view that certain forms of address may have reflected actual women's language.

[35] Schol. Pl. *Tht.* 178e; Schol. Pl. *Ap.* 25c; cf. *Suda* s.v. ὦ μέλε and ὦ τάν.

[36] On this fragment, see Campbell 1967: 448–49; Skinner 1993: 135.

to name a few.[37] These songs both accompanied the domestic tasks of women, reflecting the gender segregation characteristic of ancient Greek society, and marked major life events, thereby providing an occasion for women's public speech. Even musical modes could serve as markers of gender and social status. For example, Agathon's effeminate song in Aristophanes' *Thesmophoriazusae* (Ar. *Thesm.* 144–45), like the one sung by the crone at the end of *Ecclesiazusae* (Ar. *Eccl.* 876–83), has erotic and sensuous overtones associated with prostitutes. In the same way, Praxagora instructs the female chorus disguised as farmers to sing the type of song characteristic of rustic elders (Ar. *Eccl.* 277–78). Although these passages give us few reliable clues about the actual linguistic practices that might have characterized women's speech in the ancient world, clearly the literary tradition recognized that there were differences of sound, style, and content between male and female speech.

LAMENTATION

As much recent work on the subject has convincingly shown, the predominant, although not exclusive, speech genre assigned to female characters in both archaic and classical literature is lamentation. Socrates in the *Republic* explicitly designates lamentation and the musical modes associated with it as a female discursive practice inappropriate for men: these musical modes are deemed "worthless even for women, who are to be good, let alone men" (ἄχρηστοι γὰρ καὶ γυναιξὶν ἃς δεῖ ἐπιεικεῖς εἶναι, μὴ ὅτι ἀνδράσι, Pl. *Rep.* 398e2). Throughout the Greek tradition, ritual lament, while not exclusively feminine, remained the province and prerogative of women, in whom it was believed there was an innate affinity for weeping and sorrowful songs, as Medea remarks: "Women by nature are given to weeping" (γυνὴ δὲ θῆλυ κἀπὶ δακρύοις ἔφυ, Eur. *Med.* 928). Though the laments of women, together with funerary ritual, serve a positive function in early epic by binding together the community and affirming collective values, this view may have gradually changed in the period between epic and tragedy.[38] In the fifth century, female lamentation is construed as a source of danger and disorder

---

[37] On these songs in general, see Ath. 14.618ff.; for the *ioulos*, cf. Apollod. *Hist.* 149J; Eratosth. fr. 10; for the Linus song, see Hom. *Iliad* 18.570; Pind. fr. 126.5 Bowra; for the *humenaios*, cf. Hom. *Iliad* 18.493; Hes. *Sc.* 274; Aesch. *Ag.* 707; Eur. *IA* 1036; Pind. *Pyth.* 3.17; Eur. *Alc.* 922; Sappho 111 Voigt; on lullabies, see Waern 1960; cf. also Hesychius s.v. βαυκαλᾶν; Theoc. 24.7; Rosenmeyer (1991: 23–24) briefly discusses the lullaby as a speech act in Simonides' Danaë fragment, although she does not identify it as a specifically feminine verbal genre.

[38] As Martin (1989: 87–88) points out, both Helen and Hecuba employ lamentation as a means of conveying a *muthos* to men in the *Iliad*; as a form of authoritative speech employed by women, the use of lament perhaps has a slightly subversive connotation.

liable to undermine the stable, masculine community of the polis. Given the significance of ritual lament in ancient Greek literature and society, studies of women's laments have proliferated in recent years, influenced by Margaret Alexiou's pioneering research, which traces the form and function of female lamentation from ancient Greece to the modern Greek village.[39] These studies have also been fueled by the growing interest of anthropologists in death rituals and women's laments in contemporary cultures, particularly in rural Greece, where women's laments over the dead appear to have existed almost continuously for almost 3,000 years.[40]

Performed predominantly by women, ritual lamentation may represent an attempt, in Danforth's words, "to continue their relationship with their male kin beyond death—a relationship that gave them their identity in life."[41] Although the lament expresses private pain, it is also a collective enterprise involving a group of female mourners, either relatives or hired professionals (a role often taken by the chorus in Greek tragedy), who sing their songs in antiphony.[42] As a collective activity, women's laments draw together a subordinate group within the larger community, presenting an opportunity "to create, reflect, reinforce, and negotiate realms of experience and action that are exclusive to women."[43] In fact, as Caraveli argues, the lament in modern Greece, as perhaps in antiquity, provides a female, oral history of the village as women's foremost expressive genre.[44] Like gossip, lamentation may have provided an occasion for strengthening ties between women, and perhaps for reinforcing gender roles by means of participation in a shared female activity. As a collective performance, ritual lamentation resembles women's state religious festivals, like the Thesmophoria and the particular rites involving women at Eleusis, which, in Alexiou's view, may have been established in "consolation for their lost privileges," placing them firmly under State control.[45] While on one level ritual lamentation functions to consolidate and articulate a community's feelings of loss, on another, more subversive level it can function as a form of social protest and as a spur to revenge, a point to which I shall return later in this section.[46]

---

[39] Alexiou 1974; Vermeule 1974; see, more recently, Holst-Warhaft 1992; Foley 1993; Sultan 1993.

[40] On lamentation in contemporary rural Greece, see Danforth 1982; Seremetakis 1991; Caraveli 1980 and 1986; as well as Holst-Warhaft 1992 and Alexiou 1974. Feld (1982), examining lamentation among the Kaluli of Papua New Guinea, provides fascinating comparative material.

[41] Danforth 1982: 136–38.

[42] Alexiou 1974 repeatedly emphasizes the responsive aspect of the performance.

[43] Caraveli 1986: 178.

[44] Ibid.: 170.

[45] Alexiou 1974: 21.

[46] On blood vendetta and women's laments, see Holst-Warhaft 1992: 5–6, 33, 118; Alexiou 1974; Caraveli 1980 and 1986.

Ritual lament in ancient Greece was a highly conservative genre that produced a relatively stable pattern of thematic and stylistic conventions and accompanied rituals largely unchanged throughout the archaic and classical periods. In Vermeule's view, these death rituals were probably "the oldest and least changing art-form in Greece."[47] After the proper sacrifices and offerings were made, ritual lament occurred at the *prothesis*, laying out of the dead, with women standing closest to the body, a spatial arrangement that, in addition to the physical gestures accompanying lament, reinforced the intimate association between women's speech and the body. Attic vases show female mourners surrounding the head and body of the corpse, with men standing at a distance.[48] More lamentation accompanied the *ekphora*, the procession in which the corpse was carried out of the house to the cemetery, followed by another round of laments at the tomb. As a folk genre, the lament in ancient Greece, as in contemporary societies, formed part of an oral tradition passed down from generation to generation. As it evolves in the literary tradition, the genre conforms to a fixed set of conventions, perhaps reflecting the conservative nature of ritual practice. The terms most closely associated with the ritual lament are *goos* and *thrēnos*, terms used interchangeably by the time of tragedy.

Although men are also depicted as mourners in ancient Greek poetry, the Homeric poems distinguish between the two types of mourner. The verb κωκύω, often in combination with an adverb such as λίγα or ὀξύ, normally describes women's keening over the dead.[49] At the end of the *Iliad*, the verb appears synonymous with female speech when it is used of Cassandra's report to the Trojan people of the return of Hector's corpse (Hom. *Iliad* 24.703). The adverbs λίγα or ὀξύ when applied to the voice of the female mourner describe a piercing or shrill tone, as when Briseis falls shrieking over the dead body of Patroclus (λίγ' ἐκώκυε, 19.284).[50]

---

[47] Vermeule 1974: 12.

[48] Holst-Warhaft 1992: 103.

[49] Hall (1996: 143) observes that "men hardly ever κωκύειν in serious Greek literature," unless they are barbarian men, as in the case of Aesch. *Pers.* 427 and 468. The fact that the verb κωκύω is used of Creon at Soph. *Ant.* 1315 possibly implies his effeminized status at the end of the play.

[50] The name of the wailing river in Hades, ὁ Κωκυτός, shows the strong funerary associations of κωκύω. For the verb κωκύω and its cognates in Homer, cf. Hom. *Iliad* 18.37, 71 (Thetis); 19.284 (Briseis); 22.407 (Hecuba); 24.703 (Cassandra); *Od.* 4.259, 8.527 (Trojan women); and κωκυτός, *Iliad* 22.447 (Andromache); 22.409 (Trojan people). On the adjectives λίγυς and ὀξύς in Homer, see Kaimio 1977: 38–49. Hall (1996: 143) notes that the word λίγυς in Aeschylus normally refers to female cries (cf. Aesch. *Supp.* 114), or to the nightingale, a bird normally associated with women's laments, as discussed later in this chapter. Monsacré (1984: 231) argues that men's weeping is portrayed as more forceful and spontaneous than that of women in the Homeric poems. Although males occasionally assume a piercing tone in their laments—Achilles, for example, weeps in shrill tones over the dead Patroclus (κλαίοντα λιγέως, Hom. *Iliad* 19.5)—the term λιγέως in these contexts usually denotes loudness and authority rather than a high pitch.

That this cry is distinct from that of a male mourner is illustrated by the lamentations over the body of Patroclus: while Thetis wails piercingly (κώκυσεν, Hom. *Iliad* 18.37; ὀξὺ δὲ κωκύσασα, 18.71), Achilles lets out a terrible groan (σμερδαλέον δ' ᾤμωξεν, 18.35), the same cry of pain the Cyclops utters when blinded by Odysseus (*Od.* 9.395). Since the term σμερδαλέος normally marks "major persons and moments of the epic," as Kaimio puts it, it tends not to be applied to women in Homer.[51]

In the *Odyssey*, when Odysseus begins to weep upon hearing the story of the Trojan horse, his tears are compared to those of a woman who laments over the body of her slain husband. The simile underscores the difference between male and female weeping: whereas Odysseus merely sheds tears (δάκρυ δ' ἔδευεν . . . παρείας, *Od.* 8.522), the woman in the simile shrieks shrilly (λίγα κωκύει, *Od.* 8.527). The masculine sound of Odysseus' lament is later indicated by the phrase "groaning heavily" (βαρὺ δὲ στενάχοντος, *Od.* 8.534). The high-pitched, piercing wail, also characteristic of the female mourners of tragedy, evokes the cry of a bird, and so becomes identified with the song of Procne, the nightingale who eternally mourns her dead child: "As when the daughter of Pandareus, green nightingale . . . pours forth her melodious song, mourning her beloved child, Itylus" (ὡς δ' ὅτε Πανδαρέου κούρη, χλωρηῒς ἀηδών, | . . . χέει πολυηχέα φωνήν, | παῖδ' ὀλοφυρομένη Ἴτυλον φίλον . . ., Hom. *Od.* 19.518–22). Besides suggesting a sharp or shrill tone, the term κωκύω also implies inarticulate speech; thus Empedocles uses the verb to describe the sound of a newborn baby (κλαῦσά τε καὶ κώκυσα ἰδὼν ἀσυνήθεα χῶρον, Empedocles 118 DK).

While on the subject of sound and gender, it should be noted that sweetness of voice in early epic and lyric poetry is typically associated with women; in the few instances where this terminology is applied to male singers, almost without exception young males are described: a boy (πάϊς) in the *Iliad* sings with delicate voice (λεπταλέῃ φωνῇ, Hom. *Iliad* 18.571); here the adjective λεπταλέος implies that the voice has not yet broken. Further, the boy's singing is termed καλὸν ἄειδε, a formula normally used to describe female singing in Homer (*Iliad* 18.570). Males in early epic and lyric who are described as singing beautifully or sweetly often are engaged in singing a paean; in the *Iliad*, young men (κοῦροι) delight the god with their song (*Iliad* 1.473), whereas a similar group in Bacchylides (νέοι) sings the paean with a lovely voice (ἐρατᾷ ὀπί, Bacchyl. 17.129 Snell). Similarly, youths in Theognis are said to sing λίγεα (Thgn. 242 *IEG*).[52] Thus early epic and lyric poetry typically associate sweetness and clarity of voice with women and girls; as a result, male voices that are

---

[51] See Kaimio 1977: 62–63; for an example of σμερδαλέος applied to women, cf. Bacchyl. 38.10.56, where the maddened daughters of Proetus are described.

[52] Kaimio 1977: 136.

characterized in this way tend to belong to prepubescent males or to those engaged in a choral, religious performance. The belief that the high-pitched female voice changed and became deeper after first intercourse, a change that corresponded to the enlarging of the neck, indicates that sweetness of voice was associated specifically with virgins.[53]

In Greek tragedy, as in early epic, ritual lamentation is the principal speech genre of women; indeed, lament forms an important dramatic and thematic component in plays such as Aeschylus' *Libation Bearers* and *Seven against Thebes*, Sophocles' *Antigone* and *Electra*, and Euripides' *Suppliants* and *Trojan Women*. The standard linguistic features of ritual lament in Greek tragedy include interjectional cries such as ἒ ἒ ἔ, ἰώ, ὀτοτοῖ, οἲ or οἲ 'γω, ὤ, commands, refrain and repetition, specific forms of address (although the dead person is seldom directly named as in modern Greek laments), and metaphor or symbolic language. These laments generally assume a tripartite structure consisting of an address to the dead, a narrative, and a readdress.[54] Though refrain, repetition, invocation, metaphor, and tripartite structure appear frequently in Homeric laments, the interjectional cries so characteristic of tragic lament are conspicuously absent from epic, suggesting, perhaps, that tragic laments more closely approximated the musical sounds or spoken language found in actual funerary practice. The gestures that accompanied ritual lament also seem to have been highly stylized. Vases from the archaic through the classical periods show women with raised arms, and some scholars have suggested that patterned movements much like dance may have accompanied ritual lamentation.[55] Other movements included the tearing of hair, the laceration of cheeks, and the beating of the chest. As these gestures suggest, ritual lament perhaps approximated a state of controlled frenzy by means of which the mourner mediated between the worlds of the dead and the living, and underscored the close connection between women's speech and their bodies.[56]

As the prerogative or *geras* of the dead, both ancient and modern Greek laments are frequently associated with revenge. In the *Iliad*, for example, the angry spirit of Patroclus visits Achilles in a dream and warns him to accomplish proper burial and its attendant rites, lest his wrath be brought against the living (Hom. *Iliad* 23.65ff.). Because of the link between funerary ritual and the cult of the dead, lamentation served as a means of communication and mediation between the two worlds. Through her laments, the mourner could channel the anger of the dead into revenge against the living. The uncontrolled laments of the outcast Electra and

[53] Armstrong and Hanson 1986: 97–100; and Hanson 1990: 328–29. In an interesting parallel, Baron (1986: 73–74) discusses Havelock Ellis's claim that prostitutes have lower voices because of his theory that the size of the larynx had a direct relation to sexual activity.

[54] Alexiou 1974: 133; Holst-Warhaft 1992: 112.

[55] Alexiou 1974: 6.

[56] Caraveli 1986: 171–72.

the foreign, female chorus that incites Orestes to revenge in Aeschylus' *Libation Bearers* provide another example. Described as peculiarly excessive because foreign, these cries are particularly unrestrained (Aesch. *Cho.* 424).

The association of laments with blood vendetta, as well as their extravagant, feminine nature, perhaps contributed to the many reforms of excessive funerary displays in Athens and elsewhere. The reforms of Solon enacted at Athens during the sixth century B.C.E. were followed by later reforms at Ioulis on the island of Keos and then at Delphi, both at the end of the fifth century, and by much later legislation at Gambrion in Asia Minor during the third century B.C.E.[57] This legislation resulted in a reduced role for women in death rituals. Solon's reforms decreed that women under sixty years of age would not be allowed to attend the *prothesis*, and that women could no longer lacerate themselves or wail (κωκύειν)[58] or accompany the funerary procession. The exception made for women over sixty offers further support for the view that the lives of older women in classical Athens were less restricted than those of their younger counterparts. The silencing of women, especially younger women of childbearing age, enacted by this legislation simultaneously reduced their public visibility by restricting their movements out of doors and further confining them to the house.

The effect of these reforms can be seen both in vase painting and in tragedy during the classical period, as female lamentation gradually becomes suppressed just as the *epitaphios* or public funeral oration becomes increasingly important in consolidating political identity at Athens, a point discussed in Chapter 1.[59] White-ground lēkuthoi from the end of the fifth century showing female mourners have a markedly muted character, with the gestures more restrained, a shift that may reflect the pervasiveness of the reforms against funerary excess.[60] A perfect example of this shift in tragedy can be seen in Aeschylus' *Seven against Thebes*, a play that begins with the ominous wailing of the chorus of maidens. Their first words call attention to their state of fright and the uncontrolled sound of their wailing: "Immense the fear and pain I cry" (θρεῦμαι φοβερὰ μεγάλ' ἄχη, Aesch. *Sept.* 78).[61] But the terrified chorus must be repeatedly admonished by Eteocles to behave as proper women should, to remain indoors and keep quiet (201, 232). He maintains that their voices have an almost coercive,

[57] Alexiou 1974: 14–23; Humphreys 1983: 85–86; and Loraux 1986: 45–49; Holst-Warhaft 1992: 114–15.

[58] Cic. *Leg.* 2.59ff.; Plut. *Sol.* 21.

[59] On the shift from *thrēnos* to *epitaphios* occasioned by these reforms, see Loraux 1986: 42–44.

[60] Foley 1993: 106–7. More generally, Pollitt (1972: 111–12) has suggested that these vases may also represent the somber atmosphere of Athens and the "decay of idealism" during the Peloponnesian war.

[61] For an excellent discussion of female lamentation in this play, see Foley 1993: 129–43.

magical power that threatens to emasculate men (ἀλλ' ὡς πολίτας μὴ κακοσπλάγχνους τιθῇς, 237).[62] Aeschylus' *Seven against Thebes* shows how women's laments can unite an otherwise powerless marginal group into a collective body that may potentially resist masculine authority through its discourse. And yet because that body threatens to intrude into the public and martial sphere, it is ultimately contained.

A similar muting of women's laments is found in Euripides' *Suppliants*, a play that documents the subordination of women's ritual language to the city's collective eulogy.[63] In the beginning of the play, the lamenting chorus of Argive mothers disrupt the rituals of Demeter performed by Aethra, showing again the potentially subversive effects of uncontrolled feminine lamentation (Eur. *Supp.* 95–97, 103, 290). This disorderly women's speech becomes entirely suppressed in the course of the play as their lamentation over the individual dead is supplanted by Adrastus' public encomium, a process aided by Theseus, the Athenian culture hero, who intercedes on the city's behalf. The identification of the chorus of mothers with the city becomes complete when they repudiate Evadne's extravagant immolation over her husband's funerary fires as an extreme gesture of lamentation (Eur. *Supp.* 1072–79). The mothers are finally integrated into the city when they come to terms with "the rights of the city over the children."[64] Their appointment as guardians of Athenian memory by Theseus represents the final testament to the completeness of their transformation.

Although a socially sanctioned, women's genre, the lament can also serve as a vehicle of social protest and resistance, as mentioned earlier. In modern Greece, women's laments voice opposition to male institutions such as war, the medical profession, and even the church; indeed, in antiquity, as now, laments have "commented on, protested against, and affected social change."[65] The example of Antigone in classical drama shows how female lamentation affords a means of resisting masculine civic authority. Antigone's desire to bury her brother, while conforming to traditional expectations of female behavior, completely undermines the edicts of Creon and his regime. Antigone's extraordinary self-lament at the end of the play (Soph. *Ant.* 870ff.) further underscores the revolutionary potential of women's ritual, since Antigone "uses lamentation to carry her point assertively in a public context that might otherwise have silenced her speech."[66] By the end of the fifth century and beyond, literary and didactic texts voice increasingly negative views of women's laments; the

---

[62] Bacon 1964.

[63] On the replacement of lamentation by the *epitaphios* in this play, see Loraux 1986: 48–49; and Foley 1993: 122.

[64] Loraux 1986: 49.

[65] Caraveli 1986: 180.

[66] Foley 1993: 113.

weeping warriors depicted in the Homeric poems give way to a strictly feminine form of emotion in the classical period.[67] For this reason, Plato closely identified lamentation with tragedy and partially attributed the debilitating, emasculating effects of theatrical impersonation on male actors and spectators to their use of lamentation as a feminine verbal genre:

> We will not then allow our charges, whom we expect to prove good men, being men, to play the parts of women and imitate a woman young or old wrangling with her husband, defying heaven, loudly boasting, fortunate in her own conceit, or involved in misfortune and possessed by grief and lamentations—still less a woman that is sick, in love, or in labor. (Pl. *Rep.* 395d5–e2; trans. Shorey).

AISCHROLOGIA

Though not an exclusively female speech genre, *aischrologia*, or scurrilous joking, was a notorious feature of women-only festivals in ancient Greece, especially those in honor of Demeter, such as the Stenia, the Haloa, and the Thesmophoria. These occasions offered another opportunity for women's public speech, if only in the presence of other women, and camaraderie, an opportunity that was thought to foster human and agricultural fertility. Since many of these festivals are shrouded in secrecy, little is known about what the female participants actually said, the words they used and the structure of their exchanges, and we have only scattered allusions to the content of their speech. All that is known with any certainty is that ritual obscenity involved mocking invective, sexual joking, and expressions normally forbidden to women, or *arrhēta*, "religious secrets which may not be disclosed or . . . that which is 'unspeakable' because it violates the social norms."[68] A scholion to Lucian, describing ritual obscenity as practiced by women at the Eleusinian Haloa, corroborates this view. He describes the women's talk as *aiskhista*, "most shameful":

> On this day there is also a women's ceremony conducted at Eleusis, at which much joking (παιδιαί) and scoffing (σκώμματα) takes place. Women proceed there alone and are at liberty to say whatever they want (ἐπ' ἀδείας ἔχουσιν ἃ βούλονται λέγειν): and in fact they say the most shameful things (αἴσχιστα) to each other. The priestesses covertly sidle up to the women and whisper recommendations for adultery into their ears—as if it were a secret (ὡς ἀπόρρη-τον). All the women utter shameful (αἰσχρά) and irreverent things (ἄσεμνα) to each other."[69]

[67] Loraux 1986: 45.
[68] Zeitlin 1982: 144.
[69] Rabe 1971: 280; for a discussion of this passage, see Winkler 1990a: 195.

Like the rituals associated with lament, the religious festivals that involved *aischrologia* required women to leave the house. The scholion implies that women's speech was normally highly restricted, since on this exceptional occasion they were permitted to say whatever they wanted without fear (ἐπ' ἀδείας). By suggesting that this unregulated talk concerned erotic matters, the scholion resorts to the traditional association between women's uncontrolled speech and sexual license. The comment that ritual obscenity may encourage women's adultery indicates the suspicions it aroused in men and its potential for challenging normal social hierarchies. By congregating apart from men, the women are allowed to adopt a speech practice, sexual joking, denied them in the presence of men.[70]

At the Stenia, another women's festival, which took place on the ninth of Pyanopsion, on the day before the minor Thesmophoria at Halimos, the women also exchanged mockery (διασκώπτουσι), insults (λοιδοροῦσι), and blasphemies (βλασφημῆσαι) during the nocturnal ceremonies.[71] Men could participate in obscene exchanges at many of the festivals, including the Haloa and the Stenia. Herodotus, for example, mentions mocking female choruses led by male choregoi in honor of the goddesses Damia and Auxesia at Aigina (χοροῖσι γυναικηίοισι κερτόμοισι, Hdt. 5.83),[72] and specifies that the women never direct this ritual abuse to the men, but only to each other, a point that further underscores the importance of context for evaluating women's speech. At the Argive celebration of Demeter Mysia, from whose sanctuary not only men but even male dogs were excluded during part of the festival, the women spent the first night performing various ceremonies together. On the next day the men joined them, and both groups then took turns insulting each other (αἱ γυναῖκές τε ἐς αὐτοὺς καὶ ἀνὰ μέρος ἐς τὰς γυναῖκας οἱ ἄνδρες γέλωτί τε ἐς ἀλλήλους χρῶνται καὶ σκώμμασιν, Paus. 7.27.10).

The story of Iambe, who cheers up the grieving goddess with humorous abuse in the *Homeric Hymn to Demeter*, provides an aetiology for the practice of women's ritual obscenity.

ἀλλ' ἀγέλαστος ἄπαστος ἐδητύος ἠδὲ ποτῆτος
ἧστο πόθῳ μινύθουσα βαθυζώνοιο θυγατρός,
πρίν γ' ὅτε δὴ χλεύης μιν Ἰάμβη κέδν' εἰδυῖα
πολλὰ παρασκώπτουσ' ἐτρέψατο πότνιαν ἁγνὴν
μειδῆσαι γελάσαι τε καὶ ἵλαον σχεῖν θυμόν.   (200–204)

---

[70] Although Versnel (1993: 284) associates sexual joking with men, the literary tradition, particularly Aristophanes, depicts older women as speaking obscenely, a portrayal that possibly originates in the stories surrounding Iambe.

[71] IG II² 674.6–8; Hesychius s.v. Στήνια and Στηνιῶσαι; see Fluck 1931: 15–17; Deubner 1932: 52–53, 57–58; Parke 1977: 88; Olender 1990: 94.

[72] Paus. 2.32.2; see also Richardson 1974: 213–15; Olender 1990: 95; Buxton 1994: 31n.77.

Unsmiling, tasting neither food nor drink,
she sat wasting with desire for her deep-girt daughter,
until knowing Iambe jested with her and
mocking with many a joke moved the holy goddess
to smile and laugh and keep a gracious heart.   (Trans. Foley)

Although the text is silent about what exactly makes Demeter laugh, the association of Iambe's name with invective poetry suggests that her speech may have been obscene; further, the words χλεύη (202) and σκώπτω (203) suggest pointed insults directed at another person.[73] A later version of the Demeter story by the Hellenistic poet Philocus portrays Iambe as a rustic matron and gossip, a λάλος.[74] In this account, Iambe wanders into Eleusis from Halimos, where there was a sanctuary of Demeter and Persephone, according to Pausanius (Paus. 1.31.1), and where a minor Thesmophoria was held on the tenth of Pyanopsion. The phrase γέλοιος λόγος in line 7 of the Philocus Fragment indicates that Iambe employs comical language in her encounter with Demeter. The term λάλος, "gossiper," identifies her speech as distinctly female, since the word is frequently associated with women in Attic Old Comedy, whereas ἀπαίδευτα and δημότις suggest a woman of the lower classes, a peasant. Nicander in his *Alexipharmaca* similarly describes Iambe as loquacious: she is literally "doorless" (ἀθύροισιν) and her speech therefore "unchecked, unregulated."[75] An Athenian version of the story also puts the emphasis on Iambe's verbal skills by making her the daughter of the nymph Echo: she is thus a " 'disembodied voice' . . . a babbler, a being who is all words."[76]

Whatever the context of her talk, the various versions of Iambe's story link her with the gossip and volubility characteristically associated with women, particularly older women, from the archaic period on. In the "Orphic" version of the myth, it is Baubo, not Iambe, who cheers Demeter up with her obscene mimes.[77] In these accounts Baubo lifts her skirts in a gesture of *anasurma*, by which she exposes her genitals as an apotropaic gesture.[78] This obscene action may have served as the aetion for the handling of the *arrhēta* that accompanied ritual *aischrologia* at some festivals of Demeter.[79] Thus, whereas Iambe puts an end to Demeter's sorrow

---

[73] Foley 1994: 45–46; see also West 1974: 23–24; and Richardson 1974: 222.

[74] For the fragment, see Norsa 1927; Scarpi 1976: 150; and Foley 1994: 46.

[75] *FGrH*. 328, fr. 103.131–32; see also Olender 1990: 86.

[76] Olender 1990: 89.

[77] See Foley 1994: 46; cf. Clem. Al. *Protr.* 2.20.1–21.2 = Orphic fr. 52 Kern; Arn. *Adv. nat.* 5.25–26; Euseb. *Praep. evang.* 2.3.31–35.

[78] On Baubo generally, see Olender 1990. On *anasurma*, see Scarpi 1976: 154–56; on Artem. *Oneirocritica* 4.44, see White 1975: 227; Clem. Al. *Protr.* 2.21.1, 4; on *anasurma* as an apotropaic gesture, see Plut. *Mor.* 246A; Scarpi 1976: 151–52; on Baubo and *anasurma*, see Graf 1974: 168–71.

[79] Richardson 1974: 215.

through improper language, Baubo uses indecent gesture. The stories of Baubo and Iambe have become conflated over time, to the extent that many scholars have assumed that the Iambe of the Homeric hymn not only uses obscene speech but also makes rude gestures. In either case, the speech of Iambe and the gesture of Baubo have sexual implications appropriate to a figure associated with female reproduction, while the conflation of obscene speech and gesture found in the stories of Iambe and Baubo further underscore the relation between women's speech and their bodies. Because many of these accounts allude to qualities traditionally associated with crones, and in fact, one source actually refers to Iambe as a γραῖα, "old woman" (Apollod. 1.5.1), it is quite possible that the irreverent and abusive older women so characteristic of Attic Old Comedy originate in this figure. In fifth-century Athens, Sophocles' lost satyr drama, *Iambe*, further supports the idea of Iambe as a comic, female embodiment of indecent speech and behavior.[80]

As the largest and perhaps oldest Athenian festival celebrated by women, the Demetrian Thesmophoria figures prominently in accounts of *aischrologia*. Celebrated on the eleventh, twelfth and thirteenth of the month of Pyanopsion, at the time of the fall planting, the Thesmophoria was preceded by the Stenia on the ninth and a local version of the Thesmophoria at Halimus on the tenth. On the first day of the festival, women acting as bailers descended into pits to bring back the decaying remains of piglets; the second day, the Nesteia, probably consisted of fasting, mourning, and *aischrologia*; and the third day celebrated the reunion of mother and daughter with feasting and other activities. According to Winkler, "The Demetrian feasts were official business of the polis" and obligatory for all citizen women.[81] Sexual abstinence was required of all participants, and men, as well as children and virgins, were rigorously excluded from this festival (Ar. *Thesm*. 574–76). At the same time, men were required to finance their wives' participation in the rites (Isae. 3.80; IG II² 1261, 1290). The site of the Thesmophoria, adjacent to men's place of Assembly, the Pnyx, further suggests that the women's festival mimicked the male discursive spheres of the city, a feature comically exploited by Aristophanes' *Thesmophoriazusae*.

There are numerous references to badinage at the Demetrian festivals, particularly the Thesmophoria. Most ancient authors attribute the origins of obscene speech at the Thesmophoria to Iambe in the Demeter myth: "A certain old woman, Iambe, joked with the goddess and made her smile.

---

[80] The existence of an *Iambe* by Sophocles has been much debated; Sutton (1989: 319–20 and 326) includes the title *Iambe* in his list of plays that are "demonstrably" satyric and argues that it was produced as a pair with a tragic *Triptolemus*, for the evidence, see Soph. fr. 731 Radt.

[81] Winkler 1990a: 194; see also Zeitlin 1982: 132.

On account of this they say the women at the Thesmophoria engage in mocking insults" (γραῖά τις Ἰάμβη σκώψασα τὴν θεὸν ἐποίησε μειδιᾶσαι. διὰ τοῦτο ἐν τοῖς Θεσμοφορίοις τὰς γυναῖκας σκώπτειν λέγουσιν, Apollod. 1.5.1). Diodorus Siculus also links the practice of ritual obscenity at a Sicilian festival in honor of Demeter and Kore to Iambe's role in the myth; in this case, however, it seems that both men and women participated in the insults: "It is their custom (αὐτοῖς) during the festival days to use vulgar language (αἰσχρολογεῖν) as they associate with one another (πρὸς ἀλλήλους) because the goddess, when she was grieving over the rape of her daughter, laughed on account of obscene talk" (αἰσχρολογίαν, Diod. Sic. 5.4.7). A passage from Cleomedes, in which he criticizes Epicurus' language as indecent, affords further insight into the festival: "Some of the expressions one would say came from brothels, others are like the things said at Demetrian festivals by women celebrating the Thesmophoria" (Cleomedes *De motu circulari corporum caelestium* 2.1). The Demetrian festival at Eleusis, although not confined to women, also apparently involved obscene speech both during the procession along the Sacred Way to Eleusis and at the *pannuchis*, the all-night gathering of women. During the procession, veiled or marked figures, *gephuristai*, made obscene gestures and proffered insults to initiates as they crossed the Cephisus river.[82] These performers have been described variously as a prostitute, a veiled man—possibly a man disguised as a woman—or several men.[83] Scurrilous joking may also have been a feature of the *pannuchis*, although there is little concrete information relating to this event.[84]

At the Demetrian festivals, *aischrologia* was closely associated with female sexuality, reproduction, and fertility. Laughter and obscenity in these ritual contexts thus served as the necessary complement to the lamentations that reenacted the sorrows of Demeter. Festivals like the Thesmophoria, though state-sanctioned, allowed for the suspension of normative roles and a moment of subversion in the male-governed polis, since the festival involved "the dissolution of the family, the separation of the sexes, and the constitution of a society of women."[85] At the same time, women's ritual obscenity, while ensuring agricultural productivity and human fertility in the larger community, also allowed a rare opportunity for women's public speech. This license to speak, and particularly to use obscenity, represented the most extreme form of role inversion associated with such sex-segregated rituals, perhaps allowing, in Winkler's words, "women's realization of this

[82] Olender 1990: 95; Foley 1994: 67; see also schol. Ar. *Plut.* 1014, which mentions σκώμματα performed by women in carriages during the procession; Hesychius s.v. Γεφυρίς and Γεφυρισταί; Strabo 9.1.24.

[83] Richardson 1974: 214; Olender 1990: 95–96.

[84] Richardson 1974: 215; Foley 1994: 67; Katz 1994b: 235. For ancient references to the *pannuchis*, see Ar. *Ran.* 444ff., 451ff.; Eur. *Ion* 1074ff.; Paus. 1.38.6.

[85] Burkert 1985: 245.

counter-ideology."[86] In Aristophanes' *Ecclesiazusae*, it is in fact at the Skira,
another women's festival that involved dice-playing and wanton behavior,
that the female participants supposedly hatched their plan to take over the
city (Ar. *Eccl.* 18), a plan that involves a role reversal similar to that enacted
at the women's festivals. Although the Demetrian festivals of license may
have allowed their participants a momentary escape from the social constraints placed on them, it would be difficult to maintain that these women-
only gatherings offered any real opportunity for subversion, since rituals
of role reversal must be viewed as ultimately reinforcing dominant ideology,
as Burkert points out: "Through such grotesque negation, a person is led
to accept his or her role."[87] Whatever the reality, it is clear from the literary
sources that these exclusively female rituals aroused a certain amount of
suspicion in Greek men. Like ritual lamentation, women's obscene utterance in the Demetrian festivals had a close association with the body:
by speaking about their sexuality, participants encouraged the fertility of
the city.

CHORUSES OF GIRLS AND WOMEN

In addition to lamentation and ritual obscenity, there were other ritual
speech genres associated with women, often publicly performed, which
served to affirm social roles. Perhaps the best known of these speech
practices is the *ololugē*, a ritual cry confined to women that marked private,
domestic events such as childbirth and that also occasionally accompanied
choral song. Like lamentation, this speech genre may be considered a
socially constructive utterance executed on behalf of the larger community.
That ritual and musical performance in the archaic period required distinct
roles for men and women can be seen in a fragment from Sappho that
describes the marriage of Hector and Andromache and elaborates on a
musical occasion celebrated by male and female singers:

>]ως δ' ἄρα πάρ[θενοι
> ἄειδον μέλος ἄγγ[ον, ἴκα]νε δ' ἐς αἴθ[ερα
> ἄχω θεσπεσία γελ[. . . .
> γύναικες δ' ἐλέλυσδον ὄσαι προγενέστερα[ι
> πάντες δ' ἄνδρες ἐπήρατον ἴαχον ὄρθιον
> πάον' ὀνκαλέοντες.   (Sappho fr. 44.25–33 Voigt)

The maidens sang sweetly a sacred song,
and a divinely sounding echo reached the heavens . . .

---

[86] Winkler 1990a: 189; see also Zeitlin 1982: 145.
[87] Burkert 1985: 259.

then the older women cried out the *ololugē*,
and all the men called on Paean with a lovely, clear song.

Here the poet differentiates the ritual and musical tasks of the celebrants according to gender, age, and social role, juxtaposing the sacred song of the maidens, the *ololugē* of the older women, and the masculine hymn to Apollo. Described as divine and otherworldly in a passage from Alcaeus, the *ololugē* was thought to avert curses and evoke blessings, "the otherworldly echo of the sacred, yearly cry of women rings out" (περὶ δὲ βρέμει | ἄχω θεσπεσία γυναίκων | ἴρα[ς ὀ]λολύγας ἐνιαυσίας, Alc. 130b.18–19 Voigt).[88] In Bacchylides' account of Theseus' dive for the garland of Amphitrite, the celebratory *ololugē* is similarly juxtaposed with the masculine paean:

> ἀγλαό-
> θρονοί τε κοῦραι σὺν εὐ-
> θυμίᾳ νεοκτίτῳ
> ὠλόλυξαν, ἔ-
> κλαγεν δὲ πόντος· ἤίθεοι δ' ἐγγύθεν
> νέοι παιάνιξαν ἐρατᾷ ὀπί.   (Bacchyl. 17.124–29 Snell)

The sea-nymphs on their bright thrones
cried out the *ololugē* with new-made festivity,
and the sea, too, resounded. And close at hand
virgin youths sang a paean with lovely voice.

As these passages imply, the *ololugē* was predominantly a cry of women addressed to the gods, the feminine counterpart of the masculine paean and other ritual forms uttered by men, such as the *alalagē*. That these cries continued to distinguish the ritual language of men and women at least as late as the fourth century can be seen in a passage from Xenophon:

> ἐπεὶ δὲ καλὰ ἦν τὰ σφάγια, ἐπαιάνιζον πάντες οἱ στρατιῶται καὶ ἀνηλάλαζον, συνωλόλυζον δὲ καὶ αἱ γυναῖκες ἅπασαι. πολλαὶ γὰρ ἦσαν ἑταῖραι ἐν τῷ στρατεύματι. (Xen. *An.* 4.3.19)

After the auspicious sacrifice, all the soldiers chanted the paean and cried *alalagē*, while all the women gave the shout of *ololugē* in unison, for there was a large number of hetaeras in the camp.

These gendered, ritual cries reflect the distinct social and ritual spheres occupied by men and women in ancient Greece. Because the *alalagē* was

---

[88] For this view, see Deubner 1941: 15–16. On the *ololugē* in another wedding context, see also Pind. *Pae.* P. Berol. 13411c4, an account of the marriage of Niobe. Although over fifty years old, this article is still the best source on the *ololugē* to date.

originally a battle cry, it retains a martial and masculine sense.[89] The *ololugē*, in contrast, accompanied many of the activities that characterized female life in antiquity. In Sophocles' *Electra*, the *ololugē* occurs in a context of ritual lamentation and marks a moment of unrestrained, piercing grief (Soph. *El.* 749).[90] The cry was also uttered upon the birth of a child, as a means of facilitating a difficult labor or of protecting the vulnerable newborn from harm.[91] More commonly, however, the *ololugē* denoted a joyful cry of triumph that initiated a public sacrifice, as suggested by the passage from Xenophon above.[92] Like the other two female speech practices considered thus far, the *ololugē* was typically performed by a group of women as a means of marking an important moment in the life of the community.

More broadly, the performative context implied by the Sapphic fragment suggests that various types of ritual song in ancient Greece provided an occasion for women's public speech and served as a means of affirming the values of the community.[93] Sappho's reference to the girls' sacred song provides an example of the maiden choruses, mentioned continuously throughout the archaic and classical periods and represented in archaic lyric by the poetic genre of the *partheneion*.[94] These choruses may have offered young girls a means of education beyond what they received at home, drawing them outside of their houses to participate in a public performance; in turn they also educated other girls and women by reinforcing normative social roles through their songs.[95] Though ancient evidence points to the widespread presence of girls' choruses in ancient Greece, we hear far less about the choruses of married women; those mentioned appear to relate to childbirth.[96] The function of maiden choruses was to promote

---

[89] For *alalagē* as a battle cry, cf. Hes. *Theog.* 686; Pind. *Nem.* 3.60; Aesch. *Sept.* 497; as a cry invoking Ares, see Xen. *Cyr.* 7.1.66; expressing joy in battle, cf. Hom. *Iliad* 16.78; Aesch. *Sept.* 951; Soph. *Ant.* 133; Eur. *Supp.* 719; as a general cry of jubilation, cf. Eur. *HF* 981; *Bacch.* 1133; *El.* 859.

[90] Cf. Ap. Rhod. 3.1218.

[91] For a discussion of these contrasting views, see Deubner 1941: 14; on the harmful effect of omitting this cry at the birth of a child, see Theoc. 17.64; on the association of *ololugē* with childbirth generally, see *Hom. Hymn Ap.* 119, and *Hom. Hymn Pyth. Ap.* 45; Paus. 9.11.3.

[92] For the *ololugē* as a cry of jubilation, cf. Hom. *Od.* 22.408, 411; Bacchyl. 17.124; Aesch. *Sept.* 825; *Ag.* 27, 587; *Cho.* 387, 942; Soph. *Trach.* 205; Eur. *El.* 691; *Or.* 1137; on *ololugē* and sacrifice, see Deubner 1941: 21–22.

[93] Calame 1977, 1: 117–21. Stehle (1997: 71–118) discusses how performative occasions for women's choral song negotiated the contradiction between their public speech and their gender roles.

[94] For examples, cf. *Hom. Hymn Ap.* 186ff.; *Hom. Hymn Ven.* 259ff.; Bacchyl. 17.100ff., 3.58ff.; Pind. *Pyth.* 10.34–36. Stehle (1997: 278–79) argues that Sappho's fragment provides evidence for the actual performative context of girls' choruses.

[95] Calame 1977, 1: 385–420; Lardinois 1994: 63.

[96] Stehle (1997: 107–13) gathers the evidence for married women's choruses. This topic is considered more fully in my discussion of Euripides' *Hippolytus* in Chapter 4.

the values conducive to marriage, whether by honoring a particular deity, like Artemis, as in the *Homeric Hymn to Aphrodite* (117–20) and in Euripides' *Hippolytus* (1428–29), or as part of a more secular event, like the wedding celebration depicted in Sappho (fr. 44 Voigt). Offered as a gift to a (usually female) deity for a positive intervention in human life, the maiden choruses celebrated the principal moments in female life, marking the passage from girlhood to adulthood through marriage.[97]

The collective aspect of the performance can be seen in Alcman (fr. 1), in a *partheneion* in which the chorus repeatedly use the first-person singular pronoun to refer to the group as a whole. The surviving *partheneia*, whether actually performed in a ritual context or not, similarly affirm the values of the community by praising female excellence. In the Alcman fragment, the chorus not only glorify the physical attractiveness of two girls, Agido and Hagesichora, and their exceptional musical skill (85–87), but through oblique comparison they also celebrate the beauty of several other girls, calling upon them by name (70–76). This public naming provides a direct contrast to the classical Athenian custom of avoiding any direct allusion to respectable women, a convention found in Attic oratory and even on the comic stage of Aristophanes. The poem suggests a ritual occasion, such as a feast, that may have celebrated the passage from adolescence to adulthood through marriage.[98] These choral songs affirmed the place of female experience in both the human and divine realms, and perhaps served a pedagogical function by preparing adolescent girls for marriage. As a public performance that most likely took place before men, these girls' songs presented a social paradox in that they proclaimed verbal authority by the fact of their performance even as their narrative disavowed it, much like the maiden Macaria depicted in Euripides' *Children of Heracles*, discussed in Chapter 1.[99]

The content and context of female choruses is a subject too broad to examine fully here, but the existence of these groups confirms the idea that there were other venues beyond lamentation and ritual obscenity for women's public speech. For it appears that female choruses, whether composed of girls or mature women, performed a vital role in perpetuating the values and ideals of the community by reaffirming the social and religious roles of men and women. The choruses of girls and women, together with ritual lamentation, *aischrologia*, and other ritual utterances like the *ololugē*, suggest the existence of women's public and authoritative speech in ancient Greece. And yet, although these speech genres were

---

[97] Calame 1977, 1: 361.

[98] For this interpretation, see ibid., 2: 137.

[99] For this view, and further discussion of Alcm. fr. 1, see Stehle 1997: 73–88. Clark 1996 also examines the issue of women's authoritative speech in the poem, but specifically within the context of how ritual reinforces gender norms.

considered both necessary and propitious, the fact that they often required women to leave the house and congregate alone invested them with a subversive potential in the eyes of men, as demonstrated by the reforms restricting even women's religious speech in the Athenian polis and the representation of women's speech as dangerous in classical drama.

GOSSIP AND VOLUBILITY

We turn now from women's public, ritual speech to the literary representation of women's domestic speech. The two verbal genres most frequently associated with women outside a ritual context are gossip and what I have termed "seductive persuasion." These speech practices are not gender-exclusive, since men both engaged in marketplace gossip and employed persuasion in public contexts like the law courts and the Assembly; rather, they may be seen as dangerous corruptions of the male speech genres generally considered productive of normative social values. Nor do they consist of a clear set of formal speech practices, in contrast to some of the ritual genres; rather, gossip refers to a whole range of informal linguistic operations occurring among women mostly in a domestic context.

Throughout the Western tradition, women have been associated with loquacity and gossip; Jesperson asserts that women's talkativeness results from the "vacant chambers of the mind."[100] It is interesting, therefore, that in recent research conducted in the United States on the amount of time men and women speak, men were found to be more talkative than women.[101] Because the dominant culture may view gossip as a source of solidarity among members of a muted group, Western literary sources frequently admonish women against idle talk.[102] The association of women and volubility in ancient Greece begins with Semonides' iambic invective against women, which portrays women's talk as a series of disorderly and noisy animal sounds, including yapping and barking (Semon. fr. 7.15, 20). Only the bee woman deserves praise for her silence, since she avoids women's idle stories of love (οὐδ' ἐν γυναιξὶν ἥδεται καθημένη | ὅκου λέγουσιν ἀφροδισίους λόγους, fr. 7.90–91).[103] But even the bee woman provokes ambivalence, since, as the narrator reminds us, the woman who appears most virtuous is, in reality, the most worthy of blame (fr. 7.108–9).

---

[100] Jesperson 1922: 252; on this passage, see also Coates 1986: 31–32; for a good general discussion of Jesperson and women's language, see Baron 1986: 78–80. On gossip as a feature of women's oral culture, see Jones 1980; and Coates 1986: 114. For an interesting analysis of male gossip in a fraternity house, see Cameron 1997: 61.

[101] Tannen 1996: 38.

[102] Bornstein (1978: 135) discusses admonitions against women's gossip in medieval and Renaissance courtesy books.

[103] Note also that Xen. Oec. 7.17 describes the good wife as a queen bee, ἡγεμὼν μέλιττα.

As a speech genre that both eludes male control and unites women in intrigue, classical drama frequently represents gossip as destabilizing the normative social hierarchy not only within the domestic sphere, but also in the polis.

Since references to female gossip in archaic literature are scant, we must turn to literary sources in the classical era. The role of gossip in formulating public opinion and in policing behavior in the democratic polis has received increased attention in recent years. Discussion has centered on public and male institutions, particularly the law courts, in which slander played a prominent role.[104] Outside the law courts, it is well known that rumor could spread very quickly through such male meeting places as the agora and the barber's and the perfumer's shops.[105] Although female characters in fifth-century Athenian drama, as well as in other cultures and literary traditions, are often represented as consummate gossipers, classical scholars have paid surprisingly little attention to this issue. Hunter focuses mostly on gossip *about* women as a form of social control in her account of women and gossip; through gossip, surveillance of the female could extend from the public sphere into the very interior of the house: "Gossip penetrated into the privacy of the oikos to mark out women who did not conform to community standards."[106] In the courts, this policing assumed two forms: attacks on a woman's sexual mores and questions about her status as an Athenian, both of which reflect the male concern for legitimacy of offspring.[107] Hunter further notes that there is little historical evidence that would link the circulation of gossip more closely to females than to males. In contrast, fifth-century Athenian drama frequently portrays women as transmitters of gossip and excessive talkers.

Although women did not participate in the male discursive spheres of the city, they had frequent opportunities to converse with other women, either by paying social visits to relatives and immediate neighbors, or at gender-segregated religious festivals such as the Skira and the Thesmophoria.[108] Anecdotal evidence portrays older women, like nurses and grandmothers, as storytellers within the oikos, who passed on traditional stories of gods and heroes to the very young.[109] Ritual contexts, such as funerals,

---

[104] For the most recent and most comprehensive treatment of the role of gossip in the law courts and in public life, see Dover 1974: 30–33, and 1988; Ober 1989: 148–51; Winkler 1990a: 58–64; see Hunter 1994.

[105] Buxton 1994: 11–12.

[106] Hunter 1994: 116.

[107] Ibid.: 111–16.

[108] Ibid.: 100; see also Cohen 1991: 88 and 155–56. For literary sources that depict women as having social contact outside the house, cf. Eur. *Hipp.* 384, 395–97, 646ff.; *Andr.* 944ff.; Men. *Dys.* 481ff.; Theophrastus quoted in Stobaeus 16.30; Aeschin. 1.127–28.

[109] See Buxton 1994: 18–20; on Baubo and nurses' tales, see also Olender 1990: 98–100; cf. Pl. *Rep.* 378d and Philostr. *Imag.* 1.15.17–19.

choral performances, and women-only festivals, provided occasions for the expression of a collective female voice and may have created solidarity among women. Women's speech within the oikos, although less regulated and more individual than in a ritual context, may have served a similar purpose by reinforcing women's values and experiences. Because speech in all these instances operated outside the bounds of male control, it was felt that even in the oikos, women's speech needed to be regulated. Thus Ischomachus in Xenophon's *Oeconomicus* stresses the importance of acquiring a young wife who has been so closely supervised that, having seen and heard little, she might ask the fewest questions possible (ἐλάχιστα δ' ἔροιτο, Xen. *Oec. 7.5*).

One theory put forth by anthropologists holds that gossip binds together and maintains a community.[110] Gossip therefore functions as a means of social control, a way to reinforce normative values and to ensure social conformance. And yet, as Gluckman points out, gossip can "unite a group within a larger society, or against another group."[111] Like ritual lamentation, gossip may have a dual function: it can both reinforce the values of the dominant group and serve as a vehicle of resistance for the socially marginal: "Gossip does not conform to the official values of our society; like the operations of that system, it frequently has a subversive effect."[112] This subversiveness stems in part from the fact that gossip can never be fully contained or controlled: "One can never know quite where it goes, whom it reaches, how it changes in transmission, how and by whom it is understood."[113] Gossip may easily spread across social and class lines; in ancient Athens, for example, slaves and prostitutes often served as conduits of gossip, while in drama, the nurse is a stock figure responsible for conveying illicit messages.[114] The permeability and uncontrollability of gossip and rumor are frequently suggested by images of porousness, leakiness, and swiftness: when Clytemnestra in the *Agamemnon* describes the various rumors of her husband's death as trickling into her house, she uses the verb ὀχετεύω (Aesch. *Ag.* 867), a term that means to conduct water through a pipe and one that evokes the uncontrollability of this type of speech. Because gossip is often characterized as furtive, and because it creates a speech community among women, classical drama depicts this speech genre as potentially harmful to men and to the polis through its threat to undermine traditional social hierarchy.[115]

---

[110] Gluckman 1963: 308; see also Bailey 1971; du Boulay 1974.
[111] Gluckman 1963: 313.
[112] Spacks 1985: 43.
[113] Ibid.: 6.
[114] Ober 1989: 149.
[115] Jones 1980: 95.

Fifth-century drama frequently portrays women as insatiable gossipers and chronicles the destructive consequences of their unrestrained talk—Phaedra in Euripides' *Hippolytus* lists long conversations as one of life's pleasures for women (Eur. *Hipp*. 384). Tragic drama portrays women not only as loquacious, but also as taking particular delight in criticizing their peers. In Euripides' *Phoenician Women*, the Pedagogue signals the entry of the female chorus with a gnomic statement that condemns women for scandal-mongering:

φιλόψογον δὲ χρῆμα θηλειῶν ἔφυ,
σμικρὰς τ' ἀφορμὰς ἢν λάβωσι τῶν λόγων,
πλείους ἐπεσφέρουσιν· ἡδονὴ δέ τις
γυναιξὶ μηδὲν ὑγιὲς ἀλλήλας λέγειν.   (Eur. *Pho*. 198–201)

The host of women are by nature scandal-loving.
If they should find any slight opportunity for talk,
they expand it. For women get a certain pleasure
from speaking ill of one another.

Similarly, Hermione in the *Andromache* blames women's love of gossip for leading good wives astray and warns men not to allow women to visit their wives because they are teachers of evil bent on destroying the oikos (διδάσκαλοι κακῶν, Eur. *Andr*. 946). The virtuous Andromache in the *Trojan Women*, by contrast, shuns the clever words of women (κομψὰ θηλειῶν ἔπη, Eur. *Tro*. 651), schooling herself to keep a silent tongue and gentle demeanor (γλώσσης τε σιγὴν ὄμμα θ' ἥσυχον πόσει | παρεῖχον, 654–55). Like Semonides' iambic and the scholion to Lucian's *Dialogue of the Courtesans*, which comments on women's ritual obscenity at the Haloa, both of these Euripidean passages imply that women's private conversations revolve around *erōs* and thus encourage adultery.

But the most dangerous aspect of female gossip in classical drama is its potential to unite women against both household and city. Several scenes in classical drama show women as conspirators against men: Iphigenia in Euripides' *Iphigenia in Tauris* exhorts the female chorus to swear an oath of silence, "We are women, a race sympathetic to one another and most infallible in maintaining loyal counsel" (γυναῖκές ἐσμεν, φιλόφρον ἀλλήλαις γένος, | σῴζειν τε κοινὰ πράγματ' ἀσφαλέσταται, Eur. *IT* 1061–62). An anonymous speaker in Euripides' *Alope* states it even more simply: "A woman is naturally an ally to another woman" (γυνὴ γυναικὶ σύμμαχος πέφυκέ πως, Eur. fr. 108 *TGF*). Indeed, many tragic plots revolve around female conspiracy forged through speech, as will be seen in the example of Phaedra and the Nurse in Euripides' *Hippolytus*, discussed in Chapter 4. Lysias provides a similar view of the effects of women's oral culture on the everyday lives of men; in his oration *On the Murder of Eratosthenes*, he depicts a network of women conspiring against men, a servant in cahoots with an adulterous wife, and the wife in league with the mother of her lover (1.15 and 20).[116]

Attic Old Comedy reinforces a similar image of women as conspiratorial and garrulous; one word in particular, the verb λαλέω, conveys this idea (and it is noteworthy that this word almost never appears in tragedy).[117] Although occasionally applied to men, the verb more often describes women's speech and for this reason appears with frequency in the two plays most concerned with female speech, Aristophanes' *Thesmophoriazusae* and *Ecclesiazusae*.[118] Early in the *Ecclesiazusae*, Woman A responds to Praxagora's suggestion that the women rehearse what they are going to say at the Assembly with the rhetorical question, "My dear, who of us does not know how to gossip?" (τίς δ' ὦ μέλ' ἡμῶν οὐ λαλεῖν ἐπίσταται; Ar. *Eccl.* 120). The humor of this remark lies in the bathetic contrast between the women's chattering, conveyed by λαλεῖν, and the masculine, political speech, properly ἀγορεύειν, demanded of their disguise as speakers and auditors in the Assembly. The onomatopoeic term, which later describes the sounds made by animals such as locusts, grasshoppers, and swallows as well as musical instruments in Hellenistic poetry, also refers to the gossip of the agora and the conversations of everyday life.[119] That talkativeness belongs to the category of excess and lack of self-control is made clear in a passage from the *Thesmophoriazusae* when Woman A, in a typical comic reversal, accuses Euripides of slandering women by portraying them as adulterers, wantons, drunkards, traitors, and babblers, τὰς λάλους (Ar. *Thesm.* 393).

Garrulousness or loose talk is often equated in fifth-century drama with sexual promiscuity or adultery, since, as Spacks notes, both gossip and sex represent intimate forms of contact: "Gossip, like sexual intercourse, belongs to a hidden life."[120] To flaunt one's self in speech is, for a woman, the verbal equivalent of adultery. Hirschon observes a similar linkage between female speech and female sexuality in her study of women in modern

---

[116] Foxhall (1996: 151) discusses this passage more fully.

[117] There are no instances of the verb λαλέω in Aeschylus or Sophocles, although Creon does rebuke the male herald for his trivial talk with the cognate λάλημα (Soph. *Ant.* 320). When applied to men, therefore, the word may indicate lower-class speech, since a related term, λάλος, also describes the words of messengers in Euripides (cf. fr. 112.2, 1012 *TGF*; *Supp.* 462), whereas at *Cyc.* 315 it refers to the Cyclops.

[118] Cf. Ar. *Eccl.* 16, 119, 120, 129, 1058; *Thesm.* 138, 393, 578, 717, 1082, 1087, 1108, 1109; and *Lys.* 442, 627. For a discussion of this term and relevant bibliography, see Taaffe 1993: 86n.36 and 116n.22; cf. also Men. *Sam.* 241; Men. fr. 66.3; Lucian *Rhetorum praeceptor* 23.

[119] For example, the effeminate Cleisthenes in the *Thesmophoriazusae* reports to the women of the Thesmophoria that he has heard a rumor that a man has slipped into the festival unseen, a fact that he has heard κατ' ἀγορὰν λαλούμενον (Ar. *Thesm.* 578).

[120] Spacks 1985: 40.

Greece: "A woman's speech is held to be dangerous, her words may be irresponsible and likely to have disruptive consequences."[121] Hirschon cites the popular rebuke, "She has a tongue," as an example of the social disapproval attached to female speech in modern Greece. The dangers of female speech, like the dangers of the female body, revolve around a perceived absence of self-control: "Through uncontrolled words a woman may upset the home environment and jeopardize the unity of the family; through gossip and irresponsible chatter she may provoke ill-feeling, discord and trouble in relationships within the neighborhood."[122] This lack of self-control as a potential source of disruption necessitates external monitoring by males: areas of surveillance include the threshold of the house, the body, and the mouth.[123] Thus women's speech and volubility has a direct correlation to their bodies: to remain inside is, for the female, to curb her tongue and restrain her passions. The speech that eludes male control is seen as leading to transgressive behavior, particularly adultery, suggesting that concerns with regulating female speech stem in part from the desire to ensure the legitimacy of one's offspring, as Bergren and Rabinowitz have argued.[124]

Perhaps Plutarch should have the last word, since he makes explicit the connection between women's public speech and promiscuity:

Ἡ Θεανὼ παρέφηνε τὴν χεῖρα περιβαλλομένη τὸ ἱμάτιον. εἰπόντος δέ τινος "καλὸς ὁ πῆχυς," "ἀλλ' οὐ δημόσιος," ἔφη. δεῖ δὲ μὴ μόνον τὸν πῆχυν ἀλλὰ μηδὲ τὸν λόγον δημόσιον εἶναι τῆς σώφρονος, καὶ τὴν φωνὴν ὡς ἀπογύμνωσιν αἰδεῖσθαι καὶ φυλάττεσθαι πρὸς τοὺς ἐκτός. (Plut. *Mor.* 142C-D)

Theano exposed her arm as she was putting on her cloak. When someone said, "What a lovely arm," she replied, "But it's not for the public." Not only the arm of a virtuous woman, but even her speech ought not to be public, and she ought to restrain her voice, since it exposes her, and be modest in the presence of outsiders.

Many of the literary sources discussed in this section trivialize and derogate the verbal genre of gossip affiliated with women. As an alternative discourse that creates solidarity among women and eludes male surveillance, gossip is viewed as potentially disruptive of the traditional power hierarchies created by men, primarily because it leads to adultery and thus jeopardizes the legitimacy of male offspring. Linked to sexuality in this way, female gossip and volubility appear motivated by a lack of physical self-control frequently identified with women in the ancient world. And even though

[121] Hirschon 1978: 84.
[122] Ibid.
[123] Stallybrass (1986), in a fascinating analysis of female surveillance in Renaissance texts, raises similar issues.
[124] Bergren 1983; Rabinowitz 1987.

gossip as a verbal genre differs radically from ritual forms such as *aischrologia* and lamentation, the pervasive association of women's sexuality and speech, two spheres of activity potentially beyond male control, persists.

SEDUCTIVE PERSUASION

Like gossip, seductive persuasion as a verbal genre does not involve a set of formal linguistic practices; rather, it refers more generally to literary representations of women's deceptive use of persuasion as a means of gaining power over men, normally in a domestic and erotic context. In contrast to the masculine *peithō*, which promotes the city and civic values, this type of persuasion, as an embodiment of *dolos*, "verbal cunning," threatens to undermine social stability.[125] It also has a strong sexual component that connects it to the secular and private world beyond the polis, to the household, and to relations between individual men and women, an aspect underscored by the Attic vases that depict the goddess Peitho in the company of Aphrodite and Eros.[126] The Athenians did not really distinguish between sexual and political persuasion, however, and in fact continually conflated the two forms, although they did associate erotic and deceitful persuasion mainly with women and with womanish men, and considered more direct forms of political persuasion the province of "real" men and the polis.[127] Erotic persuasion often has connotations of *dolos*, a kind of trickery that allows one person to get the better of another who is superior in power: "If your antagonist will not be persuaded, and his superior strength also rules out force, then your only resort is cunning."[128] Fifth-century Athenian drama typically represents women, especially wives, and slaves as deploying this kind of persuasion, whereas misuses of persuasion in a political context were by definition considered feminine and feminizing, and therefore politically subversive. For this reason, the law of Solon recorded in Lysias' *On the Murder of Eratosthenes* condemns the adulterers who seduce other men's wives, persuading them to betray their domestic loyalties (Lys. 1.32–33).

Hera's seduction of Zeus in Book 14 of the *Iliad* provides one of the earliest examples of a duplicitous wife who combines physical enticement with verbal guile to gain control over her husband. Through the magical and alluring *kestos* of Aphrodite, Hera receives the gift of verbal persuasion with which to lure Zeus away from battle:

---

[125] Buxton 1982: 64.
[126] For the visual evidence, see ibid.: 45–46 and plates.
[127] For the idea of all persuasion as seductive, see ibid.: 31.
[128] Ibid.: 64.

ἔνθ' ἔνι μὲν φιλότης, ἐν δ' ἵμερος, ἐν δ' ὀαριστὺς
πάρφασις, ἥ τ' ἔκλεψε νόον πύκα περ φρονεόντων.

(Hom. *Iliad* 14.216–17)

And it contains affection, and desire, and intimate conversation,
and seductive persuasion, which steals away the mind even of the wise.

The term πάρφασις not only is "synonymous with *peithō*"[129] and deceptive speech generally, but also conveys erotic overtones. The gifts of seduction provided by Aphrodite work together with Hera's innate craftiness, a quality repeatedly suggested by the epithet δολοφρονέουσα, "crafty-minded" (Hom. *Iliad* 14.197, 300, 329). Another episode in which Hera again deceives Zeus attributes this craftiness to women in general: "But Hera, being female, deceived him with her craftiness" (ἀλλ' ἄρα καὶ τὸν | Ἥρη θῆλυς ἐοῦσα δολοφροσύνης ἀπάτησεν, Hom. *Iliad* 19.96–97; cf. 106). Conversely, the erotic escapades of Paris, the archetypal seducer, have effeminized him and branded him a deceiver: "Evil Paris, fair in form, woman-crazy, a deceiver" (Δύσπαρι, εἶδος ἄριστε, γυναιμανές, ἠπεροπευτά, Hom. *Iliad* 3.38).

This combination of seductive persuasion and deception finds it fullest archaic expression in the figure of Pandora in Hesiod's *Theogony* and *Works and Days*. The spectacle of Pandora bedecked in nuptial garments—the elaborate gifts of clothing and jewelry given by the gods—makes her the concrete embodiment of feminine guile; she is both pure body and pure artifice.[130] Adorned (κόσμησε, *Op.* 72), she herself becomes an adornment for men, a καλὸν κακόν (*Theog.* 587). The golden necklaces received from the goddess Peitho and the Graces (*Op.* 73–74) contribute to Pandora's seductive power, since Greek literature frequently imbues such ornaments with erotic power.[131] A scholion to *Works and Days* 73–74 further strengthens the link between Pandora's costly attire and her seductive persuasion: "For a woman so adorned quickly persuades a man to have sex" (ἐπειδὴ ἡ γυνὴ κεκοσμημένη πείθει τὸν ἄνδρα πρὸς συνουσίαν τάχος, schol. *Op.* 73–74). But Hermes' gift in the *Works and Days* is perhaps the most dangerous of all, since he gives the first woman voice, one full of falsehood

---

[129] Ibid.: 36. On the magical elements of Aphrodite's *kestos* and its relation to ancient magical practices, see Faraone 1990.

[130] Loraux (1978: 49) argues that because of the emphasis on her costume, Pandora is not body at all, but merely appearance. Given the strictures governing the exposure of the female body, particularly in the archaic period, we must view her clothing as a symbolic substitution for her body, a physical presence meant to provoke a seductive response in men.

[131] See *Hom. Hymn Ven.* 88–90; on the power of such *agalmata* in Greek myth and literature, see Gernet 1981. For the necklace of Eriphyle, see Apollod. *Bibl.* 3.6.2 and 3.7.2–5; for the tunic and crown given to Theseus by Amphitrite, cf. Bacchyl. 17.57–66, 74–80 Snell; for the necklace and cup given by Zeus to Alcmene, cf. Pherec. *FGrH* 3F13a and Ath. 11.49, 474d–f.

and cunning words: "And then Hermes, the slayer of Argus, gave her lies and cunning words and a thievish nature within her breast" (ἐν δ' ἄρα οἱ στήθεσσι διάκτορος Ἀργειφόντης | ψεύδεά θ' αἱμυλίους τε λόγους καὶ ἐπίκλοπον ἦθος, *Op.* 77–78).[132] Deceptive speech therefore completes Pandora's *kosmēsis*, since the creation of the first woman culminates in an account of her speech and voice, an account that introduces the possibility of deception into human life: in one reading of the poem, Pandora not only irrevocably severs mortals from gods, she also introduces verbal ambiguity and polysemy into the world.[133]

The story of Pandora as found in Hesiod's *Works and Days* foreshadows the narrator's exhortation to men to avoid seductively persuasive women:

μηδὲ γυνή σε νόον πυγοστόλος ἐξαπατάτω
αἱμύλα κωτίλλουσα, τεὴν διφῶσα καλιήν·
ὃς δὲ γυναικὶ πέποιθε, πέποιθ' ὅ γε φιλήτῃσιν.   (Hes. *Op.* 373–75)

Do not let a woman with a sexy ass trick you
with her chattering blandishments, since she only wants your property.
For he who believes a woman believes deceivers.

The hapax πυγοστόλος may refer to a seductive clothing style, the gathering up of folds of cloth in a sort of archaic bustle, a fashion both sexually suggestive and deceptive.[134] The word αἱμύλα at 374 recalls the cunning words of Pandora, the gift of Hermes, and is closely linked to the idea of falsehood in all its other contexts in Hesiod. In this passage, however, the cunning words serve to amplify the woman's deceptive physical appearance. With the participle κωτίλλουσα, a word that signifies chattering or babbling, the narrator evokes the association of women with volubility and gossip discussed earlier in this chapter.[135] Moreover, the term κωτίλος denotes words that are deceptively persuasive and even cheating; to wit, the Theognidean passage where the poet advises Cyrnus to cheat his enemy (εὖ κώτιλλε τὸν ἐχθρόν, Thgn. 363 *IEG*).[136] A passage in Aristotle reveals

[132] Calypso uses similar words on Odysseus (Hom. *Od.* 1.56), but note that cunning words are not the property of women alone; Zeus in Hes. *Theog.* 890 uses them on Metis, and at Hes. *Op.* 789 a boy born on the sixth of the month is said to favor ψεύδεά θ' αἱμυλίους τε λόγους κρυφίους τ' ὀαρισμούς.

[133] According to Leclerc (1993: 44), "La voix de Pandora lui est donneé comme condition de possibilité des mensonges et mots trompeurs."

[134] According to West (1980: 251), the word πυγοστόλος means "rigging herself out (στελλομένη) in a way that focuses on her arse." West further suggests that this might be a kind of padding to compensate for being ἄπυγος, without much padding on the buttocks, since Semonides describes the ugly woman with the same term in his iambic.

[135] Tzetzes in his commentary on this passage equates κωτίλλουσα with πολυλογοῦσα, "talking a lot," and further notes that the term is applied to the swallow by Anacreon and Simonides because the bird chatters incessantly; see Tzet. Hes. *Op.* 374. In Theognis, the term suggests talkativeness as well as drunkenness and loss of control; cf. Thgn. 296, 487 *IEG*.

[136] Cf. Thgn. 851–52 *IEG*.

the association of κωτίλος with inarticulate speech, since the adjective simply signifies animal sound (Arist. *Hist. an.* 488a33). The garrulous female unable to control her flow of speech so prevalent in later Greek literature resonates with this passage in Hesiod and continues to persist even as late as Theocritus.[137] More importantly, the poet represents this deceptive speech as potentially dangerous to men, prompting him to condemn the whole race of women with his final gnomic utterance. The emphatic repetition of πέποιθε πέποιθε here amplifies the topos of women's persuasive power and its erotic associations later central to tragedy, one that will be explored in subsequent chapters.[138]

The Greek imagination also closely linked the persuasive power attributed to women in erotic contexts to magic; throughout the literary tradition, women procure and employ drugs, chant incantations, and perform other magical acts intended to gain control over men, a point that will be discussed in greater detail in subsequent chapters. In the *Odyssey*, divine females like the Sirens, Calypso, and Circe exhibit the magical verbal ability conveyed by the verb *thelgein*, a term frequently linked to seductive persuasion. It is noteworthy, however, that the poem describes the speech of two exceptionally persuasive males, Hermes and Odysseus, with the verb *thelgein*.[139] Through their irresistible songs, the Sirens compel and detain men against their wills, luring them onto their island:[140]

> Σειρῆνας μὲν πρῶτον ἀφίξεαι, αἵ ῥά τε πάντας
> ἀνθρώπους θέλγουσιν, ὅτις σφέας εἰσαφίκηται.
> ὅς τις ἀϊδρείῃ πελάσῃ καὶ φθόγγον ἀκούσῃ
> Σειρήνων, τῷ δ' οὔ τι γυνὴ καὶ νήπια τέκνα
> οἴκαδε νοστήσαντι παρίσταται οὐδὲ γάνυνται,
> ἀλλά τε Σειρῆνες λιγυρῇ θέλγουσιν ἀοιδῇ.   (Hom. *Od.* 12.39–44)

First you will come to the Sirens, who enchant
all men, whenever anyone comes upon them.

---

[137] Theoc. 15.87 describes a male passerby who exhorts two matrons to stop their idle prattle. "My dear women, do stop that ceaseless chattering" (παύσασθ', ὦ δύστανοι, ἀνάνυτα κωτίλλοισαι).

[138] Thgn. 1367–68 *IEG*: "Indeed grace is the part of a boy; but trust is no friend to a woman" (παιδός τοι χάρις ἐστί, γυναικὶ δὲ πίστις ἑταίρος | οὐδείς).

[139] On *thelgein* and persuasion, see Buxton 1982: 51–52; for feminine contexts, the verb is used of Calypso's seduction of Odysseus, Hom. *Od.* 1.57; the Sirens' song, *Od.* 12.40, 44; Penelope's beguilement of the Suitors, *Od.* 18.282; and the *kestos* of Aphrodite, which Hera uses to seduce Zeus, *Iliad* 14.215. Significantly, the term is also applied to Odysseus several times (cf. Hom. *Od.* 14.387, 16.195, 17.514), as well as to Hermes (Hom. *Od.* 23.3, 5.47, *Iliad* 24.343); and to Zeus in the context of war (cf. Hom. *Iliad* 12.255, 13.435, and 15.594). For a discussion of *thelgein* and the concept of enchantment in early Greek poetry, see Walsh 1984: 14–15 and passim.

[140] Similar to the Sirens are the mythical Keledones, the "Charmers," who cause their listeners to forget their homelands and waste away with pleasure; cf. Pind. *Pae.* 11.9; Ath. 7.290e.

Whoever draws near them in ignorance and hears the voice
of the Sirens, to that man neither his wife nor young children
stand near nor rejoice in his homecoming,
but the Sirens enchant him with their sweet song.

The nymph Calypso represents another supernatural female in the *Odyssey* who exerts a coërcive, magical power over mortal men through her use of persuasive speech. Like the Sirens, Calypso also enchants, but with soft and flattering words rather than with sweet song (μαλακοῖσι καὶ αἱμυλίοισι λόγοισι | θέλγει, Hom. *Od.* 1.56–57). The adjective αἱμύλιος connects Calypso's words to the cunning speech of women in Hesiod, while the verb *thelgein* conveys magical associations. Similarly, the verb also applies to the nymph Circe (θέλξαι, Hom. *Od.* 10.291), whose power of enchantment takes a more concrete form since she possesses the knowledge of shape-changing drugs in addition to seductive words (πολυφάρμακος, Hom. *Od.* 10.276). Even the mortal Penelope wields this charm of speech, since she, too, utilizes sweet but deceptive words to trick the suitors (θέλγε δὲ θυμὸν | μειλιχίοις ἐπέεσσι, Hom. *Od.* 18.282–83). In all these passages, the verb *thelgein* associates women with speech that overcomes masculine reason and causes men to act contrary to their intentions. Thus when the sophist Gorgias uses the term to refer to the spellbinding power of rhetoric at end of the fifth century, he relies on the traditional affiliation of persuasion with feminine seduction incarnated by the figure of Helen (Gorg. *Hel.* 10).

In the *Odyssey*, the character of Helen also uses feminine verbal guile to deceive men: in Menelaus' narrative of the Trojan horse, she seductively imitates the voices of the absent Argive wives: "Three times you walked around the hollow trap, touching it all over; and you called by name the best of the Danaans, likening your voice to the wives of all the Argives" (πάντων Ἀργείων φωνὴν ἴσκουσ' ἀλόχοισιν, Hom. *Od.* 4.279). This feminine form of verbal mimesis, the ability to impersonate others in order to deceive men, has other parallels in early Greek epic. The Delian maidens whose songs imitate the speech of foreign men in the *Homeric Hymn to Delian Apollo* exhibit a similar facility for verbal impersonation:

πάντων δ' ἀνθρώπων φωνὰς καὶ κρεμβαλιαστὺν
μιμεῖσθ' ἴσασιν· φαίη δέ κεν αὐτὸς ἕκαστος
φθέγγεσθ'· οὕτω σφιν καλὴ συνάρηρεν ἀοιδή.   (162–64)

They know how to imitate the voices of all men,
and their clattering words. Each man would say he himself was speaking,
so fitted to them is their beautiful song.[141]

---

[141] I take φωνή here to refer to the dramatic skill of the maidens rather than to their ability to imitate dialects, as does Kaimio 1977: 105n.254; and Sörbon 1966: 58.

In another hymn, Aphrodite's seduction of Anchises involves a similar mimetic operation. By means of an elaborate *kosmēsis* reminiscent of Pandora, particularly in its reference to golden jewelry (*Hom. Hymn Ven.* 64–65), the goddess impersonates a marriageable young virgin, imitating a foreign language, like the Delian maidens above, to seduce the Trojan hero:

γλῶσσαν δ' ὑμετέρην καὶ ἡμετέρην σάφα οἶδα·
Τρῳὰς γὰρ μεγάρῳ με τροφὸς τρέφεν, ἡ δὲ διὰ πρὸ
σμικρὴν παῖδ' ἀτίταλλε φίλης παρὰ μητρὸς ἑλοῦσα.
ὣς δή τοι γλῶσσάν γε καὶ ὑμετέρην εὖ οἶδα.   (*Hom. Hymn Ven.* 113–16)

I know both of our languages very well.
For a Trojan nurse reared me in the palace, one who
brought me up from girlhood, having taken me from my dear mother.
That is why I know your language so well.

Not only does Aphrodite show a capacity for verbal dissimulation traditionally associated with women throughout the Greek literary tradition, her speech has an explicitly erotic purpose and belongs to the other enhancements of the nuptial *kosmēsis* represented elsewhere by Pandora. And yet the ability to impersonate others cannot be considered a strictly feminine skill in the world of the Homeric poems: Odysseus cleverly constructs new disguises for himself through his manipulation of words, especially in his deception of the Cyclops, his exchange with Nausicaa, and his use of disguise upon his return to Ithaca.[142]

This brief survey of feminine deception in archaic literature suggests that women's seductive speech was viewed as inextricably bound to their bodies and the desire engendered by them. As a form of ventriloquism practiced by Helen, the Delian Maidens, and Aphrodite in early epic, this speech genre has affinities with the arts of acting and rhetoric, which are sometimes figured as feminine in the classical period, when "the seductive vagaries of communication, as well as deviousness in action, are often construed as female qualities in the hierarchy of values."[143] However, it would be going to far too say that craftiness and cunning persuasion belong exclusively to women in archaic literature; Odysseus in the Homeric poems, for example, shows himself adept at gaining control over others, particularly in situations where he has a physical disadvantage, through dissimulation and verbal cleverness. In contrast, while the examples of feminine

---

[142] Though humans only rarely imitate the voices and appearances of others, gods often impersonate mortals in Homer, like Poseidon, who likens his voice to that of Calchas (Hom. *Iliad* 13.43–45); Apollo, who imitates Lycaon (*Iliad* 20.81); and Athena, who assumes the voice of Deïphobus (*Iliad* 22.227), not to mention an extended disguise as Mentor in the *Odyssey*. In practice, men could appropriate female voices, but in public genres like drama the opposite did not hold true; see Stehle 1997: 132–35.

[143] Goldhill 1986: 128.

persuasion discussed in this section represent the attempts of women to gain control over men, at least temporarily, their verbal guile normally occurs in an erotic context and deploys physical desirability as an additional tool. Although not an erotic context, the *teichoscopia* depicted in Book 3 of the *Iliad* reinforces the idea that public speech, even in the Homeric poems, where the division between the household and the political realm is less distinct than in the classical period, belongs to men: when Helen identifies Odysseus, Antenor takes over the job of describing his skill at political speaking among men (Hom. *Iliad* 3.204–27).

CONCLUSION

Although very few of the discursive practices discussed in this chapter apply exclusively to one gender, the literary sources broadly distinguish between masculine and feminine verbal genres. They also point to a few gender-specific lexical features, such as ritual cries like *ololugē* and *alalugē*. Out of all the verbal genres, ritual lamentation probably has the strongest ties to women, with the result that men who lament are often depicted as either effeminized or foreign; but gossip, obscenity, and cunning persuasion, while identified in specific instances with female speakers, clearly have a masculine equivalent. Many of the sources portray women as belonging to a speech community separate from that of men, where they gather as a group to engage in shared verbal activities such as mourning, ritual obscenity, gossip, and choral performance in both private and public contexts. The discursive practices related by these sources reinforce the idea that men and women inhabited separate social spheres, at least in the Greek imagination, if not in actual fact. In contrast, the instances of verbal guile discussed in the last section show individual women, particularly wives, prevailing on individual men through their skillful use of words, most often in an erotic and domestic context.

All of these verbal genres reflect the pervasive association of women's speech with the body and with female sexuality in ancient Greece; thus participants in the Thesmophoria and other Demetrian festivals promoted both personal and civic fertility through their use of ritual *aischrologia*, while mourners frequently accompanied their cries with wild, uncontrolled gestures. Similarly, the sources portray both female gossip and verbal guile as the product of an excessive interest in *erōs*, which encourages adultery and promiscuity. But the connection between speech and sexuality pertains not only to women: it has a correlate in the masculine, political sphere of the Athenian polis, where freedom of speech and inviolability of body are identified as the fundamental rights of the adult citizen male, distinguishing him from all others, particularly women and slaves. The equation between power and speech thus reflects a fundamental male concern about maintaining control over the bodies and speech of perceived subordinates. For this reason, fifth-century literary sources frequently represent women's verbal activities as dangerous and subversive of political stability, even when they assume a religious form. Because ritual activities provided an opportunity for women to leave their households, congregate apart from men, and speak publicly, if only to each other, they provided an alternative discursive sphere that men could not directly control. Similarly, gossip and seductive persuasion, the speech practices associated with individual women in the domestic sphere, also represented a potential source of trouble for men, because they, too, could elude male surveillance. The following chapters will examine the ways in which the dramatic poets deployed these traditional verbal genres and the associations they evoked in plays that represent women's speech, particularly their use of persuasion, as transgressive and dangerous to the male community. By assimilating fifth-century concerns about rhetoric and speech to an archaic prototype, that of women's treacherous verbal guile, the plays examined in the remainder of this book find a vehicle for meditating on the problems posed by persuasive speech of men in the democratic polis.

Chapter Three

LOGOS GUNAIKOS: SPEECH AND
GENDER IN AESCHYLUS' ORESTEIA

THE PRECEDING CHAPTER suggested the types of speech genre associated with women in the ancient Greek literary tradition and distinguished those verbal activities from the masculine, political speech of the polis discussed in Chapter 1. This chapter will show how these genres are dramatically deployed in the *Oresteia*, a trilogy that explores the place of persuasive speech within the democratic city. Produced in 458 B.C.E., the trilogy concludes with the founding of the homicide court, the Areopagus, an archaic institution originally controlled by the Eupatridae but whose jurisdiction and political influence had become increasingly restricted by the reforms of Ephialtes introduced just a few years earlier. Aeschylus' representation of the Areopagus should be considered not merely at face value as an endorsement of conservative values, but rather as a paradigm for actual judicial procedure at Athens. In this way, the trial scene may be viewed as a general symbol of democratic process in which speech and persuasion played such a major role.[1]

By giving its central female character speech practices that deviate in many respects from the conventions outlined in the last chapter, the trilogy configures the problem of speech in the polis in terms of gender. Clytemnestra's verbal practices are strikingly free of the ritual language associated with women, particularly lamentation; indeed, most of her infrequent allusions to ritual speech have very ambiguous connotations. Because her speech derives from her *kratos*, the masculine, political authority conferred upon her in her husband's absence, it is represented as public and rhetorically persuasive, a view corroborated by the fact that she almost exclusively addresses a male internal audience throughout the play. And yet, although figured as masculine, Clytemnestra's persuasive power has a distinctly femi-

---

[1] For the Greek text in this chapter, I have relied on Denniston and Page 1972 for the *Agamemnon*; Garvie 1988 for the *Choephori*, and Sommerstein 1989 for the *Eumenides*, unless otherwise noted. Parts of this chapter originally appeared as McClure 1997a and 1997b. Thanks are owed to the editors of *Helios* and *Classical Journal*, as well as to the anonymous referees, for their comments. On the relation of the trial scene in the *Eumenides* to the law courts and to the Euripidean agon, see Lloyd 1992: 14–15. Griffith 1995 also examines some of the political aspects of the *Oresteia*, focusing on how it negotiates class interests and consolidates hegemonic power. For the Areopagus as a conservative symbol, see Sinclair 1988: 208.

nine aspect in that she deploys it to deceive and gain power over men; for this reason, it has no effect on the women in the trilogy even as it subjugates men. Clytemnestra's facility for impersonation, semantic dissimulation, and magical incantation harks back to the archaic topos of women's seductive persuasiveness. This aberrant combination of public and private speech, echoed and inverted by Athena in the *Eumenides*, shows the trilogy to be fundamentally preoccupied with the problem of persuasion in a democracy. More precisely, the drama depicts a movement from the feminine, figurative, and false speech of the first play to the ideal of a masculine, unambiguous, and divinely sanctioned speech of the law court in the third. The perversion of speech genres reflects the profound disturbance of gender roles in the first play, a disturbance entailed by Clytemnestra's adulterous union with Aegisthus, her political power, and her subsequent murder of Agamemnon. Only the androgynous Athena, who rescues *peithō* and cleanses it of its female associations, may rectify the imbalance and reestablish the norms disrupted in the first play.

Clytemnestra's speech vacillates between gendered subject positions: she is by turns persuasive, like a man, and deferential, like a woman, freely reformulating herself to suit the occasion. Her ability to perform both masculine and feminine verbal genres resembles the verbal mimesis of Helen, Aphrodite, and the Delian Maidens in archaic poetry as well as exemplifies the type of linguistic "code-switching" identified with muted groups in Chapter 1. But this bilingualism, instead of reinforcing the social order, creates a category crisis that ultimately destabilizes gender roles.[2] In this sense, her character functions almost as a metaphor for the idea of performance itself, for the male actor who performs gender by impersonating women.[3] In addition to this rhetorical posturing, the abundance of polysemy and metaphor found in Clytemnestra's speech contributes to her ability to deceive and control her male interlocutors. And finally, the carpet scene links Clytemnestra with magical language characteristic of erotic incantations, another coercive verbal means traditionally deployed by women to gain control over men, and a speech genre later associated with the Erinyes, whose inauspicious utterance must be negated and transformed in the *Eumenides*. In contrast, Cassandra deploys more conventionally feminine speech genres, particularly ritual lament. Only her speech

---

[2] Garber (1992: 17) defines a category crisis as "a failure of definitional distinction, a borderline that becomes permeable, that permits of border crossings from one apparently distinct category to another." Goldhill (1984b: 14) also recognizes the same phenomenon in anthropological terms when he speaks of Clytemnestra's adultery as entailing a loss of social identity.

[3] It is tempting to correlate the queen's facile shifting of personas to Butler's notion of gender as a performance: "Gender is the repeated stylization of the body, a set of repeated acts within a rigid regulatory frame that congeal over time to produce the appearance of substance, of a natural sort of being"; see Butler 1990: 33.

can be grounded in truth because it is involuntary, beyond her control, and derives from Apollo.

In the *Choephori*, Clytemnestra's feminine and deceptive speech gradually yields to the masculine persuasion of Orestes mandated by Apollo and later associated with the law court. The *Eumenides* integrates the figurative and deceptive speech of women and the masculine discourses of the polis through the androgynous figure of Athena, whose enchanting persuasion benefits rather than harms the city. Athena converts the dangerous speech of Clytemnestra into the divinely sanctioned and truthful speech of the law court. Whereas Clytemnestra's hybrid speech is portrayed as jeopardizing political stability in Argos, Athena's performance in the law court resolves the category crisis of the first two plays by rendering the female invisible. The tragic poet possibly reinforced the similarity between these two figures by utilizing the same actor for both roles. The trilogy thus demonstrates not only that women's speech must be regulated by the polis and kept out of the public sphere, but also that persuasion, if it is to benefit the democratic city, must be stripped of deceptive, feminine guile, since this duplicitous speech potentially subverts normative social categories, categories that the masculine speech of the law court, and tragic drama, seek to produce and maintain.

The Male Chorus as Internal Audience

The chorus of male elders in the Agamemnon serve as an internal audience, corresponding to the male spectators in the theater, who comment on the speech and actions of Clytemnestra and continually reassert gender norms. Although physically infirm and reduced to a marginal position, the chorus still claim the authority and prerogative of public speech in the parodos:

> κύριός εἰμι θροεῖν ὅδιον κράτος αἴσιον ἀνδρῶν
> ἐκτελέων· ἔτι γὰρ θεόθεν καταπνείει
> πειθώ, μολπᾷ δ' ἀλκὰν σύμφυτος αἰών.   (104–6)

> I have the power to sing of the auspicious command
> ruling the expedition; for persuasion from the gods still breathes
> down upon me, and my time of life is naturally suited to a song of deeds.
>   (Adapted from Fraenkel)

The phrase κύριός εἰμι θροεῖν, which contains forensic overtones,[4] marks the chorus' speech as masculine and political; indeed, it in general contains a large number of legal terms.[5] The fact that the chorus represent their

---

[4] Fraenkel 1950, 2: 159.

[5] The following judicial terms are found in the chorus' speech: ἀντίδικος (41), ἄτιται (72), τίνει χρέος (457), προδίκοις (451), πρασσομένα (705), τεκμηρίοισιν (1366), μαρτυρήσων (1506), δίκαν . . . παρέξει (1511–12). On legal language in the *Oresteia*, see Robertson 1939.

persuasion as deriving from the gods identifies it as authoritative and truthful and prefigures the speech of Athena in the third play.[6] Similarly, they indicate that the content of their song will be concerned exclusively with men, men who have *kratos*.[7] The chorus also participate in and create public discourse as revealed by their subsequent exchange with Cassandra: although they do not understand her visions of the future, they comprehend her allusion to the past, to Atreus and Thyestes, since this is something the whole city knows (πᾶσα γὰϱ πόλις βοᾷ, 1106). The chorus of Argive elders function dramatically as an internal, male audience that evaluates and circumscribes Clytemnestra's speech; through the chorus, the play establishes a dialectical relationship between the spectators in the theater and those within the play.[8] This reflexivity extends to the *Eumenides*, where the male jurors who must decide Orestes' fate also mediate between the theatrical spectators and the dramatic action. The Areopagite judges in the third play and the Argive elders in the first are also linked verbally, since Clytemnestra at the end of the *Agamemnon* uses the term δικαστής to refer to them (1421). By establishing masculine speech as judicial and public, the chorus provide a standard against which the play measures Clytemnestra's speech.

Gender and Performance:
Clytemnestra's Shifting Verbal Genres

Although the chorus furnish in the parodos and throughout the play normative gender categories regarding speech, the Watchman has already defied gender expectations in the prologue by describing Clytemnestra as androgynous: "So a woman who thinks like a man rules with expectant heart" (ὧδε γὰϱ κϱατεῖ | γυναικὸς ἀνδϱόβουλον ἐλπίζον κέαϱ, 10–11). On a linguistic level, Aeschylus marks Clytemnestra's gender ambiguity with several oxymoronic juxtapositions of male and female terms.[9]

---

[6] According to Scott (1984: 194), the term κύϱιος "stress[es] the completeness of the entitlement"; cf. Arist. *Eth. Nic.* 3.5.8 and *Pol.* 3.16.10; Eur. *Supp.* 1189; Thuc. 4.18 and 5.63. Thalmann (1985a: 107) also notes that the chorus, in contrast to Clytemnestra and Cassandra, are "bound by the rules that usually govern speech." Thalmann concludes in the second part of this study (1985b: 233) that "an ideal speech would doubtless be perfectly expressive, without any ambiguity or other impression. But that speech would be the privilege of divinity."

[7] Goldhill 1984b: 18.

[8] Griffith (1995: 122) observes that because the chorus always survive, they serve as a tangible symbol of "collectivity affirmed and restored."

[9] Katz (1994: 89) describes Clytemnestra's character as "constructed . . . around an uncertainty regarding her sexual inscription." At the level of language, this androgyny is signified by the repeated juxtaposition of male and female terms: so the Watchman describes Clytemnestra's mind as ἀνδϱόβουλον (11), whereas the chorus speak in similar terms of her authority

Similarly, her control of public discursive practices contingent upon her possession of masculine *kratos* reflects a profound inversion of gender roles. Nonetheless, the chorus persist in treating Clytemnestra as stereotypically female, repeatedly derogating her words as trivial and unreliable.

In the chorus' first exchange with Clytemnestra, they express incredulity and distrust: they do not believe her claim that Troy has fallen (πέφευγε τοὔπος ἐξ ἀπιστίας, 268); they demand proof (τί γὰρ τὸ πιστόν; ἔστι τῶνδέ σοι τέκμαρ; 272); and they accuse her of relying on the persuasive but unreliable visions of dreams (ὀνείρων φάσματ' εὐπειθῆ, 274) or unsubstantiated rumor (ἄπτερος φάτις, 276). They contrast a masculine concern for truth, expressed by the legal term τέκμαρ and the adjective πιστός, with less reliable, and therefore more feminine, forms of speech.[10] Clytemnestra's angry response rhetorically serves to establish her credibility by distancing her from the trivial words of girls and women: "You mock my understanding as if I were a mere girl" (παιδὸς νέας ὣς κάρτ' ἐμωμήσω φρένας, 277). By associating Clytemnestra with male speech, the poet creates an incongruity between her gender and her verbal activities, a discrepancy that reveals both the control she maintains over her interlocutors and her ability to perform the role necessitated by her rhetorical goals.

The beacon speech, in turn, represents a type of masculine demonstration, an inartificial proof characteristic of the law courts, brought in to corroborate her testimony. In contrast to the self-deprecating Macaria discussed in Chapter 1, Clytemnestra boldly proclaims her verbal authority. Her speeches introduce several terms and motifs inappropriate to women that effectively combine to convince the male chorus: the emphasis on victory and defeat encompassed by the verb νικάω and its cognates (291, 314), the vivid portrayal of inverted power relations in the conquered Troy (324, 340, 342), and her insistence on proof (τέκμαρ ... σύμβολον, 315; cf. 272, 352). Clytemnestra's persuasiveness earns her praise from the chorus: "You have spoken sensibly like a self-controlled man" (γύναι, κατ' ἄνδρα σώφρον' εὐφρόνως λέγεις, 351). The chorus confirm that this self-controlled, masculine speech is implicitly credible: "Now that I have heard your plausible proofs, I am quite ready to address the gods" (ἐγὼ δ' ἀκούσας πιστά σου τεκμήρια | θεοὺς προσειπεῖν εὖ παρασκευάζομαι, 352–53). At

---

in the king's absence: δίκη γάρ ἐστι φωτὸς ἀρχηγοῦ τίειν | <u>γυναῖκ'</u> ἐρημωθέντος <u>ἄρσενος</u> θρόνου (259–60). Note that in both passages, Clytemnestra's masculine control of political power is underscored by the repetition of κρατεῖ (10) and κράτος (258) in the emphatic last position. Other examples of this oxymoronic juxtaposition include <u>γύναι</u>, κατ' <u>ἄνδρα</u> σώφρον' εὐφρόνως λέγεις (351); τὸ μὲν <u>γυναῖκα</u> πρῶτον <u>ἄρσενος</u> δίχα (861); <u>θῆλυς ἄρσενος</u> φονεύς | ἐστίν (1231–32). On Clytemnestra's androgyny in general, see Winnington-Ingram 1948; Zeitlin 1984: 163–64.

[10] Goldhill (1984b: 39) distinguishes between two epistemological modes: he defines the visible mode, or seeming, as feminine, and the noetic mode, or "the power of conceptualisation in language," as masculine.

the same time, Clytemnestra undercuts her mastery of masculine speech by calling attention to her feminine gender: "You hear this story from me, a woman" (τοιαῦτά τοι γυναικὸς ἐξ ἐμοῦ κλύεις, 348).[11] This shifting between gendered discourses, between male and female subject positions, can be understood as a type of code-switching that allows her to gain the upper hand with her interlocutors: at times, she positions herself as masculine in speech in order to establish credibility with the chorus of Argive elders; at other times, she portrays herself as typically feminine as a means of arousing the sympathy of her listeners.

Although the chorus have just praised Clytemnestra's command of rational, masculine speech, the ode that follows retracts this sentiment and underscores the queen's exceptional rhetorical ability. At the end of the first stasimon, the chorus meditate on the foolishness of women who rely not on hard evidence but on capricious, false rumors:

τίς ὦδε παιδνὸς ἢ φρενῶν κεκομμένος,
φλογὸς παραγγέλμασιν
νέοις πυρωθέντα καρδίαν ἔπειτ'
    ἀλλαγᾷ λόγου καμεῖν;
γυναικὸς αἰχμᾷ πρέπει
πρὸ τοῦ φανέντος χάριν ξυναινέσαι.(479–84)

Who is so childish or bereft of sense as to get his heart
excited by the sudden news of the beacon,
only to be disappointed by a change of story?
It's just like a woman to believe a thing before it is clear.

Although Clytemnestra in the earlier scene convinced the chorus of the truth of her words, she is now condemned with women as a group for her childishness. Rumors voiced by women, the chorus assert, are inherently unreliable: "The boundary of the overcredulous female mind is open to swift encroachment, and swift indeed does the rumor voiced by a woman disappear" (πιθανὸς ἄγαν ὁ θῆλυς ὅρος ἐπινέμεται | ταχύπορος· ἀλλὰ ταχύμορον | γυναικογήρυτον ὄλλυται κλέος, 485–87).[12] This gnome seems to attribute both garrulousness and credulity to females: easily convinced by rumors, women spread gossip rapidly. The chorus call attention not to women's ability to deceive, the more usual trope and the one most applicable to the situation, but to their own vulnerability to deception. By means of their gnomic pronouncements, the chorus derogate and dismiss female speech as trivial and lacking authority, implying that only masculine speech,

[11] Fraenkel (1950, 2: 178) observes that here Clytemnestra shows her "superior, man-like insight into the nature of human affairs."

[12] I follow Denniston and Page in taking πιθανός as well as ἐπινέμεται as passive, since the passive construction better suits the context established by the previous six lines, that the female too readily believes what others tell her; for πιθανός and women, cf. Xen. *Oec.* 13.9.

since it is based on reliable proofs, can be trusted. But the play will render these narrow observations about women's speech, later reiterated by Agamemnon, extremely ironic, since Clytemnestra through her verbal machinations will gain control over all of her male interlocutors.

Although Clytemnestra represents herself in masculine terms to the chorus in the first episode, she subsequently constructs herself as a conventional Greek wife who acts in conformity with the norms of female behavior. In fact, whenever Aeschylus shows her performing the part of an obedient and loyal wife in this way, he also implies that she acts duplicitously. The best example of her characterization as deceitful appears in her speech to the Herald at 587–614, in which Clytemnestra seeks to persuade Agamemnon and the chorus that she has been a faithful wife. The difference in her attitude to the chorus and to the messenger, who she knows will carry her message back to Agamemnon, is striking: whereas she adopts a tone of familiarity and even contempt with the chorus, she assumes a more formal and artificial pose with her new interlocutor. The poet first portrays Clytemnestra as acting in accordance with feminine norms by her conformity to the conventions of female speech. Thus she begins by stating that she has acted properly in a religious context by raising the cry of *ololugē* (ἀνωλόλυξα, 587), the ritual cry associated with women, discussed in Chapter 2.[13] Then she casts into direct speech the earlier reproaches of the chorus, "Do you think that Troy has now been vanquished, having been persuaded by the beacons? How like a woman to get her hopes up" ('φρυκτωρῶν διά | πεισθεῖσα Τροίαν νῦν πεπορθῆσθαι δοκεῖς; | ἦ κάρτα πρὸς γυναικὸς αἴρεσθαι κέαρ,' 590–92). This gnomic commonplace serves a dual function: by recounting the words of the chorus, Clytemnestra employs a familiar rhetorical move seen in her earlier exchange with them. She first portrays herself as typically feminine, and therefore gullible; then she implicitly distances herself from this characterization by showing how she herself has believed only the beacon that bears a true and unambiguous report. Clytemnestra further evokes and subverts the traditional image of female lability: "Such accounts made me appear to be astray" (λόγοις τοιούτοις πλαγκτὸς οὖσ' ἐφαινόμην, 593). And yet Clytemnestra has demonstrated her superior masculine insight by taking immediate action: she has already made the proper sacrifices and raised the ritual cry of thanksgiving, the *ololugē*, whose feminine associations she emphasizes (γυναικείῳ νόμῳ | ὀλολυγμόν, 594–95).

In the second part of her speech, the part she explicitly instructs to be delivered to Agamemnon (604), Clytemnestra deploys a discourse of sexual

---

[13] Scott (1984: 14) notes that the *ololugē* denotes "a cry of emotional release and often of triumphant joy." On the *ololugē* generally, see Deubner 1941 and the discussion in Chapter 2; in the *Oresteia*, see Goheen 1955: 124–25; Peradotto 1964: 393; Zeitlin 1965: 507; Haldane 1965b: 37–38; and Moritz 1979.

fidelity, claiming that she has been a faithful wife (γυναῖκα πιστήν, 606) and a good watchdog of the house (δωμάτων κύνα | ἐσθλήν, 607–8) and that the seal, presumably of chastity, but perhaps more prosaically the seal to the household storeroom, has not been broken (σημαντήριον | οὐδὲν διαφθείρασαν, 609–10).[14] By using the term πιστή, Clytemnestra refers to the sexual self-control that governed female life in ancient Greece. This feminine loyalty, which has both an economic and an erotic aspect, corresponds to the credible speech of the self-controlled male. Further, the term πιστή in conjunction with σημαντήριον underscores the integrity of the chaste female body, which should be bounded, uncorrupted, and impenetrable, as the feminine complement of the physical inviolability of the adult citizen male in classical Athens. The fact that the verb διαφθείρω later becomes the technical term for adulterous seduction in Attic oratory further contributes to the ambiguity.[15] Moreover, the sexual metaphor contained in Clytemnestra's penultimate words further suggests adultery even as it disavows it: "Nor have I known pleasure with another man nor the rumor that brings rebuke more than the dippings of bronze" (οὐδ' οἶδα τέρψιν οὐδ' ἐπίψογον φάτιν | ἄλλου πρὸς ἀνδρὸς μᾶλλον ἢ χαλκοῦ βαφάς, 611–12). The metaphor χαλκοῦ βαφάς not only connotes a blend of sexuality and violence later echoed at 1447, but also points forward to Agamemnon's death within the house. A general or gnomic statement concludes her speech: "Such a boast (κόμπος), full of truth, is not shameful for a wellborn woman to utter" (τοιόσδ' ὁ κόμπος, τῆς ἀληθείας γέμων, | οὐκ αἰσχρὸς ὡς γυναικὶ γενναίᾳ λακεῖν, 613–14).[16] But this statement, while affirming the propriety of her speech, at the same time undercuts it with the notion of the boast (κόμπος), a speech genre more appropriate to the battlefield than the household.[17] In this highly rhetorical speech, the poet depicts Clytemnestra as alternately establishing and subverting the ethos of a dutiful and loyal wife by means of her verbal activities.

In her first direct address to Agamemnon (855–913), a speech dense in metaphor and innuendo, Clytemnestra continues both disguising and exposing herself, undermining her feminine persona with masculine rhetoric. First, she appropriates masculine and civic speech in her opening address

---

[14] The scholiast glosses σημαντήριον as σφραγῖδα τῆς πρὸς ἄνδρα εὐνῆς. On a more literal level, the term refers to the custom of sealing up storerooms, as at Pl. *Leg.* 954 a–b. For further discussion of this term, see Denniston and Page 1972: 126.

[15] This term is discussed more fully in Chapter 4; for relevant references, see Eur. *Hipp.* 1008; for a similar usage, cf. Aesch. *Ag.* 610; Eur. *Alc.* 316; *Bacch.* 314–18; Lys. 1.16.

[16] I follow Denniston and Page and Fraenkel in ascribing these lines to Clytemnestra rather than to the herald. For a full discussion of this passage, see Fraenkel 1950, 2: 305–6.

[17] On the Homeric hero's desire to "impress himself upon the world" through his voice, especially through his use of the boast, see Murnaghan 1988a: 25. For the Homeric boast in general, see Muellner 1976. Thalmann (1985b: 226) discusses the "excess of meaning" found in this boast.

to Agamemnon, flaunting her unfeminine public appearance with an elaborate *excusatio*: "Citizen men, elders of Argos, I am not ashamed to tell
you of my man-loving ways" (ἄνδρες πολῖται, πρέσβος Ἀργείων τόδε, |
οὐκ αἰσχυνοῦμαι τοὺς φιλάνορας τρόπους | λέξαι πρὸς ὑμᾶς, 855–57).
Since public, civic speech was not normally associated with women in the
Greek literary tradition and in the Athenian polis, Clytemnestra openly
defies this convention by addressing herself to the citizens. At the same
time, her words are distinctly nonpublic in character. As Goldhill comments, the verb αἰσχύνεσθαι when used of women normally refers to
sexual behavior; in this passage, however, sexual and verbal indiscretion
are conflated by the verb in combination with the adjective φιλάνορας.[18]
Clytemnestra justifies her transgressive appearance out of doors and her
public speech before men with an overt message of wifely solicitude. Yet
the deliberate ambiguity of φιλάνορας, a term that describes Helen's erotic
misconduct earlier in the play, draws attention to Clytemnestra's adulterous
union with Aegisthus. The response this speech elicits from Agamemnon
reveals its impropriety: he censures Clytemnestra for speaking at length
and then warns her that the task of praising him, because a public genre,
more properly belongs to men (914–17), as does the job of blaming
women exemplified by the chorus' lyric invective against Helen (681–98).
But Clytemnestra, in contrast with Phaedra in Euripides' *Hippolytus*, resists
male discourses of praise and blame, both in this passage as well as after
Agamemnon's murder (1403–4).

   In her exchange with her husband, Clytemnestra again constructs herself
as acting in accordance with the conventions of feminine behavior, particularly verbal norms. At 861–65, she speaks of the hardships that await a
woman left behind in war, especially the rumors of her husband's death:

> τὸ μὲν γυναῖκα πρῶτον ἄρσενος δίχα
> ἧσθαι δόμοις ἐρῆμον ἔκπαγλον κακόν,
> πολλὰς κλύουσαν κληδόνας παλιγκότους,
> καὶ τὸν μὲν ἥκειν, τὸν δ' ἐπεισφέρειν κακοῦ
> κάκιον ἄλλο πῆμα, λάσκοντας δόμοις.   (861–65)

> First of all, it is a fearful grief that a woman should sit alone
> at home, hearing many rumors that break out afresh,
> and then one comes, and then another, bringing
> new reports of evil worse than the last, which they
> cry out for the house to hear.   (Adapted from Fraenkel)

In this passage, Clytemnestra characterizes herself as a typical wife who
sits at home in idleness, vulnerable to gossip, a portrait that draws on a

---

[18] Note that Helen's footsteps are termed φιλάνορες (411). For αἰσχύνεσθαι, see Goldhill
1984b: 89. Cf. Eur. *Andr.* 229.

commonplace about women in Greek literature, as discussed in the last chapter. These rumors seem to have a voice and agency of their own; they continually break out afresh (κληδόνας παλιγκότους, 863), and they cry aloud out to the house (λάσκοντας, 865). That these rumors cannot be controlled is further implied by the following section, in which a series of striking metaphors describes their content:

καὶ τραυμάτων μὲν εἰ τόσων ἐτύγχανεν
ἀνὴρ ὅδ' ὡς πρὸς οἶκον ὠχετεύετο
φάτις, τέτρηται δικτύου πλέω λέγειν. (866–68)

And if this man had met with as many wounds
as the rumors that trickled into the house,
he would have had more holes than a net.

The emphatic term φάτις, a word placed in the first position, recalls the male chorus' earlier gnome about the unreliability of rumors transmitted by women. In this passage, however, Clytemnestra reverses her earlier representation of herself to the male chorus as impervious to false reports, and reconstructs herself as stereotypically feminine in her readiness to believe whatever stories she hears. In the same way, she mentions dreams as another source of false information, and one perhaps characteristically female, which led her to conclude that Agamemnon had already died (891–94), even though she had earlier dismissed the chorus' speculation that her knowledge of Troy's fall had come from dreams (274). These contradictions again underscore Clytemnestra's ability to perform herself according to the rhetorical necessity of the moment.

The first part of Aeschylus' *Agamemnon*, then, represents Clytemnestra as portraying herself as conventionally feminine while her masculine control of rhetoric simultaneously undercuts this image, a strategy exhibited by Macaria's words in Euripides' *Children of Heracles*. On the one hand, Clytemnestra conforms to the conventions of proper female speech by deploying ritual cries, prayers, and gnomic statements about the correct behavior of women. On the other, her manipulation of the masculine discursive practices such as direct public address, epic boast, and persuasive proofs continually inverts the speech genres normally assigned to women. In the carpet scene, a critical dramatic juncture, we find a similar juxtaposition of masculine and feminine verbal genres. The carpet scene depicts a contest of *peithō* in which a woman conquers the conqueror of Troy, a gender-role reversal indicated by Clytemnestra's use of military vocabulary and finally accomplished with πιθοῦ at 943 (νικωμένη, 912; μάχης, 940; νικᾶσθαι, 941; and νίκην, 942).[19] Cassandra later reinforces the perverted martial imagery present in this scene when she refers to Clytemnestra's

[19] On battle imagery in this scene, see Bonnafé 1989; Taplin 1978: 82.

cry over the dead Agamemnon as an *ololugē*. In this context, however, the *ololugē* refers not to the feminine cry of jubilation, but rather to the triumph of a warrior "in the turn of battle" (ὡς δ' ἐπωλολύξατο | ἡ παντότολμος, ὥσπερ ἐν μάχης τροπῇ, 1236–37). Clytemnestra thus rejoices not as a wife at the safe return of her husband, but as a soldier victorious in battle. Although figured as a conquering warrior, Clytemnestra's use of deceptive persuasion in the carpet scene nonetheless retains feminine and feminizing qualities; her exotic and extravagant rhetoric affiliates her with the oriental courtier skilled in flattering tyrants.[20] At the same time, her expert use of persuasion allows the queen to gain control over her husband, forcing him to yield to her authority through the treading of the cloth, a victory that prefigures Athena's triumph over the Erinyes in the *Eumenides*.

Even though Agamemnon attempts to thwart Clytemnestra by reinscribing speech-related gender norms during the course of the carpet scene— "Surely, this lust for conflict is not womanlike" (οὔτοι γυναικός ἐστιν ἱμείρειν μάχης, 940)—he chronically underestimates his wife's rhetorical power. Agamemnon, like so many other tragic heroes, plays the part of the gull, deceived by his wife's irresistible verbal cunning, as Cassandra later remarks: "He does not know what sort is the speech of that hateful bitch" (οἵα γλῶσσα μισητῆς κυνός, 1228). The initial scenes of the *Agamemnon* portray Clytemnestra as a formidable speaker capable of manipulating her rhetorical ethos to suit the occasion: by "performing" herself, she shows her mastery of both masculine and feminine discursive practices and consequently subverts traditional gender roles. And yet, as the next section of this chapter will show, Aeschylus represents the queen in the carpet scene as using another verbal strategy traditionally associated with women, and also with Persians: magical incantation.

CLYTEMNESTRA'S BINDING SONG

Although metaphor is a feature of many of the speeches in the *Oresteia* trilogy, it is striking how frequently it appears in Clytemnestra's words.[21] Recent scholarship has produced a complex view of Clytemnestra as a character who skillfully exploits the ambiguities inherent in language

---

[20] Hall (1989b: 204–7) discusses how Aeschylus deploys a "vocabulary of barbarism" to affiliate Agamemnon with Persian tyranny, with Clytemnestra playing the part of a "barbarian flatterer."

[21] Thalmann 1985b: 226. In her analysis of significant metaphors in Clytemnestra's speech, Betensky (1977) argues that Clytemnestra's verbal power derives from her manipulation of metaphor. Following Betensky, Sevieri (1991) further explores Clytemnestra's capacity to control others through speech. Finally, in a fascinating but often overlooked article on the power of speech in the *Agamemnon*, Neustadt (1929) argues that Clytemnestra's control over speech represents a form of magic.

through her use of metaphor; her language is "crammed with truth"[22] and continually reveals a superabundance of meaning. Nowhere is this more apparent than in her speech at 958–74, pronounced as Agamemnon enters the house, treading on the ornate tapestries. On the level of plot, the standard view has been that the speech simply attempts to ensure that Agamemnon enters the house by allaying his fear of destroying its wealth (948–49).[23] Stanford even goes so far as to suggest that Clytemnestra in this speech is "merely babbling anything till her victim is safely in."[24] But if one views this complex speech as the penultimate expression of Clytemnestra's desire to exercise control over Agamemnon, it might best be understood not merely as idle chatter or metaphorical deception, but as a form of magical incantation, a speech genre closely associated with feminine seductive persuasion, as well as with barbarians, through the ancient Greek literary tradition.

The belief that control over language may translate into control over the physical world has traditionally been associated with magic.[25] As Neustadt has argued, Clytemnestra through her power of speech, particularly through her use of metaphor, exerts control over Agamemnon and others; by speaking about his death she causes it to happen.[26] Thus the poet combines in Clytemnestra an ability to "perform" herself by shifting her ethical representation to suit the moment with powerful performative utterances or speech acts analogous to those of the Erinyes. The belief in the efficacy and power of language appears at several points in the *Oresteia* trilogy, most notably in the *kommos* of the *Choephori* and in the binding song of the Erinyes in the *Eumenides*. In the *Agamemnon*, when Cassandra first names Agamemnon as the queen's intended victim, the chorus caution her to keep an auspicious silence (εὔφημον, ὦ τάλαινα, κοίμησον στόμα, 1247).[27] The chorus' use of εὔφημον suggests that by speaking of Agamemnon's death, Cassandra may actually induce it.[28] Such unpropitious speech, whether uttered casually or on purpose, was thought to bring about

---

[22] Thalmann 1985b: 226.

[23] For this view, see Jones 1962: 87; Thomson 1966: 76. The more recent and, in my view, less convincing interpretation of Crane (1993: 132) holds that Clytemnestra in this speech shows herself to be a sort of Aristotelian gentleman, one who "assumes the great-heartedness that her husband cannot himself achieve."

[24] Stanford 1942: 118.

[25] Neustadt 1929: 247–48. See also Tambiah 1968: 179. In this commentary on the *Homeric Hymn to Demeter*, Scarpi (1976: 165–69) observes that the *magos* or magician maintains control over nature through his knowledge of magical names.

[26] Neustadt (1929: 261) argues that when Clytemnestra uses the metaphor of the net in speaking about Agamemnon's death (866–68), she reveals her secret intention to kill her husband and seeks to guarantee her success.

[27] For a fuller discussion of this idea, see Neustadt 1929: 251; Thalmann 1985b: 222.

[28] Thalmann (1985b: 229) remarks upon the chorus' "fruitless attempt to suppress terrible knowledge."

catastrophic events.[29] Building on these views, I shall establish that Clytemnestra's speech has magical associations and, more precisely, that the
final two lines of this speech are in fact modeled on traditional closing
formulas of magical incantations, thus realizing the many incantatory features of repetition, assonance, alliteration, and metaphor found in the
earlier part of the speech. And yet, although this approximates magical
language, it must be viewed as a perversion of feminine erotic magic in
that it seduces in order to kill rather than to promote or maintain a sexual
relationship. Such erotic spells typically sought to enervate or control their
male objects while putting their female authors in the dominant position,
at least temporarily, thus inverting normal gender roles in a dynamic similar
to the one enacted in the carpet scene.

The link between magic and the power of persuasion, and even of song
itself, was widely known in antiquity.[30] As knowledge of magical practices in
the ancient world has increased, scholars have begun to identify traditional
magical formulas in poetic texts. Examples of literary adaptations of magical
language in the Greek tradition are found in the *Homeric Hymn to Demeter*,
in Sappho 1 (Voigt), in the binding song of the Erinyes in Aeschylus'
Eumenides, and in various literary fragments.[31] Richardson observes that
Demeter in the *Homeric Hymn to Demeter* employs language suggestive
of magical incantations when she promises to protect Demophoön from
witchcraft (228–30). He singles out triple repetition, double chiasmus,
anaphora, and assonance as stylistic features that contribute to the incantatory effect of Demeter's speech.[32] Line 228 also resembles in both form
and content a couplet near the end of a hexametrical incantation inscribed
on a lead amulet from Phalasarna, Crete (c. 400), suggesting that the poet
of the hymn was reflecting traditional incantatory language.[33] Cameron
notes as well several similar features characteristic of magical formulas
in Sappho 1. 21–28 (Voigt), including the peculiar use of antithetical
repetitions, or conditional clauses followed by reversals in combination

---

[29] Peradotto (1969) argues along the lines of Neustadt that seemingly casual phrases such
as χαλκοῦ βαφάς (612) bring about disastrous consequences.

[30] See Segal 1974: 139; de Romilly 1975; Buxton 1982: 12, 40, 52, 153–54. In his *Helen*,
Gorgias compares rhetoric to magic and witchcraft; see 11.10 DK. For a similar idea, see
Pl. *Soph.* 234e–f; *Plt.* 303c; *Euthydemus* 289e–f; and *Rep.* 358b. On the link between poetry
and enchantment more generally, see Walsh 1984.

[31] See Richardson 1974: 229–31; Scarpi 1976: 159–73. Faraone (1985) argues that the
binding song of the Furies in Aeschylus' *Eumenides* reflects the fifth-century practice of
judicial curses aimed at binding the wits of one's opponent. For a different interpretation,
see Moritz 1979: 187.

[32] Richardson 1974: 229.

[33] The Cretan amulet probably does not imitate the *Hymn* because the poem was not
widely known in antiquity; see Richardson 1974: 67–68. Maas (1944: 36–37) discusses the
parallels between the *Hymn* and the amulet. For the text and the most recent bibliography,
see Jordan 1992: 191–94.

with the repetition of ταχέως.[34] Most recently, Faraone has argued that these stylistic elements, particularly the double repetition of τελέω in the coda, with the final example in imperative form, τέλεσον, precisely echo the traditional closure of erotic spells.[35] The fact that Aristophanes parodies this coda indicates that it would have been well known to a late fifth-/ early fourth-century Athenian audience, and lends support to the notion that Clytemnestra, by using a similar formulation at the end of her speech, evokes traditional magical language.

These literary texts clearly associate magic with women, corroborating a pattern of representation within the broader literary tradition, where familiar female activities, such as administering drugs or producing cloth, are depicted as coercive, magical practices.[36] As discussed in the last chapter, cloth and drugs figure prominently in women persuading and gaining control over men in the *Odyssey*: both Calypso, who detains Odysseus for several years, and Circe, who transforms his men into pigs through her skillful use of herbs (Hom. *Od.* 10.235–36; 276; 290–92), are represented as singing and weaving in their houses, and both use words that seduce and enchant. Helen, also conspicuously surrounded by her weaving, possesses knowledge of magical drugs brought back from Egypt (*Od.* 4.227–32).[37] Even the weaving of Penelope can be seen as a magical action that renders the suitors powerless until Odysseus returns. Whereas weaving suggests feminine wiles, the finished product, cloth, may also exert power as an *agalma* or magical object: so the *kestos* of Aphrodite works erotic magic for Hera (*Iliad* 14.214–21),[38] whereas the *krēdemnon* or veil that Ino/ Leucothea gives to Odysseus averts his death (*Od.* 5.343–47; cf. 373).

The pervasive association of textiles with feminine powers of binding and entrapment also finds expression in Attic tragedy; in the stories of

---

[34] On magic and Sappho 1, see Cameron 1939; Putnam 1960: 79–83; Segal 1974; and Burnett 1983: 254–55.

[35] The standard formula is τέλει τελέαν ἐπαοιδήν; on this see Faraone 1992a: 323–24. For a nonliterary example of this form of closure, see Brashear 1979; Maltomini 1988: 247–48; and Janko 1988: 293. On erotic incantations in Pindar's *Fourth Pythian Ode*, see Faraone 1993.

[36] On female characters and magic in classical literature, see Gager 1992: 79 and 244. Note also that the curse tablets at times contradict the picture of women and magic presented in the literary tradition. In fact, men were just as likely, if not more likely, to compose or commission a defixio, especially given that many of the activities for which a spell might be required—athletic competitions, the law court, or the marketplace—were the province of men; see Gager 1992: 244–45. For incantations pronounced by women, cf. Theoc. 2.17 and passim; Ap. Rhod. 1665ff.; Luc. *Pharsalia* 6.413ff.

[37] Attic tragedy normally associates the use of *pharmaka* with persons of lower status, usually women; cf. Eur. *Andr.* 156–58; *Ion* 616–17, 843–46, 1185, 1220–21, 1286; *Hec.* 876–78. I discuss *pharmaka* in more detail in Chapters 4 and 5.

[38] On the garment, see Faraone 1990. For a more extensive discussion on female craftiness and cloth, see Bergren 1983. Jenkins 1985 further explores the motif of dangerous cloth in Greek literature, using Gernet's interpretation of the meaning of *agalma*.

Deianeira and Heracles, Medea and Glauce, and perhaps Procne and Philomela in Sophocles' lost *Tereus*,[39] they function as instruments of retribution and seduction. In Sophocles' *Trachiniae*, Deianeira attempts to seduce her husband but unwittingly works the opposite effect with her handiwork, the robe she has rubbed with love potions (φίλτρα) and spells (θέλκτρα, Soph. *Trach*. 584–85).[40] The charm, activated by exposure to the sun, binds and clings to Heracles' body, eating away at his flesh (Soph. *Trach*. 767ff.). In Euripides' *Medea*, it is the cloth itself that destroys, when Medea's gifts, the ornate robe (ποικίλος, Eur. *Med*. 1159) and the golden diadem, actually kill her rival by means of a smothering spontaneous combustion (Eur. *Med*. 1168ff.). In several other texts, including Euripides' *Hippolytus*, Theocritus' second *Idyll*, and Lucian's *Dialogue of the Courtesans*, erotic spells practiced by women require a garment or a scrap of cloth.[41] In all these instances, cloth helps women to seduce and gain control over men, by either detaining, destroying, or seducing them; its presence in these texts represents the subversive potential of an ordinary, feminine activity to overturn the normal social order.

Given this association of magical cloth with women controlling men, it is significant that Clytemnestra's speech at 958–74 follows the climactic carpet scene in which she persuades her husband to enter the house by walking on ornate and luxurious tapestries.[42] Cloth indeed figures prominently in the *Agamemnon* as well as in the rest of the *Oresteia* trilogy: the tapestries of the carpet scene both recall the trailing saffron robes of Iphigenia in the parodos and prefigure the fatal πέπλοι that later entrap Agamemnon in his bath (*Ag.* 1126–27). Related also are the many allusions to nets, traps, and coverings that recur throughout the play.[43] In the *Choephori*, Electra's elaborate woven garment brings about the recognition

---

[39] For fragments of Sophocles' *Tereus*, see fr. 523–37 *TGF* = Radt fr. 581–95b; cf. Ov. *Met*. 6.411–676.

[40] On erotic magic in this play, see Faraone 1994.

[41] Eur. *Hipp*. 513–15; Theoc. 2.23–25, 53; and Lucian *Dial. meret*. 4.4. These magical operations perhaps reflected actual practice, since some of the folded curse tablets were found to contain hair and other fibers; see Gager 1992: 16–17.

[42] Scholars disagree about what exactly Agamemnon walks on. The most common term for the cloth is εἷμα (cf. *Ag*. 921, 960, 963, 1383), which LSJ defines as "carpets," based on an erroneous reading of Soph. *Aj*. 1145. The term εἷμα has led some scholars to conjecture that textiles are finished clothing—not carpets, but fine cloth to be worn by the members of the royal household; see Flintoff 1987: 121. Other terms for the cloth that Agamemnon treads are πέπλος (1126, 1580), ὕφασμα (1492, 1516), ὑφή (949), and πέτασμα (909). Agamemnon thus walks on finished cloth, whether coverings or actual garments.

[43] Consider the terms χλαῖνα (872), δίκτυον (868, 1115), ἄγρευμα (1048), ἄρκυς (1116), ἀρκύστατα (1375), ἀράχνης ὕφασμα (1492), ἀμφίβληστρον (1382); related are the references to veils: προκαλύμματα (691) and καλύμματα (1178). On this set of images, see Lebeck (1971: 68 and passim), who argues that they symbolize the strands of fate that bind mortals to death: "The carpet, the entangling robe, and all related images are themselves symbols of the interwoven strands of fate by which Agamemnon is held fast."

between brother and sister (*Cho.* 231–32), whereas the scene in which Orestes later holds out to the sun the cloth used by Clytemnestra to kill her husband functions as an inversion of the carpet scene (*Cho.* 973ff.). At the end of the *Eumenides*, Athena instructs the propitiated Erinyes to don their festal robes (1028), a gesture that in part signals the restoration of order in the trilogy.[44]

Closer inspection of the scene's language confirms the link between the tapestries and magic. For example, three times Agamemnon calls the garments ποικίλος (923, 926, 936), a term used either for clothing offered to or worn by deities,[45] or for the ornately embroidered and luxuriously patterned cloth of barbarians.[46] But the term ποικίλος may also associate the cloth with magical power, since the term may designate a love charm in early Greek poetry.[47] In a more contemporary parallel, it also describes the destructive, magical garment that Medea uses to eliminate a sexual rival in Euripides' *Medea*. The adjective ποικίλος also frequently refers to speech that is treacherous and deceptive.[48] Similarly, Clytemnestra speaks of the spreading of the cloth as a τέλος (908; later echoed by Agamemnon at 934), a word that symbolically recurs throughout the play and one that repeatedly appears in magical incantations from the fifth century B.C.E. on.[49] Clytemnestra's use of the imperative γενέσθω in instructing the servants to unfurl the tapestries is reminiscent on a purely verbal level of the language of fifth- and fourth-century curse tablets or *defixionum tabellae*: "Let there spring up at once a purple-strewn path" (εὐθὺς γενέσθω πορφυρόστρωτος πόρος, 910).[50] The associations between magic and the spreading of the

---

[44] See Macleod 1975: 201–3; and Griffith 1988: 552–54. On the carpet scene and its resonances, see also Taplin 1977: 314–16; on cloth in the *Choephori* and its relation to the first play, see ibid.: 358–59.

[45] In Homer, fine clothing comes from Olympus or Troy; see Taplin 1980: 10. Taplin points out that the gods wear clothing that is ποικίλος (Hom. *Iliad* 5.735 and 8.385–86). That such garments could provoke divine φθόνος is shown by the law that forbade participants in the Peloponnesian cults of Demeter to wear embroidered or purple robes and golden jewelry; see Parker 1983: 144.

[46] The associations with Persia in this passage are unmistakable; for ornate garments as oriental, see *Pers.* 836, where Xerxes' clothing is described as ποικίλων ἐσθημάτων. See also Crane 1993: 122–25.

[47] Putnam (1960: 81–82) argues that ποικίλος has magical associations in the descriptions of the *kestos* of Aphrodite in Hom. *Iliad* 14.215 and 220, the earrings of Aphrodite in Hom. Hymn *Ven.* 89, and the robe of Aphrodite in Sappho 1.1, contexts in which the term may refer to "the charms of love."

[48] Johnston 1995: 189n.26.

[49] On the importance of τέλος in the trilogy, see Lebeck 1971: 68–73; also Goldhill 1984a. For τέλος in magical incantations, see Faraone 1992a; for examples of defixiones in which the verb τελέω appears, see Audollent 1967, esp. 7a.16, 32.29, 33.32, 35.28, 37.28, 38.14–15; Wünsch 1897; and Jordan 1985: n. 42.

[50] The passage cannot represent a contextual or semantic parallel, because the victim of the curse in defixiones usually appears as the subject of the third-person verb. For examples,

cloth and the sheer force of the queen's persuasive skills have prompted many scholars to conclude that Clytemnestra in the carpet scene assumes an "almost supernatural power," or even works a form of magical fascination.[51]

Although persuasion and cloth are not in themselves elements of magical practice, their use in this scene resonates with the aforementioned examples of female characters in the Greek literary tradition who use magic and verbal guile to gain control over men. It is therefore not surprising that Clytemnestra's speech at lines 958–74 picks up and develops in a more concrete form the echoes of incantatory language found in the carpet scene. The lead curse tablets employed throughout the Mediterranean world, with the earliest found in Sicily and Attica in the fifth century B.C.E., provide many examples of magical language. According to Gager, these tablets expressed a "formalized wish to bring other persons . . . under the client's power."[52] The fact that the defixiones were employed by people of various social classes and both genders points to widespread use in Athens.[53] The language and style of the curse tablets are highly formulaic and include such commonly recurrent features as repetition, alliteration and assonance, isocola, personification, metaphor and simile, and rhythmic phrasing.[54] Since many Athenians would have been acquainted with the practice of binding spells as well as with their language, it is not improbable that similar features found in Clytemnestra's speech may have had magical connotations for a fifth-century audience.

> ἔστιν θάλασσα· τίς δέ νιν κατασβέσει;
> τρέφουσα πολλῆς πορφύρας ἰσάργυρον
> κηκῖδα παγκαίνιστον, εἱμάτων βαφάς·   960
> οἶκος δ' ὑπάρχει τῶνδε σὺν θεοῖς, ἄναξ,
> ἔχειν· πένεσθαι δ' οὐκ ἐπίσταται δόμος.
> πολλῶν πατησμὸν δ' εἱμάτων ἂν ηὐξάμην,
> δόμοισι προυνεχθέντος ἐν χρηστηρίοις

---

see Jordan 1985, noting γενέσθω (no. 168), γένοιτο (no. 40), γ]ένοιτο (no. 46). See also γένοιτο in Audollent 1967: nos. 7a.20, 7b.1–2, 44.9, 66.6, 208 (where the phrase is repeated nine times in about ten lines); and Wünsch 1897: no. 65.8. On the third-person optative used in a wish formula, apparently as early as the mid-fifth century B.C.E., see Faraone 1991: 5.

[51] Kuhns (1962: 36), the first exponent of this view, refers to Clytemnestra as a "priestess of black magic." Taplin (1977: 314n.2) also speaks of her "more than masculine, almost supernatural, power," although he rejects without elaboration Dingels' passing suggestion of magic, "Klytaimestra hier eine magische Praxis übt"; see Dingels 1967: 166. Moreau (1976–77: 56–57) argues that the treading of the cloth results from magical fascination. On the related idea of Agamemnon's *atē* as the work of the ancestral curse, see Lloyd-Jones 1970: 67; Hammond 1965: 42–43; and Easterling 1973: 16–17.

[52] Gager 1992: 244.

[53] Ibid.: 21 and 24.

[54] Ibid.: 13. For a list of the characteristics of defixiones, see Kagarow 1929: 34–44.

ψυχῆς κόμιστρα τῆσδε μηχανωμένῃ·   965
ῥίζης γὰρ οὔσης φυλλὰς ἵκετ' ἐς δόμους,
σκιὰν ὑπερτείνασα σειρίου κυνός·
καὶ σοῦ μολόντος δωματῖτιν ἑστίαν,
θάλπος μὲν ἐν χειμῶνι σημαίνει μολόν,
ὅταν δὲ τεύχῃ Ζεὺς ἀπ' ὄμφακος πικρᾶς   970
οἶνον, τότ' ἤδη ψῦχος ἐν δόμοις πέλει,
ἀνδρὸς τελείου δῶμ' ἐπιστρωφωμένου.
Ζεῦ Ζεῦ τέλειε, τὰς ἐμὰς εὐχὰς τέλει·
μέλοι δέ τοί σοι τῶνπερ ἂν μέλλῃς τελεῖν.

There is a sea; who shall drain it dry?
Breeding an ever-renewing spring of abundant purple,
precious as silver, for the dying of cloth.
Our house has a supply of these things from the gods, my lord,
and this house does not know poverty.
For I would have vowed the treading of many robes
if it had been proposed to our house by the oracles
when I was devising a safe return of this man's life.
For when the root exists, leafage comes to the house,
stretching forth its shade against the dog-star;
so, now that you have come back to the hearth of our house,
your arrival signals the coming of heat in winter;
but whenever Zeus makes wine from the bitter grape,
then at once cold comes into the house
when the lord and master moves about the house.
Zeus, Zeus Accomplisher, accomplish my prayers.
Take thought for whatsoever you intend to fulfill. (Adapted from Fraenkel)

As suggested above, one of the salient characteristics of Clytemnestra's speech is the polysemy created by an abundance of metaphors. But this stylistic feature can be specifically linked to the incantatory nature of the speech. Metaphor allows Clytemnestra to say what she means in a way that eludes the other characters, particularly the chorus, who are continually baffled by her words. Given the belief in the efficacy of language that reappears at several critical junctures in the play, the repeated use of metaphors centered on themes of death suggests that more than flowery rhetoric is at work here. Metaphor allows Clytemnestra both to allude to her husband's death, functioning as a kind of speech act that sets in motion the disastrous events of the end of the play, and to keep her intentions concealed from both Agamemnon and the chorus. The appearance of language modeled on magical incantations in the coda further confirms the function of this speech as a form of efficacious language or performative utterance. That the chorus later attempt to block this magical imprecation with a plea for its negation lends further support to the idea that this speech potentially exerts an effective power.

For this reason, Clytemnestra's quasi-incantatory manipulation of metaphor as an instrument of control warrants closer examination. The speech begins with "a tone of magnificent emphasis,"[55] one created by the extended metaphor of the cloth and its dye. Through metaphor, Clytemnestra ambiguously invokes both the richness of the cloth, flattering to Agamemnon, and its dangerous, deadly qualities: its vastness (θάλασσα, 958), its purple color (πορφύρα, 959), its costliness (ἰσάργυρος, 959), and its liquidity (κηκίς, βαφαί, 960). These terms powerfully suggest the flow of blood, since κηκίς means any substance that spurts or oozes, whereas βαφή can be used metaphorically of blood.[56] The dark purple color of the cloth (πορφύρεος, cf. πορφυρόστρωτος, 910; πορφύρα, 957, 959; ἁλουργής, 946) implies not only the endless flow of blood in the house, but also death.[57] Moreover, the adjective βαφαί carries ominous associations, since it recalls both Iphigenia's yellow robes (κρόκου βαφάς, 239) and, ambiguously, either Clytemnestra's sexual conduct or the violence to come (χαλκοῦ βαφάς, 612). The queen expands on this theme of economic prosperity with personification, making δόμος the subject of the verb ἐπίσταται at 962. She again returns to the idea of the treading of the cloth at 963–65, here barely veiling her intentions revealed by the word pair that frames the line, ψυχῆς and μηχανωμένη (965). Rather than devising a means of saving Agamemnon's life, the queen has plotted his death.

From the subject of the house and its property described by metaphors portending death (958–65), Clytemnestra turns to agricultural and harvest metaphors associated with preservation and protection and, ultimately, the idea of completion (966–71). The continued repetition of δόμος/δῶμα links these sections, although the focus shifts from the inside of the house to its exterior. The images of the circling seasons, of summer and winter, and of fall harvest recall Clytemnestra's earlier speech (895–903), in which she flatters Agamemnon with a series of increasingly ornate, oriental metaphors, comparing him first to a farm watchdog, then to the mast of a ship, the roof beam of the house, and so on, ending with a comparison to a spring that greets the thirsty traveler.[58] The images of the movement of

---

[55] Fraenkel 1950, 1: 433.

[56] Aesch. *Pers.* 317; see Lebeck 1971: 39–40 and n. 19.

[57] Hom. *Iliad* 5.82–83, 16.333–34, 20.476–77, "Mighty fate and purple death took hold over his eyes" (τὸν δὲ κατ' ὄσσε ἔλλαβε πορφύρεος θάνατος καὶ μοῖρα κραταιή). Kirk (1990, 2: 62) notes that "the 'purple death over the eyes' is associated with blood in all three contexts." Goheen (1955: 116) argues on the basis of Aesch. *Pers.* 314–17 that πορφύρεος indicates "an ambiguous blood color." Interesting in this context is Artemidorus' assertion at *Oneirocritica* 1.77 that "garlands of dark blue violets signify even death. For the color dark blue has a certain affinity with death"; see White 1975: 57 and n. 85.

[58] Fraenkel (1950, 1: 410) discusses the close parallels, originally observed by Wilamowitz (1927: 287–88 [= 1962: 4.442–43]), between Clytemnestra's metaphors of deliverance at

the seasons toward harvest have at their root the concept of completion, and at first glance seem to contrast with the preceding metaphors of death; nonetheless, as Lebeck points out, the underlying idea is death: "As leaves are the telos of the root, as wine is the telos of the grape, Agamemnon's death is the telos for which Clytemnestra prays."[59] In one sense, this passage offers an elaborate and flattering metaphor for Clytemnestra's machinations by obliquely comparing her persuasive power to the cyclical movements of nature. The final ambiguity, the use of τέλειος at 972 in reference to the master of the house, again reveals her singular purpose: Agamemnon will enter the house not as its master, but as a sacrificial victim.[60]

The incantatory effect of the first part of the speech is further enhanced by the presence of several other striking stylistic features. For instance, the speech reveals multiple instances of repetition, including the word pairs μολόντος (968) and μολόν (969), πολλῆς (959) and πολλῶν (963), and εἱμάτων (960, 963). These pairs, although not always closely juxtaposed, focus our attention on the movement of Agamemnon toward the house and on its economic prosperity, earlier dramatized by the spreading of the cloth. Even more striking, however, is the repetition of the related terms δόμος/δῶμα/οἶκος, which appear seven times in seventeen lines, heightening the incantatory effect and identifying Clytemnestra with the house, its past, and the events about to unfold within it.[61] Just as the final instance of δῶμα at 972 completes the pattern of repetition established in the first part of the speech, so the term τελείου, although semantically distinct from what follows, points forward to the triple repetition of τέλος in the coda. Thus the pattern of repetition in the first part of the speech (958–72) creates an incantatory effect and prefigures the triple repetition of semantically similar terms in the final two lines of the speech. This unique pattern of repetition in the closing couplet closely resembles traditional magical formulas.

The first part of this speech also contains alliteration and assonance, which, like repetition, are incantatory elements. Alliteration appears with *p* in 959 and in 962–63, and with *k* in 960, followed by several examples of assonance: *ura* and *argu* in 959, *ōn* in 963, *ois* in 964, *k* and *kh* in 965

Aesch. *Ag.* 895–902 and 968–72 and an Egyptian hymn of the Middle Kingdom, which he quotes in full; for further discussion, see Hall 1989b: 206.

[59] Lebeck 1971: 73.

[60] The interpretation of τέλειος as a sacrificial term, meaning "unblemished, perfect," was first suggested by Verrall, and later found its way into almost all scholarship on this passage; see Zeitlin 1965 and 1966. For the most recent treatment, see Rosivach (1994: 150–51), who argues that the word refers to the animal's age as "full grown," not to its ritual purity.

[61] Cf. οἶκος (961), δόμος (962), δόμοισι (964), δόμους (966), δωματῖτιν (968), δόμοις (971), δῶμα (972). For a close stylistic parallel, see Hom. *Od.* 6.296–303. On the idea of words as a means of bringing about action, see Neustadt 1929: 257–58; also Betensky 1977: 19–20; and Sevieri 1991: 28.

and 970, *m* in 965, *ē* in 965 and 966, *s* in 967, as well as the *ō* and *ou* sounds in 972. The intensification of assonance in 965 clearly reflects its semantic importance, since this line contains a thinly disguised reference to the intended murder of Agamemnon. The first part of the speech also exhibits one additional peculiar feature, four genitive absolutes, three of which are roughly the same length, and all of which juxtapose the participle with the word δῶμα or δόμος: δόμοισι προυνεχθέντος (964), ῥίζης γὰρ οὔσης . . . δόμους (966), σοῦ μολόντος δωματῖτιν (968), δῶμ' ἐπιστρωφω-μένου (972). The last two constructions, of similar length and content, form a ring that rhetorically completes the first part of the speech and on a thematic level brings into focus the house and Agamemnon's fateful progression toward its interior. The acoustic and stylistic features used in this speech—metaphor, repetition, alliteration, assonance, and rhythmic phrasing—produce an incantatory effect perhaps suggestive of traditional magical formulations, an effect that intensifies in the coda.

The asyndeton between 972 and 973 introduces a shift in tone, content, and style so pronounced that we may conclude, as Taplin does, that Agamemnon has actually entered the house and therefore can no longer hear Clytemnestra in lines 973–74.[62] He further shows how this pattern of action prefigures what later becomes a common formula in tragedy: "The avenger lures the victim inside, and then after he has gone stays on for few lines of prayer and vengeful gloating."[63] In this sense, the incantation parallels the formulation of the end of Sappho 1 and other erotic spells where the speaker appeals to a deity for aid in bringing about some plan.[64] The coda may be viewed as the logical culmination of the incantatory effects found in the body of the speech, since it most closely approximates magical language through emphatic repetition, rhythmical phrasing, and similarity of sounds: Ζεῦ Ζεῦ τέλειε, τὰς ἐμὰς εὐχὰς τέλει· | μέλοι δέ τοί σοι τῶνπερ ἂν μέλλῃς τελεῖν (973–74). Clytemnestra calls her request an εὐχή, the usual term for a prayer, since the phrase τὰς ἐμὰς εὐχάς regularly occurs in traditional prayer formulations. However, the term also suggests a magical incantation, revealing how fluid the distinctions between prayers and magical formulas were in classical antiquity.[65]

The coda is marked by the emphatic triple repetition of τέλος: τέλειε (973), τέλει (973), and τελεῖν (974). This repetition builds upon the two earlier occurrences of the word, first when Clytemnestra terms the spreading of the cloth a τέλος (908), and few lines later when Agamemnon

---

[62] Taplin 1977: 309; see also Denniston and Page 1972: 154; Fraenkel 1950, 2: 440.

[63] Taplin 1977: 310.

[64] Faraone (1992a: 322) argues that this type of formulation is typically found in erotic incantations, although he also adduces a couple of nonerotic parallels.

[65] On εὐχή as an imprecation, cf. Aesch. *Sept.* 821; Eur. *Phoen.* 70. A fifth-century defixio from Sicily refers to itself as an εὐχή, for which see Jordan 1985: no. 91; Miller 1973: 1–30 cites some other parallels; see also Gager 1992: 12.

declares that to walk on the carpet is a τέλος (934). Just as the previous description of the tapestries simultaneously evokes other metaphors of cloth, so, too, the triple repetition of τέλος in this passage consolidates all the earlier occurrences of the word. The term simultaneously conflates the treading of the cloth, Clytemnestra's imprecations, and Agamemnon's death, which Cassandra identifies as a τέλος (1109) later in the play. In the coda, Clytemnestra calls upon Zeus Τέλειος, an aspect of Zeus Σωτήρ, the deity responsible for perpetuating and preserving the family line; and yet Zeus Τέλειος was also connected with the dead, since the third and final libation at the symposium, drunk to Zeus Τέλειος, was offered to the dead.[66] By invoking Zeus Τέλειος, Clytemnestra exploits an ambiguity implicit in the god's dual function. Calling upon Zeus in his capacity as guardian of the male family line, she asks for his help in obliterating it. The term is doubly ironic when we consider that the master of the house in the verse before the prayer has been called τέλειος ("sacrificial victim," 972). At the same time, the fact that the word τέλειος has strong nuptial overtones that Apollo evokes in the *Eumenides*, albeit in relation to Hera, suggests that Clytemnestra's "spell" has an erotic dimension, a point to which I later return.[67] In the coda, then, Clytemnestra seeks not merely to persuade, but also to realize her plans through a performative utterance addressed to Zeus. Clytemnestra's ability to control others through her coercive speech is later borne out by the chorus' attempt to avert a disaster they are not yet able to comprehend: they try to block or negate her magical imprecation with their own impotent plea: "I pray that contrary to my expectation it fall to the ground as a falsehood and thus not bring fulfillment" (εὔχομαι . . . | ἐς τὸ μὴ τελεσφόρον, 998–1000).[68]

The heavy use of assonance and alliteration contributes to an unmistakably rhythmic pattern also suggestive of magical language in the coda. For instance, three of the final four lines conclude with the same sound, *elei* (πέλει, 971; τέλει, 973; τελεῖν, 974); in verse 973, the effect is even more pronounced with the repetitions of Ζεῦ Ζεῦ and τέλειε . . . τέλει, while the wordplay created by τὰς ἐμὰς εὐχάς heightens the incantatory effect. In the next line, we find a repetition of sounds in μέλοι and μέλλῃς (974), although the words are from different verbs, as well as a similar type of wordplay with the sound *oi* in the phrase μέλοι δέ τοί σοι (974). By repeating words and sounds in the coda, Clytemnestra closes her speech with a traditional closing formula used in incantations of the type Aristophanes parodies in a fragment from his *Amphiaraus*: τελέει δ' ἀγαθὴν ἐπαοιδήν (Ar. fr. 29 KA).[69] The vagueness of the final line of her speech, moreover,

---

[66] Fraenkel (1950, 1: 973) notes the widespread cult of Zeus the Fulfiller in the Greek world. For the idea of Zeus as the fulfiller of prayers, cf. Aesch. *Cho.* 246; Eur. *Hipp.* 1363.

[67] Aesch. *Eum.* 214–15: Ἥρας τελείας καὶ Διὸς πιστώματα.

[68] On the chorus' failure to articulate their thoughts, see Thalmann 1985b.

[69] Faraone 1992a provides a complete discussion of the restored imperative in this fragment.

is reminiscent of the wish at the end of Sappho's incantatory hymn to Aphrodite: ὅσσα δέ μοι τέλεσσαι | θῦμος ἰμέρρει, τέλεσον (Sappho. fr. 1.26–27 Voigt). The use of triple repetition of relative words also closely parallels in form the incantatory passage in the *Homeric Hymn to Demeter* (ὑποταμνόν | . . . ἀντίτομον . . . ὑλοτόμοιο, 228–29). Finally, the erotic associations of this type of prayer closure should not be overlooked. Given the dramatic context capped by these lines, that of a dispute between a husband and his adulterous wife, Clytemnestra's incantation represents a perverted form of an erotic spell that works death rather than love and consequently secures her liaison with Aegisthus. Aphrodisiac spells directed toward men in everyday life often attempted to enervate and debilitate them even as they empowered the women who used them, thus effecting a gender-role reversal similar to the one depicted in the carpet scene.[70] The power of Clytemnestra's speech derives in part from her status as an adulteress, a betrayal that requires verbal duplicity and undermines traditional structures of authority, as we shall see in the next chapter.

THE LAMENT OF CASSANDRA

If Clytemnestra represents the deceptive potential of language to disrupt and overturn gender norms, Cassandra may be viewed as serving the opposite function; though a foreigner, she ironically embodies conformity to Greek social norms through her use of the feminine verbal genres, silence and lamentation. Scholars frequently point out that Aeschylus characterizes the two women as opposites, especially in their relation to speech: Cassandra's uncontrolled, involuntary, and divinely inspired speech contrasts with Clytemnestra's rhetorical mastery.[71] The Argive queen never tells the truth, whereas the barbarian slave never lies; Clytemnestra easily persuades men, although not women, whereas Cassandra is neither able nor willing to persuade (1212, 1239). Clytemnestra shows a mastery and control of masculine discourse, whereas Cassandra's speech alternates between restraint and agitated lyric outbursts characteristic of a state of divinely inspired madness. These differing relations to speech reflect the social status of the two women: although Clytemnestra claims to be the loyal wife of Agamemnon (γυναῖκα πιστήν, 606), and her words to be

---

[70] Faraone (1992b) argues that spells directed toward men had an enervating effect, putting them under the woman's power; for a literary example, consider the *kestos* of Aphrodite at Hom. *Iliad* 14.214–17. By debilitating their objects, these spells reversed normal gender roles by rendering the male passive and the female active. For other examples of male-targeting aphrodisiacs, cf. Antiph. 1.9.2; Plut. *Mor.* 256C.

[71] Goldhill 1984b: 57–58. According to Thalmann (1985b: 229), "Cassandra represents the inverse of Clytemnestra."

deemed trustworthy by the chorus (πιστά, 352), in fact she proves the opposite. Cassandra, on the other hand, earns the title of Agamemnon's faithful spouse at the end of the play (πιστὴ ξύνευνος, 1442). Finally, Clytemnestra's striking lack of words and gestures of lament, a normative speech genre for women in tragedy, contrasts with the number of exclamations characteristic of lament found in Cassandra's speech, including her last self-lament at 1322–30.

Significant, and often overlooked, are the several verbal motifs that closely link the two characters. Both women are likened to dogs—Clytemnestra to the trusty guardian of the house (δωμάτων κύνα, 607), and Cassandra to a keen hunting dog, able to track down the truth about the past (κυνὸς δίκην, 1093). In the minds of their male interlocutors, both excessively prolong their speeches; thus Agamemnon rebukes Clytemnestra for her lengthy welcome (μακρὰν γὰρ ἐξέτεινας, 916), whereas the chorus admonish Cassandra that her speech has been too drawn out (μακρὰν ἔτεινας, 1296). The chorus also express amazement at both women, first at Cassandra's uncanny knowledge of the past (θαυμάζω δέ σου, 1199), then later at the brazenness of Clytemnestra's speech (θαυμάζομέν σου γλῶσσαν, 1399). And although both defend themselves against charges of vain, unreliable, or worthless speech (Clytemnestra, 277, 1401; Cassandra, 1195), they eventually convince men of their credibility.

A negation of speech initially marks Cassandra's presence, since she stands silently onstage for 300 lines before speaking. Her silence, unparalleled in extant Attic drama, distinguishes her character as unique,[72] contrasting with Clytemnestra's verbal surfeit. When Cassandra does speak, her words shift from obscurity to clarity, a progression expressed metrically by the shift from lyric to dialogue meters starting at 1178ff.[73] From a dramatic perspective, Aeschylus constructs the scene between the two women as another contest of *peithō*, one that echoes the carpet scene; here, however, Cassandra refuses to fall under the spell of Clytemnestra's language, which, because erotic, works only on men.[74] Cassandra's defiant silence compels the chorus to intervene on her behalf: they translate Clytemnestra's instructions and later interpret the Trojan princess's prophetic visions. By instructing her to make a sign if she cannot understand Greek, Clytemnestra draws attention to her otherness (1060–61). Cassandra's silence thus has a double significance in that it shows her conformity to

[72] Taplin 1978: 104.

[73] On this progression, see ibid.: 104, 143.

[74] Note the preponderance of πειθ* words in the first part of this scene: πείθοιο, πείθοιο, ἀπειθοίης (1049); πείθω (1052); πειθοῦ (1054); cf. Clytemnestra's final πιθοῦ in the carpet scene, also in the first position (943). On the function of *peithō* in the trilogy, see Buxton 1982: 105–14. On the Cassandra scene, see Lebeck 1971: 52–58; Knox 1979: 42–55; and Schein 1982: 13–14.

prescribed gender roles and simultaneously reflects her social status as barbarian and other (1050–52). But Cassandra's silence serves another purpose; it temporarily hinders Clytemnestra by rendering her fatal weapon, her control of language, ineffectual.[75]

Another distinctive feature of Cassandra's speech is her use of lyric meters, in contrast with Clytemnestra, who utters only iambic trimeter and recitative anapaests.[76] According to Aristotle's *Rhetoric*, iambic trimeter, as the "meter of the masses," most closely approximates the rhythm of everyday conversation (Arist. *Rhet.* 1408b34–36). Lyric meters, on the other hand, not only express emotion but also convey high or royal status.[77] In between these two metrical forms is recitative, or anapaests (and possibly trochaic tetrameter), a form of chanting or intoning that has an emotive affect and that functions as sort of "poor man's" lyric verse, as suggested by the rhythm of the Nurses' speeches in Euripides' *Medea* and *Hippolytus*.[78] Similarly, fifth-century Athenian drama shows a strong tendency to "gender song as feminine," a tendency that may reflect the fact that these songs were understood as principally threnodic.[79] Thus the poet's refusal to assign Clytemnestra lyric speech, giving her iambic trimeter and anapaestic recitative instead, reinforces her masculine characterization. Much later, Euripides appears to imitate this pattern in his *Iphigenia in Aulis*, a play in which he depicts a more sympathetic Clytemnestra refusing to join in her daughter's piteous lyric monody, but responding in anapaests (Eur. *IA* 1276–1310).[80]

In further contrast with Clytemnestra, Cassandra's first words reveal her speech as uncontrolled: frenzied, she is under the spell of the god, Apollo (ἦ μαίνεταί γε, 1064).[81] The onslaught of prophetic vision also causes a physical disturbance, a sensation of heat or fever (παπαῖ· οἷον τὸ πῦρ· ἐπέρχεται δέ μοι, 1256), accompanied by delirium ("This terrible prophet's work whirls me around again, confusing me with its ominous preludes," ὑπ' αὖ με δεινὸς ὀρθομαντείας πόνος | στροβεῖ ταράσσων φροιμίοις ⟨δυσφροιμίοις⟩, 1215–16), and effects that closely associate her utterance with

---

[75] Thalmann 1985b: 228.

[76] Scott (1984: 66) notes that the meter in this scene is largely dochmiac, a rhythm "traditionally associated in Greek tragedy with a high level of excitement or vexation." From 1080ff., Cassandra speaks in lyric meters broken by at least one iambic trimeter, a stylistic feature that reveals a "note of restraint" in the view of Denniston and Page (1972: 165). On the alteration of lyric and trimeter verses in this scene, see Fraenkel 1964: 345; and Schein 1982: 13–14.

[77] Hall 1999. If slaves sing lyric verses, they are freeborn slaves, like Andromache and Hecuba in Euripides, and even Cassandra here.

[78] Maas 1962: 53; Hall 1999.

[79] Hall 1999.

[80] Ibid.

[81] Goldhill 1984b: 87.

her body.[82] The shift from iambic trimeter in the carpet scene to the lyric meters that accompany Cassandra's speech signals a heightened emotional state. This change in meter is accompanied by an increase in pathetic utterance, interjections of pure sound that mark tragic emotion, particularly lamentation; thus Cassandra initially breaks her long silence with a cry of horror, ὀτοτοτοτοῖ πόποι δᾶ (1072).[83] These features identify Cassandra's speech as emotional, involuntary, and therefore without guile.

In a play in which lamentation is conspicuously absent, it is noteworthy that the chorus immediately identify Cassandra as a mourner (θρηνητής, 1075) who laments things that have happened in the remote past and things that have not yet happened; indeed, the scene is full of the language of lament.[84] The numerous expressions of pity introduce an element of pathos not found in the verbal sparring between Clytemnestra and Agamemnon in the carpet scene. A central image in Cassandra's song identifies her not simply with mourning, but with maternal mourning. Just as Procne mourns the child she killed and served to his father, Itys (1144ff.), so Cassandra laments Thyestes' dead children, who suffered a similar fate.[85] The reference to the Procne myth is interesting from another perspective as well, since the story chronicles the silencing of a woman for infanticide; when transformed into a bird, her speech is restored and takes the form of a lament, a socially accepted speech genre for women in ancient Greece. So, too, Apollo silences Cassandra by rendering her prophecies ineffectual. The fact that bird cries often function as a metaphor for ritual lamentation, perhaps because the high-pitched, piercing wail of female mourners evokes the cry of a bird,[86] explains the numerous bird images and sounds in Cassandra's speech: her barbarian voice is like a swallow's (χελιδόνος δίκην, 1050), her lament is like that of a swan (κύκνου δίκην, 1444), she is like

[82] Although line 1172 is hopelessly corrupt, the presence of θερμόνους may further suggest a feverish state; on this term, see also Fraenkel 1950, 3: 536.

[83] Knox (1979: 43) observes that Cassandra's utterance "is a formulaic cry of grief and terror." The term δᾶ signifies an expression of horror, and is not to be taken, as in earlier interpretations, as a Doric form for γᾶ or γῆ; see Denniston and Page 1972: 167; and Fraenkel 1950, 3: 490–91.

[84] Later in the play, Clytemnestra refers to Cassandra's lyrics as a γόος or lament (1445). Within the scene itself, several terms identify her song as a lament: γόοις (1079); γοερά (1176); ἰώ (1136, 1146, 1156, 1167); ἰοὺ ἰού, ὢ ὢ κακά (1214); οἳ ἐγὼ ἐγώ (1257); θροῶ (1137); θρεομένας (1165); ἀναστένω (1285); κωκύσουσα (1313); θρῆνον (1322). Expressions of pity also suggest a mourning context; cf. ἐποικτίρω (1069) and τάλαινα (1070, 1136, 1138, 1143, 1158, 1260, 1274, 1295). On Cassandra's lament generally, see Bollack 1981.

[85] As discussed in Chapter 2, at Hom. *Od*. 19.518–22 Penelope's mourning is compared to the nightingale's song. Note that Cassandra returns several times to the theme of children in her speech; cf. 1096, 1218, 1219ff.

[86] For the comparison of female mourning to the sound of birds, cf. the passage cited above, Hom. *Od*. 19.518–22; and Soph. *Ant*. 423–24 (Antigone).

a nightingale in her sorrow (ἀηδών, 1145), whose piercing strains (ὀρθίοις ἐν νόμοις, 1153) are shrill (ξουθά, 1142)[87] and high-pitched (λιγείας, 1146).

Although it is the tangible symbol of her powerlessness and her low status, the play suggests that Cassandra's speech, because inauspicious, is potentially dangerous. So the chorus caution Cassandra against naming Apollo, in whose presence, as in the case of the other gods, lamentation was considered inappropriate (ἥδ' αὖτε δυσφημοῦσα τὸν θεὸν καλεῖ | οὐδὲν προσήκοντ' ἐν γόοις παραστατεῖν, 1078–79). They describe her song as unmusical and therefore ill-omened, since any sound without the accompaniment of musical instruments is normally represented as inharmonious and dissonant in Aeschylus: she sings a "melody which is no melody" (θροεῖς | νόμον ἄνομον, 1141–42). It is δύσφατος (1152), a term related to δύσφημος and to κακορρήμονας (1155) in its suggestion of improper or sacrilegious speech. Later, when Cassandra names Agamemnon as the intended murder victim for the first time, the chorus again caution her to keep an auspicious silence (εὔφημον, ὦ τάλαινα, κοίμησον στόμα, 1247). Because the chorus deem Cassandra's laments dangerous and ill-omened, they try in vain to suppress them.[88]

In the final part of the scene, Cassandra moves away from her lamentation and directly addresses the chorus at 1178ff., a transition marked by her shift from lyric to speech meters. This metrical change underscores the movement from involuntary speech to voluntary speech. Accordingly, Cassandra begins by comparing the revelation of her prophecies to the unveiling of the bride: "And no longer will my prophecy look out from under veils like a newly married bride" (καὶ μὴν ὁ χρησμὸς οὐκέτ' ἐκ καλυμμάτων | ἔσται δεδορκὼς νεογάμου νύμφης δίκην, 1178–79). The idea of sexual exposure entailed by public female speech evokes the conflation of sexuality and speech inherent in Clytemnestra's earlier use of the verb αἰσχύνεσθαι (856), but whereas the queen flaunts her public words, Cassandra underscores their impropriety. As the anecdote from Plutarch discussed in the preceding chapter makes clear, nonritual public speech points to a lack of shame or *aidōs* in women much like the public display of the female body, as illustrated by Plutarch's story about Theano (Plut. *Mor.* 142D). Perhaps for this reason, Cassandra's initial silence more than anything else signifies her conformity to conventional female behavior. Just as she has accurately defined Clytemnestra, so Clytemnestra at the end of the play truly names

---

[87] Though ξουθά in fifth-century Attic Greek can denote either a color or a sound, it surely refers, in this context, to sound, since Cassandra later describes the nightingale as λιγεία (1146), a term that also suggests a high-pitched tone. In Aeschylus, the term λιγύς is mostly used of wailing or lamentation; cf. *Pers.* 322, 468; *Supp.* 112ff. See also Kaimio 1977: 165.

[88] Thalmann (1985b: 229) remarks upon the chorus' "fruitless attempt to suppress terrible knowledge."

Cassandra: "Captive of the spear, portent-reader, who shared the bed of this man, prophecy-speaker, his true wife" (1440–42).

CLYTEMNESTRA'S HEROIC SPEECH AND THE FEMINIZED CHORUS

Interposed between the carpet scene and Clytemnestra's revelation, the feminine speech genres of Cassandra temporarily reinscribe normative gender roles. The scene creates a profound contrast with Clytemnestra's final appearance onstage when she reveals her dissimulations to the chorus. The speech she employs throughout this scene has strong epic overtones, beginning with her opening line: "Much have I said before to serve the moment, but now I shall not be ashamed to say the opposite" (πολλῶν πάροιθεν καιρίως εἰρημένων | τἀναντί' εἰπεῖν οὐκ ἐπαισχυνθήσομαι, 1372–73). The infinitive ἐπαισχύνεσθαι plays against her earlier and ambiguous use of the verb in her previous address to Agamemnon (856), and again conflates sexual promiscuity with women's public speech. Clytemnestra now reverses the commonplaces of wifely solicitude so painstakingly constructed in her earlier words to the messenger (587–614), concluding here as before with an epic boast (ἐγὼ δὲ ἐπεύχομαι, 1394) that undoes the feminine κόμπος of 613–14.[89] The chorus' description of her gloating over Agamemnon's corpse further reflects her boastful tone (1424). Clytemnestra's outrageous words provoke a harsh response from the chorus because they represent a linguistic transgression: "I am amazed at your speech—how brash it is! You who make such a boastful speech over the man" (θαυμάζομέν σου γλῶσσαν, ὡς θρασύστομος, | ἥτις τοιόνδ' ἐπ' ἀνδρὶ κομπάζεις λόγον, 1399–1400). In fact, the male chorus, like Cassandra before them, seem to censure above all Clytemnestra's brash transgressive speech even before they condemn her crime.

Her response to their disapproval further shows that her speech violates gender norms as she distances herself from the chorus' feminine verbal stereotype: "You make trial of me as if I were a senseless woman" (πειρᾶσθέ μου γυναικὸς ὡς ἀφράσμονος, 1401). This assertion recalls Clytemnestra's earlier response to the chorus in which she derides them for treating her as a silly girl (παιδὸς νέας, 277). Now, however, Clytemnestra does not mitigate her verbal dominance with feminine posturing; instead, she continues to maintain discursive control over the male chorus, who deride her as haughty (μεγαλόμητις, 1426), an arrogant speaker (περίφρονα, 1427), and an ally of dark Ares (1511), terms that identify her more as a

---

[89] On the inappropriateness of vaunting over a corpse, cf. Hom. *Od.* 22.412: "It is not pious to vaunt over dead men" (οὐχ ὁσίη κταμένοισιν ἐπ' ἀνδράσιν εὐχετάασθαι); and Archil. fr. 65D: "It is not good to jeer over dead men" (οὐ γὰρ ἐσθλὰ κατθανοῦσι κερτομεῖν ἐπ' ἀνδράσιν).

warrior than a wife. This association persists until the end of the trilogy, when Clytemnestra reappears in *Eumenides* as a ghost who goads the Erinyes with her heroic indignation, proclaiming her public humiliation and outrage (ἀπητιμασμένη, *Eum.* 95; ὄνειδος, 97; αἰσχρῶς, 98). In the same way, Clytemnestra's use of recitative, instead of lyric, anapaests in this scene further reinforces her masculine characterization; instead of joining in the lament of the male chorus, which could be viewed as feminine, she uses the anapaests typically associated with marching.[90] Indeed, recitative anapaests "could be recited in a grand and declamatory manner more suitable than lyric song for indomitable, masculinized females."[91]

Just as the murder of Agamemnon fully realizes Clytemnestra as a heroic figure with corresponding epic speech practices, so, too, it reduces the chorus to less than masculine status; they perform the laments neglected by the queen, who will bury her husband without "the accompaniment of mourning by the people from his own home" (οὐχ ὑπὸ κλαυθμῶν τῶν ἐξ οἴκων, 1554). Although decrepit and powerless in the beginning of the play, the male chorus nonetheless attempt to maintain normative gender categories by means of their assertions on speech and gender; but their verbal unity soon begins to fragment after the death of Agamemnon. Powerless, they are unable to help the dying Agamemnon, delaying decision until it is too late, forced to acknowledge that even words can provide no remedy: "I am at a loss as to how words might bring the dead back to life" (δυσμηχανῶ | λόγοισι τὸν θανόντ' ἀνιστάναι πάλιν, 1360–61), a sentiment that strikingly contrasts with the magical and efficacious feminine language that contributed to his death. With the murder of Agamemnon, the chorus lose their social identity as well as their civic authority, and their voice becomes increasingly disjointed as the play progresses. The disorderly shifting of meters in the final part of the play replicates the social collapse present in Argos as the discord between the chorus and Clytemnestra escalates.[92] Structurally, the play lacks an exodos, a feature found in every other Aeschylean play except *Prometheus Bound*; the absence of an exit song "conveys a sense of incompleteness" and further reinforces the idea of the disintegration of the chorus.[93] The silent departure of the chorus thus becomes a visual emblem of their political disenfranchisement and verbal impotence, creating a conspicuous contrast with the processional ending of the *Eumenides* that celebrates civic collectivity.[94]

---

[90] Parker (1997: 57) observes that lyric anapaests in Attic tragedy are normally associated with mourning, particularly the laments of women; for examples, cf. Soph. *El.* 86–250; Eur. *Med.* 96–183; *Hec.* 59–196; *Tro.* 98–229; *IT* 123–235; and *Ion* 859–922.

[91] Hall 1999; for recitative anapaests in connection with masculinized women, e.g., Clytemnestra and Medea, see also Pintacuda 1978: 114, 171–73.

[92] Scott 1984: 74.

[93] Ibid.: 76.

[94] Taplin 1978: 35–40.

In their silence, the chorus also come to resemble women, for their silence reflects a loss of political status. Aegisthus has marginalized them by depriving them of effective speech; unlike the musical Orpheus, they can neither persuade nor raise the dead (1629). Their speech has become impotent (ματαίαν γλῶσσαν, 1662), it has become a bestial, helpless barking (νηπίοις ὑλάγμασιν, 1631; ματαίων τῶνδ' ὑλαγμάτων, 1672).[95] The term ὕλαγμα not only evokes the comparison of Clytemnestra and Cassandra to dogs, but also points forward to the Erinyes, creatures on the margins of the polis, denied access to the free speech that is the prerogative of democratic citizens, as we saw in Chapter 1. Thus the members of the chorus, enfeebled by age, become powerless in that most gendered of acts, speech: they, too, have become like women.

This chapter has examined the effects of Clytemnestra's duplicitous bilingualism both in the construction of her character and in the category crisis brought about by her speech. And yet her ability to manipulate speech genres fundamentally identifies her as feminine, since the Greek literary tradition repeatedly associates women with disguise and deception, as discussed in the previous two chapters and exemplified by Aegisthus' confession, "Deceit was clearly the woman's part" (τὸ γὰρ δολῶσαι πρὸς γυναικὸς ἦν σαφῶς, 1636). Only the women in the trilogy can see through this deceptive exterior: Cassandra reveals Clytemnestra as a consummate actor, a clever speaker who misleads her audience by means of her false appearance, who feigns joy (φαιδρόνους δίκην, 1229) even as she convinces Agamemnon to enter the house. And although the chorus and Agamemnon attempt to maintain normative gender categories in response to Clytemnestra's public and transgressive speech, they ultimately fail to do so. At the same time, her speech has an erotic component in that she employs the language of amatory incantations to bring about her husband's death in the carpet scene. This deceptive speech leads to a category crisis that disturbs the social order and leads to the final anomaly, that of a woman killing a man, as Cassandra remarks in another oxymoronic juxtaposition of male and female terms: "The woman is the slayer of the man" (θῆλυς ἄρσενος φονεύς | ἐστίν, 1231–32). And even though Clytemnestra adopts the strongest masculine speech in the final scene, it is ironized by her final reference to herself as a female speaker. Warning Aegisthus to avoid further bloodshed, she states, "This is the speech of a woman, if anyone should think it worthwhile to listen" (ὧδ' ἔχει λόγος γυναικός, εἴ τις ἀξιοῖ μαθεῖν, 1661).[96] Not only may this statement, and others like it, be read

---

[95] For this word applied to the barking of a dog, cf. Hom. *Od.* 21.575; Eur. *IT* 293; Xen. *Cyn.* 4.5 and 6.7; Arist. *Hist. an.* 536b30.

[96] Aesch. *Ag.* 348. Scholars without exception seem almost as taken in by Clytemnestra's words as Agamemnon: Stanford (1942: 117), for example, sees it as a statement of "womanish modesty"; for a more recent but similar view, see Taplin 1978: 144. Others interpret this

metatheatrically, as I have argued elsewhere, it also foregrounds Clytemnestra's dissimulations by calling attention to her constant shifting between gendered forms of speech.[97]

SPEECH AND GENDER IN THE *CHOEPHORI*

Although scholars have maintained that Clytemnestra relinquishes her duplicitous characterization in the *Choephori* to play the part of a conventional wife and mother, especially in the dramatic climax of the play, when she bares her breasts and beseeches Orestes for her very life, I argue in this part of the chapter that the second play represents her much more ambiguously. In fact, it is another female character, the Nurse, Cilissa, who discloses her deceptive demeanor and duplicitous speech. In contrast with the first play, however, the *Choephori* depicts a man not easily taken in by the words of a woman through the figure of Orestes, whose task and speech represent a divinely sanctioned form of *dolos*.

As Taplin and others have noticed, the return of Orestes to his natal oikos both resembles and inverts the carpet scene in the *Agamemnon*.[98] In the *Choephori*, Clytemnestra again supervises the entry of the male into the house. Yet whereas the queen deceived her husband in the first play, now she is the one deceived; the male now succeeds where before he failed. Further, Orestes' second exit at 930 mirrors Agamemnon's exit at 972, and the stichomythic dispute between a man and a woman, this time mother and son, echoes that of Clytemnestra and Agamemnon, only the outcome is different in that the woman now yields to the man. For many scholars, however, the greatest sign of role reversal in this play is Clytemnestra's singular lack of guile: "Clytemnestra still appears to control the palace door; but, just as she has lost her strength of rhetoric and deceit, she has really lost her power over the house."[99] The emphasis should fall on the word "appears," since Clytemnestra, here as in the first play, only seems to play the part of the dutiful wife and bereaved mother in a performance whose persuasiveness is undercut by a series of linguistic contradictions.

As in the *Agamemnon*, several characters in the *Choephori* establish gender norms for speech, distinguishing masculine speech as concerned with public and political matters and portraying feminine speech as inherently unreliable, norms that Clytemnestra once again violates. For instance, Orestes twice remarks on the impropriety of a man speaking with a woman

---

assertion as either a statement of superiority (Denniston and Page 1972: 223) or a protest against prejudice (Fraenkel 1950, 3: 796).

[97] McClure 1997b.
[98] Taplin 1978: 104.
[99] Ibid.: 124.

(of course, it should be noted that the dramatic action requires these remarks, since Orestes must find a way to confront Aegisthus alone). In his instructions to the servants, his juxtaposition of gendered terms, τελεσφόρος | γυνὴ τόπαρχος, ἄνδρα (663–64), evokes the aberrant role inversion of husband and wife in the first play, and implies that Clytemnestra still retains control of the house. But then Orestes asserts that conversation between men is more appropriate, since men naturally have *aidōs* in speaking in front of women (665). Only a man can give a clear indication of what he means to another man (ἐσήμηνεν ἐμφανὲς τέκμαρ, 667). The criterion of proof, *tekmar*, has been associated with men at *Agamemnon* 352, when the chorus praise Clytemnestra for providing them with convincing evidence of the fall of Troy. Masculine speech is thus depicted as concerned with truth, properly occurring in a male space, the *andrōn* (712), and among men. The exchange between Orestes and the servant establishes a norm that will be swiftly inverted by the entrance of Clytemnestra: a female head of household receives a male visitor and participates in a conversation reserved for men.

Many of the elements of Clytemnestra's welcoming speech to the disguised Orestes recall her earlier speeches in the *Agamemnon*. Clytemnestra's first words associate her intimately with the house and its provisions: her prosaic statement, "For we have the sorts of things that are fitting for a house such as ours" (πάρεστι γάρ | ὁποῖάπερ δόμοισι τοῖσδ' ἐπεικότα, 668–69), echoes faintly the proclamation of the house's wealth at *Agamemnon* 961–62. Her talk of warm baths (θερμὰ λουτρά, 670), inviting beds (θελκτήρια | στρωμνή, 670–71), and "honest faces" further recalls the first play, especially the bath that accomplished Agamemnon's murder and the adulterous bed Clytemnestra shared with Aegisthus. The unexpected third term, "the presence of honest faces" (δικαίων τ' ὀμμάτων παρουσία, 671), has a double meaning like many of her earlier phrases and evokes her association with false appearance in the *Agamemnon* (*Ag.* 1229). As in the first play, Clytemnestra also calls attention to her gender a number of times, first with her assertion that politics are the business of men: "But if you must engage in more political business, this is the work of men" (εἰ δ' ἄλλο πρᾶξαι δεῖ τι βουλιώτερον, | ἀνδρῶν τόδ' ἐστὶν ἔργον, 672–73). The term βουλιώτερον not only alludes to the Watchman's description of Clytemnestra's "male counsels" (ἀνδρόβουλον, 11) in the beginning of the *Agamemnon*, but also points forward to the tribunal, βουλευτήριον, established by Athena in the *Eumenides* (570). On a stylistic level, the term signals one of Clytemnestra's familiar rhetorical moves: she disassociates herself from a masculine role by positioning herself as a loyal and obedient wife even as she participates in the male world normally prohibited to women.

Consistent also with Clytemnestra's characterization in the *Agamemnon* is the doubleness of her speech. In her first exchange with Orestes, she claims at one moment that she has plenty of friends (717) and then in the next that the curse placed on the house has stripped her of them (695). Similarly, she states that she will take part in the deliberations with Aegisthus (βουλευσόμεσθα, 718), when she has just said that such talk is the province of men (672). The phrase τοῖς κρατοῦσι (716), which presumably includes Clytemnestra, returns to the question of who is really in charge of the house, raised first by Orestes (663) and later by Cilissa (ἡ κρατοῦσα, 734). This doubleness confirms that we encounter the same Clytemnestra in the *Choephori* as in the *Agamemnon*, that in fact Clytemnestra continues to perform herself, to construct and deconstruct by turns a feminine persona. In contrast with his father, however, Orestes is not taken in by his mother's machinations, but rather carries out deceptions of his own.

Clytemnestra's reaction upon learning of Aegisthus' death similarly reveals her deceptive, feminine posturing. She cries οἲ 'γώ (691), a feminine ritual cry associated with lament, used earlier by Cassandra (*Ag.* 1257), and only uttered by women in Greek tragedy.[100] For Taplin, this phrase signifies genuine grief: "She reacts convincingly as a mother. It is hard to detect any vindictive ambiguity here . . . this seems to be, rather, the wiser, less assertive Clytemnestra of the end of the *Agamemnon*. This Clytemnestra is hardly to be written off as an unnatural villainess."[101] On the contrary, this exclamation works in much the same way as her ambiguous use of the *ololugē* in the *Agamemnon*. Although on one level it betokens compliance with normative feminine verbal genres, it also discloses her manipulative control of language. Cilissa corroborates the falseness of Clytemnestra's response by claiming that she faked her grief in front of the servants:

> πρὸς μὲν οἰκέτας
> θέτο σκυθρωπῶν πένθος ὀμμάτων, γέλων
> κεύθους' ἐπ' ἔργοις διαπεπραγμένοις καλῶς
> κείνῃ.[102]   (737–40)

To the servants she put on the grief of a sad countenance,
concealing her laughter over the deed
that had been performed so well for her.

---

[100] Cf. Aesch. *Pers.* 445, 515; *Sept.* 808; *Cho.* 691, 887, 893, 928; Soph. *Aj.* 803 (Tecmessa); *El.* 674, 1115 (Electra). All nineteen occurrences in Euripides are spoken by women; see McClure 1995. Note that the only instances of οἲ alone are found in the speech of the Persian elders in Aesch. *Pers.* 663, 671, 1003, 1045, 1053.

[101] Taplin 1978: 144.

[102] This passage contains many textual problems. Although I have adopted Garvie's reading (1988) as the best way to make sense of the manuscript's σκυθρωπὸν ἐντὸς ὀμμάτων, I think that σκυθρωπός must imply sorrow rather than "scowling," as he maintains; otherwise the sense of the rest of the line is lost.

In this context, therefore, Clytemnestra's οἲ 'γώ may be viewed as highly ambiguous, as part of the mask she assumes in the presence of others. The word ὀμμάτων further strengthens this idea of a disguise, recalling as it does the queen's own highly ironic words at 671. Cilissa thus assumes a role similar to that of Cassandra in that she sees through Clytemnestra's false appearance, unlike the male characters, and portrays her as a consummate performer who adopts whatever disguise best suits her purpose. At the same time, Cilissa's own cry upon hearing the news of Orestes' death, ὦ τάλαιν' ἐγώ (743), displaces the idea of maternity onto her as his nurse in infancy.[103]

Several general assertions about speech and gender elsewhere in the play further identify Clytemnestra's speech as deceptive and therefore feminine. Cilissa prefaces her account of the queen's duplicity with the assertion that only speech between men can be deemed truly clear (σαφέστερον, 735), reconfirming the importance of man-to-man speech earlier voiced by Orestes (666–67). Aegisthus echoes this view of women's speech when he demands proof that the report of Orestes' death represents not merely the idle rumors of women, but something more reliable:

πῶς ταῦτ' ἀληθῆ καὶ βλέποντα δοξάσω;
ἢ πρὸς γυναικῶν δειματούμενοι λόγοι
πεδάρσιοι θρῴσκουσι, θνῄσκοντες μάτην;   (844–46)

How shall I know whether this report is really true?
Or whether it is only frightened words that come from women,
leaping in the air and dying to no effect?[104]

As in the *Agamemnon*, women's speech is portrayed as trivial and ineffectual, belonging to the shadowy realm of rumor (ἐξ ἀμαυρᾶς κληδόνος, 853). Conspiring with Orestes, the female chorus further reiterate the importance of messages communicated from one man to another (849–50). Aegisthus then demands the chance to cross-examine, in juridical fashion, the messenger (ἐλέγξαι, 851); in this sense, he resembles the male chorus in the *Agamemnon*, who also question the reliability of female speech, ask for proof, and deploy an arsenal of legal terms. And also like the male chorus of the first play, his ironic disparagement of women's speech works against him in the end: by believing this rumor, Aegisthus is shown to play the part of a woman, duped into facilitating his own death.

In the dénouement, Clytemnestra is again represented as vacillating between masculine and feminine speech genres. Once Orestes makes clear his intention to murder her, she acts in characteristic epic fashion:

δοίη τις ἀνδροκμῆτα πέλεκυν ὡς τάχος·
εἰδῶμεν εἰ νικῶμεν ἢ νικώμεθα.   (889–90)

---

[103] Taplin 1978: 145.
[104] I have followed Garvie (1988: 278–79) in this translation.

> Let someone give me a man-killing ax in all haste—
> let us see whether I will conquer or be conquered.

Clytemnestra juxtaposes this martial vocabulary, seen earlier in her beacon speech and in the carpet scene, with the language of ritual lamentation, οἲ 'γώ, a cry she repeats three times in this scene (887, 893, 928). In this context, therefore, we must understand her final gesture, the baring of her breasts that accompanies her plea that Orestes spare her life, as inherently problematic:

> ἐπίσχες, ὦ παῖ, τόνδε δ' αἴδεσαι, τέκνον,
> μαστόν, πρὸς ᾧ σὺ πολλὰ δὴ βρίζων ἅμα
> οὔλοισιν ἐξήμελξας εὐτραφὲς γάλα.   (896–98)

> Stop, my son, and respect, child, this breast
> at which you often drowsily sucked the nourishing milk
> with your toothless gums.

As Taplin comments, this gesture may have strained the limits of dramatic verisimilitude, although Attic drama was not known for its naturalism in its physical depiction of characters: "At this point, Clytemnestra cannot bare her breasts because the part is played by a male actor."[105] The contrast between her masculine speech and her feminine gesture not only jeopardizes the illusion of the female onstage; it both plays up the masculine aspects of her ethos and reinforces the duplicity connected with her character from the very beginning of the trilogy. And while Clytemnestra understands Orestes' actions in familial terms, Orestes views it from a purely legal perspective by stating that her death serves as the penalty for Agamemnon's murder (ὁρίζει, 927).

ORESTES AND JUDICIAL SPEECH

The disguised Orestes, who uses *peithō* to gain entrance to his natal household, occupies the same dramatic position as Agamemnon, since he, too, has returned to reclaim his birthright, and he, too, assumes a mixed status in regard to gender. Orestes may be seen as superficially feminine in his use of disguise, sometimes understood in Greek literature as a compromised form of masculinity, and in his use of feminine *dolos*.[106] However, we must view Orestes' deployment of "cunning Persuasion," or Πειθὼ δολίαν (726), as distinct from that of Clytemnestra, since his persuasive power derives not from self-interest, but from Apollo, who has compelled him

[105] Taplin 1978: 61.
[106] Bassi 1995.

under threat of death to murder his mother.[107] Viewed in this light, *Choephori* heralds Orestes' deception as the beginning of a more constructive, collective aspect of persuasion that is fully realized through the figure of Athena in the *Eumenides*.

The second play also foreshadows the trial scene in the *Eumenides* by using judicial actions and language in connection with this positive use of *peithō*. At 972–1076, Orestes leaves the house and addresses the chorus, accompanied by attendants who carry the garment that Clytemnestra threw over Agamemnon before killing him. At the level of staging, Orestes probably describes an object that is physically present.[108] The unfolding of the blood-stained robe recalls the tapestries that Agamemnon crossed and reverses the action of the carpet scene by bringing the object outside.[109] In this scene, Orestes defines the garment in legal terms as the murder weapon (μήχανημα, 981) that will serve as evidence (μάρτυς, 987) of his mother's crime when he is brought to trial (μετῆλθον, 988).[110] Further, by removing the garment from the house, Orestes places the cloth, and therefore the crime, into the public and masculine sphere. Orestes' masculine, judicial language thus circumscribes the entangling robe, the tangible reminder of Clytemnestra's duplicitous, ambiguous speech, and points forward to the function of persuasion in the law court established in the *Eumenides*.

WOMEN'S SPEECH IN THE POLIS: THE *EUMENIDES*

In the foregoing, I have shown how the first two plays of the *Oresteia* trilogy construct Clytemnestra's speech as androgynous and duplicitous; importantly, this rhetorical posturing is directed almost entirely to a male internal audience—the chorus of Argive elders, the messenger, Agamemnon, and Orestes. By representing Clytemnestra as deliberately manipulating discourses to gain control over others, particularly men, the first two plays explore the dangerous potential of persuasion to upset the social and political norms established and maintained by them. In order to better understand this point, this section will examine Clytemnestra's rhetorical counterpart, Athena, and the function of persuasive speech in the trilogy's third play, the *Eumenides*.

---

[107] *Pace* Goldhill (1984b: 206), who relates Orestes' use of deceptive persuasion to Clytemnestra and her ambiguous use of language.

[108] Hansen 1977: 239–40. Τόδε at 1003 suggests an object physically present. As Hansen explains, νιν at 997 is weak, since the audience actually sees the robe. See also Fraenkel 1950, 3: 809–15; Garvie 1988: 316–17.

[109] Whallon (1980: 87) even suggests that the robe is displayed in the same stage position as Agamemnon's tapestries.

[110] Cf. ἔχει . . . δίκην (990); on these legal terms, see Robertson 1939.

In the *Eumenides*, Clytemnestra's duplicitous performance yields to an entirely new kind of public spectacle, that of the law court. This civic drama restores the dramatic illusion imperiled by Clytemnestra's compromised gender identity in the first two plays and establishes a dialectical relation between the discursive spheres of the tragic theater and Athenian political institutions, as considered in Chapter 1. The *Eumenides* reconstructs the idea of persuasion, represented in the first play as inherently deceptive and subversive through the figure of Clytemnestra, as a public performance based on unambiguous, truthful speech and therefore exclusive of women. The format of the trial thus replicates the contest of words in the *Agamemnon*; but instead of Clytemnestra's victory of *peithō* over Agamemnon, the *Eumenides* celebrates Athena's conversion of the Erinyes from hostile to propitious deities: she embodies the principle of persuasion, now cleansed of feminine guile, necessary to the political and judicial procedures of the polis. As a result, the *Eumenides* resolves the category crisis brought about in the first play and, in a self-censoring gesture, substitutes the drama that makes men for the one that undoes them.

Yet the play that celebrates masculine, political speech opens with terrifying female creatures whose power resides in their coercive, magical, and barbarian use of language, creatures closely identified with Clytemnestra, whose ghost goads them into action at the play's beginning, much like the Homeric Agamemnon marshaling his troops. We have seen that Clytemnestra's speech in *Agamemnon* 958–74 exhibits some of the features that a fifth-century audience might have associated with magical language, especially her emphatic use of repetition, metaphor, assonance and alliteration, and rhythmic phrasing. These techniques reach their fullest expression in the two-line coda in which Clytemnestra invokes Zeus in his capacity as guardian of the dead to fulfill her prayers. The close parallel between this formulation and magical incantations found in other literary texts points to the coercive power of Clytemnestra's language; it thus represents another aspect of the dangers of *peithō* described by the chorus in the first stasimon (ἁ τάλαινα Πειθώ, *Ag*. 385).

The evocation of magical ritual in *Agamemnon* 958–74 also forges a link between Clytemnestra and the Erinyes, revealing another aspect of the underlying unity of the trilogy. Indeed, Aegisthus associates Clytemnestra with the Erinyes at the end of the *Agamemnon* when he identifies the fatal garment used by Clytemnestra to kill Agamemnon as belonging to the Erinyes (ὑφαντοῖς ἐν πέπλοις Ἐρινύων, *Ag*. 1580). A stronger parallel, however, lies in the fact that both characters employ magical incantations to compel others to act against their wills, Clytemnestra by means of her imprecation, and the Erinyes by means of their binding song (*Eum*. 328–33, 341–46). The Erinyes sing a refrain that Faraone has identified as sharing similarities with Attic judicial curse tablets. He argues that Erinyes

accusative in the phrase ὕμνον ὑμνεῖν recalls the song of the Erinyes, whom Cassandra has earlier described with a similar phrase, ὑμνοῦσι δ' ὕμνον (1191). Further, the adjective ἐκνόμως, "out of tune," suggests an unpleasant cacophony similar to that of the Erinyes, whose dissonant and unmusical tones (οὐκ εὔφωνος, *Ag.* 1187; ἄνευ λύρας, 990; cf. ἀφόρμικτος, *Eum.* 332–33, 345–46) suggest improper or sacrilegious speech.[115] The Erinyes' speech also resembles the barking of dogs (κλαγγαίνεις δ' ἄπερ | κύων, *Eum.* 131–32) and in this way recalls the prophecies of Cassandra, the clever speech of Clytemnestra, and the male chorus' ineffectual words at the end of the *Agamemnon*. This bestial, ill-omened speech marks the Erinyes' status as outsiders in the polis, since they are "so remote from the world of civilization that they cannot even speak except in bloodcurdling noises."[116] Both Clytemnestra and the Erinyes in the *Oresteia* practice a perverted, destructive form of *peithō* that exerts an irresistible coercive power over others and is represented as harmful to the polis. The beginning of the *Eumenides* therefore distinguishes between the inauspicious, extra-political, and feminine speech of the Erinyes and the auspicious, judicial speech of men in the law court.

Like the male chorus in the *Agamemnon*, Orestes claims that his speech has been divinely sanctioned, in this case by Apollo (φωνεῖν ἐτάχθην, 279). In his prayer to Athena, he characterizes his speech as ritually correct (εὐφήμως, 287) and pure (ἁγνοῦ, 287); similarly, he remains silent (ἄφθογγον) in observance of the laws governing homicide (448–50). Orestes' speech also contains many legal terms reminiscent of those occurring at the end of the *Choephori*: after inviting Athena to decide his case (κρῖνον δίκην, 468), he speaks of proofs (τεκμήριον, 447; cf. 485) and witnesses (ἐξεμαρτύρει, 461), language that foreshadows the judicial speeches of Athena and Apollo. The fact that there are twice as many legal terms in the *Eumenides* as in the first two plays demonstrates, at least at the level of diction, a move away from the figurative, metaphorical speech of the *Agamemnon* to a more public type of discourse.[117]

In response to Orestes' request, Athena establishes a jury of male citizens, dikasts, sworn by oath to vote according to the laws (ὁρκίων, 483) and to pursue the truth (ἐτητύμως, 488). She then enjoins the speakers to

---

classical literature, see Thompson 1936: 159–64. In poetry, the crow is frequently portrayed as a ravenous predator who preys on corpses; cf. Thgn. 833; Pind. *Ol.* 2.87; Aesch. *Supp.* 751.

I take Clytemnestra as the subject of this passage, reading, with Denniston and Page, σταθεῖσα instead of στάθεις. It is hard to see how Fraenkel's suggestion, that the subject is the δαίμων invoked at 1468, would work in performance, since it is Clytemnestra who stands onstage gloating over the corpses.

[115] On the ritual correctness of sound and its negation in Aeschylus, see Kaimio 1977: 116–17.

[116] Taplin 1978: 107.

[117] Robertson 1939: 217.

are represented as "litigants in a forthcoming murder trial" wh render their opponent speechless by means of a magical incanta

ἐπὶ δὲ τῷ τεθυμένῳ
τόδε μέλος, παρακοπά,
παραφορὰ φρενοδαλής,
ὕμνος ἐξ Ἐρινύων
δέσμιος φρενῶν, ἀφόρ-
μικτος, αὑονὰ βροτοῖς. (327–33 = 34

Over the sacrificial victim,
this is the chant, maddening,
distracting, mind-rending,
the binding song of the Erinyes,
without melody, withering to mortals.

This imprecation perhaps more closely adheres to the pattern of de than does the passage at *Agamemnon* 958–74 in two significant v it addresses the intended victim rather than a deity, and 2) it th the victim with physical suffering, a notorious feature of the curse ta The Erinyes' use of magical language also affiliates them with for particularly barbarians, celebrated for their knowledge of magic. link between the speech of Clytemnestra and that of the Erinyes is strengthened when we consider that both are associated with disc unmusical sound. At the end of the *Agamemnon*, for example, the compare the sound of Clytemnestra's voice to that of a crow that tuneless song:

ἐπὶ δὲ σώματος δίκαν [μοι]
κόρακος ἐχθροῦ σταθεῖσ' ἐκνόμως
ὕμνον ὑμνεῖν ἐπεύχεται. (*Ag.* 1472-

Standing over the body like a hateful crow,
she revels and sings her tuneless song.

The harsh cry of the crow, as well as its penchant for scavenging, commonplace in antiquity; even the mimetic term κόραξ conno croaking sound.[114] The rhythmic combination of the verb and co

[111] See Faraone 1985: 152. Prins 1991 also examines the coercive power of the speech from the broader perspective of speech-act theory.

[112] The word αὑονά, "dryness," suggests an unpleasant physical sensation; cf. Archil. Ar. *Eccl.* 146; Hdt. 8.2. Faraone (1985: 152n.13) further notes that the repetition ephymnion "may indicate a literary rendering of magical formulas."

[113] On the Erinyes as barbarians, see Hall 1989b: 205.

[114] See Denniston and Page 1972: 206; and Fraenkel 1950, 3: 700. On mimetic and animal sounds, see Stanford 1967: 102–3; on the sound and meaning of the cr

present their witnesses and evidence (μαρτύριά τε καὶ τεκμήρια, 485). This public tribunal, βουλευτήριον (570), mandated by Athena, fixes deliberation as the province of males in the democratic city (572) and negates the masculine counsels of Clytemnestra first mentioned by the Watchman in the *Agamemnon* (11). Apollo as a prophet exemplifies the standard of true and unequivocal speech (Eum. 615) in this arena, speech that issues from Zeus himself (618). Although emanating from the gods, this judicial discourse represents a kind of social contract between citizen males, as symbolized by the importance of the oath in the proceedings; the jural or heliastic oath ensured truthfulness not only of the litigants, but especially of the Areopagite judges (indeed, their oath is mentioned no less than three times in the course of this scene: 483, 680, 710). Significantly, the trial concludes with Orestes' oath promising eternal peace between Argos and Athens (764).

The trial scene is instructive in another way, since the Erinyes react to Athena's verdict with a curse, another example of coercive, magical speech. This curse resembles the binding song in that it takes the form of an identical pair of strophes (780–90 = 810–20). But the judicial speech of the trial scene is incapable of surmounting this resistance; instead, Athena must intervene to mediate between the two parties. Athena clearly represents the positive, socially constructive power of persuasion necessary for the proper functioning of the polis. Early in the *Eumenides*, Apollo instructs Orestes to journey to Athens for the purpose of finding charming words, θελκτηρίους μύθους (81–82), words that recall the erotic and magical persuasion of women. Athena later characterizes her speech in the same terms as she attempts to reconcile the Erinyes to their new role:

ἀλλ' εἰ μὲν ἁγνόν ἐστί σοι Πειθοῦς σέβας,
γλώσσης ἐμῆς μείλιγμα καὶ θελκτήριον—
σὺ δ' οὖν μένοις ἄν.   (885–87)

But if you have reverence for sacred Persuasion,
the soothing charm of my words,
then you might stay.

Using the verb *thelgein*, "to enchant," the Erinyes assert that Athena's persuasiveness has charmed them into compliance (θέλξειν μ' ἔοικας, 900), although her threat of bodily harm may also have influenced their change of heart.[118] And yet the erotic feminine connotations of *thelgein* are negated by Athena's maiden status and her masculine birth. Her enchanting persuasion has been cleansed of its destructive and feminine aspects and

---

[118] Bers (1994: 185) observes that Athena's victory "both had to be, and still might have been allowed to fail, for Athena holds bolts of lightning in reserve (827–28)." But Gagarin (1976: 83) argues that Athena's persuasion holds greater sway over the Erinyes than her threat of force.

appropriated by the polis because she herself is not really a woman, "not reared in the darkness of the womb" (οὐδ' ἐν σκότοισι νηδύος τεθραμμένη, 665).[119] The story of Athena's birth from Zeus' head reminds us that her speech lacks deception because her loyalty lies with the group, not the individual, with the male, not the female, as she later states (736). The fact that Athena credits Zeus *agoraios*, or forensic Zeus, for her victory over the Erinyes links her persuasive power not only to her unique, masculine birth, but also to the law courts (ἐκράτησε Ζεὺς 'αγοραῖος, 973). Her triumph effects one further transformation: not only do the Erinyes abandon their anger, but their speech is converted from curses into blessings and words of grace (921ff.). This efficacious speech will benefit rather than harm the city, for the Erinyes have found "the path of good speech" (γλώσσης ἀγαθῆς | ὁδόν, 988–89). The androgynous Athena, female in gender but masculine in birth and speech, presides over the civic drama enacted in the *Eumenides*; her benevolent, divine gift of persuasion supplants the ambiguous and deceptive speech of Clytemnestra and serves as the basis for speech in the law court.

The social order restored by Athena reaches its ultimate expression in the choral procession that concludes the *Eumenides*. The Erinyes' final farewell to the citizens as they depart (ἀστικὸς λεώς, 997; cf. 1014–16) serves to strengthen civic unity by drawing the spectators, as citizens of Athens, into the world of the drama. The procession, composed principally of Athena, her cult priestesses, the Areopagites, the herald, the trumpeter, and perhaps others,[120] escorts the Erinyes to their new underground home. Their song is both propitious and triumphant: they urge the assembled company to speak auspiciously (εὐφαμεῖτε, 1035, 1038) and to utter the cry of *ololugē* (1043, 1047). This public, religious song reverses the fragmented silent exit of the male chorus in the *Agamemnon*: now the duplicitous and tainted feminine *ololugē* of the first two plays "can be raised in true and unsullied joy."[121] And from the perspective of staging, it is quite possible, as Sommerstein suggests, that the whole community in the theater joined in the song: "The *Oresteia* ends with a united cry of triumphant joy from

[119] Goldhill (1984b: 213) links the θελκτηρίους μύθους of Athena to Clytemnestra's πόνων θελκτηρία | στρωμνή at *Cho.* 670–71.

[120] Because of possible lacunae before and after v. 1027, it is unclear to whom the εὐκλεὴς λόχος of 1026 refers; it might possibly include the "maidens, wives, and old women" of v. 1027, but the presence of στόλος in connection with them provides another ambiguity (παίδων, γυναικῶν, καὶ στόλος πρεσβυτίδων, 1027). The passage also is unclear about whether the women are participants in the cult of the Erinyes-Semnai, or the cult personnel of Athena, the πρόσπολοι mentioned at 1024. In any case, it does not seem likely that the line refers to figures actually present onstage: for a discussion, see Sommerstein 1989: 275–78.

[121] Sommerstein 1989: 285. As Haldane notes (1965b), the *ololugē* marks several catastrophic events in the trilogy: the capture of Troy (*Ag.* 28, 587, 595), the murder of Agamemnon (*Ag.* 1118, 1236), and the murders of Clytemnestra and Aegisthus (*Cho.* 942, 386).

over 10,000 mouths as all Athenians hail the birth of a new era."[122] But as Sommerstein neglects to point out, most, if not all, of these mouths were male, as described in Chapter 1. The third play of the *Oresteia* trilogy celebrates the erasure of women's speech from the polis, both in the theater and in the law court, and further suggests that the only proper speech for women in public, onstage as well as in the polis, is religious.

CONCLUSION

The *Oresteia* trilogy depicts a movement from the deceptive, figurative, and erotic speech of Clytemnestra in the *Agamemnon* to the divinely sanctioned judicial speech of men in the *Eumenides*. The androgynous figure of Athena mediates and integrates these two discourses: her male birth results in a powerful form of persuasion stripped of feminine guile. The trilogy implicitly problematizes the role of deception and mimesis in the democratic polis, associating a dangerous, coercive form of *peithō* with women and a politically beneficial one with men. However, the problem resides not so much in women's speech, but in a noncitizen's manipulation of public and persuasive speech genres out of self-interest rather than for the good of the community. The trilogy represents the speech of outsiders as potentially subversive of normative social categories, categories created and maintained by civic institutions, such as the law court and even the theater, under the guidance of the gods. The trilogy partially resolves this dilemma by dramatizing the creation of a new type of performance in the *Eumenides*, the trial, a performance based on truthful speech and one that conspires to erase women's speech from the polis.

[122] Sommerstein 1989: 286.

Chapter Four

AT THE HOUSE DOOR: PHAEDRA AND
THE POLITICS OF REPUTATION

FOR AESCHYLUS, composing the *Oresteia* shortly after Ephialtes' reforms, persuasive speech in a juridical context provides a means of consolidating male civic identity, a process that necessitates the exclusion of women's dangerous and deceptive erotic speech. In the post-Periclean age, however, the art of persuasion is viewed with increasing suspicion by the Athenian elite; rhetoric takes center stage in the courts and Assembly as well as in the theater of Dionysus, a shift underscored by Aristotle, who observes that the characters in the earlier tragedies spoke politically, *politikos*, while those in the newer ones speak more rhetorically, *rhētorikos* (Arist. *Poet.* 1450b7–8). Euripides therefore engages more directly than Aeschylus does with the problem of demagogues and their teachers through his use of sophistic arguments and techniques, as well as through his anachronistic representation of democratic institutions. Rhetoric in his plays, in contrast with rhetoric in those of Sophocles, wears "almost the same clothing it wore outside the Theater of Dionysus," whether deployed by a male or female character.[1] In the two plays considered in the next two chapters, Euripides' *Hippolytus* and *Andromache*, produced about thirty years after the *Oresteia* trilogy, the poet explores the destructive effects of women's domestic, erotic speech on the male discursive spaces of the city. In contrast to Aeschlyus, however, Euripides joins the archaic topos of women's verbal guile to a late fifth-century concern about the increased importance of rhetoric to the democratic polis.

Through the figures of Phaedra and the Nurse, the *Hippolytus* represents women's speech both as private and intimately concerned with *erōs*, and yet at the same time as rhetorically sophisticated, since both characters deploy sophistic arguments and terminology similar to that found in contemporary Athenian law courts. By inserting this cunning, feminine speech into a highly forensic agon between men, a domain from which women's testimony was normally excluded, the play provides, on one level at least, a metadiscourse on contemporary judicial process. This legal focus also provides a framework for understanding how women's gossip, depicted

---

[1] Bers 1994: 182. Reinhardt (1960: 231) describes Euripidean drama as the "Barometer der Krise" that registers the social and political tensions posed by a new generation of leaders instructed by the sophists. The Greek text quoted in this chapter is taken from Barrett 1964, unless otherwise noted.

formally as operating in a discursive sphere separate from that of men in the first half of the play, both polices feminine sexual norms in the house and negotiates masculine political identity outside it. A parallel is found in a passage of the *Politics* (1313b30–35) in which Aristotle cites as one of the shortcomings of the worst form of democracy the fact that men's reputations depend too much on the gossip of women, since under such governments women rule the household and carry abroad reports of men.[2]

καὶ τὰ περὶ τὴν δημοκρατίαν δὲ γιγνόμενα τὴν τελευταίαν τυραννικὰ πάντα, γυναικοκρατία τε περὶ τὰς οἰκίας, ἵν' ἐξαγγέλλωσι κατὰ τῶν ἀνδρῶν, καὶ δούλων ἄνεσις διὰ τὴν αὐτὴν αἰτίαν. (Arist. *Pol.* 1313b32–35)

And the things that come about in the last (and worst) form of democracy are all characteristic of tyrannies. Women rule supreme in the house with the result that they betray their husband's secrets, while for the very same reason license is the part of slaves.

Here Aristotle seems to have in mind Sparta as a model, a state whose government he earlier characterizes as a form of gynaecocracy (Arist. *Pol.* 1269b25), where women exhibit verbal dominance to an unprecedented degree, an issue explored in greater detail in the next chapter. In his treatment of timocracy in the *Republic*, a discussion also based on Sparta, Plato examines the effects of women's domestic speech on political life. In a state where the typical male uncharacteristically avoids public speaking (ῥητορικὸν δ' οὐδαμῶς, Pl. *Rep.* 548e) and seldom appears in the courts or assembly (Pl. *Rep.* 549d2–4), in marked contrast to classical Athenian practice, women's querulous speech within the oikos has a great impact on public life, albeit indirectly.

The false rumors produced by women and their effect on men is a central issue in Euripides' *Hippolytus*, one that pertains to the larger thematic problem of speech and its dangers, first treated at length in Knox's seminal 1952 article.[3] More recently, critics have considered the impact of gender on speech, arguing that the play depicts the subversive potential of women's speech and its ultimate containment by men.[4] A recurrent issue in some of this scholarship is how the play's critique of rhetoric and deceptive speech engages with contemporary intellectual debates on the relation between *phusis* and *nomos*, language and truth, and appearance and reality, controversies closely associated with the sophists and their movement.[5] For these critics, Phaedra's abiding concern with *eukleia* affiliates her with *nomos* and the world of appearance, in contrast to the aristocratic Hippolytus, who

[2] See Cohen 1991: 161.

[3] Now reprinted in Knox 1979: 205–30; Turato 1976.

[4] Rabinowitz 1987; Zeitlin 1985b; Goff 1990; Segal 1993: 103, cf. 1992: 443.

[5] Berns 1973; Michelini 1987: 40–41; Luschnig 1988: 35–36; Gill 1990: 77; Goff 1990: 78–81; Segal 1992: 421 and 450–51n.3; Meltzer 1996: 189.

embodies the principle of *phusis*.[6] Viewed from the perspective of women's speech, Euripides' *Hippolytus* first shows men and women as operating in separate discursive spheres, then demonstrates how the lies generated by women infiltrate and ultimately subvert the judicial discourse of men. At the end of the play, the ritual song of girls reverses this movement, providing a public, feminine song that reinforces normative gender roles. At the same time, the *Hippolytus* contradicts the model of women's silence and seclusion discussed in Chapter 1, suggesting instead that women played a complex role behind the scenes in negotiating male identity and relationships in the democratic polis.

As discussed in Chapter 2, gossip, exchanged in the agora and in the other places where men congregated and conversed, significantly influenced the reputations of adult citizen males and their female kin. Such rumors formed the basis of slander, which could be brought against an individual both in the law courts and in the formal procedure known as *dokimasia*, a hearing at which prospective magistrates were publicly scrutinized before assuming office.[7] At least in the orators, much of this hearsay concerned not merely the behavior of the individual in question, but the activity of his female relatives, and particularly his mother.[8] At issue were her status as an Athenian and her sexual mores, reflecting concerns about legitimacy and citizen rights.[9] As Hunter points out, "Gossip about women could have devastating effects on the individuals against whom it was directed as well as on their families."[10] The role played by slander in the courts is comically portrayed by Aristophanes in *Wasps*, when Bdelycleon complains about the difficulty of defending a dog who has been slandered (διαβεβλημένου, 950). Against this backdrop, we can better understand Phaedra's concern for *eukleia* and its effect on her children, as well as the role of women in shaping the reputations of men in the democratic polis.

As a play about discourse, it is significant that the *Hippolytus* both commences and ends with an act of slander broadly understood: Hippolytus defames and incites the wrath of Aphrodite by calling her the basest

---

[6] Phaedra's concern with reputation, *eukleia*, has long been established as the action for her actions; see Knox 1952 [= 1979]; Winnington-Ingram 1960; Segal 1970: 282 and passim; Reckford 1973; Gill 1990. On Phaedra as the embodiment of *nomos*, see Winnington-Ingram 1960: 186; Segal (1970: 291) remarks, "Through Phaedra's concern with appearance, reputation, the 'outside' world, Euripides raises the questions beginning to be asked in his time about the adequacy of an ethic based entirely upon external, social sanctions, the *nomoi*."

[7] Hunter 1994: 106–8.

[8] Ibid.: 111; Henderson 1987b: 112–13.

[9] On foreign birth, see Aeschin. 2.78, 93, 180; 3.172; Din. 1.15; on sexual promiscuity, Isae. 3. See also Hunter 1994: 112.

[10] Hunter 1994: 113.

of the gods (λέγει κακίστην δαιμόνων πεφυκέναι, 13), whereas Phaedra later impugns the character of Hippolytus by falsely accusing him of rape. Framed by these two speech acts, a world unfolds in which *muthoi*, associated with women throughout the play, freely circulate.[11] The drama begins within the private, domestic sphere of women, where rumors proliferate and invite complicity, and where slaves typically serve as go-betweens in conducting their mistresses' adulterous affairs, as depicted both in the theater and in the law court.[12] It concludes with a trial scene in which the evidence consists only of written words that preclude interrogation.

Yet the domestic sphere is also the realm of *doxa*, "appearance," governed by Aphrodite, who works through the power of sight, and embodied by Phaedra, her mortal agent, who privileges fair appearance; inherently unstable, *doxa* provides the medium for persuasive and deceptive speech, not unlike the sophistic model provided by Gorgias in his *Helen*.[13] Facilitated by the chorus and the Nurse, whose association with Aphrodite may have been reinforced by having the same actor play both roles, Phaedra's speech produces the false *doxa* that misleads Theseus and causes him to condemn his son in the final scene of adjudication (δόξης ... ἐσφαλμένοι, 1414). Hippolytus, who has maligned both Aphrodite and womankind in general in his bitter invective, is repaid in the same coin: Phaedra defames him with accusations of rape, and Theseus, as a gullible recipient of her false *muthos*, further slanders his son (διαβαλών, 932). The device for conveying this slander, however, is exceedingly clever: Phaedra uses writing, a new technology associated with the sophists and depicted as primarily visual in the play, to transmit her falsehood.

In contrast to the *Eumenides*, where the trial celebrates the human capacity for justly resolving social conflict with the help of the gods, the *Hippolytus* shows a new world in which there is no benevolent, remedial form of persuasion to counteract the endless duplicities spawned by human discourse, one in which mortal adjudication is implicitly flawed. In the *Hippolytus*, the poet feminizes the art of rhetoric, in a manner similar to that of Aristophanes, as a means of conveying the dangers and seductions of persuasive speech in a polis increasingly vulnerable to demagogues. But religious utterance, collective and divinely inspired, may check the falsehoods and fictions manufactured in the household and imported into the political sphere; the cult song of virgins and the civic laments of men contain the destructive speech of matrons and restore stability to the polis.

---

[11] In contrast to Martin's observation, discussed in Chapter 2, that *muthos* refers mostly to the speeches of men in the Homeric poems, the word in the *Hippolytus* is only used by women or about women's speech: cf. 9, 197, 609, 1288, 1313.

[12] Ar. *Thesm.* 339–41, *Eccl.* 610; Lys. 1; Hyp. 1b fr. 1. See Cohen 1991: 164; and Hunter 1994: 85–86 and 217n.28.

[13] Gorg. *Hel.* 9; Segal 1962: 111.

PHAEDRA'S CONCERN FOR REPUTATION

The play situates the problem of the politics of reputation in Phaedra, whose desperate struggle to maintain appearances leads not only to her own death but also to that of Hippolytus. This overvaluation of *eukleia* correlates not to the epic values exemplified by an Achilles, but to a more contemporary concern with protecting one's name in an increasingly litigious political environment where rumor and slander could defame and even disenfranchise the best of citizens. The ascendancy of the politics of reputation in the last half of the fifth century promoted an atmosphere in which appearances became more important than reality. Phaedra's doubleness, remarked upon by many scholars, stems from just such a desire to maintain appearances under an increasing threat of public exposure and criticism.[14] Her character may therefore be viewed as a metaphor for the complex role played by speech in constructing personal reputation in the democratic polis, suggesting the influence of women exerted, albeit indirectly, on the masculine political sphere.

Phaedra confronts the critic with an interpretive Gordian knot: her complexity and ambiguity manifest a sophistic fascination with manipulating conceptual categories that renders any absolute interpretation of her character inadequate. It is as if Euripides had set himself the task of creating an *apologia* for his first play, similar to that of Gorgias for Helen, and had marshaled in its service the most intricate strands of contemporary sophistic debate. Thus the poet affiliates Phaedra with a principle of equivocation, with apparent rather than genuine virtue; in this sense she simultaneously reinforces Hippolytus' philosophy of *phusis*, that women cannot be taught morality, as well as incarnates the Gorgian doctrine of deception: since reality cannot be known, the important thing is to appear to conform to the dictates of conventional law.[15] In addition, her ethical and linguistic

---

[14] The fact that scholarship on the *Hippolytus* is divided between viewing Phaedra as "a figure of deep moral hypocrisy" and as "a paragon of female virtue" discloses a central feature of her character, her ambiguity. For the view of Phaedra as a self-serving hypocrite, see Fitzgerald 1973: 26; and Orban 1981a: 17, where her hypocrisy is linked to the sophists. Those who argue for the second *Hippolytus* as a palinode for the first play tend to see Phaedra as a virtuous incarnation of her predecessor; see Zeitlin 1985b: 52; cf. Michelini 1987: 288. Others have emphasized the similarities between Phaedra and Hippolytus, e.g., their foreign birth, the sexual prehistories of their mothers, and their scenes of bodily suffering; see Knox 1979: 212–13; Winnington-Ingram 1960: 176, 179–80; Turato 1976; Frischer 1978; Michelini, 1987: 277–320. On the two as exponents of aristocratic values, see Segal 1992: 442; Kovacs 1987; Gill 1990: 87.

[15] Most of the references to *doxa* and *eukleia* in the *Hippolytus* pertain to Phaedra: she receives a fair reputation from the chorus first for her struggle to resist desire (δόξαν ἐσθλήν, 432) and then for her resolution to die and save herself from shame (εὐδόξον . . . φήμαν, 773). The concept of *doxa*, however, is intimately associated with falsehood, as Theseus suggests at the end of the play: *doxa* led him astray to place curses upon his son (δόξης . . .

ambiguity derive in part from her status as a potential adulteress, just as Clytemnestra's ambiguity in Aeschylus' *Agamemnon* reflects her extramarital liaison with Aegisthus.[16] But Phaedra's ambiguity differs qualitatively from that of her Aeschylean counterpart: whereas Clytemnestra's double signification reflects a complete mastery over language, Phaedra's conveys a loss of self-control brought about by her sickness. She vacillates involuntarily, not from masculine to feminine poles, as does Clytemnestra, but from virtuous wife to incipient betrayer of the oikos.[17] At the level of ethos, her use of innuendo and euphemism identifies her speech as that of an aristocratic, wellborn woman, in contrast to the blunt, crass speech of the Nurse.

Phaedra's quest for a good name, *eukleia*, provides a central paradox around which the dramatic action is organized. On the one hand, some critics have viewed her desire to protect her reputation as masculine, given that this type of acclaim is normally associated in Athenian drama with men or with heroized women such as Alcestis or Antigone.[18] On the other, this struggle can be seen as a desire to conform to the norms of feminine behavior, which involve avoiding the rebuke or *psogos* normally incurred by women who venture outside the house, as defined by Andromache in Euripides' *Trojan Women:*

πρῶτον μέν, ἔνθα—κἂν προσῇ κἂν μὴ προσῇ
ψόγος γυναιξίν—αὐτὸ τοῦτ' ἐφέλκεται
κακῶς ἀκούειν, ἥτις οὐκ ἔνδον μένει,
τούτου παρεῖσα πόθον ἔμμνον ἐν δόμοις.   (Eur. *Tro.* 647–50)

ἐσφαλμένοι, 1414); for other references to the word, cf. 432, 773, 1115. More predominant, however, are *eukleia* words, most of which are linked to Phaedra, beginning in the prologue, where Aphrodite refers to her as *eukleēs* (47). At 489, Phaedra puts the principle of *eukleia* above pleasure in response to the Nurse's suggestion of magic, while at 687 she fears she will no longer die *eukleēs* now that Hippolytus knows her secret. Significantly, her sense of *eukleia* is intimately bound to her sons and their reputations: twice she affirms the importance of preserving her honor for their sake (423, 717). In fact, her desire to protect them results in the final stratagem that destroys Hippolytus (717). By the end of the play, Artemis *ex machina* sets things aright to ensure that Hippolytus may die *eukleēs* (1299).

[16] On the ambiguity of Phaedra's language, see Segal 1970: 289; 1992: 427 and 433; 1993: 98; Zeitlin 1985b: 84–85, on Phaedra's "double-speaking"; Luschnig (1988: 35) speaks of her concern for "the shifting meanings of words"; see also Craik 1993: 51; Meltzer 1996: 180.

[17] On Phaedra's tendency to vacillate, see Avery 1968: 30.

[18] Scholars have persisted in seeing Phaedra as an epic hero, including Claus 1972: 236; Kovacs 1980c: 301–2; Segal (1970: 284 and 290; 1988b: 274) compares her to Achilles; see also Mitchell 1991: 114. Although it is true that the term *eukleia* in Euripides normally refers to the martial valor of men, it can also describe heroic female actions, such as those of Alcestis (as below), Iphigeneia (*IA* 1376, 1440), Medea (*Med.* 810), and Antigone (*Phoen.* 1742). But the term seems to have been undergoing some change during last part of the fifth century: for example, at *Med.* 236, Medea claims that divorce is not *eukleēs* for women,

First, whether blame belongs to women or not,
this very thing attracts slander, not remaining within the house.
Putting aside a desire for this, I remained within the house.

The phrase κακῶς ἀκούειν, "to be ill spoken of," is a technical term for slander found in the orators and alludes to the type of public censure a woman invites if she does not exhibit self-control.[19] By remaining within, the prudent wife also avoids the crafty speech of other women that may potentially induce adultery (κομψὰ θηλειῶν ἔπη, Eur. *Tro.* 651), a major theme in the next chapter. Phaedra's desire for *eukleia* therefore may be viewed as largely negative: public acclaim, for women, almost always has pejorative connotations in the Athenian polis; because she breaches her silence in order to protect her reputation, Phaedra brings disaster on her house.[20] And the fact that the final instance of the word *eukleia* occurs in relation to the ritual song Artemis confers upon Hippolytus at the end of the play (1299) further suggests that instead of the positive *kleos* of men, Phaedra receives its feminine, negative version, the *psogos* that advertises her betrayal and that condemns all women to a discourse of infamy.

The play develops the association between Phaedra and illusory appearance by gradually revealing a discrepancy between what she professes to be and what she actually is.[21] Overwhelmed by the sickness of desire, Phaedra can neither maintain her original silence nor remain within the house; instead, she wavers between disclosure and concealment, one of the many polarities explored by the play.[22] While the chorus, upon hearing her long speech, applaud Phaedra for her apparent self-control, their ambivalent reference to her noble *doxa* (δόξαν ἐσθλήν, 432) undercuts this praise by suggesting the potential for appearances to mislead, since in the end it is a false *doxa* that undoes Theseus. As Gorgias argues in his *Helen*, a text probably composed at least a decade after this play, *doxa* is inherently precarious and unstable (σφαλερὰ καὶ ἀβεβαίος, *Hel.* 11), a concept underscored in the *Hippolytus* by the recurrence of σφάλλω and its cognates, especially in connection with Aphrodite.[23] After Phaedra's confession, the Nurse exposes the insecure and illusory nature of Phaedra's reputation

---

whereas the chorus at 415 speak of a future time when gender roles will be reversed and women will receive *eukleia*, both contexts that lack any masculine or military associations.

[19] Hunter 1994: 221–22n.14; cf. Antiph. 5.75; Dem. 37.37; and Lys. 10.11.

[20] Goff 1990: 15 also cites Pericles' funeral oration in connection with Phaedra's desire for fair repute.

[21] On Phaedra's concern with the appearance of virtue and not its reality, see Calder 1979; Braund 1980; Gilula 1981; Kawashima 1986.

[22] Goff 1990: 1–26 provides an excellent discussion of oppositions within the play and their relation to the speech-silence polarity.

[23] On Gorgias' treatment of *doxa*, see Segal 1962: 112; for a discussion of σφάλλω and its cognates, see Fowler 1978: 16–17; cf. Eur. *Hipp.* 6, 100, 183, 262, 671, 785, 871, 1231, 1414.

with her assertion that she lacked sexual self-control (σώφρων δ' οὖσ' ἐτύγχανες γυνή, 494). Hippolytus later encapsulates this paradox in his denunciation of Phaedra as a woman "chaste, although not able to be chaste" (ἐσωφρόνησε δ' οὐκ ἔχουσα σωφρονεῖν, 1034). In contrast, Hippolytus embodies the real virtue of self-control expressed by the term *sōphrōn* and its cognates.[24]

ERŌS AND ILLUSION: APHRODITE'S PROLOGUE

From Homer to classical drama, a man's prolonged absence from the house and his inability to superintend his wife is viewed as a potent source of danger. Euripides' *Hippolytus* begins with the same commonplace: Theseus, on a visit to the oracle, has left his wife alone in their palace at Troezen (281, 807). In turn, Phaedra violates social convention by leaving the house, a gesture that augurs domestic upheaval in Attic drama, specifically adultery. Citizen women's putative seclusion in classical Athens restricted opportunities for illicit sex: literary sources depict weddings and funerals as events in which women were likely to encounter men outside the family, but more often, the object of desire tended to be a near relative or neighbor.[25] Phaedra's initial departure from the house to attend the festival of Demeter and her subsequent attraction to Hippolytus (24–28) reflect this model and reinforce the idea of the dangers of women leaving the house. At the same time, feminine spatial transgressions frequently involve a violation of the verbal restrictions placed on women, as discussed in Chapter 1.

The first part of the play links the public role of gossip as promulgated by women to women's desire to protect their reputations from the derogations of men. The prologue establishes slander, particularly what men say about women in public, as a central issue in the play, for Aphrodite stresses, with her emphatic λέγει, that Hippolytus has deprecated her in speech by calling her the basest of gods (λέγει κακίστην δαιμόνων πεφυκέναι, 13). Invective comprises Hippolytus' primary speech genre, since he will later subject Phaedra and the Nurse to similar abuse in his bitter attack on women. At the same time, women's gossip and their private speech are portrayed as irreparably damaging the reputations of men. Aphrodite, like her victim, also exhibits an extreme concern with publicity: she refers to herself as "not nameless" with the litotes κοὐκ ἀνώνυμος (1), a phrase Artemis later uses to describe Phaedra's immortalization in song (1429). The goddess's use of the verb κέκλημαι (2) in naming herself correlates

---

[24] Cf. Eur. *Hipp.* 949, 995, 1007, 1013, 1100.

[25] Cohen 1991: 155; cf. Arist. *Eth. Nic.* 1137a5; *Mag. mor.* 1188b17, on the sexual availability of the wives of neighbors or friends.

her desire for renown to Phaedra, whom she calls εὐκλεής (47).[26] As discussed above, the play transmutes this positive form of fame into the notoriety of the maidens' choral song later established by Artemis.

The preponderance of words for seeing and showing in the prologue identifies the goddess with the faculty of sight (4, 9, 25, 27, 30, 41, 42, 51, 57); she is Aphrodite Κατασκοπία, her Troezen cult title.[27] Because Aphrodite arouses desire through the eyes, Phaedra falls in love upon first seeing Hippolytus, ἰδοῦσα (27), whereas the chorus later sing of Eros' effect on the eyes in the first stasimon (525).[28] And just as Aphrodite has produced Phaedra's love at first sight, so, too, will she deprive Hippolytus of his sight, and life, by the end of the play (φάος δὲ λοίσθιον βλέπων τόδε, 57). The erotic dimension of this cognitive mode and its relation to Aphrodite has roots in early epic: in Hesiod's *Works and Days*, the goddess imbues Pandora with golden grace (χάρις, *Op.* 65) and desire (πόθον, *Op.* 66), fashioning a creature of pure appearance, a wonder to behold.[29] The *Homeric Hymns* also establish a structural similarity between Aphrodite and Pandora; she who suffuses others with sexual beauty herself undergoes a *kosmēsis* that arouses the gods' visual pleasure (οἱ δ' ἠσπάζοντο ἰδόντες, *Hom. Hymn Ven.* 6.15).[30] A similar role reversal occurs in the account of her dalliance with Anchises: like Phaedra, she falls in love with him at first sight (ἰδοῦσα, *Hom. Hymn Ven.* 5.56); elaborately costumed, she inspires wonder and desire in her lover (θαῦμα ἰδέσθαι, *Hom. Hymn Ven.* 5.90–91).[31] Deceit also plays an important role in this erotic encounter, since Aphrodite disguises herself as a young girl in order to entice her mortal lover (παρθένῳ ἀδμήτῃ μέγεθος καὶ εἶδος ὁμοίη, *Hom. Hymn Ven.* 5.82). In the same way, the prologue of the *Hippolytus* affiliates the seductions of Aphrodite with deception: her vow to bring everything to light in the course of the play's action is deliberately ambiguous ("I will show the matter to Theseus and it will be revealed," δείξω δὲ Θησεῖ πρᾶγμα, κἀκφανήσεται, 42), because what she reveals is not the truth, but a lie that will provoke Theseus' fatal curse (43–46). This equivocal statement implicates

---

[26] On the cult of Artemis *eukleia*, see Braund 1980.

[27] Halleran 1995: 149–50.

[28] Luschnig (1988: 4) remarks, "Seeing and being seen are necessary to Aphrodite's *modus operandi*." She also tries somewhat less successfully to link the adjective κατόψιον (30), a word that describes the temple Phaedra builds in honor of Aphrodite, to the erotics of sight.

[29] As discussed in Chapters 1 and 2, Pandora herself is repeatedly described as pure appearance, an ἴκελον (Hes. *Theog.* 572; *Op.* 71) or εἶδος (*Theog.* 589; *Op.* 63), delightful to look at (θαῦμα ἰδέσθαι, Hes. *Theog.* 575, 581; θαῦμα, 588).

[30] Schwabl 1966: 80; Loraux 1993: 80.

[31] Segal (1993: 113 and n. 8) argues that ἰδοῦσα is a direct verbal echo of the hymn. The emphasis on sight continues in the rest of the poem: when Aphrodite and Anchises go to bed, she averts her gaze (*Hom. Hymn Ven.* 5.156); on the next day she commands Anchises to look her in the eye (*Hom. Hymn Ven.* 5.179). He then recognizes the goddess and averts his gaze (*Hom. Hymn Ven.* 5.181).

the goddess, like all of the other females in the play, in a process of deception and verbal manipulation destructive to men.[32] Only Artemis, as a female whose virginity affiliates her with truth, can expose and expunge this feminine duplicity; Cassandra, because of her mantic status, plays a similar role in the *Agamemnon*.

Because of her ability to incite sexual desire through deceptive appearance and cunning words, Aphrodite figures prominently in the archetypal story of adultery, Paris' abduction of Helen: in the *Iliad*, the goddess compels Helen to seduce Paris under threat of death.[33] Aphrodite's role in promulgating the adulterous liaisons of myth recalls the sophistic argument in which human responsibility for malefactions devolves upon the gods. In his encomium, Gorgias justifies Helen's adultery by shifting the blame first to the gods and then to the art of persuasion itself. In the second *Hippolytus*, Euripides makes a similar move: relocating the source of promiscuity in Aphrodite, he transforms the character of Phaedra from a shameless seductress into an unwitting victim. Not only the gods but also the persuasive power of images and words, which may mislead and deceive the listener, exculpate Helen, according to Gorgias (Gorg. *Hel.* 19).[34] Indeed, strong aesthetic stimulants, like physical attractiveness and seductive words, engender in the recipient such a state of mental confusion, ἔκπληξις (Gorg. *Hel.* 17), as to overpower all sense of social obligation or duty. The sight of Hippolytus has worked a similar response in Phaedra: thrown into confusion by the spurs of love (ἐκπεπληγμένη, 38), she is represented as unable to adhere to the social norms prescribed for women. The strong association between the persuasive power of images and words is evidenced by the shrines apparently established by Theseus in honor of Aphrodite *Pandēmos* and Peitho during the synoecism of Attica.[35] This equivalency of sight and verbal persuasion finds its fullest expression in Phaedra's fatal writing, since the written word is depicted as uniting both visual and verbal modes.

HIPPOLYTUS AND THE LANGUAGE OF PRAYER

Whereas Aphrodite works through the faculty of sight, Hippolytus' mode is strictly aural, as his first words show. The imagery that accompanies Hippolytus' arrival onstage embodies a paradox: as an erotic figure, like

[32] Barrett (1964: 165) views these words as the poet's attempt to mislead the audience without overtly lying.

[33] Cf. Sappho. fr. 16.10–12 Voigt; Hom. *Iliad* 3.395–420.

[34] Segal 1962: 105–6.

[35] Paus. 1.22.3; another tradition held that the temple was established on the profits of prostitution, since Peitho was the patroness of hetaeras; see Buxton 1982: 32–33.

Phaëthon or Adonis, who inspires the bridal rivalry of maidens, he also symbolizes the virginity that must be lost upon consummation of that marriage.[36] His pristine meadow consecrated to Artemis is at once the site of wild purity and of erotic encounter, like those found in lyric poetry.[37] In contrast to the speech of women, his language is direct, unequivocal, and ritually correct.[38] This scene establishes a contrast between religious language, here gendered as masculine, and Phaedra's ambiguous and erotically charged utterances. His oath later sworn on behalf of a woman, his social inferior, provides the drama with an absolute and unchanging moral center that respects both mortal laws and divine imperatives. Avoiding the world of politics and its deceptions typically associated with adult males, he claims to lack the rhetorical ability of his peers (988–89), reserving his speech solely for Artemis.[39]

Hippolytus' entrance assumes a lyric form, like that of Phaedra, but his song is collective rather than individual; as a pious hymn delivered up to the goddess, his song represents an authoritative form of language communally recognized, and one answered by the maidens' ritual song instituted by Artemis at the end of the play (59–61). He and his huntsmen enter honoring the goddess Artemis with a hymn (Ἄρτεμιν τιμῶν θεὰν | ὕμνοισιν, 55–56) that conforms to traditional prayer formulations. His address to the goddess signifies an exclusive relationship with her:

> μόνῳ γάρ ἐστι τοῦτ' ἐμοὶ γέρας βροτῶν·
> σοὶ καὶ ξύνειμι καὶ λόγοις ἀμείβομαι,
> κλύων μὲν αὐδῆς, ὄμμα δ' οὐχ ὁρῶν τὸ σόν.
> τέλος δὲ κάμψαιμ' ὥσπερ ἠρξάμην βίου.   (84–87)

I alone among mortals have this privilege:
I may accompany and converse with you,
hearing your voice but not seeing your face.
May I end my life just as I began it.

This relationship is characterized by an aural, not visual, mode, in contrast to the relationships between Aphrodite and the individuals through whom she works.[40] Hippolytus' preference for this mode is indicated later in the play, when he claims his distaste for visual representations of sexual

---

[36] Reckford 1972: 415 and 422.

[37] Bremer 1975; Pigeaud 1976: 3–4.

[38] Segal (1988b: 268) remarks that Hippolytus' speech "asserts a simplicity and clarity of belonging. It exudes confidence about definition and boundary and establishes his firm directness in his ritual approach to his goddess." Luschnig (1988: 6) makes a similar observation: "His tools are words, prayers, hymn, oath, denunciation, the argument from probability."

[39] On Hippolytus' desire to avoid the world of politics and his denial of rhetoric, see Zeitlin 1985b: 87; Kovacs 1987: 29; Luschnig 1988: 20–21; Goff 1990: 42–43.

[40] Turato 1976; Zeitlin 1985b: 90; Luschnig 1988: 5.

encounters: "Nor am I eager to view them, since I have a virgin soul" (οὐδὲ ταῦτα γὰρ σκοπεῖν | πρόθυμός εἰμι, παρθένον ψυχὴν ἔχων, 1005–6). And just as he honors Artemis through his prayer, he rebuffs Aphrodite by refusing to pronounce her name, cautioning the Servant to watch his words, lest he pollute Hippolytus by any reference to sexual matters (εὐλαβοῦ δὲ μή τι σου σφαλῇ στόμα, 100).[41] His subsequent reservations about her "night worship" (106) again suggest his denial of her power, which he consigns to women's hidden and erotic sphere. Hippolytus' verbal reticence, and his deployment of religious speech modes such as prayers, hymns, and oaths, provide a contrast to the deceptive and subversive speech of women as well as to the political discourse of men.

WOMEN'S TRAFFIC IN SPEECH: THE CHORUS

Just as an act of slander initiates Aphrodite's scheme for revenge, so, too, the circulation of stories among women at their washing (φάτις, 130) contributes to the tragic chain of events and serves as the medium by which false rumors are generated in the *Hippolytus*. The report or φάτις that leads the women to the palace to inquire after Phaedra also prefigures the speech they overhear in the Nurse's interview with Hippolytus (φήμα, 572). Even Phaedra in her lengthy rhesis recognizes gossip or conversation as one of the pleasures of female life (μακραί τε λέσχαι, 384). But thus far she has managed to evade women's idle talk by remaining silent and concealing her true thoughts from others: neither the Nurse nor the chorus knows what afflicts her (cf. servants: σιγῇ, 40; chorus: ἄσημα, 269; Nurse: οὐκ οἶδα, 271). When Phaedra and the women do converse, their subject is *erōs*, like that of the women described in Semonides' iambic (ἀφροδισίους λόγους, fr. 7.91 *IEG*). The troubles engendered by such speech are a commonplace of Euripidean drama: as discussed in the next chapter, Hermione blames her betrayal of her husband on the Siren's song of women's gossip (Eur. *Andr.* 946), just as Andromache in *Trojan Women* claims to avoid their crafty words altogether (Eur. *Tro.* 651). The private speech of wives as a form of gossip creates solidarity: united outside the world of men, and eventually sworn to silence by Phaedra (712), the chorus stalwartly refuse to divulge the truth upon Theseus' return (804–5). This feminine complicity, forged on behalf of *erōs*, also underlies two of Aristophanes' plots to be discussed in Chapter 6.

As mature, married women, the chorus contrast with the group of girls who will memorialize Phaedra and Hippolytus with their songs at the end

---

[41] I agree with Barrett (1964: 178) that Hippolytus here suspects that the Servant refers to Aphrodite; Halleran (1995: 158) reads this verse as a comment on Hippolytus' scrupulous concern for ritually pure speech.

of the play. Many of their odes focus on *erōs*, beginning with Phaedra's difficulties in the parodos (121–69) and turning to the theme of its destructive power in subsequent odes, particularly in the first stasimon (525–64), a hymn to Eros that commemorates the violent unions of Iole and Semele, and in the fourth stasimon (1268–81), a hymn celebrating Aphrodite's universal power. The parodos not only presents a picture of women's domestic life, but also calls attention to the important part played by women's conversation about *erōs* in the play. The term φίλα (125), placed in the emphatic position at line end, stresses that the talk has circulated among women only while the allusion to φάτις (131) establishes speech as the medium for transmitting and creating appearances.[42]

The content of the parodos identifies women's speech as private and preoccupied with feminine concerns: the chorus speculate that Phaedra's illness might be brought on by demonic possession, neglect of a deity (Artemis-Dictynna), her husband's adultery, bad news from her natal family, or pregnancy and impending childbirth (141–69). Their subject reflects their status as matrons and evokes the women's choruses, such as those in honor of Eileithyia at Elis, that celebrated the reproductive role of women.[43] And yet, this knowledge of sexual matters renders their speech more dangerous than the regulated song of maidens at the end of the play.

> φιλεῖ δὲ τᾷ δυστρόπῳ γυναικῶν
> ἁρμονίᾳ κακὰ δύ-
> στανος ἀμηχανία συνοικεῖν
> ὠδίνων τε καὶ ἀφροσύνας.　　　　　　　　　　(161–64)

An unfortunate, evil incompetence,
the result of childbirth and foolishness,
tends to dwell along with women's wayward temperament.

The terms ἀφροσύνη, a word falsely derived from Aphrodite to describe Meneleus' senseless pursuit of Helen in the *Trojan Women* (Eur. *Tro.* 990), and ὠδίς assimilate the two opposing realms of Aphrodite and Artemis as aspects of mature female experience. Claiming that they also have experience of pregnancy and birth (165–66), the chorus invoke Artemis in her capacity not as virgin, as Hippolytus does, but as goddess of childbirth, who brings about an easy labor for women (εὔλοχον, 166). The fact that the topics of childbirth and female sexuality are considered secret and unmentionable in the presence of men (293) reinforces the idea of the chorus and their interactions with the Nurse and Phaedra as a separate speech community.[44]

---

[42] Luschnig (1988: 6) sees in τις . . . φίλα a variation on the witness theme.

[43] Stehle 1997: 108–13.

[44] Goff (1990: 6) relates this description of a woman's physical interior to the interior of the house.

The talk of the women at their wash and their desire to verify the report brings the chorus to the palace out of concern for Phaedra, a desire expressed by the verb ἔραμαι (173), a word that further links their speech to *erōs* and one that will figure prominently in Phaedra's delirium. Their eagerness for news, twice reiterated in their exchange with the Nurse (πυθέσθαι, 270, 283), and their suggestion that the Nurse force a confession from Phaedra (ἀνάγκην, 282) again call attention to the prominent role assigned to the circulation of speech in the play. But it is the character of the Nurse, as one who mediates the space between outside and inside, who incarnates the idea of the traffic in words. Her medium is purely verbal, as she herself acknowledges: "Indeed, we are borne along by mere idle tales" (μύθοις δ' ἄλλως φερόμεσθα, 197). The servant's ability to leave the palace and transport messages between households renders her indispensable for the forging of adulterous unions, as Aristophanes comically reminds his audience (Ar. *Thesm.* 340–42). Because of their low social status and ambiguous loyalties, such figures were considered inherently untrustworthy, since they could betray secrets and transmit false information. The double loyalties of the Nurse are expressed by her facility for verbal ambiguity and rhetorical manipulation. She exhibits a bilingualism similar to that of Clytemnestra in her mixture of the verbal strategies typically wielded by persons of low status to compel compliance from superiors, like magical language and ritual supplication (325ff., 605ff.) and the sophisticated and high-flown rhetoric more characteristic of men.

PHAEDRA'S SHAMEFUL SPEECH

Because eroticized, Phaedra's speech may be metaphorically likened to the ritual *aischrologia* that characterized single-sex festivals in honor of Demeter, and perhaps celebrations such as the Adonia in honor of Aphrodite.[45] The scholion to Lucian's *Dialogue of the Courtesans* describes the content of this talk as "shameful," *aiskhra*, and "not to be spoken," *apporhēta*, because it concerned illicit sex, as we saw in Chapter 2. In the same way, the term *aiskhra* alludes to Phaedra's adulterous secret in the first half of Euripides' *Hippolytus*. She begs the Nurse not to repeat her extremely shameful tale (αἰσχίστους λόγους, 499) and later rebukes her for confessing her secret to Hippolytus, who, she believes, will "fill the whole land with the most disgraceful speeches" (αἰσχίστων λόγων, 692).[46] Indeed, Phaedra's very presence outside the house has erotic implications: the loosening

---

[45] On the idea of Phaedra's double speaking as a form of *aischrologia*, see Zeitlin 1985b: 84–86; on ritual *aischrologia* generally, and the significance of the term *aporrhēta*, see also Zeitlin 1982: 144, 146–47; and the discussion in Chapter 2.

[46] For other examples of *aiskhros*, cf. Eur. *Hipp.* 331, 404, 411–12, 500, 503, 505–6, 511.

of her veil can be interpreted as a gesture toward Eros *lusimelēs*,[47] whereas standing at the house door, as discussed in Chapters 1 and 6, also has associations with promiscuity and even prostitution.[48] Because this speech, once it breaches the discursive sphere of men, becomes transgressive both in its content and in the fact of its public disclosure, it must be confined to the house. The Nurse thus openly rebukes Phaedra for her inappropriate, public speech (212–14) and later warns Hippolytus that Phaedra's confession is utterly private and not for others' ears, even as she betrays it (κοινὸς οὐδαμῶς ὅδε, 609). And for the same reason, Theseus denounces the content of Phaedra's written tablet as unspeakable.[49]

But unlike the brazen catcalls of the crones who await their lovers at the end of Aristophanes' *Ecclesiazusae*, Phaedra's speech is riddling and enigmatic: it both discloses her erotic state and conceals it.[50] Her longing for the grassy meadow watered by dewy springs (208–11) overtly recalls Hippolytus' chaste field.[51] Instead of suggesting virginity, Phaedra's meadow evokes the site of erotic encounter familiar from lyric poetry, particularly given her repetition of ἔραμαι (219, 225, 235; cf. πόθον, 234).[52] In the same way, the erotic connotations of horses at 231 invert the image of Hippolytus' chaste equestrian pursuits.[53] The fact that Phaedra feels shame, once she has regained reason, further confirms that her fantasy has an erotic dimension: "I am ashamed at the things I have said" (αἰδούμεθα γὰρ τὰ λελεγμένα μοι, 244); and "My face turns toward shame" (καὶ ἐπ' αἰσχύνην ὄμμα τέτραπται, 246). Whereas αἰσχύνη in other Euripidean contexts suggests the disgrace incurred by a woman who ventures outside, particularly in the presence of men, and may even connote adultery,[54] the explicit application of this word to speech not only indicates a taboo subject, but also reveals a degree of ambiguity that will repeatedly characterize her language. As we saw in the prologue, this type of ambiguity is explicitly associated with the deceptions engendered by Aphrodite in her capacity as guardian of women's erotic endeavors.

---

[47] Pigeaud 1976: 8; Goff 1990: 7.

[48] Cohen 1991: 148; cf. Ar. *Eccl.* 876–1111; Lycurg. *Leoc.* 40; Theophr. *Char.* 28.3.

[49] Theseus responds to Phaedra's tablet in similar fashion, οὐδὲ ῥητόν (846) and οὐδὲ λέκτον (875), although Wilamowitz and Barrett delete the line; see Zeitlin 1985b: 85. The chorus also speak of her desire as οὐχ ὁσίων (764).

[50] On the multiple polarities inherent in Phaedra's speech, see Goff 1990: 1–10.

[51] Verbal echoes link the two speeches: cf. λειμών (211, 74, and 77); δροσερός (208 and 78).

[52] For examples from lyric poetry, see Bremer 1975; on the erotic allusions in Phaedra's delirium, see Segal 1965: 124.

[53] Segal 1965: 125; cf. Sappho. fr. 2.9 Voigt and Alcm. fr. 1.45–51; schol. Hom. *Iliad* 2.820.

[54] Cf. Eur. *Phoen.* 1276; *IA* 188; *Andr.* 877; *Tro.* 172.

The erotic and illicit aspects of women's conversation are further underscored by another important and much-discussed passage in the first episode:[55]

κεἰ μὲν νοσεῖς τι τῶν ἀπορρήτων κακῶν,
γυναῖκες αἵδε συγκαθιστάναι νόσον·
εἰ δ' ἔκφορός σοι συμφορὰ πρὸς ἄρσενας,
λέγ', ὡς ἰατροῖς πρᾶγμα μηνυθῇ τόδε.   (293–96)

And if you are sick with any of the unspeakable troubles,
these women are here to manage your sickness.
But if your illness may be carried forth to men,
tell me, so that this thing may be disclosed to doctors.

Pigeaud relates this passage to one in the Hippocratic corpus that describes women's reticence in speaking about their illnesses.[56] The word ἀπόρρητα, although ambiguous, implies a gynecological disorder, since it can be used of the female genitals in both literary and ritual contexts.[57] As discussed in Chapter 2, the term can also refer to the ritual objects, probably clay representations of genitalia, used in the Demetrian festivals, as well as to the adulterous secrets confided between women in the sex-segregated celebrations. Similarly, Hippolytus, in his refusal to pronounce the name of Aphrodite, has assimilated the idea of the forbidden and unmentionable to female sexuality.

Erōs AND RHETORIC: PHAEDRA'S GREAT SPEECH

In the speech that follows her delirium and confession (373–430), Phaedra moves from erōs to logos, from an involuntary erotic discourse with parallels in women's ritual aischrologia to a sophistic mastery of rhetoric.[58] Although it has traditionally been interpreted as an apologia, Phaedra's great speech has been viewed by recent scholars as setting forth the moral standards

[55] Both Goff (1990: 1) and Segal (1993: 89) begin their discussions of female speech in the play with this passage.
[56] Pigeaud 1976: 8–9; for detailed discussions of this passage, see Goff 1990: 1–2; and Segal 1993: 92–93.
[57] At Ar. Eccl. 12, the double entendre ἀπορρήτους μυχούς refers to women's private parts; in connection with male and female genitals, cf. Plut. Mor. 284A, and Longinus 43.5. See also Dean-Jones 1994: 34n.102, for the view that the Nurse speaks here not of a biological problem, but of the distress entailed by socially unacceptable feelings; for a similar use, cf. Eur. Or. 14.
[58] Segal (1992: 433 [= 1993: 98]) argues that women's speech in this play vacillates "between a language of ambiguous erotic signs on the one hand and a bestial language on the other."

that will ultimately require her to die and that will preserve her reputation.[59] But I argue in this section that the speech also is designed to show that for all her apparent self-control, reflected in careful rhetoric and philosophical generalizations, Phaedra has in fact lost control, and yields to adulterous impulses even as she denounces them. In this sense, the speech corroborates Hippolytus' view that women cannot be schooled in self-control because they lack it innately. The central theme of the speech is the duplicity adultery induces in married women: women who traffic in sex outside marriage give birth to brazen lies and bastard children.[60] The many linguistic and semantic puzzles in this passage further instantiate and reinforce the idea of doubleness associated with Phaedra's character throughout the play, suggesting that she simultaneously resists and yields to her adulterous impulses. At the same time, the obscurity of her thought may be intended to portray her as speaking discretely and euphemistically about sexual matters in a manner appropriate to a wellborn woman.

A good parallel for this speech is provided by Pasiphaë's *adikos logos* in Euripides' fragmentary *Cretans*, a fascinating play from the standpoint of rhetoric, probably produced some time in the mid-430s and perhaps as late as 430, a date that would explain its apparent similarities to the *Hippolytus*.[61] In a speech addressing her husband, Pasiphaë glibly justifies her own bestial adultery using familiar rhetorical techniques: she blames the gods, not herself, for her actions (Eur. *Cretans* fr. 82.9, 21 Austin); she employs the argument from probability (11); she describes her trouble as involuntary (10) and proclaims her passion a divinely inflicted sickness that brings shame (αἰσχίστῃ νόσῳ, 12; cf. 35); and, like Phaedra, she expresses a desire to die (35–36). As Rivier observes, Pasiphaë's speech has many affinities with judicial rhetoric, while her main rhetorical strategy, that of justifying corrupt and illicit behavior, has parallels in sophistic argumentation. Although Phaedra's argument is less blatantly self-serving, she defends herself in a similar manner, using legal techniques and terminology that foreshadow the forensic agon between father and son later in the play.[62]

---

[59] Craik 1993: 48. Halleran (1995: 180–81) provides a good summary of these two views: for Phaedra's speech as an *apologia*, see Dodds 1925; Winnington-Ingram 1960; Barrett 1964: 227–28; Segal 1970; for the more recent idea that she justifies her suicide in this speech, see Willink 1968; Claus 1972; Kovacs 1980c; Craik 1993. I think we can safely put to rest, as most recent scholars have, the notion that Phaedra here engages directly with Socratic polemic.

[60] As discussed in Chapter 1, Bergren (1983) argues that the Greek imagination locates women's duplicity in their reproductive power, since men can never know for certain the true paternity of their children.

[61] For the text, see Austin 1968: 55–59.

[62] On the juridical and sophistic elements of this speech, see Rivier 1958: 58–59 and 69; Reckford 1973: 319–22.

As critics have noted, this speech has the overall effect of a sophistic or forensic pleading.[63] The speech divides neatly into four sections, consisting of an introduction (373–87), a narratio (388–402), a discussion of implications (403–25), and a peroration (426–30). The speech also contains several legal terms (e.g., ξυμμαρτυρῇς, 286; μηνυθῇ, 296; ἐλέγχειν, 298), as well as technical or semitechnical legal language (e.g., ἄλλως, 375; μάρτυρας, 404; ἁλῶ, 420). This juridical language prefigures the agon between Theseus and Hippolytus, and identifies Phaedra's pleading with the process of ethical manipulation familiar from the courts.[64] Her double signification begins with a generalization about human behavior:

ἤδη ποτ' ἄλλως νυκτὸς ἐν μακρῷ χρόνῳ
θνητῶν ἐφρόντισ' ᾗ διέφθαρται βίος.　　　　　　　　(375–76)

Already at other times during night's long expanse,
I have pondered how the life of mortals is ruined.

The term νυκτός recalls Hippolytus' earlier rejection of Aphrodite's night worship, whereas darkness (σκότον, 417) appears later in the speech explicitly in connection to adultery. The ambiguity created by these words does not necessarily suggest that Phaedra here actively contemplates yielding to her impulses, but rather may foreshadow on a literary level her inevitable capitulation. Similarly, a double meaning inheres in the verb διαφθερεῖν, a word that can mean both economic ruin and moral corruption; it is also a technical term for seducing a woman, as noted in regard to Clytemnestra in Chapter 3.[65] The term later reappears together with *pharmaka*, a word with obvious erotic associations, when Phaedra states her resolve to resist her adulterous proclivities:

ταῦτ' οὖν ἐπειδὴ τυγχάνω φρονοῦσ' ἐγὼ
οὐκ ἔσθ' ὁποίῳ φαρμάκῳ διαφθερεῖν
ἔμελλον, ὥστε τοὔμπαλιν πεσεῖν φρενῶν.　　　　　(388–90)

Since this, then, is what I happen to think,
there is no drug by which I was going to weaken my resolve
and fall into the opposite frame of mind.

The phrase οὐκ φαρμάκῳ διαφθερεῖν both affirms Phaedra's resistance and discloses her weakened resolve, since she is unable to stray far from the subject that preoccupies her. Moreover, her allusion to mind-altering

---

[63] Orban 1981a: 17; Craik 1993: 57–58.

[64] For other locutions appropriate to litigation, cf. 379, 388–90, 395–97, 402, 407 and 413; see Craik 1993: 48.

[65] On the ambiguity of διέφθαρται, see Barrett 1964: 227; as a term for seduction, see Goff 1990: 49. It is also used later in the play of the alleged adultery, cf. Eur. *Hipp.* 1008; for similar usage, cf. Aesch. *Ag.* 610; Eur. *Alc.* 316; *Bacch.* 314–18; Lys. 1.16.

pharmaka prefigures the Nurse's charm of speech that will later compel her compliance.

An even more striking ambiguity, one that has been much discussed, similarly uncovers and obscures Phaedra's amatory distress, the double αἰδώς at 385 that caps the string of erotic innuendoes:

τὰ χρήστ' ἐπιστάμεσθα καὶ γιγνώσκομεν,
οὐκ ἐκπονοῦμεν δ', οἱ μὲν ἀργίας ὕπο,
οἱ δ' ἡδονὴν προθέντες ἀντὶ τοῦ καλοῦ
ἄλλην τιν'· εἰσὶ δ' ἡδοναὶ πολλαὶ βίου,
μακραί τε λέσχαι καὶ σχολή, τερπνὸν κακόν,
αἰδώς τε· δισσαὶ δ' εἰσίν, ἡ μὲν οὐ κακή,
ἡ δ' ἄχθος οἴκων.   (380–86)

We know what is right and we recognize it,
but we do not always do it, some out of laziness,
others by putting some other pleasure before the good.
There are many pleasures in life: long conversations and leisure,
a piquant evil, and desire. And there are two kinds:
one is not bad, the other is a grief for the house.

Phaedra's list of pleasures is strictly feminine, since many of its elements relate to female sexual conduct.[66] The term λέσχη, gossip, has already been associated with women in the parodos and their talk of Phaedra's troubles, and ἀργία evokes the idleness that stereotypically leads women to adultery.[67] Similarly, the terms τερπνόν and ἡδονή have strong erotic overtones.[68] More puzzling, however, has been the question of how αἰδώς fits into this list and whether δισσαί modifies it. The standard view, first proposed by Dodds, understands αἰδώς as the antecedent of δισσαί, whereas more recent scholarship has argued for ἡδοναί.[69] Because there is no indication of a subject change in these lines, I concur with the traditional interpretation that δισσαί refers back to αἰδώς. But even with that problem solved, the question remains: Exactly what does Phaedra mean by her reference to a double αἰδώς, one that is harmless and one that destroys the house (385–86)? Many difficulties are removed if we adopt Craik's

[66] Wilamowitz (1891: 203) first introduced this idea; see also Winnington-Ingram 1960: 174–75; Solmsen 1973: 420.

[67] Craik (1993: 52) also discusses λέσχη as gossip (cf. Eur. *IA* 1001) and ἀργία as leading to scandalous behavior (cf. Eur. *Andr.* 943–53; *Hipp.* 645–50).

[68] Craik (1993: 52) describes τερπνόν as "the *mot juste* for sensual and especially sexual delight"; on this term, see also Michelini 1987: 299. She further observes that ἡδονή is a common euphemism for sex; cf. Eur. *Phoen.* 21, 338; *Supp.* 453–54; and *Hipp.* 495, εὐνῆς οὕνεχ' ἡδονῆς τε σῆς.

[69] On dual *aidōs*, see Dodds 1925; Barrett ad loc; Segal 1970: 283–88; Halleran 1995: 183; cf. Plut. *Mor.* 448F; Hes. *Op.* 317–19. On δισσαί as referring to ἡδοναί, see Willink 1968: 15–17; Kovacs 1980c: 294–95; for a critique of this position, see Craik 1993: 47–48.

recent suggestion that αἰδώς represents "a euphemistic metonymy for ἔρως."[70] Craik equates αἰδώς with αἰσχυνή, a term commonly used of adultery, as we earlier saw, following the sense in which Phaedra employs it at 408.[71] By using *aidōs* in the colloquial sense to refer to sex, Phaedra's list of pleasures moves from the general to her primary preoccupation: sex, or Cypris, whom she ironically invokes in her condemnation of adulterous wives (415). As the goddess of sexuality, Aphrodite plays an indispensable role within the confines of marriage, particularly in the production of male heirs; but outside of marriage, she produces the illicit sex that destroys the oikos.[72] In any case, the allusion to *aidōs* is meant to be puzzling and enigmatic, in keeping with the ambiguous tone of the rest of the speech.[73]

Phaedra's subsequent words are equally obscure, but once again join her erotic ambiguity to sophistic rhetoric: "If what is appropriate were clear, the two kinds would not have the same letters" (εἰ δ' ὁ καιρὸς ἦν σαφὴς | οὐκ ἂν δύ' ἤστην ταῦτ' ἔχοντε γράμματα, 386–87). Phaedra continues her meditation on *aidōs* by making a further distinction: her use of καιρός again hints at adultery, since Hesiod in the *Works and Days*, ten lines after he discusses double αἰδώς, refers to adultery as παρακαίρια ῥέζων, "doing immoderate things" (Hes. *Op.* 329). Phaedra thus maintains that the appropriate context for each type of *aidōs* cannot always be determined. This assertion perhaps reflects contemporary intellectual interest in semantics and equivocation found in sophists like Prodicus, and in the anonymous sophistic treatise *Dissoi logoi*, a text attributed to Protagoras and his school.[74] There is also evidence for sophistic interest in the concept of ὁ καιρός as something that cannot be attained by knowledge, but that resides in opinion.[75] The dual signification in this passage and in the previous one demonstrates the ambiguous nature and sophistic affinities of Phaedra's speech. Moreover, her anachronistic reference to γράμματα can be viewed as another manifestation of sophistic technique, since almost all of the allusions to writing in this play appear in connection with socially marginal figures like women and slaves.

[70] Craik 1993: 56; cf. Ath. 564b, where the *aidōs* that resides in the eyes embodies the ideas of both modesty or shame and sexual attractiveness.

[71] Craik 1993: 56; see also Solmsen 1973: 423, citing Thuc. 6.13.1 and 24.4.

[72] Craik 1993: 52, and 56, where she argues that αἰδώς means " 'sex,' that sex about which αἰδώς is commonly felt."

[73] Segal (1970: 288) and Craik (1993: 52) discuss the view that Phaedra's ambiguous reference to *aidōs* reflects her confusion between appearance and reality, while Michelini (1987: 300n.99) asserts that it "is designed to be imprecise and puzzling." Goff (1990: 36) understands Phaedra's ambiguity as the product of desire, which simultaneously thwarts language and generates it.

[74] For the *Dissoi logoi*, see 90 DK and Guthrie 1971: 84–85; for its relationship to this play, see Luschnig 1988: 46, 70; Craik 1993: 56–57. A contemporary dramatization of the *Dissoi logoi* is found in the debate between the "Just" and "Unjust" Arguments in Aristophanes' *Clouds*, first produced in 423 B.C.E.

[75] This interest has been attributed to Gorgias: see Segal 1962: 128; Kerferd 1981: 82.

These individuals in fact were not likely to possess such skills; even in the fictional world of Attic drama, women are very rarely portrayed as literate. Theseus further reinforces the link between the new technology of writing and the deceptive rhetoric of the sophists in the agon.[76]

Even Phaedra's plans to escape the destructive force of *erōs*—silence, self-control, and finally suicide—are ambiguous. By concealing her sickness with silence, Phaedra has successfully thwarted gossip among her peers. She thus denounces gossip, contrasting didactic, masculine speech, which has the power to chasten other people's thoughts, with reckless feminine utterance:

γλώσσῃ γὰρ οὐδὲν πιστόν, ἣ θυραῖα μὲν
φρονήματ' ἀνδρῶν νουθετεῖν ἐπίσταται
αὐτὴ δ' ὑφ' αὑτῆς πλεῖστα κέκτηται κακά.   (395–97)

For nothing can be trusted to the tongue:
while it can advise the thoughts in the minds of other men,
left to its own devices it procures the greatest number of evils.

The term θυραῖα prefigures the men who are the object of women's adulterous passions and who are termed θυραῖοι (409) a few lines later. Her next assertion reveals more fully the preoccupation that underlies her speech: "May it be mine neither to conceal my noble deeds, nor to have many witnesses should I do something scandalous" (403–4). For Willink, these verses are tantamount to a confession that Phaedra had seriously considered committing adultery.[77] Whether true or not, the statement again creates ambiguity about her real moral position and introduces a brief *psogos gunaikon* in which Phaedra chastises women who stray from the nuptial couch:

τὸ δ' ἔργον ἤδη τὴν νόσον τε δυσκλεᾶ,
γυνή τε πρὸς τοῖσδ' οὖσ' ἐγίγνωσκον καλῶς,
μίσημα πᾶσιν. ὡς ὄλοιτο παγκάκως
ἥτις πρὸς ἄνδρας ἤρξατ' αἰσχύνειν λέχη
πρώτη θυραίους. ἐκ δὲ γενναίων δόμων
τόδ' ἦρξε θηλείαισι γίγνεσθαι κακόν.   (405–10)

I knew the act, and the sickness, brought dishonor,
and in addition, I fully recognized that I was a woman,
a hateful thing to all men. May she be utterly damned,
whoever first began to corrupt her marriage bed
with strangers. From noble houses
this evil first came to be among women.

Like much of the rest of Phaedra's speech, this passage evokes multiple and even contradictory interpretations. As a rhetorical strategy, Phaedra

---

[76] On women and literacy, see Harvey 1966; Cole 1981; Harris 1989: 106–9.

[77] Willink 1968: 20: "There could be no plainer indication that she had indeed contemplated indulgence of her passion."

uses the condemnation of adulterous women as a means of distancing herself from them, in a manner similar to Andromache's strategy in *Trojan Women*, as discussed above.[78] From a dramatic standpoint, however, the rebuke simultaneously anticipates Hippolytus' sweeping denunciation of women and reminds the spectators of the terrible sexual crimes committed by Phaedra's mother and sister, crimes that have invited reproach even from Phaedra (337–41), thereby reinforcing the theme of women's lack of sexual self-control.[79]

In this miniature *psogos*, Phaedra employs the standard elements of invective against women familiar from Hesiod and Semonides. She begins by cursing the mythical inventor of adultery in much the same way that Hippolytus will later curse the Nurse and women in general (407). Locating the origins of adultery among aristocrats, Phaedra returns to the idea of leisure introduced at 384 by explicitly identifying adultery as the product of the excessive idleness found among noble women. She acknowledges the hatred directed toward women generally, and potentially toward herself (μίσημα, 407), and then turns that hatred against an imagined group of adulterous and duplicitous women:

> μισῶ δὲ καὶ τὰς σώφρονας μὲν ἐν λόγοις
> λάθρα δὲ τόλμας οὐ καλὰς κεκτημένας.
> αἳ πῶς ποτ', ὦ δέσποινα ποντία Κύπρι,
> βλέπουσιν εἰς πρόσωπα τῶν ξυνευνετῶν
> οὐδὲ σκότον φρίσσουσι τὸν ξυνεργάτην
> τέραμνά τ' οἴκων μή ποτε φθογγὴν ἀφῆ;   (413–18)

I hate those who are chaste in words
but who secretly possess ignoble daring.
O lady of the sea Cypris, how can they look at the faces
of their husbands, and not fear that their accomplice,
darkness, or the rafters of the house, might speak?

Although Phaedra outwardly chastises adulterous wives in this passage, her rhetorical question raises the issue of her own inability to confront her husband face-to-face, a fear that will prompt her to commit suicide and leave a false letter instead. At the same time, she attributes to adulterous women the discrepancy between appearance and reality that her letter fosters at the end of the play.

The final part of Phaedra's speech returns to the issue of *eukleia* and confirms her keen awareness of the role played by the politics of reputation in the polis:

---

[78] Cf. Eur. *Tro.* 667–68; *Andr.* 269–73.

[79] Reckford (1973: 314) argues that Phaedra in this passage voices an involuntary fascination with becoming the kind of woman she denounces.

ἡμᾶς γὰρ αὐτὸ τοῦτ' ἀποκτείνει, φίλαι,
ὡς μήποτ' ἄνδρα τὸν ἐμὸν αἰσχύνασ' ἁλῶ,
μὴ παῖδας οὓς ἔτικτον· ἀλλ' ἐλεύθεροι
παρρησίᾳ θάλλοντες οἰκοῖεν πόλιν
κλεινῶν Ἀθηνῶν, μητρὸς οὕνεκ' εὐκλεεῖς.   (419–23)

This very thing is killing me, friends,
that I may never be caught shaming my husband with adultery,
nor the children whom I bore. But as free men
prospering with free speech may they dwell
in famous Athens, reputable because of their mother.

By protecting herself from rumors of adultery, Phaedra anachronistically ensures that her sons will enjoy the full rights of adult male citizens in the democratic polis.[80] As we saw in Chapter 1, Pericles' citizenship laws of 451/50 made the mother's Attic birth essential in conferring the benefits of citizenship upon her male offspring; as a result, a mother's reputation for promiscuity could facilitate charges of illegitimacy against her son in the law courts and in the procedure of *dokimasia*. By dying, Phaedra seeks to guarantee that damaging rumors about her conduct will not spill over to her sons. Her concern for her children is further evidenced by the fact that she reveals her secret only when the Nurse appeals to her maternal status and suggests that her death might result in her children's dispossession (305–6; cf. 314–15); indeed, her penultimate words reiterate her desire to secure a noble reputation for her sons (717–18). The cognates κλεινῶν and εὐκλεεῖς underscore the importance of women, particularly mothers, in shaping the reputations of men in the democratic polis, a view corroborated by the observation of Aristotle mentioned at the beginning of the chapter. But the prospect of Phaedra's death, like her speech, poses a paradox: women's silence engenders the free speech of adult citizen males, while their speech potentially jeopardizes it.

Phaedra concludes her rhesis with a highly ambiguous simile that unites many of the earlier strands of her speech—*erōs*, appearance, and deception:

κακοὺς δὲ θνητῶν ἐξέφην' ὅταν τύχῃ,
προθεὶς κάτοπτρον ὥστε παρθένῳ νέᾳ,
χρόνος· παρ' οἶσι μήποτ' ὀφθείην ἐγώ.   (428–30)

But time reveals the base among mortals whenever it happens to,
placing before them a mirror as before a young girl.
May I never be seen among them!

Although the meaning of this passage has been much debated, at the very least the mirror symbolizes Phaedra's concern for reputation and

---

[80] Segal (1988b: 275) argues that Phaedra's regard for *parrhēsia* represents a masculine concern and reflects her vacillation between male and female poles in this passage; for a different view, see Goff 1990: 7.

appearance; indeed, the chorus treat it as such by relating it to noble *doxa* (431–32).[81] The verb ὀφθείην in the last line recalls her earlier wish not to appear base in the eyes of her husband and her desire to appear to conform to conventional precepts of female behavior (cf. ὀφθείην, 321). As an object essential to feminine *kosmēsis*, mirrors are intimately associated with female life; they frequently occur on red figure vases depicting scenes of the women's quarters. The importance of mirrors for women prompted Artemidorus to assert that in dreams, mirrors symbolize women.[82] Elsewhere in Euripides, the mirror, as the site of feminine vanity, connotes promiscuity; in this regard, it is significant that the image follows upon the heels of Phaedra's own denunciation of adulterous wives.[83] Finally, the girl gazing in Phaedra's mirror prefigures the *parthenoi* at the end of the play whose song warns against the destructive consequences of adulterous passion: as a cautionary tale for women, their ritual song contains and checks the private conversations of married women.

The high degree of rhetorical proficiency and semantic ambiguity present in Phaedra's rhesis precludes a single, monolithic interpretation, instead facilitating multiple and even contradictory readings. Speaking with almost Gorgian equivocation about matters exclusively feminine, Phaedra both discloses and conceals the true cause of her sickness. By overlaying a sophistic veneer, however, the poet evokes an atmosphere of erudition and rationalization that prefigures Hippolytus' subsequent critique of excessively clever women. At the same time, Phaedra's use of innuendo and euphemism are deliberately evasive, connoting a degree of politeness and discretion appropriate to an aristocratic woman and forming a strong contrast to the crass and direct speech of the Nurse.

THE NURSE'S CHARM OF SPEECH

The low social status of the Nurse potentially equips her with comic traits, evidenced by her almost parodic reaction to Phaedra's confession, while her subversive rhetoric associates her with the sophists.[84] Affiliated with

---

[81] Zeitlin 1985b: 100; Luschnig 1988: 26.

[82] White 1975: 185, in the introduction to Book 4; cf. Artem. 2.7, 3.30, 5.67; on the legitimacy of offspring, 2.7.

[83] A relevant passage in Euripides' *Electra* identifies looking into a mirror inside the house with being promiscuously conspicuous outside the house; hence the mirror at which Clytemnestra primped after her husband left for Troy is synonymous with her subsequent adultery and deception (Eur. *El.* 1069–75). A curious passage in Aristotle states that a mirror will cloud if a menstruating woman looks into it; cf. Arist. *De insomniis* 459b24–460a23; Dean-Jones 1994: 229. On adultery and the mirror, see Goff 1990: 23.

[84] Michelini 1987: 312; on her lower-class status, see Turato 1976; Knox (1979: 218) calls her "democratic"; cf. Thuc. 2.41. Knox (1979: 210) also refers to her rhesis as a "masterpiece of sophistic rhetoric."

clever speech by the term *sophos* and its cognates (436, 518, 700; cf. ὦ δεινὰ λέξασα, 498), the Nurse employs sophistic terms, like βελτίω λόγον (292); arguments, like those of advantage and nature (442, 471–72); and techniques, such as antithesis, evident in her contrast between words and deeds (490–91, 500–502).[85] The fact that she is given anapaests, not lyric speech, further corroborates her low social status.[86] At the same time, the tragic poet assigns to this servile character one of the largest speaking parts in the play, a phenomenon without parallel in the rest of extant tragedy.[87]

In his portrayal of the Nurse, Euripides draws on a traditional tragic plot pattern, in which two characters in need of the guidance of a kurios, or male guardian, are left to their own devices, a plot device that emanates from "a social anxiety about the lethal effect of manipulative slaves on susceptible women lacking the judgment of a free male to steer their own."[88] This combination of marginal social status, doubly so as a woman and a servant, and sophistic outlook has affinities both with the women of Attic Old Comedy, whose seductive and crafty words threaten to undermine the social order, as discussed in Chapter 6, and with the demagogues of low birth and their ascent to power in the post-Periclean age.

As an agent of Aphrodite, the Nurse also deploys rhetorical proficiency in the service of *erōs:* her task is to persuade Phaedra to do something against her will, even though she has earlier described her mistress as recalcitrant (304–5) and immune to persuasion, "For neither then was she softened by means of words nor is she now persuaded" (οὔτε γὰρ τότε |λόγοις ἐτέγγεθ' ἥδε νῦν τ' οὐ πείθεται, 302–3). This stock scene, not unlike Clytemnestra's persuading of Agamemnon in Aeschylus' play, requires a degree of compulsion above and beyond that of ordinary persuasion as well as the complicity of her interlocutor. Thus it is not surprising that we find a central component of this scene to be the Nurse's recourse to magic, and indeed, her conflation of rhetoric and magic. By using the charm of speech, as Clytemnestra also does, the Nurse gradually erodes Phaedra's stalwart resolve with her final πιθοῦ at 508.

Like most sophists, the Nurse is a moral relativist: she, for whom second thoughts are wiser (αἱ δεύτεραί πως φροντίδες σοφώτεραι, 436), changes her mind three times within the course of the drama.[89] In her response to Phaedra's rhesis, the Nurse asserts that nothing falls outside the compass of rational speech (437), while her repeated juxtaposition of *logos* and *erōs*

---

[85] Meltzer 1996: 180.
[86] Maas 1962: 53; Hall 1999.
[87] Hall 1997: 117.
[88] Ibid.: 116.
[89] Knox 1979: 218.

assimilates erotic concerns to sophistic rhetoric.[90] No one can withstand the vagaries of Aphrodite, she argues, because the goddess is omnipotent (443): in contrast to Artemis, who is confined to a remote and sterile meadow, Aphrodite is everywhere and in everything (447–48). Unlike the ascetic gardener who irrigates Artemis' realm, Aphrodite sows (σπείϱουσα, 449) and propagates (ἔϰγονοι, 450). Her brief homage, which answers Hippolytus' chaste prayer, identifies her persuasive power with the seductions of the goddess. The acknowledgment of Aphrodite's power to compel individuals to act against their wills introduces a specious argument, found in Gorgias and elsewhere in Euripides, in which the responsibility for human actions is sloughed off onto a deity or abstraction, typically Aphrodite.[91] This praise of Cypris conjoins sophistic rhetoric and erotic subject matter in a manner reminiscent of Phaedra and in stark contrast to that of Hippolytus, whose pious prayer and unambiguous speech exalted Artemis, a goddess remote from the arts of civilization.

After her tribute, the Nurse uses another well-known sophistic argument: she adduces mythic examples of divine behavior as a means of rationalizing human sexual license.[92] And it is no coincidence that in doing so she alludes to the new technology of writing, a skill incommensurate with her social status, as we saw earlier in connection with Phaedra.

ὅσοι μὲν οὖν γϱαφάς τε τῶν παλαιτέϱων
ἔχουσιν αὐτοί τ' εἰσὶν ἐν μούσαις ἀεὶ
ἴσασι μὲν Ζεὺς ὥς ποτ' ἠϱάσθη γάμων
Σεμέλης, ἴσασι δ' ὡς ἀνήϱπασέν ποτε
ἡ ϰαλλιφεγγὴς Κέφαλον εἰς θεοὺς Ἕως
ἔϱωτος οὕνεϰ'.   (451–56)

Whoever possess the writings of the ancient poets
and are always among the Muses,
know how Zeus once desired a union with Semele,
and they know how once lovely-shining Eos
abducted Cephalus into the company of gods
because of *erōs*.

The fact that the term γϱαφαί may allude either to writing or to vase paintings indicates how closely associated writing was with the visual mode in the Greek mind.[93] Significantly, the word later has a purely visual

---

[90] For *erōs* and its cognates, cf. Eur. *Hipp.* 439, 440, 441, 453, 456, 476; Κύπϱις, cf. 443, 448, 465; for λόγος, cf. 288, 292, 298, 299, 303 (and earlier, 332, 336, 342, 345, 353, and passim).

[91] Gorg. *Hel.* 6 (= 82 11.6 DK); Eur. *Med.* 527–31; *Tro.* 946–51; *Cretans* fr. 82 Austin.

[92] Knox 1979: 219–20; Turato 1976: 159–60; Michelini 1987: 312.

[93] Both Barrett (1964: 241–42) and Halleran (1995: 188–89) take γϱαφαί to refer to writings; for the view that it refers to paintings, see Easterling 1985: 6n.25.

meaning for Hippolytus, who uses it to refer to sexually explicit pictures (1005). Clearly an exponent of *nomoi*, a term she uses of these mythic misdeeds (461), the Nurse downplays the problem of ill repute entailed by sexual indiscretion: sensible people turn a blind eye on an illicit affair (462–63), while even fathers abet their sons in procuring sex (465), a role the Nurse assumes in the next scene. The power of persuasion to blur ethical distinctions and justify illicit behavior is again seen in the Nurse's principle of concealing misdeeds: "For this is held among the wise principles of mortals: that which is not good goes unnoticed" (λανθάνειν τὰ μὴ καλά, 466). The undercurrent of self-justification found in Phaedra's achieves its fullest expression in the words of the Nurse; she dispenses with semantic hair-splitting and hinting ambiguities and instead conveys her arguments quite bluntly.

After exhorting Phaedra to endure, and presumably not eliminate, her passion (τόλμα δ' ἐρῶσα, 476), the Nurse then turns, as a final resort, to erotic magic:

εἰσὶν δ' ἐπῳδαὶ καὶ λόγοι θελκτήριοι·
φανήσεταί τι τῆσδε φάρμακον νόσου.
ἦ τἄρ' ἂν ὀψέ γ' ἄνδρες ἐξεύροιεν ἂν
εἰ μὴ γυναῖκες μηχανὰς εὑρήσομεν.   (478–81)

There are incantations and magical words.
Some drug for this sickness will appear.
It would take men a long time to discover contrivances
if we women did not discover them.

The reference to ἐπῳδαί and λόγοι θελκτήριοι indicates a purely verbal magical operation consonant with the Nurse's unswerving faith in the power of persuasive words, whereas *pharmakon* is the *mot juste* for the salves or potion used in erotic magic (cf. 516). Faraone identifies love magic for gaining or restoring affection as typically feminine, a type that normally involves *pharmaka*.[94] Medea's use of *pharmaka* in Euripides' play can be viewed as a perverted form of feminine love magic because she intends by means of it not to regain her husband's affections, but to destroy her rival. The fact that these potions were often used not only by women to attract men, but also by persons of low social status, such as male slaves,

---

[94] Faraone (1992b and 1994) distinguishes between two types of erotic magical operation in antiquity, those targeted at women and those aimed at attracting men; see the note on Clytemnestra's magical language in Chapter 3. In a later work, Plutarch advises brides against using such *pharmaka* to sustain their husband's affections on the grounds that they may emasculate and enervate them; cf. Plut. *Mor.* 139A. Antiphon speaks of a mistress advised to use *pharmaka* to regain her lover's affections; Antiph. 1.14, 1.19. Cf. Soph. *Trach.* 584–85; Arist. *Mag. mor.* 1188b30–38.

who may have wished to secure the affections of their masters, further sheds light on this part of the speech: the Nurse's words serve as a kind of rhetorical charm that seduces Phaedra.[95] As we saw in the *Agamemnon*, persuasive speech and magical incantation are similarly conflated: as a means of reinforcing her verbal victory over Agamemnon, Clytemnestra completes her act with language modeled on a magical incantation after he treads the fatal tapestries. The Nurse's reference to *pharmaka* marks a change in her relation to Phaedra: her increasingly imprecise and allusive language, all in relation to *pharmaka*, reveals that she is now actively deceiving her. Her allusion to φάρμακον νόσου is therefore suitably vague: it may signal her intention to cure the disease either by procuring Hippolytus or by eliminating Phaedra's desire for him.

The link between magic and rhetoric forged by this speech also reflects contemporary sophistic thought: as Turato has shown, the Nurse's speech shares many affinities with Gorgias' *Helen*, a speech in defense of another famous adulteress.[96] Gorgias attributes a palliative effect to persuasive speech that both induces pleasure and alleviates pain, casting a spell over the listener and compelling him to act against his better judgment (*Gorg. Hel.* 10–13). There is also an element of complicity in that the one persuaded must serve as "an accomplice to the act of persuasion."[97] In the same way, the Nurse gradually erodes Phaedra's resolve by giving voice to her suppressed desires: she says the name that Phaedra cannot utter and specifies the deed she cannot mention. The Nurse's final reference to magic, therefore, fully assimilates persuasion to erotic magic and its power to seduce and coerce.[98]

Utilizing the charm of speech, the Nurse gradually erodes the moral standard to which Phaedra clings by appealing to her baser instincts. In language evocative of later criticism of the sophists, Phaedra denounces the Nurse's "too fair words" as destructive of the well-governed cities and houses of men (οἱ καλοὶ λίαν λόγοι, 487). By appealing to pleasure rather than to reason in Gorgian fashion (note the use of τερπνά, 488), the Nurse rejects the aristocratic concern for reputation, substituting a callous pragmatism characteristic of the lower classes. She crassly chastises Phaedra for her "lofty talk," σεμνομυθεῖν (490; cf. Eur. *Andr.* 234) and strips away her euphemisms with her blunt retort: "You do not require fine words, but the man" (490–91). Dismissing her mistress's

---

[95] Goff 1990: 49.

[96] Turato 1976: 166–67.

[97] Segal 1962: 122.

[98] As Segal remarks, "The little scene between Phaedra and the Nurse might even be viewed, perhaps, as a displaced version of Gorgias' theories of language itself as a quasi-incantatory magic that charms its hearer by a kind of hypnotic spell." Segal 1992: 454n.56. For a similar idea, see Goff 1990: 48–49.

pretenses of chastity and self-control, the Nurse metaphorically assumes
the role of procuress:

σώφρων δ' οὖσ' ἐτύγχανες γυνή,
οὐκ ἄν ποτ' εὐνῆς οὕνεχ' ἡδονῆς τε σῆς
προῆγον ἄν σε δεῦρο.   (494–96)

If you were in fact a chaste woman,
I never would have led you to this point
for the sake of your sexual pleasure.

The term ἡδονή recalls the ambiguous pleasures of Phaedra, whose true
meaning the Nurse now clearly reveals by conjoining it with εὐνή. Similarly,
the verb προῆγον suggests procuring, since the cognate προαγωγός may
be used of pandering (cf. Ar. *Thesm.* 341). This blunt speech draws reproach
from Phaedra, who exhorts the Nurse to stop her coarse and shameful
talk (αἰσχίστους λόγους, 499). Just as the Nurse mediates discourses by
drawing forth Phaedra's inner secrets and by inverting the normative
categories of αἰσχρά and καλά (εὖ λέγεις γὰρ αἰσχρὰ δέ, 503; and ταἰσχρὰ
δ' ἢν λέγῃς καλῶς, 505), so, too, she will confound social and spatial
boundaries by confronting Hippolytus within the house. Phaedra's acknowledgment that she will be consumed by that which she flees (εἰς τοῦθ'
ὃ φεύγω νῦν ἀναλωθήσομαι, 506) reveals her vulnerability to this specious
rhetoric and signals the Nurse's victory in this contest of words, finally
conceded with πιθοῦ at 508.

Like her suggestion of magic at the end of the rhesis, the Nurse's final
words concern *pharmaka* and are similarly riddled with equivocation. For
example, the phrase δευτέρα γὰρ ἡ χάρις (508) raises the question of
whether the Nurse means that the favor of compliance is the next best
thing to satisfying Phaedra's passion, a reading that assumes χάρις contains
erotic overtones, or to not being in love at all.[99] She again broaches the
subject of magic with φίλτρα (509), a term that may denote a love charm
or simply a charm (cf. Aesch. *Cho.* 1029) whereas the phrase θελκτήρια
ἔρωτος may mean either something that induces love or something that
eliminates it. Similarly, the expression οὔτ' ἐπ' αἰσχροῖς (511) can be taken
to mean either that this magic will not involve adultery or that it will not
create scandal. The Nurse's allusion to νόσου τῆσδε (512) is also quite
vague, since it can suggest either Phaedra's illness or her love, whereas ἢν
σὺ μὴ γένῃ κακή in the same line may denote either the courage needed
to drink the potion or the resolve required to consecrate her love. A final
ambiguity relates directly to the Nurse's proposal of magic: she states that
she will join together one delight from two (συνάψαι τ' ἐκ δυοῖν μίαν

---

[99] On the ambiguities of this speech, see Barrett 1964: 253–54; and Halleran 1995: 193.

χάριν, 515); but the phrase can signify either the joining of two lovers or, more prosaically, the joining of the *philtra* and *semeion*. But χάρις, as we saw earlier, probably has an erotic sense, particularly in conjunction with συνάπτω, a word that suggests sexual union.[100] The excessive ambiguity in this speech shows that the Nurse is actively deceiving Phaedra, in a manner not unlike that of Clytemnestra: she also invokes a deity, Aphrodite, to aid her in accomplishing her task (συνεργὸς εἴης, 523), just as the Argive queen summoned Zeus at the end of the carpet scene. The Nurse thus seduces Phaedra by means of her "principle of evasion and discreet wrong-doing," a principle that comes to direct Phaedra's actions as well, and one that her increasingly equivocal language reflects.[101]

After the first stasimon, in which the chorus invoke Eros and recount his destructive effects in the unions of Semele and Dionysus and Iole and Heracles, the scene of eavesdropping that follows returns to the problem of rumor introduced in the parodos. The term φάτις (579) recalls the chorus' initial entrance and their reliance upon vague reports circulated among women. By calling attention to the fact that the chorus cannot move to the stage door (577), the poet exploits theatrical convention to convey their incomplete access to the conversation unfolding within the house and their dependence upon Phaedra for relaying it. Phaedra's subsequent characterization of the Nurse as a προμνήστρια, "matchmaker of evils" (589), simultaneously underscores her role as a mediatrix of speech and as a broker of sexual liaisons (cf. Ar. *Nub.* 41). This brief scene juxtaposes the circulation of rumor among women and its erotic themes with Hippolytus' unilateral denunciation of women, which Phaedra, who does not exit, also overhears.[102]

---

[100] Although few scholars, including Barrett, have objected to Reiske's emendation of πλόκον for λόγον, the word found in most of the manuscripts, on the grounds that one would expect a physical object to complete this act of material magic, it is tempting to resurrect Fitton's (1967) suggestion (most recently discussed in Segal 1993: 255n.19) that the original word be retained because of the Nurse's repeated emphasis on *logos*, verbal magic, and her assimilation of *erōs* to speech. Indeed, the subsequent scene confirms that she intends to bring about Hippolytus' compliance by means of persuasion. Nonetheless, I follow Barrett (1964: 255) in adopting Reiske's πλόκον as the more plausible of the two alternatives.

[101] Segal 1970: 291. Reckford (1973: 317 and n. 12) argues that Phaedra's "very language changes, becoming tricky and equivocal like that of the Nurse earlier." He mentions her allusions to an "unjust act" (675–77), her "new words" (688), her move to deceit (709), the "ill deeds" (714), the "one life" (719–22), and the chorus' oath of silence (722ff.).

[102] I follow the majority of scholars, especially Barrett (1964: 272), Reckford (1973: 316–17n.11), and Halleran (1995: 200–201), in maintaining that Phaedra remains onstage during Hippolytus' speech and that she sings the dochmiacs that follow his outburst at 669–79. For the view that Phaedra does not overhear Hippolytus' speech, see Smith 1960; Østerud 1970; and Kovacs 1987: 54–60.

Hippolytus' Invective against Women

By leaving the house, Hippolytus carries Phaedra's tale to the outside world, thereby exposing the private and shameful speech of women. Into ears suited only for a goddess's speech (εἰσήκουσα, 602; ἀκούσας, 604; εἰς ὦτα κλύζων, 654), the Nurse now pours the shameful words of Phaedra's desire. In turn, Hippolytus rejects this speech as ritually impure, ἄρρητον (602), as something that requires cleansing with water as unsullied as that of Artemis' meadow (653). To the Nurse's suggestion that such a speech should remain private (ὁ μῦθος, ὦ παῖ, κοινὸς οὐδαμῶς ὅδε, 609), he replies, "Fair things become fairer when spoken in public" (τά τοι κάλ' ἐν πολλοῖσι κάλλιον λέγειν, 610). While earlier τὰ καλά had signified the apparent good in the exchange between Phaedra and the Nurse, Hippolytus here insists on an absolute, collective, and masculine standard of public discourse that will disclose rather than obscure the truth. Through his invective, he replaces the *aiskhra* disseminated by women in the first part of the play with a discourse that denounces them.

Hippolytus' invective against women and marriage at 616–68 represents the type of slander, *kakōs legein*, comically criticized by the female celebrants of the Thesmophoria in Aristophanes' *Thesmophoriazusae*; this discourse shows men to be in control of speech in the theater if not in their own houses. This invective has affinities with similar discourses in Hesiod, Semonides, and, much later, authors like Athenaeus and Stobaeus, who collects examples in a chapter entitled *Psogos gunaikon*.[103] By the end of the fifth century, the invective against women was apparently recognized as a self-contained genre, for Aristophanes has the female chorus in his *Thesmophoriazusae* playfully mock the Hesiodic idea of woman as a curse by their ironic repetition of the word *kakon*, "evil thing" (Ar. *Thesm.* 786–99). Though critics have observed a generic similarity between Hippolytus' speech and the earlier texts, the extent of the debt has not been fully recognized.

Hippolytus' speech contains many elements characteristic of the traditional invective against women: his opening metaphor of coinage, κίβδηλος, "counterfeit" (616), implicitly compares the circulation of women to currency and suggests an equivalency between women and artifice.[104] This equation is central to the two stories of Pandora's creation, as discussed earlier: she is a semblance, consisting of pure appearance (cf. ἴκελον, Hes. *Theog.* 572, *Op.* 71; καλὸν εἶδος, *Op.* 63). Yet the term has a self-referential

---

[103] Nancy 1984: 113–15 and passim; Zeitlin 1985b: 71; Goff 1990: 11.

[104] Rabinowitz 1987; Goff 1990: 45–46. In her discussion of Theognis 117–24, Kurke (1995: 48 and n. 27) argues that the term κίβδηλος conveys not merely "the indistinguishable mixing of good and bad qualities," but "a thoroughly base interior (heart or soul) concealed beneath an apparently noble surface."

dimension in that Hippolytus, as a bastard, may also be considered in some sense spurious (cf. 310, 962, 1083). For just as women's promiscuity breeds falsehood, so illicit passion produces misbegotten children. In his fantasy of purchasing children from temples, Hippolytus not only eliminates the need for women as reproductive agents, the only ameliorative function allotted to them in the Hesiodic vision, he also eliminates the problem of illegitimacy (Hes. *Theog.* 603–12). His emphasis on sowing (σπεῖραι, 618; cf. 628) contains a further irony, since earlier the Nurse had used the term of Aphrodite and her generative power (618; cf. 449); for Hippolytus, however, the word refers not to female fertility, but to paternity. Whereas for Phaedra, the sign of freedom for her sons was free speech, *parrhēsia* (421), for Hippolytus men may only be free when they reside apart from women (624) and their speech.

Chronicling the troubles brought about by marriage, Hippolytus begins with a Hesiodic allusion to women as a *kakon mega*, "great evil," a motif that recurs several times in the course of his speech (627; cf. 616, 629, 632, 649, 651, 666).[105] Continuing with the economic metaphor, he characterizes women as a drain on domestic resources, an idea that also originates in Hesiod (cf. Hes. *Theog.* 598–99):

τούτῳ δὲ δῆλον ὡς γυνὴ κακὸν μέγα·
προσθεὶς γὰρ ὁ σπείρας τε καὶ θρέψας πατὴρ
φερνὰς ἀπῴκισ', ὡς ἀπαλλαχθῇ κακοῦ.
ὁ δ' αὖ λαβὼν ἀτηρὸν εἰς δόμους φυτὸν
γέγηθε κόσμον προστιθεὶς ἀγάλματι
καλὸν κακίστῳ καὶ πέπλοισιν ἐκπονεῖ
δύστηνος, ὄλβον δωμάτων ὑπεξελών.   (627–33)

And from this it is clear that a woman is a great evil:
Her father, having begotten and reared her, sends her out of the house
with a dowry, so that he can be rid of the evil.
And the husband takes the ruinous creature into his house
and delights in adding a beautiful ornament to this most evil statue,
and the poor wretch expends the wealth of the house
in attempting to outfit her in clothes.

Hippolytus' allusion to female *kosmēsis* recalls the nuptial adorning of Pandora and the deceptions it engenders; at the same time, it evokes Phaedra's mirror and the erotics of sight thought to lead to adultery (κόσμον, 631; cf. Hes. *Theog.* 587; *Op.* 72, 76). His use of the oxymoron καλὸν κακίστῳ (632) suggests Hesiod's famous formulation of Pandora as a *kalon kakon*, "beautiful evil" (Hes. *Theog.* 585), while the

---

[105] Hesiod uses the term κακόν six times in the two accounts of Pandora's creation (cf. Hes. *Theog.* 570, 585, 600; *Op.* 57, 58, 88).

superlative evokes his condemnation of Aphrodite as κακίστη δαιμόνων in the prologue.

Next Hippolytus denounces the clever woman, σοφή (640), a word that Phaedra earlier used to describe the Nurse (518) as duplicitous and promiscuous: "For Aphrodite is more likely to engender mischief in clever women" (τὸ γὰρ κακοῦργον μᾶλλον ἐντίκτει Κύπρις | ἐν ταῖς σοφαῖσιν, 642–43). In contrast, the "nobody" or simpleton lacks the intellectual resources to betray her husband (644). Hippolytus' emphatic hatred, denoted by the phrase σοφὴν δὲ μισῶ (640), also recalls Phaedra's own miniature invective against adulterous women (413). Since clever women, like Pandora, possess the art of seductive and persuasive speech (Hes. *Theog.* 582; *Op.* 67, 78–79), Hippolytus imagines a separate community of women, in which there is no speech, only mute animals. Condemned to silent companionship, women are prevented from carrying out their wicked plans:[106]

χρῆν δ' εἰς γυναῖκα πρόσπολον μὲν οὐ περᾶν
ἄφθογγα δ' αὐταῖς συγκατοικίζειν δάκη
θηρῶν, ἵν' εἶχον μήτε προσφωνεῖν τινα
μήτ' ἐξ ἐκείνων φθέγμα δέξασθαι πάλιν.
νῦν δ' † αἱ μὲν ἔνδον δρῶσιν αἱ κακαὶ † κακὰ
βουλεύματ', ἔξω δ' ἐκφέρουσι πρόσπολοι.   (645–50)

A servant should not approach a woman,
rather, they should dwell together with voiceless beasts,
that they might not converse with anyone,
and from these hear another voice in answer.
As it is, base women within the house accomplish their base schemes,
while their servants carry them outside.

The play itself demonstrates the irony behind Hippolytus' words: far from being like brutes, women are figured as extremely capable of subtle verbal machinations. At the same time, Hippolytus explicitly identifies their speech as concerned exclusively with *erōs*; by depriving them of discourse, he wishes to put an end to the deceptions that promulgate adultery. The idea of traffic or movement conveyed by the verbs περᾶν and ἐκφέρουσι alludes to the Nurse's liminal status as one who transgresses social and spatial boundaries, eluding masculine surveillance. Just as she has inverted linguistic categories in her earlier exchange with Phaedra, the Nurse's spatial mobility and flexibility align her with a principle of social subversion.

In the final part of his speech, Hippolytus expresses his contempt for women in the strongest terms; first he curses them, just as Phaedra had

---

[106] On the idea of a separate community of women, a *genos gunaikōn*, its origin in Pandora, and the problem of integrating women into the polis, see Loraux 1993: 72–110.

earlier cursed adulteresses (507), and then he states his intention never to
stop slandering them:

ὄλοισθε. μισῶν δ' οὔποτ' ἐμπλησθήσομαι
γυναῖκας, οὐδ' εἴ φησί τις μ' ἀεὶ λέγειν·
ἀεὶ γὰρ οὖν πώς εἰσι κἀκεῖναι κακαί.
ἢ νυν τις αὐτὰς σωφρονεῖν διδαξάτω,
ἢ κἄμ' ἐάτω ταῖσδ' ἐπεμβαίνειν ἀεί.   (664–68)

May you perish. Not ever will I have my fill of hating women,
not even if someone says that I never stop talking about it.
For truly they, too, will always be somehow base.
Either let someone teach them to be chaste,
or let me always trample on them.

Hippolytus construes his hatred of women not as a physical action, as the
final verb, ἐπεμβαίνειν, might suggest, but as a speech act, a form of slander
that reenacts his original crime against Aphrodite (οὐδ' εἴ φησί τις μ' ἀεὶ
λέγειν, 665). Depriving women of discourse, he substitutes the public
genre of invective for their erotic speech in a move similar to that of
Artemis, who transforms Phaedra's story into a didactic song for virgins.
His triple repetition of ἀεί emphasizes a fixed and unchanging standard
of blame that contrasts with the Nurse's more flexible system of values.
The final thought, that women must be taught *sōphrosunē* (667–68), implies that they do not possess this virtue by nature but must be taught it
by men, or, even more pessimistically, that they cannot be taught it at all.[107]

Hippolytus' invective against women provokes a new kind of speech
from Phaedra; persuaded by the Nurse, she fabricates a story in an attempt
to stave off infamy.[108] After twice cursing the Nurse for making her appear
base and depriving her of a noble death (684, 693), Phaedra vows to find
a new discourse that will supplant both the imagined words of Hippolytus
to his father (690–92) and those just overheard: "No longer will I die
with fair repute, but instead I have need of new words" (καινῶν λόγων,
688). Phaedra terms her new discourse an εὕρημα, "trick," a word that
echoes the Nurse's earlier commonplace about the resourcefulness of
women: "I have a remedy for this misfortune that will engender a reputable
life for my children" (716–17). Through her written stratagem, Phaedra
transcends the treachery of the Nurse by exhibiting an even greater facility
for betrayal. Her ironic concession, "Now I will arrange my affairs
beautifully" (ἐγὼ δὲ τἀμὰ θήσομαι καλῶς, 709), indicates how fully she
has come to confuse *aiskhra* with *kala*, for her use of the latter now signifies

---

[107] On *sōphrosunē* and its relation to *phusis*, see Berns 1973: 178 and 183.

[108] Reckford (1973: 317) argues that Phaedra's speech becomes increasingly "tricky and
equivocal" after Hippolytus' invective, citing the following passages as evidence: 675–77,
688, 709, 714, 719–21, 722ff.

a spurious rather than a genuine good, as it did previously for the Nurse. With her death, Phaedra confirms the "truth' of Hippolytus' invective, that women are indeed a curse set on earth to plague men; as she herself says, "In death I will become a curse, *kakon*, to the other" (728–29).

THE AGON AND JUDICIAL DISCOURSE

In the first part of the play, Euripides' *Hippolytus* establishes rumor and persuasive speech as feminine tools for manipulating appearance; the poet shows us Aphrodite's role in manufacturing falsehood and the mediating function of the Nurse, whose cunning rhetoric forces Phaedra's own equivocation. In the agon, however, Euripides explores how the *muthoi* manufactured within the household unsettle the discourses of men.[109] The circulation of speech among women produces the final falsehood, Phaedra's slanderous letter convicting Hippolytus of rape. Indeed, the formal structure of the play reinforces this dynamic by depicting women and men as operating in two distinct discursive spheres mediated only by the Nurse, who breaches and blurs these gendered verbal boundaries.

The scene between Hippolytus and Theseus takes the form of a forensic agon, a formal structure that reflects one aspect of the dialectical relation between the theater and the courts. The literary development of the agon, a standard feature of post-Aeschylean drama, coincides with important changes in Athenian legal administration, including jury pay and a growth in litigation brought about by the expanding city.[110] Increasingly detached from its dramatic context by the end of the fifth century, the Euripidean agon frequently showcases contemporary issues in the form of a sophistic debate in which two people defend opposite points of view.[111] The agon in the *Hippolytus* seems to reflect a trend in Euripidean drama toward increasingly legalistic agones: "Euripides seems to have responded to rhetorical influences with particular immediacy in the 420s, and the whole question of rhetorical expertise is itself a prominent subject in the plays of this period."[112]

The agon at 902–1101 is structured like a trial in which Theseus serves as both a jury and a judge who must weigh conflicting accounts, one written and one oral.[113] He pronounces Phaedra's body and written text

---

[109] Segal (1988b: 270–71; 1993: 103) argues that in addition to her false writing, the presence of Phaedra's body, as the site of women's forbidden eroticism, subverts the public and forensic discourse of men. For Zeitlin (1985b: 93), Phaedra's corpse is literally a "speaking sign," an ambiguous and dangerous erotic cipher.

[110] Garner 1987: 96.

[111] Conacher 1981: 22.

[112] Lloyd 1992: 130–31.

[113] Garner 1987: 102; Segal 1992: 426; Meltzer 1996: 175.

as the most reliable witness (μάρτυρος σαφεστάτου, 972) while rejecting the oral testimony of Hippolytus, who serves as his own witness (μάρτυς, 1022). Indeed, the theme of witnesses and witnessing, expressed by the term μάρτυς and its cognates, recurs several times throughout the play.[114] In the courts, witness testimony served as a privileged source of evidentiary material, along with oaths, laws, and oracles, what Aristotle describes as belonging to the category of inartificial or *atechnos* proof (Arist. *Rhet.* 1.2.2–11, 1.2.14–18).[115] But Euripides departs from judicial and social reality in two important ways. First, he portrays the witness as a woman, thus inserting her words into a context from which women were normally debarred. Second, Phaedra's account assumes a written, rather than oral, form, in contrast with normal judicial procedure, wherein witnesses spoke their testimony themselves, at least until the first quarter of the fourth century. In his innovative use of the tablet, Euripides joins the archaic topos of women's duplicity to contemporary fifth-century concerns about the potential of persuasive speech to mislead and about the new technology of writing.

The idea of a trial is further supported by the many legal terms that appear in this scene, including ἐξελέγχω, ἁλίσκομαι, μάρτυς, and μηνύω; in fact, more forensic terminology is contained in this scene than in any other play.[116] This legal language continues a pattern established earlier in the speeches of Phaedra and the Nurse.[117] Finally, the scene concludes with a legal action: Hippolytus absolves Theseus of the legal consequences of his crime, as any victim could under Attic homicide law.[118] This gesture returns in ring form to the prologue, where Aphrodite explains how Theseus had been earlier banished from Athens for a justifiable and voluntary homicide (34–37).[119]

The dynamics of this legal drama hinge upon the characterization of Theseus as a man keenly susceptible to false appearances. His mythical association with Athens and popular presence in Attic drama identifies him

---

[114] Eur. *Hipp.* 404, 972, 977, 1022, 1075, 1076, 1451.

[115] On the relation between the rhetorical proofs found in court speeches and those found in drama, see Eden 1986: 10–15. Gagarin (1990: 24–25) defines inartificial proof as the "evidentiary material" out of which the orator constructs his arguments.

[116] For legal language in general, see Segal 1992: 426; Meltzer (1996: 175–76n.9) discusses the relevant legal referents. Important legal words are as follows: ἐξελέγχω and cognates (930, 944, 1056, 1310, 1322, 1337); μάρτυς (922); ἁλίσκομαι (959); τεκμήριον (925); ὅρκοι (960); αἰτίαν φυγεῖν (961); cf. αἴτιοι (933); μηνύω and cognates (1051, 1077); ἄκριτον (1056); κατηγορέω (1058); ὑβρίζειν, in its technical sense of rape (1073). On the legal implications of this scene generally, see Lloyd 1992: 45–51. But Bers (1994: 181–82) cautions against the tendency to see too close a link between the plays and the courts, noting that connections are often "looser and less consistent than they seem at first."

[117] Meltzer (1996: 176n.9), who singles out 403–4 and 505–6.

[118] Garner 1987: 102.

[119] On the legal term ἐναυσίαν φυγήν and Attic homicide law, see Barrett 1964: 163.

with the democratic ideal.[120] In this play, however, he has more in common with the Athenian speech-goers condemned by Cleon, passive auditors motivated by pleasure who are easily deceived by sophistic displays (Thuc. 3.38.4–7), than with the wise and beneficent leader depicted in Euripides' *Suppliants*. Like the comic audience burlesqued in Aristophanes' plays, he is vulnerable to deception, unable to distinguish truth from falsehood, or appearance from reality. Moreover, the lyric lament he utters upon discovering the body of his dead wife suggests a compromised gender status, since tragedy does not typically depict adult Athenian men as engaging in lyric utterance.[121] Theseus' misguided belief that Phaedra's tablet gives a true account and requires no further examination is shown by the fact that he curses his son as soon as its contents are disclosed (886–90). By personifying the tablet as possessed of a human voice (877, 880), Theseus conflates visual and oral modes and establishes Phaedra's written words as a credible, "just voice" that will not deceive him:[122]

> δισσάς τε φωνὰς πάντας ἀνθρώπους ἔχειν,
> τὴν μὲν δικαίαν τὴν δ' ὅπως ἐτύγχανεν,
> ὡς ἡ φρονοῦσα τἄδικ' ἐξηλέγχετο
> πρὸς τῆς δικαίας, κοὐκ ἂν ἠπατώμεθα. (928–31)

[All men should] have two voices, one the just voice,
and one as chance would have it. In this way,
the treacherous scheming would be revealed
by justice, and we should never be deceived.

Although Theseus condemns the deceptions engendered by false and sophistic speech, he shows himself completely persuaded by them: his reliance on the corpse as the surest form of proof "indicates how complete a triumph of 'appearance' Phaedra has won."[123] By means of Phaedra's false testimony, Aphrodite has fashioned a tale of ignominy for Hippolytus, one that repays him in the same coin for his invective against women:

> ὅστις ἐξ ἐμοῦ γεγὼς
> ᾔσχυνε τἀμὰ λέκτρα κἀξελέγχεται
> πρὸς τῆς θανούσης ἐμφανῶς κάκιστος ὤν. (943–45)

---

[120] Knox (1979: 222) characterizes Theseus as a "statesman" and compares him to Themistocles.

[121] The effect of these lyrics is somewhat mitigated by the fact that they are delivered in couplets alternating with couplets in iambic trimeter. Hall (1999) observes that Theseus in Euripides' *Hippolytus* and Sophocles' Salaminian *Ajax* are the only two tragic adult males who are not barbarians to sing lyrics in extant tragedy.

[122] It is quite possible that Theseus' distinction between the two types of voice reflects the contemporary sophistic notion of the *orthos logos* associated with Protagoras in which one speech is characterized as straighter or stronger than the other; for the idea, see Kerferd 1981: 73.

[123] Segal 1970: 290.

You, my very own son,
have shamed my marriage bed and are clearly convicted
of being the basest sort of man by this dead woman.

Because of a woman's slander (διαβαλών, 932), Hippolytus has outwardly become that which he condemned in the deity, and in womankind in general; he who has referred to Aphrodite as the basest of the gods and who has denounced all women as a *kakon* now receives in return as a putative seducer the name *kakistos* and the censure of his father. This slander threatens to deprive him of his good name and to thrust him into obscurity (ἀκλεὴς ἀνώνυμος, 1028) in much the same way he wished both Aphrodite and Phaedra to incur reproach. The false tale engendered by Aphrodite and circulated by Phaedra after her death depends for its full effect on finding an auditor, like Theseus, vulnerable to deception. This cycle of slander illustrates how the free circulation of rumor in the democratic polis, sanctioned by *parrhēsia* and perpetuated by politicians, sycophants, and other individuals who freely manipulated appearances for their own gain, and even women, could destroy even the most unassailable of characters.

The salvaging of Phaedra's reputation must cost Hippolytus his, and so the speech Theseus delivers heaps further infamy upon him. Theseus' depiction of the reticent and chaste Hippolytus as a sophist and womanizer is further indicative of his inability to differentiate appearance and reality:

ἤδη νυν αὔχει καὶ δι' ἀψύχου βορᾶς
σίτοις καπήλευ' Ὀρφέα τ' ἄνακτ' ἔχων
βάκχευε πολλῶν γραμμάτων τιμῶν καπνούς·
ἐπεί γ' ἐλήφθης. τοὺς δὲ τοιούτους ἐγὼ
φεύγειν προφωνῶ πᾶσι· θηρεύουσι γὰρ
σεμνοῖς λόγοισιν, αἰσχρὰ μηχανώμενοι.   (952–57)

Now pride yourself and through your vegetarian diet
traffic in food, and, holding Orpheus as your leader,
revel, honoring the smoke of many words,
since you've been caught. And I encourage everyone
to avoid such men as these. For they hunt
with lofty words even as they contrive shameful deeds.

A similar analogy between sophism and religious mysticism is found in Aristophanes' *Clouds*, where the Student, questioned about his studies, describes Socrates' flea-measuring experiment as a version of the "mysteries" (μυστήρια, Ar. *Nub.* 143).[124] In addition to denouncing Hippolytus for his mysticism, many of the words in this passage suggest persons of low birth. For instance, the phrase αἰσχρὰ μηχανώμενοι evokes the stratagems of the Nurse and their effect on Phaedra, and the term λόγοισιν

---

[124] I would like to acknowledge Charles Segal for calling this passage to my attention.

reminds us that her power over others resides in her verbal cunning. The metaphors connected with trade, καπήλευε (953) and later ἔμπορον (964), further associate tricky speech with low social status, and potentially with demagogues and sophists, whom Plato compares to merchants and trades-men in his *Sophist* (Pl. *Soph.* 224a–225).

Theseus also draws an analogy between writing and sophistic manipula-tion of the truth; his allusion to γράμματα as that which conceals meaning and conjures illusion again evokes the sophists and their students. As we have seen, the play repeatedly attributes the knowledge of letters to the marginal figures least likely to have such skills in everyday life, women and slaves, suggesting a correspondence between writing and deception.[125] And perhaps Aristophanes also has this idea in mind when he attributes the skill of speech-writing to a dog, who serves as a stand-in for the demagogue Cleon, in the *Wasps*' mock domestic trial (Ar. *Vesp.* 960). Both scenes mock the idea of an educated lower class, yet darkly underscore the dangers of this contemporary trend. When Theseus later refers to Hippolytus as a sorcerer or enchanter who possesses the charm of speech (ἐπῳδός καὶ γόης, 1038; note the term πέποιθεν in the next line), he implicitly allies him with the sophistic utterance of the Nurse. Theseus' denunciation of Hippolytus demonstrates his inability to disentangle truth from falsehood and shows, in the words of the chorus, how Phaedra's false words have turned everything upside down (τὰ γὰρ δὴ πρῶτ' ἀνέστραπται πάλιν, 982). The allusions to writing in Euripides' *Hippolytus* must be understood in the context of the Athenian democracy during a period when this new technology was becoming increasingly important in administering the eco-nomic and legal business of the Athenian polis. Although it is impossible to know the extent of Athenian literacy during this period, it is likely that it was beginning to play some role, however small, in the courts.[126] At the same time, orality remained the privileged and most reliable form of proof until well into the fourth century, when written pleadings and depositions became the norm in the courts.[127] Even then, however, witnesses were still required to verify their accounts orally at the trial.[128]

The play validates orality through the character of Hippolytus, who relies not on written but on oral communication as the language of prayer,

---

[125] For references to writing, cf. Eur. *Hipp.* 387 (Phaedra), 451 (the Nurse), 1253–54 (Theseus' slave). According to Greene (1951: 40–44), the sophists were the first to develop prose writing, as evidenced by the philosophical treatises of Parmenides, Empedocles, and Anaxagoras, and by the rhetorical handbooks produced by either Corax or his pupil Tisias.

[126] There is some evidence of the composition of law-court speeches as well as written pleadings in the late 430s, just prior to the production of the *Hippolytus*; see Thomas 1989: 40; Gagarin 1994: 60.

[127] Hdt. 3.128, 8.120; Thuc. 1.128, 129, 137.

[128] MacDowell 1978: 119; Dem. 46.6.

while the means of ascertaining the truth that Artemis promulgates—pledges, mantic utterance, and refutation—are also strictly oral (1321–22). Nor does Hippolytus have any use for public oration: he first chastises his father for his excessive speech (924) and then suavely claims a reluctance to speak in his own defense (990–91). His skillful proemium, which makes use of a technique familiar from forensic oratory, gives the first clue of the great amount of rhetorical sophistication present throughout his "defense" speech.[129] He distances himself from the accomplished and erudite speaker, the *mousikos* (989), a term that implies basic literacy. The Nurse, too, we will remember, places herself among the educated, "those who are always among the Muses" (451–53). Hippolytus' disavowal of rhetorical ability and his claim that he is inexperienced in speaking before a crowd (ὄχλος, 986) identify him as anti-democratic; instead, he styles himself as an aristocrat who wishes not to compel others by means of rhetorical tricks, but rather to persuade by means of his innate *aidōs* (998).

In addition to prayer, Hippolytus deploys one other significant verbal genre, the oath; indeed, he swears three oaths in the course of the play.[130] As a strictly oral phenomenon, the oath played an important role in the democratic polis.[131] As we saw in the *Eumenides*, Athenian jurors were required to swear an oath upon assuming office at the beginning of the year.[132] Aristotle also mentions oaths as an example of artificial proof that might aid a litigant in fashioning his argument.[133] Hippolytus' refusal to contravene his oath (1060–62) provides the play's moral center, one that is divinely derived and religiously required (θέμις, 1033). The truthful, oral discourse exemplified by his oath-taking contrasts with the deceptive writing engendered by Aphrodite and women.

The importance of orality is further reinforced by the idea that face-to-face interrogation elicits the truth, an idea still prevalent in contemporary American courtrooms. The belief that a glance at a person's face will reveal the truth is reiterated several times in the course of the play; for example, the chorus wonder how Theseus, after one glance at his wife, could fail to perceive her condition (ὁ δ' εἰς πρόσωπον οὐ τεκμαίρεται βλέπων, 280). Phaedra's fear of scrutiny compels her to take her own life (416, 720–21) and to charge Hippolytus with rape:

---

[129] Lloyd (1992: 47) points out that Hippolytus' speech "evokes the law courts to a greater extent than any other speech in Euripides." And yet, paradoxically, the eloquent speaker is put into a position where he cannot win; for a parallel, cf. Eur. *Andr.* 147–273.

[130] Eur. *Hipp.* 611, mentioned again at 657–58; 1025–31; and 1191. The second oath can also be read as a curse, for which view see Segal 1972: 170.

[131] Burkert (1985: 250) describes the oath as linking together "religion, morality and the very organization of society"; cf. Lycurg. *Leoc.* 79.

[132] On the oath sworn by Athenian jurors, see MacDowell 1978: 44 and 248.

[133] On exculpatory oaths, see Kennedy 1963: 10; cf. Arist. *Rh.* 1366b35.

ἡ δ' εἰς ἔλεγχον μὴ πέσῃ φοβουμένη
ψευδεῖς γραφὰς ἔγραψε καὶ διώλεσεν
δόλοισι σὸν παῖδ', ἀλλ' ὅμως ἔπεισέ σε.   (1310–12)

Afraid that she would fall under scrutiny,
she wrote the false letter and destroyed
your child by her cunning. Nonetheless she persuaded you.

The emphatic phrase ἀλλ' ὅμως ἔπεισέ σε (1312; cf. 1287–88) places the
blame squarely on Theseus and suggests that only an extraordinarily gullible
person could be persuaded by a written text. The tablet, eroticized by the
presence of corpse, exhibits a seductive and persuasive power typically
associated with women in the earlier literary tradition, suggesting that
Phaedra's body "speaks" more eloquently than her words.

By dying, Phaedra deprives Theseus of an important means of ascertaining the truth, the process of refutation and cross-examination (ἔπειτα δ'
ἡ θανοῦσ' ἀνήλωσεν γυνὴ | λόγων ἐλέγχους, 1336–37). As Hippolytus and
Artemis both point out, all of the problems posed in the second half of
the play might have been resolved if Phaedra were present and able to
be interrogated (1022–24). As a consequence of her absence, Theseus
privileges the written words of Phaedra while rejecting the oral testimony
of Hippolytus, and all other types of oral evidence, including oaths, pledges,
and oracles:

σὺ δ' ἔν τ' ἐκείνῳ κἀν ἐμοὶ φαίνῃ κακός,
ὃς οὔτε πίστιν οὔτε μαντέων ὄπα
ἔμεινας, οὐκ ἤλεγξας, οὐ χρόνῳ μακρῷ
σκέψιν παρέσχες.   (1320–23; cf. 1055–56)

But you appear evil both in that one's eyes and in mine,
since you awaited neither proof nor mantic utterance,
nor did you scrutinize the situation, nor did a long expanse of time
furnish reflection.

Most of these modes of inquiry are oral and existed as forms of proof well
into the fourth century, when the main purpose of writing in the courts
was to fix the accounts of witnesses, as well as other types of proof, so
they could not be changed.[134] And yet, as Plato reminds us in the *Protagoras*, written texts are inherently unreliable in a judicial setting because,
like Phaedra, they cannot answer questions (Pl. *Prt.* 329a). By killing
herself, Phaedra eradicates the only human medium available for uncover-
ing the truth; in this respect, her written tablet may reflect the dangers
of cunning persuasion promulgated by the sophists and its potential for
deception in the democratic polis.

[134] Thomas 1989: 44.

As a play about discourse, the *Hippolytus* continually shows how stories as they pass from one speech community to another fluctuate and metamorphose: "We are borne along by *muthoi*," the Nurse has earlier claimed (197). Incited by Aphrodite, Phaedra's illicit passion produces and perpetuates an impenetrable world of appearances. It is Phaedra's false *muthoi* that have persuaded Theseus of things unclear (1288). Hippolytus, who has heaped a discourse of blame upon women, receives in return a tale of ignominy from the hand of a dead woman and is in turn vilified by his own father. Artemis, who appears from the machine, dissolves the world of illusion created by the false manipulation of discourse under the sign of Aphrodite. She creates a new discourse of praise for Hippolytus, confirming that he dies with fair repute (εὐκλείας, 1299), and concedes to Phaedra a measure of nobility (τινὰ | γενναιότητα, 1300–1). This final, truthful *muthos*, which Artemis declares will bring pain to Theseus (1313), restores order to the community and perpetuates the discourse of blame deployed by Hippolytus: as the subject of cult song, Hippolytus will receive the adoration of girls, while Phaedra will serve as a cautionary tale about the destructive consequences of women's adultery.

THE SONG OF GIRLS AND THE LAMENTS OF MEN

The agon shows the subversive effects wrought by the Nurse's transgression of social and discursive boundaries and Phaedra's overvaluation of *eukleia*: women's duplicitous and destructive speech drives a wedge between the most important homosocial bond in ancient Greece, that of father and son, with the result that Theseus, unable to distinguish appearance from reality, condemns his son to death. The cunning speech associated with marginal figures in the play, whether it takes the form of persuasion, magic, or writing, subverts the masculine, judicial discourse exemplified by the agon to such an extent that only divine intervention may set things aright. But a reversion to normal gender roles is signaled by the third stasimon: in this ode, the huntsmen addressed by Hippolytus (ἴτε ὦ νέοι μοι τῆσδε γῆς ὁμήλικες, 1098) join the women of the chorus in song.[135] By merging male and female voices in an ode that concludes with an allusion to marriage, Euripides fashions a kind of literary epithalamium similar to Catullus 62.[136]

---

[135] Almost all scholars except Barrett believe that the third stasimon included a subsidiary chorus of men because of the masculine participles at 1105 and 1107; see Reckford 1972: 417 and n. 14; Dimock 1977: 248–49, n. 3; and Segal 1993: 129. According to Dimock, the women thus sing 1111–19, 1120–30, and 1131–50, whereas the men sing the other verses. For the opposing view, see Barrett 1964: 366–69.

[136] Reckford 1972: 418.

ἀστέφανοι δὲ κόρας ἀνάπαυλαι
Λατοῦς βαθεῖαν ἀνὰ χλόαν·
νυμφιδία δ' ἀπόλωλε φυγᾶ σᾶ
λέκτρων ἄμιλλα κούραις.   (1138–41)

And ungarlanded are the resting places
of Leto's daughter in the deep greenery;
and by your exile the girls have lost
their bridal rivalry for your bed.

By alluding to the lost bridal rivalry of maidens entailed by Hippolytus' exile and death, the chorus of matrons affirm his status as a liminal figure who governs the transition from girlhood to adulthood, offsetting the tainted nuptial bed of Theseus and Phaedra with the untouched marital couch of virgins. Their final appeal to the yoking Charites, figures often depicted as companions of Aphrodite in art, to escort Hippolytus on his journey not only connotes the farewell at the wedding but also suggests the positive conjugal role played by Aphrodite.[137] The presence of mourning imagery in the ode, like the cessation of music, the futility of childbirth, and the lost marriage day, further identifies it with the genre of the epithalamium, which often included elements of lament.[138] The chorus thus reconcile opposites by uniting the warring aspects of sexuality and chastity embodied by Aphrodite and Artemis.

The maidens mentioned in the third stasimon assume an even larger role at the end of the play: their welfare is the special concern of the unmarried, virgin Artemis, who is herself described interchangeably as a *korē* or a *parthenos*.[139] The pleasure she takes in virginity contrasts with the voluptuous and erotic delights of Aphrodite and Phaedra; Hippolytus, with his maiden soul, properly belongs to her (1006). He fits the pattern of the great mother goddess and her mortal, early-dying consort and has been compared to mythical figures like Ialemos, Linos, and Hymenaios as the virginity that must disappear upon marriage.[140] The play also provides a mythic parallel in the figure of Phaëthon, similarly figured as an athletic, adolescent boy who, reluctant to marry, dies before his time. He is mourned by his unmarried sisters, the Heliades, who commemorate his life with tears of amber (735–41). A second such youth, indirectly alluded to by Artemis at 1420–22, is Adonis, consort of Aphrodite, whose untimely death in a boar hunt will repay Aphrodite for her revenge against Hippoly-

---

[137] Burnett 1986: 173–74. On σύζυγος as active in meaning, see Bushala 1969.

[138] Halleran 1995: 248.

[139] On Artemis *korē*, cf. Eur. *Hipp*. 15, 64, 713, 1092, 1285. It is striking that even Phaedra is called a *korē* at one point in the play (141). For the term *parthenos*, cf. Eur. *Hipp*. 1006 (Hippolytus); 17, 66, 72, and 1440 (Artemis); 1428 (maiden chorus); *partheneios*, 1302.

[140] Séchan 1911: 117. On Hymenaios and lost virginity, see Reckford 1972: 415.

tus.[141] Like these figures, Hippolytus will receive a memorializing song sung by young girls just before marriage:

σοὶ δ', ὦ ταλαίπωρ', ἀντὶ τῶνδε τῶν κακῶν
τιμὰς μεγίστας ἐν πόλει Τροζηνίᾳ
δώσω· κόραι γὰρ ἄζυγες γάμων πάρος
κόμας κεροῦνταί σοι, δι' αἰῶνος μακροῦ
πένθη μέγιστα δακρύων καρπουμένῳ·
ἀεὶ δὲ μουσοποιὸς εἴς σὲ παρθένων
ἔσται μέριμνα, κοὐκ ἀνώνυμος πεσὼν
ἔρως ὁ Φαίδρας εἴς σε σιγηθήσεται.   (1423–30)

To you, oh wretched one, I will give
the greatest honors in the Troezen city
in return for these troubles. For unyoked girls before marriage
will cut their hair for you, who will harvest for generations
the greatest laments of tears. And it will always be
the concern of maidens to make songs for you,
nor will Phaedra's love for you fall away nameless
and be silent.

This collective song elevates the domestic problems of the first part of the play to the level of myth and literary creation while, as ritual, it negates Phaedra's original silence and transforms her erotic and subversive speech into the public discourse of girls, which sanctions and supports the male institution of marriage.[142] Like the female speakers of the *partheneia*, the chorus do not construct a female subject position separate from that prescribed for them by men, since they both position themselves as speakers for the community and downplay their own authority.[143]

Some critics have viewed the song in a more positive light as a means of integrating women into the polis, preparing them for marriage and reconciling the adverse principles of Aphrodite (female sexuality) and Artemis (childbirth).[144] At the same time, the girls' song also serves as a

[141] Reckford 1972 explores at length the connections between Hippolytus and Phaëthon; see also Pigeaud 1976: 6–7. Apollodorus 3.14.4 gives the anger of Artemis as the cause of his death.

[142] Goff 1990: 117. For the idea of song as a remedial discourse, see Pucci 1977b. Pucci sees the cult and ritual song, as well as the final allusion to the lament of the citizens, as a monument that confers honor upon Hippolytus.

[143] On the function of girls' songs generally, see Stehle 1997: 38. Rabinowitz (1987: 136) argues that this song effectively denies subjectivity by forcing the maidens to reinforce gender ideology.

[144] According to Dimock (1977: 242), the purpose of this song is "to help girls submit to marriage." Goff (1990: 115) argues that "the rite and song can be seen as a means of bringing the marginal figures of unmarried females into the heart of the polis"; see also Segal 1993: 121.

didactic tale meant to teach women chastity by recalling the danger of uncontrolled, feminine *erōs*, which Hippolytus condemned at 667–68. The negative version of fame conferred upon Phaedra for her *erōs* suggests that the only public song that can be awarded to women is the one that denounces them. The play therefore depicts the containment of the dangerous, erotic speech of mature women and replaces it with the religious speech of girls, whose virgin status precludes the possibility of deceit and allows them to deliver the canonized, "male" version of Phaedra's story as a morality tale for other girls.

But Hippolytus will receive another type of commemoration; while the girls' song serves as a cautionary tale about the destructive effects of uncontrolled female desire, the lament of the male citizens affirms the importance of this figure to the polis (1462). As the Messenger makes clear, Hippolytus' death is a public event significant not only to the citizens of Troezen, but also to those of Athens (πολίταις οἵ τ' Ἀθηναίων πόλιν | ναίουσι, 1158–59), who join in a civic lament:

κοινὸν τόδ' ἄχος πᾶσι πολίταις
ἦλθεν ἀέλπτως.
πολλῶν δακρύων ἔσται πίτυλος·
τῶν γὰρ μεγάλων ἀξιοπενθεῖς
   φῆμαι μᾶλλον κατέχουσιν.   (1462–66)

A common grief has come, unexpectedly,
to all the citizens.
There will be a splashing of many tears.
For sorrowful tales about the great
will hold greater sway.

Segal argues that the supernumerary chorus of hunting companions who joined the female chorus in the third stasimon reenter and sing the tailpiece.[145] Understood in this way, they restore the masculine subject position and masculine collectivity to the play's narrative: Hippolytus, not Phaedra, becomes a civic figure who engenders the lamentations of the city. The play thus moves from the private grief of Theseus for Phaedra toward "a more restrained, ritualized expression of grief," and from the ritual laments of women to a collective, civic sorrow.[146] Instead of the rumors of women that circulate outside the boundaries of masculine political control, the play fashions a new story that commemorates the stories of great men in the civic space of the city, especially in the theater of Dionysus.

---

[145] The male chorus also sing Eur. *Hipp.* 58ff., 1102–52, and then enter again at 1342; see Segal 1993: 129.

[146] Segal 1993: 121.

CONCLUSION

In the *Hippolytus*, Euripides complicates Aeschylus' evolutionary model in which an ambiguous, deceptive, feminine speech yields to a more public and benevolent form of persuasion associated with men. As represented by the forensic agon between Theseus and Hippolytus, the judicial process commands a tenuous authority, one easily undermined by verbal guile and sophistic manipulation of appearance. In depicting mortals as unable to access the truth without the help of the gods, the play plunges its characters into an almost Gorgian universe in which only appearances can be known. It portrays women as the purveyors of reputation, who skillfully manipulate appearance through their cunning and sophistic words, easily duping a powerful yet gullible man who is the embodiment of Athenian democracy. By establishing a legal framework for the dramatic action, the poet suggests an affinity between this feminine persuasion and the contemporary use of rhetoric in the masculine discursive sphere, particularly in the courts.

In contrast to the *Eumenides*, women's speech in the *Hippolytus* cannot be fully contained and kept out of the masculine political sphere, but rather threatens continually to breach discursive boundaries, disrupting and interfering with male civic identity, a phenomenon with parallels in the role played by gossip in the contemporary Athenian law courts. But the play also sanctions women's public speech through ritual song in a manner reminiscent of the *Eumenides*: this song reinforces gender roles through the negative example of one woman's adulterous passions. At the same time, the ritual context and the virgin status of the chorus of girls ensures the truthfulness of their speech, in contrast to the duplicitous tales spawned by adulterous matrons. By reinstating masculine collectivity at the end of the play, however, Euripides privileges Hippolytus' discourse of invective and creates a structural equation between the world of the play and that of the theater. Euripides thus does not provide for Phaedra in his second *Hippolytus* the same kind of tragic palinode he later fashions for Helen; instead, Phaedra embodies the slanderous stories associated with the tragic poet and comically derided by the female characters of Aristophanes' *Thesmophoriazusae*.

Chapter Five

WOMEN'S WORDY STRIFE: GOSSIP AND
INVECTIVE IN EURIPIDES'
ANDROMACHE

IN CONTRAST TO his *Hippolytus*, Euripides' *Andromache* has received remarkably little scholarly attention. Debate has centered on a few main issues: its venue and production date, ancient assessments of the play, its anachronistic polemic against Sparta, and its lack of dramatic unity. Most recent criticism has attempted to reverse earlier assessments of the play as disjointed, second-rate, and an inferior poetic product in every way.[1] Euripides' *Andromache* was probably produced in the mid-420s, although Storey's suggestion of a proximity to the *Hippolytus* is attractive, given the similarity of issues and of dramatic structure between the two plays.[2] According to a scholion, the play was never performed at Athens, a view reiterated by Schmid-Stählin and one still occasionally encountered.[3] More damaging has been Aristophanes of Byzantium's comment in the second hypothesis, τὸ δὲ δρᾶμα τῶν δευτέρων, a phrase most critics have glossed as "a second-rate play" and one that has contributed to the reputation of the *Andromache* as worthless and hastily executed.[4]

These criticisms aside, the issue that has preoccupied scholars more than any other has been the question of the play's dramatic unity. Instead of a single, simple plot, the *Andromache* consists of three discrete actions: a

[1] For Wilamowitz' view that Euripides did not write the play, see Stevens 1971: 20. All Greek passages quoted in this chapter are taken from Stevens 1971.

[2] Storey (1989: 25) speculates that a production date of 427–426 would closely affiliate the *Andromache* with the *Hippolytus*, a play that shares the theme of *sophrosunē* and women's sexuality.

[3] The scholion to Eur. *Andr.* 445 dates the drama to the beginning of the Peloponnesian war and specifies that it was not performed at Athens (οὐ διδάκται γὰρ ᾿Αθήνησιν); see Schmid and Stählin 1929–48, 1: 3.400. Speculation about the play's venue has ranged from the court of the Molossian king Tharyps to Argos. Robertson (1923) first suggested Tharyps' court as a venue because the play attempts to prove the Hellenic origins of the Molossians. Hall (1989b: 181) agrees that the play compliments the Molossians, but argues that it need not have been performed outside Athens to do so and suggests that Tharyps may even have attended an Athenian production of the play. Page (1936: 223–28) proposes Argos on the basis of Andromache's unparalleled elegiac lament.

[4] Stevens (1971: 27–28) reviews the possibilities and argues that the phrase may actually be more laudatory than previously recognized.

suppliant and rescue drama concluded by a story of divine punishment. The play's repeated overturns, and the large number of characters required to enact them, create a disjointed and dizzying effect, one that Burnett has termed a "sickening fluidity."[5] Scholarly analysis of the *Andromache*, therefore, has predominantly attempted to find an underlying, coherent ideal or thematic system that might unify its disparate parts. Critics have proposed a single figure, such as Hermione or Andromache, or even Neoptolemus, as that which joins together the play's three separate actions.[6] Others have noted structural similarities between the various parts of the play: for example, it concludes with a murder committed to recover a spouse, an action that replicates Hermione's unsuccessful attempt to restore her husband's affections by killing her rival in the first episode.[7] Another solution frequently put forward has been to identify a recurrent pattern of images or ideas as a basis for thematic unity, such as the juxtaposition of two opposing concepts of morality, like *sophia* and *sophrosunē*, or *phusis* and *nomos*, or the issue of family ties and domestic tensions.[8]

[5] Burnett 1971: 131.

[6] Both Kamerbeek (1943:47–55) and Erbse (1966: 291ff.) view Andromache as the unifying character (hence their insistence upon her silent presence at the end of the play), whereas Garzya (1952) posits Hermione. Other critics have gone so far as to claim that honor for Neoptolemus, who arrives only at the very end of the play as a corpse: see most recently Mossman 1996. The long-standing yet unsubstantiated assumption that Andromache remains onstage as a mute figure from 765ff. must be viewed as an attempt to support the view that her character unifies the play. Most scholars assume Andromache remains onstage even after she has voiced her intention to depart at 750–56 together with Peleus, who does in fact leave, as we know from his greeting at 1047. They base their argument for the most part on the presence of the deictic pronouns καὶ παῖδα τόνδε at 1246 and τοῦδε at 1247, and the choral reference to an unnamed female at 1041 denoted by the phrase σοὶ μόνᾳ; see Kamerbeek 1943; Erbse 1966; Golder 1983; Storey 1989: 16. Although the evidence is inconclusive, as Stevens (1971: 219) observes, I follow Steidle (1968: 119–23) in assuming that Andromache is *not* present after 765, mainly because Thetis describes her in the third person at 1243, "The captive woman, I mean Andromache" (γυναῖκα δ' αἰχμάλωτον, Ἀνδρομάχην λέγω). It seems inherently implausible and dramatically unnecessary to have her onstage during Hermione's scene of contrition and her subsequent exchange with Orestes. There is also a question about when exactly Orestes arrives; although his entrance is clearly marked at 881 with his salutation ξέναι γυναῖκες, he later claims that he has been secretly hanging around the palace (961ff.), an admission that raises the alarming possibility that he has even witnessed Hermione's strip scene. If Orestes functions as a kind of voyeuristic *prosōpon kōphon* in this scene, then Andromache obviously cannot be present.

[7] Kovacs 1980a: 54.

[8] On the *sophia-sophrosunē* antithesis, see Boulter (1966), who oddly does not mention the relevance of these concepts to the sophistic movement; for the confusion of *phusis-nomos* as the underlying theme of the play, see Lee 1975. Storey (1989) and Phillippo (1995) have both recently argued that family relationships provide a unifying theme for the play's different actions. However, Mossman (1996: 144) rightly criticizes the idea of thematic integration on the grounds that many of Euripides' plays are structured around such oppositions, as we saw in the last chapter.

More convincing, however, is Burnett's argument that the episodic and fragmented quality of the play must be viewed as deliberate.[9] By means of disjointed actions and rapid reversals, the poet exemplifies the idea of fortune's overturn suffered by almost all of the play's major characters.

But in a play that contains as its main action a domestic dispute between a female slave and her mistress, it is surprising that few critics have focused on the role of gender. Examining the *Andromache* from an ideological perspective, Rabinowitz has argued that the play critiques the institution of marriage, with the episodic structure of the play reflecting "disorders in the gender system."[10] Although Rabinowitz provides insight into the functioning of gender dynamics within the play, her treatment completely neglects the issue of women's speech. In the *Andromache* as in the *Hippolytus*, women's gossip and slander, although separate from the male political sphere and largely confined to the oikos, nonetheless manages to permeate and disrupt the world of men because it is allowed to circulate unchecked in the absence of the male kurios. The artificially formal structure of the play also reinforces this dynamic: its inclusion of three agones, the first between women only, the second between a woman and a man, and third between men only, suggests a pervasive concern with rhetorical and persuasive speech.[11] By establishing women's speech as a context for the disaster that subsequently unfolds, the poet suggests a correlation between gossip in the household and male slander in the polis: both types of speech appear to have no discernible origin and thus operate beyond the bounds of social control.

The similarities between the *Hippolytus* and the *Andromache*, both structural and thematic, are striking: each play begins with an exchange between women in the domestic sphere that is answered by a subsequent agon staged exclusively between men, and ends with the suppression of women's

---

[9] Although Aldrich (1961: 61) was the first to take seriously the episodic structure of the play as part of its dramatic purpose, Burnett (1971: 130–56) develops this idea more fully. See also Lee (1975: 5), who argues that the question of dramatic unity is irrelevant. This innovative and complex dramatic structure has prompted many critics to view Euripides as a playwright of the avant garde; see Garzya 1952; Mossman 1996.

[10] Rabinowitz 1984: 112. Although I find Rabinowitz' analysis of Andromache as a woman "beaten down by patriarchy" (114) anachronistic, her argument that the two women are basically alike and placed in the same position by male institutions is incisive. For example, she notes that both Andromache and Hermione are depicted at various points as alone (87, 805, 855) and as suppliants (11, 115, 859). Both characters join themselves to the men who murdered their first husbands. Although not specifically concerned with the issue of gender in the play, Sorum (1995: 374) argues that the play represents women's sexuality as "the source of toil and suffering for men."

[11] Conacher 1967: 173. Although Eur. *Andr.* 309–463 is not technically an agon, but rather an epideixis scene, it has elements of the agon, particularly its use of legal terms and blame speech and its generally contentious tone. See Lloyd 1992: 10.

destructive speech.[12] Both conclude with a *kommos* in which a father delivers a lament for his son (or grandson, as in the case of the *Andromache*), a masculine lament with civic relevance, while a goddess from the machine promises immortality or cult recognition for one or both. Like the *Hippolytus*, the *Andromache* includes a quasi-forensic agon, albeit one between women only, in which an unjust individual attempts to defend herself before a person of superior status who serves as both judge and jury. The first part of the play identifies women's speech as deceptive and unscrupulous, whereas subsequent episodes evoke it as a paradigm for the corrupt speech practices of men, embodied by the sophistic Menelaus and the immoral Orestes cast in the role of seducer. Hermione may be seen as a product of Athenian speculation about Spartan gynaecocracy: she represents the inverted role of women in Spartan society and their access to public speech. Neoptolemus' prolonged absence from his house compounds the power imbalance and demonstrates the problem of women left unsupervised in the oikos in wartime and its lasting effects on the polis, an issue that might have been uppermost in the minds of Athenian men in the mid-420s. Moreover, by constructing Sparta as "other" in the Athenian imagination and by imputing women's speech to men, the play returns to the problem of rhetorical skill and its use by lower class or disreputable figures, earlier explored in the *Hippolytus*.

THE STATUS OF SPEECH IN THE *ANDROMACHE*

Like the *Hippolytus*, the *Andromache* depicts both male and female discursive practices as largely negative, beginning with Hermione's baseless accusations against Andromache and her boast that paternal wealth and Spartan birth have granted her freedom of speech. The unscrupulous end to which she puts this prerogative resembles the verbal stratagem later employed by Menelaus to pry the slave woman off the altar. Finally, Orestes' treacherous plans to murder Neoptolemus hinge upon the successful dissemination of false slander among the citizens of Delphi. In all of these cases, an individual of questionable moral character employs verbal treachery to eliminate a sexual rival and to secure personal gratification, rather than to further the interests of the family or city. By beginning with a domestic scene among women and concluding with Hermione's condemnation of female gossip, the poet uses women's speech as a framework for evaluating the discourse of men. The first scene shows their speech to be implicitly concerned with sexual matters and to result from an inability to control

[12] Boulter 1966 and Storey 1989: 25 discuss thematic overlaps in the *Hippolytus* and the *Andromache*.

erotic impulses. The baseless allegations of Hermione engender not only the suppliant drama of Andromache, but also the subsequent three agones and, finally, the murder of Neoptolemus. As we learn at the end of the play, Hermione's false allegations have as their source the Siren song of other women, whose talk she blames for her own misguided and corrupt behavior.

In both the *Hippolytus* and the *Andromache*, women's speech signals a disorder, *nosos*, related to the conjugal bed. In the previous play, Phaedra's *nosos* derived from the fact that she directed her desire away from her husband toward an improper object. Hermione's "sickness" can be read as an inversion and complement of Phaedra's: although properly directed toward her husband, Hermione's desire ultimately undermines her marriage, as well as her husband's oikos, by its very excessiveness. Like Phaedra, Hermione inherits her lack of sexual restraint from a notorious mother; throughout the play, the figure of Helen provides a paradigm for the human destruction engendered by female promiscuity. Thus in both plays, women's unruly speech is viewed as resulting from a lack of sexual self-control; because eroticized in this way, it must be hidden from men and contained within the house (cf. 220–21, 955–56). Hermione's unrestrained verbal activities therefore mirror her sexual proclivities; not only does she complain about her sex life, but she does so directly before men, involving both Menelaus and Orestes in the affairs of her boudoir (cf. 906). According to Peleus, the sickness that has pervaded the house has both a sexual and a verbal origin: "From what *logos* does this house grow diseased?" (ἐκ τίνος λόγου νοσεῖ | δόμος; 548–49). The figure of the *erōsa gunē* deplored by the character of Aeschylus in Aristophanes' *Frogs* (Ar. *Ran.* 1042) and by Socrates in the *Republic* (Pl. *Rep.* 395e2) demonstrates that women's speech, like female sexuality, perpetually operates outside the boundaries of male control and can therefore never be completely controlled by men.

The comparison of the women's quarrel to the Trojan war, and especially the judgment of Paris, also reveals the close connection between female speech and sexuality and indicts it as the source not only of domestic strife but also of broad-scale political upheaval. Significantly, the first stasimon attributes Aphrodite's victory over the other goddesses in the judgment of Paris to her use of *peithō:* her words, while pleasant to her male auditor, spell disaster for Troy.[13]

ἔβαν δὲ Πριαμίδαν ὑπερ-
βολαῖς λόγων δυσφρόνων
παραβαλλόμεναι, δολίοις ⟨δ'⟩ ἕλε Κύπρις λόγοις,

---

[13] Kovacs (1980a: 60) briefly discusses the passage. On the judgment of Paris as a narrative model for the *Andromache*, see Sorum 1995.

τερπνοῖς μὲν ἀκοῦσαι,
πικρὰν δὲ σύγχυσιν βίου Φρυγῶν πόλει ταλαίνα
περγάμοις τε Τροίας.   (287–92)

[The goddesses] came to the son of Priam
vying with each other with excesses of bitter words,
But Cypris prevailed with cunning words, pleasant to hear,
but blending a bitter future for the poor city of the Phrygians
and the citadel of Troy.

This choral ode, with its emphasis on *logoi*, retells the story of the judgment of Paris as an oral event in which women, unable to resolve a dispute among themselves, must appeal to a male authority. In this version of the judgment, women's speech, underscored by the repetition of *logos*, gives rise to a catastrophic war among men.[14] Although traditional accounts specify the competing goddesses and the gifts they offered to Paris, Euripides mentions only Aphrodite, whom he represents not as tendering a bribe, but as employing cunning and seductive words, δολίοις λόγοις, to secure her victory. And yet the ode cautions that Paris, by succumbing to her, compromises the welfare of his people for the sake of self-interest. From a dramatic standpoint, the allusion to quarreling women points forward to the agon between Hermione and Andromache and the subsequent intervention of Menelaus, who serves as adjudicator in their dispute.

At the same time, Aphrodite's act of feminine verbal guile provides a paradigm for the play's representation of male speech as treacherous, since it is frequently characterized by the terms *dolos* and *mēchanē*. In an inversion of the judgment of Paris, Menelaus, rather than Aphrodite, employs cunning words to convince Andromache to leave the altar, and she in turn denounces his false promise as a *dolos* and all Spartans as cunning counselors (δόλια βουλευτήρια, 446). In the same way, the play sets up an equivalence between the idea of *mēchanē*, "craftiness," and women, and then applies the word to men. Thus Andromache first identifies this type of cleverness with women through her gnomic pronouncement to a fellow slave: "You may discover many stratagems, for you are a woman" (πολλὰς ἂν εὕροις μηχανάς· γυνὴ γὰρ εἶ, 85). She has already attributed this feminine verbal treachery to Menelaus, who "weaves a plot" with his daughter (μηχανὰς πλέκουσιν, 66) and whose lies Peleus condemns with the same word (μηχανώμενοι, 549). In similar and suitably Aeschylean language, Orestes speaks of his plan for killing Neoptolemus as a "plot woven of immovable

---

[14] Stevens (1971: 130–31) takes the phrase ὑπερβολαῖς λόγων as referring to the extravagant offers made by the goddesses to Paris, whereas the participle παραβαλλόμεναι must be taken as an absolute middle, meaning "vying with each other." He then glosses the problematic δυσφρόνων as referring "to the ill-will of the contestants towards each other." However, a paraphrase in the scholia, and one adopted by other editors, makes more sense: the goddesses, disputing among themselves, revile and disparage each other's charms.

meshes," one that requires verbal guile for its success (τοία γὰρ αὐτῷ μηχανὴ πεπλεγμένη | βρόχοις ἀκινήτοισιν, 995–96). Finally, Andromache denounces the Spartans in her invective as μηχανορράφοι, "craft-contriving" (447), a term later used of Orestes for plotting Neoptolemus' murder (1116).

The allusion to the judgment of Paris reinforces another aspect of women's speech explored in the chapter on the *Hippolytus*, the dynamic and sometimes destructive interrelation between domestic and civic life. Although ostensibly a domestic drama, and not very high tragedy at that,[15] the polis is ubiquitous; indeed, the word "polis" occurs almost three times as frequently in this play as in the *Hippolytus*.[16] Such references imply an intimate connection between the activities and governance of the house and those of the city. Several times we find this reciprocity reinforced by the repeated juxtaposition of the word "polis" with words relating to the oikos. For example, in the second stasimon, the chorus compare women's nuptial rivalry to the presence of competing rulers in the city, a situation that results in strife among the citizens (471–77). They conclude that "the political power both in the house and in the city should belong to one man" (ἑνὸς ἁ δύνασις ἀνά τε μέλαθρα | κατά τε πόλιας, 483–84).[17] And by characterizing the destructive effects of the Trojan war as a sickness or *nosos*, the chorus assimilate the disease afflicting women to the Trojan war itself at the end of the play (νόσον Ἑλλὰς ἔτλα, νόσον, 1044). The emphasis on the interdependence of the city and the household found in these passages suggests that the speech of women has important implications for the whole polis.

SPARTAN WOMEN AND THEIR SPEECH

A point that has been almost completely overlooked by scholars, and one that is essential for understanding the representation of women's speech in the *Andromache*, is the extent to which Euripides draws upon contemporary Athenian views of Sparta in his depiction of Hermione. What distinguishes her, above all, is her bold speech: she is portrayed as a gossip and

---

[15] A point raised early on and one too often overlooked are the moments of comedy in the play. Aldrich (1961: 12) argues that the plot belongs to comedy, rather than to tragedy, and identifies many comic moments, including the scene where Peleus threatens to hit Menelaus with his staff. Kovacs (1980a: 78) also sees the play's comic potential. Surprisingly, Knox (1979: 250–74) does not discuss the *Andromache* in his essay on Euripidean comedy, even though it exhibits many of the same features as the plays he discusses.

[16] In the *Andromache*, the term πόλις is used of Troy: 1, 97, 291, 298, 363, 455, 796, 970; Phthia: 16, 138, 1176, 1187, 1211, 1222; Sparta: 194, 197, 209, 243, 873; Delphi: 1090, 1096, 1263; Hellas: 169; other: 388, 471, 484, 734, 788.

[17] Consider also other similar juxtapositions between the household and city: "May no unjust power reign in the bedroom and the city" (μηδὲν δίκας ἔξω κράτος ἐν <u>θαλάμοις</u> | καὶ

a scold, a characterization that continually borders on the comic. This portrayal meshes well with the widespread belief, voiced by Aristotle and others, that Spartan women were more licentious and undisciplined, especially in their speech, than Athenian women.[18] Plato, in his discussion of the timocratic youth, briefly touched upon in the last chapter, depicts Spartan mothers as incessantly railing at their husbands:

"Ὅταν, ἦν δ' ἐγώ, πρῶτον μὲν τῆς μητρὸς ἀκούῃ ἀχθομένης ὅτι οὐ τῶν ἀρχόντων αὐτῇ ὁ ἀνήρ ἐστιν, καὶ ἐλαττουμένης διὰ ταῦτα ἐν ταῖς ἄλλαις γυναιξίν, ἔπειτα ὁρώσης μὴ σφόδρα περὶ χρήματα σπουδάζοντα μηδὲ μαχόμενον καὶ λοιδορούμενον ἰδίᾳ τε ἐν δικαστηρίοις καὶ δημοσίᾳ, ἀλλὰ ῥᾳθύμως πάντα τὰ τοιαῦτα φέροντα, καὶ ἑαυτῷ μὲν τὸν νοῦν προσέχοντα ἀεὶ αἰσθάνηται, ἑαυτὴν δὲ μήτε πάνυ τιμῶντα μήτε ἀτιμάζοντα, ἐξ ἁπάντων τούτων ἀχθομένης τε καὶ λεγούσης ὡς ἄνανδρός τε αὐτῷ ὁ πατὴρ καὶ λίαν ἀνειμένος, καὶ ἄλλα δὴ ὅσα καὶ οἷα φιλοῦσιν αἱ γυναῖκες περὶ τῶν τοιούτων ὑμνεῖν. (Pl. *Rep.* 549c–e)

"Whenever," I said, "the boy first hears his mother complaining that her husband is not among the leaders, and that she has a lower status among the other women because of it, and then that she sees her husband is not very interested in making money nor in fighting and reviling privately in the courts or in the assembly, but takes all of these matters in stride, and she perceives that he always pays attention only to himself, while neither respecting nor disrespecting her; aggrieved by all these things, she says that the boy's father is not really a man and is exceedingly undisciplined, and all the other sort of things women love to harp on in regard to this kind of situation."

This passage depicts Spartan women as verbally dominating and outspoken, a linguistic inversion that has a direct impact on the masculine political sphere by producing avaricious and prestige-seeking children who value money over virtue (Pl. *Rep.* 551a). Moreover, this domestic climate, in Plato's view, eventually leads, through oligarchy, to democracy, a type of government that, in its worst form, fosters *isonomia*, a principle of parity among all men, a principle that abolishes the "natural" hierarchies of fathers and sons, masters and slaves, and, ultimately, that of men and women (Pl. *Rep.* 562e–563b).

A similar view of Spartan women is found in Aristotle's *Politics*, which characterizes Sparta as a city ruled by women, *gunaikokratia* (γυναικοκρατούμεναι, Arist. *Pol.* 1269b25). He cites *anesis*, license or indulgence, as the salient feature of Spartan women, a quality compounded by the frequent

---

πόλει δύνασθαι, 786–87); and, "O marriage, marriage, you who have destroyed my house and my city" (ὦ γάμος, ὦ γάμος, ὃς τάδε δώματα | καὶ πόλιν ἀμὰν ὤλεσας, 1186–87).

[18] Although most accounts of Sparta are late, they seem to agree on several key points; Redfield 1977–78; Cartledge 1981; Kunstler 1987; and Mossé 1991 all discuss the evidence for the status of women in Sparta.

absence of men on military campaigns (1270a1–8), as well as a characteristic of women and slaves in the worst form of democracy. This lack of discipline in Aristotle's view instilled an excessive regard for wealth in Spartan women and caused them to refuse to comply with Lycurgus' reforms (ἀντέκρουον, 1270a1). Spartan inheritance laws, by liberally allowing women to own property, further contributed to the prominence of Spartan women in public and political life; according to Aristotle, about two-fifths of the land in Sparta was controlled by women (Arist. *Pol.* 1270a23). Similarly, women's dowries, *proikes*, that consisted of landed property and movables given by father to daughter upon marriage, were apparently very large in Sparta.[19] And in contrast to Athenian practice, *epiklēroi* or heiresses were also free to marry outside their paternal line and still retain a portion of their patrimony (Arist. *Pol.* 1270a23–29). Euripides' *Andromache* seems to have relied on a similar view of Sparta, since it depicts Hermione as bringing a large dowry into her relatively poor husband's household, and expecting to be able to speak her mind in return.

Spartan marriage customs also seem to have reinforced the idea of gender-role inversion associated with Sparta in the Athenian imagination. Laconian girls received athletic training in addition to participating in dances and choruses, an education meant to prepare them for the rigors of childbirth and the production of vigorous male heirs (Xen. *Lac.* 2.7–9, 3.1–5; Plut. *Lyc.* 14).[20] They were also notorious for public nudity, a feature of Spartan life attested in sources as early as Ibycus, as well as in our play.[21] Similarly, Laconian marriage customs must have appeared quite barbarian to residents of classical Athens: for example, the laws provided that an older Spartan husband could introduce into his home a younger woman for the purpose of procreation if his marriage had no issue (Xen. *Lac.* 1.7–8; Plut. *Lyc.* 15.6–7). A man not wishing to marry might "borrow" another man's wife for the production of heirs, as long as he received the husband's permission. As Mossé points out, these Spartan practices suggest that a child's legitimacy and his citizen status was not as strongly correlated in Sparta as in Athens.[22] Given the similarity between Spartan customs and a contemporary Athenian law recorded by Diogenes Laertius that may have permitted men to have two wives in order to replace a population rapidly becoming depleted by the Peloponnesian war, it is perhaps no coincidence that a central issue in the *Andromache* is legitimacy of offspring.[23]

---

[19] Cartledge 1981: 98.

[20] On the education of Laconian girls, see ibid.: 92–93.

[21] On girls' public nudity, see Plut. *Lyc.* 14.6–7; at *Mor.* 232C, Plutarch comments that Spartan girls did not wear veils; Poll. 7.54–55; Ibyc. fr. 58P (φαινομηρίδες). On their sayings, see Plut. *Mor.* 240C–242D; and Cartledge 1981: 91–92.

[22] Mossé 1991: 143.

[23] Some scholars view 177–80 as an allusion to an Athenian law by which Athenian men were allowed to have two wives or by means of which the children of a second woman were deemed

The ancient evidence also indicates that Spartans placed fewer restrictions on the public presence of women and their public speech, perhaps because they configured public and private spheres in a manner very different from that of the Athenians. Girls' choruses, such as those represented in the *partheneia* discussed in Chapter 2, were a regular feature of Spartan life and frequently took place before a mixed audience of both genders. Occasionally, the female choral members would engage in playful badinage with their male audience, rebuking some young men and praising others (σκώμματα λέγουσαι, Plut. *Lyc.* 14.15). We also know of at least two female Spartan poets: Cleitagora, mentioned by Aristophanes, and Megalostrata, who was a contemporary of Alcman.[24] Literary sources depict Spartan women as gifted speakers: according to Plato, they received the same education as men, one especially strong in philosophy and rhetoric (Pl. *Prt.* 342d), and the *Laws* refers to their skill in *mousikē* (Pl. *Leg.* 806a; cf. *Rep.* 5.452a). By imputing outspokenness to Spartan women alongside physical immodesty, these sources rely on a familiar equation between women's speech and sexuality.

Although very late, the apophthegms of Laconian women recorded by Plutarch provide further support for the idea that women's speech was perceived to have been less restricted in Sparta; these sayings echo, in their tone and content, Plato's account of complaining mothers in the *Republic*. Consisting mostly of mothers exhorting their sons to martial valor or rebuking them for cowardice, the apophthegms represent Spartan women as fiercely patriotic, indifferent to pain, and yet obedient and deferential to their husbands (in contrast to Aristotle's representation). In one famous saying, Gorgo, the wife of Leonidas, when asked by an Athenian, "Why do Laconian women alone rule over men?" responded, "Because we alone bear real men" (Plut. *Mor.* 240E). The discovery of ex voto dedications from Sparta inscribed with the name of the dedicatrix and offered to female deities has also been cited as indicating an unusual degree of literacy among Spartan women, although it is quite possible that these women could have commissioned the inscriptions from literate men.[25] And yet, as Mossé remarks, the portrayal of Spartan women in these texts reflects not so much their historical condition, but a very old social and literary construct, in which women simultaneously served as "mistress of the oikos and in that role as an agent of stability, but also, in opposition, as a person who retained considerable powers which associated her with all that was subversive of the social order."[26] Although Mossé here has in mind

---

legitimate because of a population shortage during the war. For the decree, see Diog. Laert. 2.5.26; Ath. 13.556; cf. Eur. *Or.* 909. For further discussion, see Storey 1989: 19–20.

[24] Two passages in Aristophanes allude to a female Spartan poet, Cleitagora; cf. Ar. *Lys.* 1237; *Vesp.* 1245–47. For Megalostrata, see Ath. 13.600–601.

[25] Cartledge 1981: 93n.54.

[26] Mossé 1991: 149 and 153n.29.

Aristophanes' Praxagora, a character who will be discussed at length in the next chapter, this observation might be said to apply to Clytemnestra, Phaedra, and, in the present play, the Spartan Hermione.

HERMIONE'S FALSE ACCUSATIONS

Like the other plays already discussed, Euripides' *Andromache* makes use of a familiar plot pattern in which the absence of the male head of household provides an opportunity for women's speech to circulate freely. The play repeatedly recalls the events surrounding the Trojan war as the mythic prototype for this situation: by leaving his hearth unguarded, Menelaus courted his wife's seduction (ἄκλῃστ' ἄδουλα δώματα, 593). Similarly, the presence of Orestes at the end of the play evokes the transgressions wrought by Clytemnestra while her husband fought at Troy. In the *Andromache*, the prologue confirms the absence of the kurios: Neoptolemus has departed for Delphi, leaving no male member of his family to supervise Hermione and to ensure the safety of his concubine and her child (75–78). In his absence, the Spartan princess has assumed control of the house: by publicizing and acting on her false charges, she asserts her verbal dominance (50–55). The guarding imagery associated with Hermione throughout the play, and marked by φύλαξ and its cognates, shows how normative male surveillance of women has become inverted within the world of the play. As the servant remarks, Hermione herself has become a formidable guard of the palace (οὐ σμικρὸν φύλαξ, 86).[27] And in an effective moment of hyperbole, Andromache criticizes the Spartan princess for her vigilant watch over the nuptial couch: "You are so jealous that you would not permit even one drop of heavenly dew to come near your husband" (σὺ δ' οὐδὲ ῥανίδ' ὑπαιθρίας δρόσου | τῷ σῷ προσίζειν ἀνδρὶ δειμαίνουσ' ἐᾷς, 227–28).

Organized around the antithesis of aging concubine and youthful, legitimate spouse, the prologue uttered by Andromache specifies women's speech as the source of domestic trouble. Juxtaposing her former wealth and social position with her present life, Andromache makes use of the motif of fortune's overturn that prefigures the reversal of Hermione's own status within her husband's house:

'Ασιάτιδος γῆς σχῆμα, Θηβαία πόλι
ὅθεν ποθ' ἕδνων σὺν πολυχρύσῳ χλιδῇ
Πριάμου τύραννον ἑστίαν ἀφικόμην
δάμαρ δοθεῖσα παιδοποιὸς Ἕκτορι.   (1–4)

---

[27] On the difficulties imposed on women by masculine surveillance within the oikos, see Ar. *Thesm.* 414–17, where the festival celebrants complain that Euripides' plays have made their husbands even more vigilant than usual, a passage discussed more fully in Chapter 6. For other references to guarding in the play, cf. φύλαξ (86, 812); φυλάσσειν (939, 950, 1130); and φυλακή (961).

O Asian land, o city of Thebes,
where once with gilded bride wealth
I came to Priam's royal hearth,
having been given as child-bearing wife to Hector.

The first part of the speech draws upon the traditional Homeric portrayal of Andromache as a loyal wife and mother in order to heighten the contrast between the slave woman and her haughty mistress. Although Andromache begins by invoking her natal city, she places more emphasis on the bridal procession to Priam's household: the terms δοθεῖσα and παιδοποιός indicate her status as a legitimate wife whose task was to produce male heirs.[28] Her allusion to Astyanax as "the child whom I bore my husband" (παῖδά θ' ὃν τίκτω πόσει, 9) underscores her fulfillment of this conjugal duty and shows her complete assimilation to her former husband's household, in pointed contrast to Hermione, who has yet to bear a child and who speaks as if she still belongs to her natal home.[29] But Andromache also describes her journey to Greece as a kind of bridal procession, similar to the one that had earlier taken her to the house of Priam (Ἑλλάδ' εἰσαφικόμην, 13).[30] The repetition of δοθεῖσα, which had described her betrothal to Hector, further imparts an air of legitimacy to her relationship with Neoptolemus (15). Moreover, the fact that she has produced a male child in her new oikos (ἄρσεν' ἐντίκτω κόρον, 24) places her in the position of legitimate wife and potentially protects her from harm (27–28).

After establishing her position as a loyal wife and slave by contrasting herself with her mistress, Andromache identifies Hermione's false speech as the source of her problems:

κακοῖς πρὸς αὐτῆς σχετλίοις ἐλαύνομαι.
λέγει γὰρ ὥς νιν φαρμάκοις κεκρυμμένοις
τίθημ' ἄπαιδα καὶ πόσει μισουμένην,
αὐτὴ δὲ ναίειν οἶκον ἀντ' αὐτῆς θέλω
τόνδ', ἐκβαλοῦσα λέκτρα τἀκείνης βίᾳ.   (31–35)

I am persecuted by her cruel reproaches.
For she alleges that by means of secret drugs
I made her childless and hated by her husband,
and that I wish to dwell in this house with him,
instead of her, casting out her bridal couch by force.

---

[28] On lines 1–5 as referring to a bridal procession, see Storey 1989: 18. According to Stevens (1971: 88), who cites Dem. 69.122, the term παιδοποιός distinguished the legitimate spouse from hetaeras and other sexual partners.

[29] Rabinowitz 1984: 112.

[30] Andromache's repeated allusions to Hector, and particularly her striking apostrophe to him, ὦ φίλταθ' Ἕκτορ, at 222, indicate that she in some sense still regards herself as his wife. Storey (1989: 18) notes that when Andromache uses the word πόσις, "husband," it always refers to Hector.

This accusation of *pharmaka* probably represents a piece of domestic realism, since one finds in the fourth century and later binding spells composed by women aimed at hindering a man's affection for a rival. A story surrounding the Sicilian tyrant Dionysius relates that the mother of one of his two wives attempted to administer contraceptive drugs to the other wife in the hope of preventing the birth of an heir.[31] However, Andromache puts the emphasis not on actual *pharmaka*, but on her mistress's allegations as a speech act: the verb λέγει (32; cf. 356) foreshadows her argument in the agon that Hermione's brazen speech has served as the prophylaxis that has kept Neoptolemus away from her bed. The term κακοῖς in conjunction with λέγει further suggests that the mistress of the house has subjected the slave woman to verbal raillery rather than physical abuse.[32] The domestic disorder entailed by Hermione's accusations, prompted by the gossip of other women, as we later find out, leads to a general gnomic pronouncement about women's garrulousness and love of conversation: "For women naturally take pleasure in having present evils on their mouths and tongues" (ἐμπέφυκε γὰρ | γυναιξὶ τέρψις τῶν παρεστώτων κακῶν, | ἀνὰ στόμ' ἀεὶ καὶ διὰ γλώσσης ἔχειν, 93–95). The fact that the gnome appears in Andromache's elegiac lament prompted Stevens to assume it referred to the pleasure in giving expression to grief, a Homeric commonplace;[33] however, the absence of any specific words for lament suggest rather that she refers generally to women's lack of verbal self-control and to their penchant for gossip, a problem Hermione will later address in her invective against women.

FEMALE NATURE ON TRIAL: THE FIRST AGON

Given the domestic situation presented in the prologue and the choral allusion to the judgment of Paris in the ode that follows the first agon, one might expect an exchange of insults between Andromache and Hermione, perhaps of the sort described by the simile in Book 20 of the *Iliad*:[34]

> ὥς τε γυναῖκας,
> αἵ τε χολωσάμεναι ἔριδος πέρι θυμοβόροιο
> νεικεῦσ' ἀλλήλῃσι μέσην ἐς ἄγυιαν ἰοῦσαι. . . .   (Hom. *Iliad* 20.252–54)

---

[31] I am grateful to C. A. Faraone for providing the following examples of women's binding spells directed toward a rival: see Wünsch 1897: no. 78; Audollent 1967: no. 271.46; Preisendanz 1973: V304–69. Caven (1990: 175) describes how the tyrant Dionysius married two women, a Locrian named Doris and another named Aristomache, both of whom lived in his palace. He later put Doris' mother to death on the grounds that she had given contraceptive drugs to Aristomache, her daughter's rival.

[32] Stevens 1971: 95.

[33] Stevens (ibid.: 105–6) cites as parallels the Homeric phrase τεταρπώμεσθα γόοιο; for a similar idea in tragedy, cf. Eur. *El.* 125–26, *Tro.* 608–9. At *Phlb.* 48a and *Rep.* 605d, Plato suggests that not only women enjoyed the pleasures of lamentation, but also male spectators in the theater.

[34] I am indebted to André Lardinois for drawing this passage to my attention.

Like women,
who, embittered by a soul-devouring quarrel,
fight with one another, going into the middle of the street. . . .

Or, for a more contemporary example, one might turn to Aristophanes' *Ecclesiazusae*, where the crone competes with a young girl for the attentions of a youth and the two engage in risqué and mutually insulting badinage (Ar. *Eccl.* 890–937). The Athenians associated this type of raillery, whether directed toward a husband or another woman, with women; Aristotle attributes a tendency toward nagging complaint to the female generally (φιλολοίδορον, *Hist. an.* 608b). Socrates similarly condemns the dramatic impersonation of the verbally abusive shrew, the *loidoroumenē*, as unsuitable for men (Pl. *Rep.* 395d5–e2). Moreover, this type of shrewish rivalry between women was considered by the ancients more appropriate to the comic genre, according to the scholion to *Andromache* 32.[35]

In Euripides' *Andromache*, however, we find a formal and quasi-judicial agon structured like the agon between Theseus and his son in the *Hippolytus*, with the antagonist resolved upon a punitive course of action and deaf to the eloquent rhetoric of the accused.[36] At issue is a question of fact, whether Andromache prevented Hermione from bearing children by means of destructive *pharmaka*, as stated in the prologue (32–35) and reiterated in this scene (156–58). Another element of the scene that resembles the agon between Theseus and Hippolytus is the fact that the judge and prosecutor are one and the same: both "defendants" argue against and before a person of greater social status than themselves. The question of *pharmaka*, however, soon yields to an almost sophistic debate about the proper conduct of women.

Despite Kovacs' observation that Euripidean characters tend to act like "seasoned barristers" regardless of their gender and social standing,[37] this agon is only one of three staged between women in extant Euripidean drama.[38] The juxtaposition of antithetical characters who express opposing views conjures the public "contests of arguments," introduced by

---

[35] The scholion to Eur. *Andr.* 32 reads as follows: "The mutual suspicions of women, their rivalry and abuse, and the other elements that make up a comedy, every last one of these, is included in this play" (γυναικῶν τε γὰρ ὑπονοίας κατ' ἀλλήλων καὶ ζήλους καὶ λοιδορίας καὶ ἄλλα ὅσα εἰς κωμῳδίαν συντελεῖ, ἐνταῦθα ἀπαξάπαντα τοῦτο τὸ δρᾶμα περιειληφέναι).

[36] On the resemblance between the two agones, see Lloyd 1992: 51–54. He argues that although the two defendants are doomed before they make their arguments, Euripides misleads the audience into thinking that they might convince their opponents of their innocence.

[37] Kovacs (1980a: 81) partly explains this phenomenon as reflecting the Athenian love of debate.

[38] Lloyd (1992: 3) lists thirteen scenes in Euripides' plays generally acknowledged to be formal agones: most occur between men (*Alc.* 614–733; *Heracl.* 120–283; *Hipp.* 902–1089; *Andr.* 547–746; *Supp.* 399–580; *Phoen.* 446–635; *Or.* 470–629; *IA* 317–414); two take place between a woman and a man (*Med.* 446–622; *Hec.* 1109–1292) and only three between two women (*Andr.* 147–273; *Tro.* 895–1059; *El.* 988–1138).

Protagoras, in which competing speakers debated a single issue from opposite sides.[39] In this scene, Euripides has staged a controversy about *phusis* and *nomos* and dressed it in feminine clothing: "The poet has made his women introduce the unsettling idea that morals may be relative."[40] The repeated recurrence of λέγω and its cognates indicates that the central issue explored by the agon is the status and function of speech itself, particularly the speech of women, and its relation of their speech to men.[41] At the same time, the discrepancy between the characters' gender and the scene's legal structure and language continually verges on bathos.

The lack of rhetorical sophistication and intellectual substance in Hermione's rhesis show her to be concerned mostly with superficial appearance.[42] Appropriately, she enters dressed in the elaborate finery befitting a well-dowered bride (note that Helen at Eur. *Tro.* 1023 makes a similar entrance). The first word of her speech, κόσμον, "ornament" (146), affiliates her with the archetypal bride, Pandora, whose gilded and lovely exterior masked a corrupt interior.

> κόσμον μὲν ἀμφὶ κρατὶ χρυσέας χλιδῆς
> στολμόν τε χρωτὸς τόνδε ποικίλων πέπλων
> οὐ τῶν Ἀχιλλέως οὐδὲ Πηλέως ἄπο
> δόμων ἀπαρχὰς δεῦρ' ἔχουσ' ἀφικόμην,
> ἀλλ' ἐκ Λακαίνης Σπαρτιάτιδος χθονὸς
> Μενέλαος ἡμῖν ταῦτα δωρεῖται πατὴρ
> πολλοῖς σὺν ἕδνοις, ὥστ' ἐλευθεροστομεῖν.   (147–53)

With a crown of golden abundance around my head,
and the fabric of brocaded robes here against my skin,
not from the house of Achilles nor of Peleus
have I come here bearing offerings,
but from the Laconian land of Sparta.
My father Menelaus gives these things to me
along with a great dowry, that I might speak freely.

The word κόσμον also indicates a concern for appearance reminiscent of Pandora, a creature of pure artifice, and even Phaedra in the last play.[43] Hermione shares Pandora's golden ornaments, her elaborate costume, and her verbal guile.[44] The emphasis placed on her attire also recalls Hippolytus'

---

[39] Kerferd 1981: 29; cf. Diog. Laert. 9.52 [= 801A DK].

[40] Burnett (1971: 137) cites in support of her claim Eur. *Andr.* 173–76, 215ff.; cf. 437 and 693.

[41] For λέγω and λόγος in this scene, cf. Eur. *Andr.* 154, 187, 189, 192, 233, 234, 236, 238, 239, 251, 252, 264.

[42] Lloyd 1992: 52–53, and 99.

[43] Hes. *Theog.* 573, 587; *Op.* 72.

[44] On Pandora's golden jewelry, cf. Hes. *Theog.* 578; *Op.* 65, 73–74; on her clothing, cf. *Theog.* 575: δαιδαλέην; and on her craftiness, cf. *Op.* 67–68.

critique of women and their expensive taste for adornment in the earlier play (Eur. *Hipp.* 630–40). Moreover, the choice of the term ἀπαρχαί to describe the ornaments purchased by her father's wealth suggests sacrificial offerings appropriate to a deity, elevating her above mortal status and making her into a rival of Thetis herself.

The evocation of the wedding procession recalls the prologue, inviting a comparison between the young Spartan bride and the Trojan Andromache in her former life. But Hermione in her describing nuptial journey (ἀφικόμην, 150; cf. 3) focuses instead on wealth, her costly jewelry (χρυσέας χλιδῆς, 147; cf. 2), and her large dowry (πολλοῖς σὺν ἕδνοις, 153; cf. 2). Her affinity with her natal oikos also strikingly contrasts with the prologue: she describes herself as the daughter of Spartan Menelaus, to whom she devotes two full verses, while relegating her references to Achilles and Peleus to a half line each. Unlike Andromache, Hermione emphatically refuses to assimilate herself to the house of Aeacus, a refusal underscored by her inability to bear children to Neoptolemus and by the repeated reference to her as the daughter of Menelaus.[45] In addition, the present tense of the verb δωρεῖται implies an ongoing economic relationship with her father. Foxhall has recently made the argument that a dowry, especially that of a wealthy woman, provided a wife with a certain amount of protection within her husband's household in classical Athens, since a husband had to return it to the woman's father or kurios upon divorce; this law may have served as an incentive for men to treat their wives well.[46]

Though the play's general didactic message about the perils of marrying wealthy women may reflect this economic reality at Athens, Hermione's large dowry brings about a power imbalance within the oikos, one that may reflect contemporary ideas about Sparta. According to Hermione, this wealth and power imbues her with a special access to speech denied most Greek women, particularly Athenian women. She claims as her prerogative *eleutherostomia*, "freedom of speech"; though not a technical term like *parrhēsia*, it nonetheless suggests unrestrained male political speech rather than women's private talk.[47] The frame formed by the first and final terms of Hermione's speech, κόσμος and ἐλευθεροστομεῖν, evokes a contrast between the Sophoclean ideal of silence as an adornment for women and the verbal license and dominance associated with women in Sparta. In contrast, the futility of Andromache's speech, indicated by the unanswered messages she has sent to Peleus (79–81, 560–62), reinforces her marginal status.

---

[45] On the use of the patronym to identify her, see also Phillippo 1995: 365; cf. Eur. *Andr.* 486–89, 897; 1049–50.

[46] Foxhall 1989.

[47] Although the verb ἐλευθεροστομέω and its cognates appear infrequently in the fifth century, two Aeschylean examples refer exclusively to male speech, e.g., Prometheus' bold speech, cf. [Aesch.] *PV* 182 (ἄγαν δ' ἐλευθεροστομεῖς); and the speech of the Argive king,

Although Hermione accuses Andromache of rendering her infertile by means of drugs, most of her speech actually consists of an attack on her rival's barbarian nature and the perversions, sexual and otherwise, engendered by it. In recounting the charges, she links the knowledge of *pharmaka* with Andromache's barbarian origins, a topos that originates in Homer and recurs throughout the literary tradition.

δόμους κατασχεῖν ἐκβαλοῦσ' ἡμᾶς θέλεις
τούσδε, στυγοῦμαι δ' ἀνδρὶ φαρμάκοισι σοῖς,
νηδὺς δ' ἀκύμων διὰ σέ μοι διόλλυται·
δεινὴ γὰρ ἠπειρῶτις εἰς τὰ τοιάδε
ψυχὴ γυναικῶν.   (156–60)

Once you have cast me out, you wish to occupy this house:
I am hated by my husband because of your drugs,
and my womb is ruined and without offspring because of you.
For skilled at these things are the minds of Asiatic women.

The charge of magic is suitably vague and for this reason, difficult to counter: by specifying a physical effect worked by the *pharmaka*, Hermione implies Andromache has used some sort of salve or potion, much like that of the Nurse in the *Hippolytus*, to hinder her fertility (Eur. *Hipp.* 516).[48] This association of *pharmaka* with foreigners introduces Hermione's main rhetorical strategy, and one that ultimately fails, an attack on barbarian *phusis*.

A pronounced element of bathos undercuts not only Hermione's *phusis* argument in its various stages, as we shall see, but the whole speech. Her demand that Andromache either die or sweep her floors reveals a ridiculous incongruity between her self-representation as a sort of cult icon and her very pedestrian, domestic concerns:

δεῖ σ' ἀντὶ τῶν πρὶν ὀλβίων φρονημάτων
πτῆξαι ταπεινὴν προσπεσεῖν τ' ἐμὸν γόνυ,
σαίρειν τε δῶμα τοὐμὸν ἐκ χρυσηλάτων
τευχέων χερὶ σπείρουσαν Ἀχελῴου δρόσον,
γνῶναί θ' ἵν' εἶ γῆς.   (164–68)

In place of your once lofty thoughts you must,
humbled, grovel and fall abject at my knee,

---

cf. Aesch. *Supp.* 948–49 (ἐξ ἐλευθεροστόμου | γλώσσης). Cf. also *Philo* 1.474; Dion. Hal. 6.72.

[48] On the association of magical *pharmaka* with foreigners and remote places, cf. Hom. *Od.* 4.230 and 4.394; their role in fertility is seen in Medea's promise to cure Aegeus' infertility by means of potent *pharmaka* in exchange for refuge at Athens; cf. Eur. *Med.* 717–18. For a more extensive discussion of women and magic, see Chapter 3.

and sweep my house and sprinkle dewy water with your hands
from golden urns and know exactly where on earth you are.

This incongruity of extremes—die, or else sweep my floor—is almost comic. The elevated expression, τοὐμὸν ἐκ χρυσηλάτων | τευχέων χερὶ σπείρουσαν Ἀχελῴου δρόσον, to speak of banal housework similarly contributes to the effect of bathos.[49] Hermione's quotidian concerns strip away her illusory grandeur to reveal a foolish lack of circumspection. A similar technique is employed with the character of Menelaus, whose blustery arrogance is exposed and deflated through the insults of Andromache and Peleus in the next scene.

The association of magical *pharmaka* with barbarian women introduces the issue of *phusis* central to the rest of Hermione's speech. With ἀμαθία at 170, she imputes to barbarians an ignorance of proper kin relations, adducing as an example Andromache's willingness to share the bed of the son of her husband's murderer. The interlacing terms παιδὶ πατρός, πόσιν, and τέκνα exemplify the scrambled family ties that result from a barbarian proclivity for lawless behavior like incest and kin murder:

πατήρ τε θυγατρὶ παῖς τε μητρὶ μίγνυται
κόρη τ' ἀδελφῷ, διὰ φόνου δ' οἱ φίλτατοι
χωροῦσι, καὶ τῶνδ' οὐδὲν ἐξείργει νόμος.   (174–76)

Father mixes with daughter and child with mother,
and sister with brother; the closest kin advance
through murder and there is no law to stop them.

Yet even as Hermione enumerates the criminal consequences of privileging family over community, her association with the house of Atreus and its murders, as well as her future liaison with Orestes, almost comically undercuts her position. The barbarian *phusis* that overvalues blood ties and leads to incest and murder contrasts with a civilizing Greek *nomos* whose central institution is marriage:

οὐδὲ γὰρ καλὸν
δυοῖν γυναικοῖν ἄνδρ' ἕν' ἡνίας ἔχειν,
ἀλλ' εἰς μίαν βλέποντες εὐναίαν Κύπριν
στέργουσιν, ὅστις μὴ κακῶς οἰκεῖν θέλει.   (177–80)

Nor is it a good thing
for one man to hold the reins of two wives,
but looking toward one wedded Cypris
they are content, whoever do not wish to live badly.

---

[49] Knox (1979: 252) singles out as a characteristic of "Euripidean comedy" domestic situations that involve pedestrian characters and activities; for an example of menial labor used comically in Euripides, cf. Eur. *El.* 54ff.

Hermione here juxtaposes the Greek *nomos* regarding marriage with the barbarian license of Andromache, while simultaneously inverting the traditional Greek view of marriage as a restraint for women by suggesting that it is in fact wives who exert control over men. Her assertion may also anachronistically condemn the contemporary Athenian law discussed earlier that may have permitted men to have two wives. The allusion to εὔναια Κύπρις, conjugal sex, links Hermione to her mother, Helen, who is ironically termed εὐναία at 104 in the context of her elopement with Paris, and reveals her true concern to be *erōs*, not offspring. Hermione's defense of conventional law as a means of masking self-interest and an overvaluation of *erōs* potentially affiliates her character with the sophists and their arguments, represented in the world of the play by her father, Menelaus.

Whereas Hermione allies herself with a principle of *nomos*, by means of which she establishes the superiority of the Greeks, Andromache skillfully turns her argument against her, showing her behavior to be the product of a bad *phusis*.[50] Although ultimately unsuccessful, her speech contains a great degree of rhetorical sophistication and an abundance of legal terms that anachronistically associate it with the Athenian courts.[51] Her rhetorical proficiency and "almost sophistic skill" resemble those of contemporary Athenian demagogues and politicians, although in contrast to her opponent, she marshals this expertise in the service of justice.[52] In characteristic fashion, Euripides inverts dramatic and social norms by making the slave woman and her aging rescuer embody the noble values of a bygone era, while the Spartan Menelaus and his daughter project a vulgar and bourgeois attitude characteristic of demagogues in contemporary Athens.

Andromache's speech has a clear rhetorical structure, beginning with a proemium in which she ponders the advisability of speaking (184–91), followed by a series of rhetorical questions that culminates in a *reductio ad absurdum* (191–203). She then refutes the charges by impugning Hermione's character (205–14), especially her arrogant and boastful speech. The whole rhesis possesses vivid color and immediacy achieved by her use of rhetorical questions, hypothetical statements, emotional appeal, hyperbole, and gnomic assertions. As its main rhetorical strategy, the speech attempts to collapse the social and cultural distinctions between Andromache and her rival by appealing to their universal status as women. Once Andromache puts the argument on these terms, she then turns Hermione's *phusis* argument against her by showing how Hermione's own nature, inherited from Helen, has led to an excessive and destructive overvaluing of *erōs*.

---

[50] On Andromache as the victim of *nomos*, see Lee 1975: 10.

[51] The terms ἔνδικα (Eur. *Andr.* 187), κρατήσω, ὄφλω βλάβην (188), ἁλώσομαι (191), and ἐχεγγύῳ (192) represent examples of legal language in Andromache's speech.

[52] On Andromache's affiliation with the sophists, see Conacher 1967: 177.

Using a typical law-court technique, Andromache tries to overcome the prejudice of her interlocutors by contrasting her lack of credibility as a slave with Hermione's inappropriate arrogation of speech:

ἐγὼ δὲ τάρβῶ μὴ τὸ δουλεύειν μέ σοι
λόγων ἀπώσῃ πόλλ' ἔχουσαν ἔνδικα,
ἢν δ' αὖ κρατήσω, μὴ 'πὶ τῷδ' ὄφλω βλάβην·
οἱ γὰρ πνέοντες μεγάλα τοὺς κρείσσους λόγους
πικρῶς φέρουσι τῶν ἐλασσόνων ὕπο.   (186–90)

I fear that my servile status might in your eyes deny me
the privilege of speech, even though I have many just points.
If I win the suit, I fear that I might actually lose because of this.
For those who are high-spirited chafe
when inferiors make the stronger argument.

Andromache openly acknowledges her low social status: the phrase τὸ δουλεύειν reinforces the contemporary Athenian idea that slaves and other noncitizens had no claim to *parrhēsia* in the polis, nor any right to speak in court, in contrast to Hermione's boast of *eleutherostomia*.[53] At the same time, the slave woman implicitly asserts her rhetorical power to be superior to that of her rival; her use of technical and legal terms like ἔνδικα, κρατήσω, and ὄφλω βλάβην invests her speech with the authority of the courts.

In the subsequent lines (192–204), Andromache continues to exhibit a rhetorical sophistication incommensurate with her social status. Using an argument about possibility in order to deny a possible motive,[54] she states that her children, because illegitimate, pose no threat to any children and heirs Hermione might bear. But because the provision made in Athenian law for childless men recorded by Diogenes suggests that legitimacy in such a case would be a real question, this argument is inherently suspect. Indeed, Peleus will later claim that in the absence of any children born to Hermione and Neoptolemus, Andromache's offspring would be considered legitimate (714, 724), and even Hermione reluctantly recognizes these children as only "half-slave" (ἡμιδούλους, 942).

In the next part of her speech, Andromache moves from logical argument to an ad feminam attack, accusing Hermione of an excessive regard for sexual love. Drugs, she claims, have not rendered Hermione sterile; instead, her boasting has caused her husband's affections to stray:

---

[53] On *parrhēsia* and this passage, see Stevens 1971: 119; cf. Eur. *Phoen.* 392; *Ion* 674–75.
[54] I follow Goebel (1989) in believing that these lines should not be rearranged, *contra* Kovacs (1980a: 20–28). Andromache's argument, as Goebel points out, is exactly paralleled in Gorgias' *Palamedes*. Hippolytus also uses a similar type of argument from probability at Eur. *Hipp.* 1009–21. See also Stevens 1971: 119–20; and Lloyd 1992: 53.

οὐκ ἐξ ἐμῶν σε φαρμάκων στυγεῖ πόσις,
ἀλλ' εἰ ξυνεῖναι μὴ 'πιτηδεία κυρεῖς.
φίλτρον δὲ καὶ τόδ'· οὐ τὸ κάλλος, ὦ γύναι,
ἀλλ' ἀρεταὶ τέρπουσι τοὺς ξυνευνέτας.   (205–8)

Your husband does not hate you because of my drugs,
but only if you prove to be unfriendly company.
And this is the charm: not beauty, o woman,
but virtues delight husbands.

Andromache responds to the allegations of *pharmaka* by implying that
Hermione's arrogance has kept Neoptolemus away from the nuptial bed.
Drawing on the *phusis-nomos* distinction earlier employed by her rival, she
contrasts Hermione's fair appearance and costly attire with her lack of
inner virtue. The allusion to *philtron* evokes not only the erotic magic
associated with women in the Greek literary tradition, but also the charm
of speech, as illustrated by the character of the Nurse in Euripides' *Hippolytus*.[55] Instead of winning her husband's affections with seductive words
like those of Aphrodite in the judgment of Paris, Hermione drives him
away him with her shrewish goading:

σὺ δ' ἤν τι κνισθῇς, ἡ Λάκαινα μὲν πόλις
μέγ' ἐστί, τὴν δὲ Σκῦρον οὐδαμοῦ τίθης·
πλουτεῖς δ' ἐν οὐ πλουτοῦσι· Μενέλεως δέ σοι
μείζων Ἀχιλλέως. ταῦτά τοί σ' ἔχθει πόσις.   (209–12)

If you are at all aggravated, [you say] the Laconian city
is great, while you put Scyros nowhere. [You say]
you are wealthy among the poor. Menelaus in your opinion
is greater than Achilles. No wonder your husband hates you for this.

The abusive ranting attributed to Hermione strongly resembles the passages from Plato, Aristotle, and Plutarch discussed at the beginning of the
chapter that depict Spartan women as disdainful and deprecating toward
their husbands. Similarly, these sources frequently depict their complaints
as pecuniary in nature. The outspokenness of Spartan women diverges from
contemporary Athenian views, embodied by the character of Andromache,
which expected women to remain silent and indoors. Hermione's disparagement of her husband has resulted in an inversion of gender roles that
disrupts the normal relationship between married couples: "A wife ought
to be content even if she is given to a bad man, and not engage in
arrogant rivalry" (χρὴ γὰρ γυναῖκα, κἂν κακῷ πόσει δοθῇ, | στέργειν,
ἅμιλλάν τ' οὐκ ἔχειν φρονήματος, 213–14). On a rhetorical level, Andro-

---

[55] For the idea that a *philtron* may be purely verbal, cf. Eur. *IT* 1182, where Thoas asks
whether the Argive strangers are using news of Argos as a *philtron*. On the idea of female
decorum as a type of love charm, see Plut. *Mor.* 141C.

mache's generalizations about what constitutes appropriate behavior for women establish her character as a paragon of domestic virtue, in contrast to Hermione, whose speech largely lacks these commonplaces, at least until much later in the play.

Again resorting to the *phusis-nomos* opposition, Andromache in almost Herodotean fashion adduces the hypothetical account of a Thracian king as an example of non-Asiatic polygamy (215–18).[56] Posed as a rhetorical question illustrating the principle of domestic tolerance just put forth, this passage is clearly calculated to use a foreign *nomos* as a means of exposing Hermione's promiscuity. Andromache thus turns Hermione's *phusis* argument about barbarians against her by showing her jealousy to be the product of her own sexual license.

εἰ δ' ἀμφὶ Θρήκην χιόνι τὴν κατάρρυτον
τύραννον ἔσχες ἄνδρ', ἵν' ἐν μέρει λέχος
δίδωσι πολλαῖς εἷς ἀνὴρ κοινούμενος,
ἔκτεινας ἂν τάσδ'; εἶτ' ἀπληστίαν λέχους
πάσαις γυναιξὶ προστιθεῖσ' ἂν ηὑρέθης.
αἰσχρόν γε· καίτοι χεῖρον' ἀρσένων νόσον
ταύτην νοσοῦμεν, ἀλλὰ προύστημεν καλῶς.   (215–21)

If from Thrace overflowing with snow
you had a royal husband, where by turns
one man shared his bed in common with many women,
would you kill them all? Then would you be discovered
attributing to all women an insatiate desire for sex.
How shameful! Indeed, we have this sickness
worse than men, but we conceal it well.

By rebuking her behavior as *aiskhron*, Andromache condemns Hermione not only for her licentiousness, but also for her inability to hide it from men. As in the *Hippolytus*, feminine *erōs* is configured as that which ought to be concealed from men, while feminine speech is portrayed as the vehicle that threatens to expose this *nosos* to them. The concentrated repetition of *logos* in the subsequent stichomythia confirms that women's speech, as an expression of their sexual proclivities, is the real issue.[57] Andromache thus denounces Hermione not merely for her lack of sexual self-control, but also for publicizing it through speech in a phrase reminiscent of Phaedra (λέγεις αἰσχρῶν πέρι, 238); this sexual license, she argues, brings universal disgrace on a woman, whether she is Greek or barbarian (κἀκεῖ τά γ' αἰσχρὰ

---

[56] Kerferd (1981: 112) notes that interest in barbarian customs seems to have been a fad among the sophists, citing as examples Herodotus, the *Dissoi logoi*, and a lost treatise of Aristotle entitled *Nomima barbarika*.

[57] For *logos* in the stichomythic exchange, cf. λόγοις (233), λόγων (234), λόγοις (236), λέγεις (238), λέγεις (239), λέξον (251), λέγω (252).

κἀνθάδ' αἰσχύνην ἔχει, 244). In the stichomythic exchange, Andromache further rebukes Hermione for her open and unrestrained discussion of sexual matters—"Will you not suffer in silence about your *Kupris*?" (οὐκ αὖ σιωπῇ Κύπριδος ἀλγήσεις πέρι; 240)—and contrasts this with her own resolve to remain silent (ἰδοὺ σιωπῶ κἀπιλάζυμαι στόμα, 250).

At the end of her rhesis, Andromache juxtaposes Hermione's bold speech and sexual license with a depiction of her former life as the wife of Hector: not only did she silently tolerate his liaisons with other women, but she actually promoted them:

> ὦ φίλταθ' Ἕκτορ, ἀλλ' ἐγὼ τὴν σὴν χάριν
> σοὶ καὶ ξυνήρων, εἴ τί σε σφάλλοι Κύπρις,
> καὶ μαστὸν ἤδη πολλάκις νόθοισι σοῖς
> ἐπέσχον, ἵνα σοι μηδὲν ἐνδοίην πικρόν.
> καὶ ταῦτα δρῶσα τῇ ἀρετῇ προσηγόμην
> πόσιν.   (222–27)

O dearest Hector, I both helped you
in your love affairs, if Cypris tripped you up,
and often to my breast I held
your bastard children, so as not to give you pain.
And in so doing, with my virtue I won over
my husband.

Andromache's account of nursing Hector's bastards functions rhetorically on several levels. First, it serves as a means of persuading Hermione to spare Andromache's own bastard child, whether motivated by self-interest or principle.[58] Second, the maternal associations of *mastos* both in this passage and in her subsequent address to Molossos (μαστοῖς ματέρος, 511) contrast with the promiscuity of mother and daughter, since the term later refers to the seductive beauty of Helen at 629 that caused Menelaus to drop his sword, and prefigure Hermione's shocking public nudity later in the play.[59] Finally, the fact that these lines make no reference to Andromache's speech in the presence of her husband but rather imply her silent compliance again distinguishes her behavior from that of Hermione.

In her final lines, Andromache explicitly assimilates the actions of the daughter to those of her notorious mother as a means of encapsulating her main argument based on *phusis*, that Hermione, as the progeny of Helen, cannot possibly possess the virtue of sexual self-control:

> μὴ τὴν τεκοῦσαν τῇ φιλανδρίᾳ, γύναι,
> ζήτει παρελθεῖν· τῶν κακῶν γὰρ μητέρων
> φεύγειν τρόπους χρὴ τέκν', ⟨ὅσ⟩οις ἔνεστι νοῦς.   (229–31)

---

[58] Burnett 1971: 135.

[59] For another example of barbarian female nudity, cf. Eur. *Hec.* 560, where Polyxena bares her chest in front of the assembled Hellenic host before being sacrificed.

Don't strive to surpass your mother in love for men.
For children ought to flee the traits of bad mothers
if they have any sense at all.

Here Andromache exploits the double signification inherent in the term φιλανδρία, just as we saw in the case of Clytemnestra in Aeschylus' *Agamemnon*: she implies both the excessive love for a husband exhibited by Hermione and Helen's adulterous promiscuity.[60] Both meanings imply an innate lack of sexual self-control potentially dangerous to the household.

In the stichomythic exchange that follows, the sophistic display of rhetoric organized around oppositions of *phusis* and *nomos*, word and deed, continence and incontinence, escalates into name-calling and abuse like that of the Homeric simile cited at the beginning of this section: "O you barbarian creature and stubborn arrogance," exclaims Hermione (ὦ βάρβαρον σὺ θρέμμα καὶ σκληρὸν θράσος, 261). This harsh apostrophe reinforces the characterization of Hermione as verbally dominating and unrestrained, particularly because female characters in Euripidean drama typically do not employ this form of negative address.[61] Andromache accomplishes what she fears in her proemium: she "wins" in the sense that her rival eventually concedes a verbal victory to her (σοφὴ σοφὴ σύ, 245),[62] and yet she loses in that Hermione, in flagrant disregard for her husband's authority, decides to act before his return, resorting to threats of violence (κοὐ μενῶ πόσιν μολεῖν, 255). Although both characters have employed sophistic techniques and arguments—indeed, the whole scene can be understand as a sophistic contest of words—only Hermione resorts to duplicity: after insulting Andromache, she cryptically alludes to a new plan: "I have a sort of lure for you. But I will hide my words" (τοιόνδ' ἔχω σου δέλεαρ. ἀλλὰ γὰρ λόγους | κρύψω, 264–65). The word δέλεαρ points forward to the verbal treachery ultimately employed by Menelaus, yet traditionally associated with women.

This underhanded treachery prompts Andromache's gnomic denunciation of all women. By viewing herself and other women with the distrust characteristic of men, Andromache not only affirms her own probity but also serves as a mouthpiece for the play's didactic message about the perils engendered by women and marriage:

δεινὸν δ' ἑρπετῶν μὲν ἀγρίων
ἄκη βροτοῖσι θεῶν καταστῆσαί τινα·
ὃ δ' ἔστ' ἐχίδνης καὶ πυρὸς περαιτέρω,

---

[60] At Pl. *Symp.* 191e, φιλανδρία is explicitly connected with adultery: "promiscuous and adulterous women" (γυναῖκες φίλανδροί τε καὶ μοιχεύτριαι).

[61] One form of negative address, ὦ + κάκιστος, is twice as likely to appear in male speech in Euripides (McClure 1995: 54–55); Hermione's address, because abusive, also belongs to this category.

[62] On the phrase σοφὴ σοφὴ σύ as conceding a verbal victory, cf. Eur. *Bacch.* 655.

οὐδεὶς γυναικὸς φάρμακ' ἐξηύρηκέ πω
κακῆς· τοσοῦτόν ἐσμεν ἀνθρώποις κακόν.   (269–73)

It is strange that some god has given to mortals
a cure for creeping beasts;
yet no one has discovered healing drugs
for the evil woman, a thing beyond snakes or fire.
Such a great evil are we to men.

The slave woman's earlier commonplaces about appropriate female behavior find their fullest expression in this invective. Like Hippolytus, Andromache uses the wayward behavior of one woman to denounce all women, including herself, while the familiar comparison of women to beasts underscores women's inherent lack of self-control. The double allusion to remedial *akē* and *pharmaka* returns to the idea of women's sexuality as a disease earlier introduced by Andromache (220); yet here the female becomes synonymous with an uncontrollable *nosos* that plagues men. Moreover, the gnome associates Hermione with both Pandora, whom Hesiod credited with introducing disease among mortals (Hes. *Op.* 90–95), and Clytemnestra, whose domestic treachery earned her an association with snakes in the *Choephori*, a comparison further amplified at the end of the play.[63] This blame discourse, condemning women for their duplicity and sexual license, in part counteracts women's gossip; it reinforces social norms and privileges a male subject position, whereas female gossip implicitly subverts the world of men by presenting a female perspective.

As a debate staged between women and one concerned with female virtue, the first agon in the *Andromache* deals explicitly with the problem of women's speech in the oikos. The scene identifies their speech as largely preoccupied with Aphrodite, a point summed up by Hermione's rhetorical question, "Isn't this the most important thing to women everywhere?" (οὐ γυναιξὶ ταῦτα πρῶτα πανταχοῦ; 241). Moreover, women's voluble and shameless talk is viewed as resulting from a lack of self-control, particularly sexual self-control. When this speech is not adequately held in check, either by a woman's own sense of modesty or by the authority of her husband, it threatens to subvert the stability and continuity of the oikos. We see just such an overturn at the end of the play, when Hermione abandons her husband's house for a liaison with Orestes, who has destroyed Neoptolemus because of a sexual rivalry.

The traditional invective against women, a discourse that adopts a male subject position, attempts to counteract women's licentious speech and behavior. By assigning this blame discourse to a woman, Euripides distinguishes her from her wicked peers, a technique also used with Phaedra in

---

[63] On snakes and domestic intrigue, cf. Aesch. *Cho.* 249, 992 (Clytemnestra); Soph. *Ant.* 531 (Ismene); *Ion* 1262 (Creusa); see also Stevens 1971: 126–27.

the *Hippolytus*, and suggests that the only woman who can be trusted is the one who condemns her peers. Because women's speech largely concerns *erōs*, it represents a principle of unbridled self-interest that poses a threat not only to the family, but also to the larger community, a concern expressed by other late fifth-century texts. The unrestrained and shameless speech of women, while almost comically staged in the first agon, provides a paradigm for darker destruction engendered by the dishonest and self-promoting speech of men in the subsequent episodes.

THE MALE INTRUDER: THE SECOND AGON

Although the departure of women from the house normally occasions disaster in Attic tragedy, Euripides' *Andromache* reverses this pattern with equally destructive consequences. Hermione remains at home while Menelaus arrives at her husband's house in a sort of perversion of typical wedding ritual.[64] He intrudes into a realm usually confined to women and meddles in matters that ought to be kept hidden from men. Whereas entry into the public sphere invests women with power, according to Shaw's model,[65] Menelaus' intrusion into the female domestic sphere has the opposite effect: he becomes effeminate and almost comically absurd, like the figure of Paris, to whom he is implicitly compared in the ode that immediately precedes this scene. Through him, callous opportunism intrudes into the world of epic heroism, downgrading its values and perhaps reflecting the changing political and social realities in contemporary Athens: he is a *phaulos*, a vulgar man whose wealth is perhaps meant to associate him with the manufacturing classes (cf. 325–79).[66] Only in the women's quarters could Menelaus pose any threat.[67]

Although staged between a man and a woman, the second agon involves a dynamic similar to that of the first: Andromache continually exposes Menelaus' buffoonish cowardice and self-interest, berating him for his involvement in the trivial affairs of women. The discrepancy that emerges between Menelaus' heroic pretensions and his unscrupulous and absurd pursuit of a helpless female enemy continues to contribute to an atmosphere of bathos. Whereas she had earlier chided Hermione for her bold and inappropriate talk, now her own insolent speech addressed to a male of much higher social standing draws sharp criticism from the chorus: "You have said too much as a woman speaking to a man, for it is no

[64] Storey 1989: 19.

[65] Shaw 1975.

[66] Burnett (1971: 140) remarks that with Menelaus, "the real world has invaded the tragic stage."

[67] Ibid.: 138–39.

womanly modesty that has let fly such words as these" (ἄγαν ἔλεξας ὡς γυνὴ πρὸς ἄρσενας, | καί σου τὸ σῶφρον ἐξετόξευσεν φρενός, 364–65). This aggressive speech effects a gender-role inversion, identifies Andromache as the verbally dominant of the two characters, and almost comically exposes how Menelaus, by squabbling with women, makes himself womanish:

οὐ χρὴ 'πὶ μικροῖς μεγάλα πορσύνειν κακὰ
οὐδ', εἰ γυναῖκές ἐσμεν ἀτηρὸν κακόν,
ἄνδρας γυναιξὶν ἐξομοιοῦσθαι φύσιν.   (352–54)

One should not make something great out of something small,
nor, if we women are a ruinous evil,
should men make their natures like women.

This commonplace about women—and it is no coincidence that Hippolytus uses the very same word, ἀτηρός, to describe them (Eur. *Hipp*. 630)—serves a purpose similar to Andromache's earlier invective: by reestablishing gender norms, it shows how the interlocutor, this time male, fails to meet them. But Menelaus' ruthlessness undercuts much of the comedy supplied by his figure: his part in this child murder chillingly evokes his association with the house of Atreus, specifically with the sacrifice of Iphigeneia, whose death, according to this play, he in fact commanded (σφάξαι κελεύσας θυγατέρα, 625). Joined to this criminality is the duplicitous verbal treachery illustrated in the first part of the play by Hermione's false charges, to which Andromache again alludes in this scene (ὡς αὐτὴ λέγει, 356). Like his daughter, Menelaus is a creature of *doxa*, of false appearance, who has undeservedly won fair repute (319–23) and who invites comparison to a sophist.[68]

By staging a second quarrel, the poet returns to the issue of speech raised in the first part of the play: this second "trial" makes a further mockery of the first one, since Menelaus must resort to cheating in order to bring about the death of his pathetic opponent, an aging female slave. As in the previous agon, an innocent litigant pleads before a judge who simultaneously serves as prosecutor: the numerous legal terms indicate a juridical process (ἀγωνιῇ, 336; συνδρῶν, 337; τὴν δίκην ὑφέξομεν, 358; βλάβην ὀφείλω, 360; ψήφῳ, 496), but a corrupt one, since, as we learn at the end of the scene, the woman had already been condemned to die at its inception (517–19). Menelaus' cheap victory over the female slave may be viewed as a "revolting show of legal scrupulosity,"[69] a display that suggests the vulnerability of the legal system to clever speakers who put self-interest and personal ambition above the good of the community and

---

[68] Kovacs 1980a: 68; his character "shows affinities with the Sophistic . . . and its belief in the power of reason and education."

[69] Ibid.: 63.

the difficulty of even gifted rhetoricians to overcome them by means of persuasion alone.

This principle of self-interest, which appears as an exaggerated form of Hermione's overvaluation of *erōs*, finds expression mainly through the observation that Menelaus, by dabbling in the affairs of women, makes much ado about nothing (cf. 352–54, 366–67, 387). The prototype for this type of overreaction is the Trojan war, a quarrel fought for a woman, as Andromache reminds him (διὰ γυναικείαν ἔριν, 362). Although he concedes that such matters are beneath him, Menelaus nonetheless articulates the underlying principle of lawless self-interest that motivates all his actions: "Whatever one's need happens to be, that's his Troy" (ὅτου τις τυγχάνει χρείαν ἔχων, | τοῦτ' ἔσθ' ἑκάστῳ μεῖζον ἢ Τροίαν ἑλεῖν, 368–69). This self-serving and relativistic principle is further amplified by the repeated elision of domestic and military spheres: Menelaus calls himself the *summachos* or "ally" of his daughter (371); he fights Andromache like a "grim hoplite" (γοργὸς ὁπλίτης, 458); and his defense of his daughter is characterized as a form of martial "plundering" (πορθεῖς, 633). By juxtaposing epic and quotidian concerns, the scene continually verges on comic bathos, a technique that exposes the very little man behind the self-important bluster and dramatically links his character to that of his daughter.

Perhaps the fullest expression of Menelaus' womanish nature, however, is the verbal trick he employs to persuade Andromache to leave the altar. Given the choice between saving herself and rescuing her son (381–82), she heroically chooses to die, employing the standard language of Euripidean sacrifice heroines; but as soon as she has surrendered herself, Menelaus reneges on his promise and condemns both of them to death (425–29). This *dolos* both recalls and inverts the crafty words of Aphrodite in the judgment of Paris, since here a man resolves a dispute among women by deceiving one of them. Menelaus' verbal treachery fulfills Hermione's promise of a new trick, but instead of concealing it, he shamelessly urges that it be publicly proclaimed (κήρυσσ' ἅπασιν, 436).

Like the first agon, this scene concludes with an invective delivered by Andromache against her opponent. But instead of using the example of women to denounce Menelaus, as she had earlier, Andromache derides his sophistic perfidy as characteristically Spartan.[70]

ὦ πᾶσιν ἀνθρώποισιν ἔχθιστοι βροτῶν
Σπάρτης ἔνοικοι, δόλια βουλευτήρια,
ψευδῶν ἄνακτες, μηχανορράφοι κακῶν,
ἑλικτὰ κοὐδὲν ὑγιές, ἀλλὰ πᾶν πέριξ

[70] Hall 1989b: 164 and n. 14 remarks that the large amount of anti-Spartan invective in this play represents one of the rare moments in tragedy in which criticism is directed toward another Greek state rather than toward barbarians.

φρονοῦντες, ἀδίκως εὐτυχεῖτ' ἀν' Ἑλλάδα.
τί δ' οὐκ ἐν ὑμῖν ἐστιν; οὐ πλεῖστοι φόνοι;
οὐκ αἰσχροκερδεῖς; οὐ λέγοντες ἄλλα μὲν
γλώσσῃ, φρονοῦντες δ' ἄλλ' ἐφευρίσκεσθ' ἀεί;   (445–52)

O dwellers of Sparta, you who are the most hateful mortals
to all human beings, treacherous schemers,
princes of lies, contrivers of evils,
crooked, unsound, twisting everything around in your minds,
unjustly do you prosper in Hellas.
What is *not* among you? Are most not murderers?
Are you not sordidly greedy of gain? Are you not detected saying
one thing with your tongue while always thinking something else?

This anachronistic invective specifies duplicity, particularly self-serving deceit, as the supreme characteristic of Spartans.[71] It echoes Andromache's earlier brief invective against women, especially the phrase οὐδὲν ὑγιές, which continues the motif of the "other" as a *nosos*, and it simultaneously points forward to Peleus' diatribe against Spartan women and to Hermione's final castigation of their gossip. Although the dramatic action in this scene emanates from the unrestrained and shameless speech of women, this second debate shifts the focus to the verbal treachery of men and figures it as feminine. Andromache's invective against Spartans thus proves that there is indeed something worse on earth than a woman—a man who acts like a woman.

HELEN AND THE EDUCATION OF WOMEN: THE THIRD AGON

After winning an easy and pathetic victory over the female slave, Menelaus encounters the aging aristocrat, Peleus, whose status as patriarch of the remaining Aeacid line furnishes him with authority over his grandson's house and invests him with the power to act as kurios over Andromache. Peleus brings to this world of debased mores and sexual license the epic values celebrated by the almost Pindaric encomium of the third stasimon. As we saw earlier, his opening question returns to the problem of speech as the cause of domestic disease, not only the speech of wayward women, but also that of treacherous men in a juridical context (ἐκ τίνος λόγου νοσεῖ | δόμος; 548–49). Staged between men, the third and final agon reverses the outcomes of the earlier two and makes use of yet a third type of invective in Peleus' scathing denunciation of Spartan women, a blame discourse that combines elements of the previous two.

---

[71] On contemporary views of Spartans as treacherous and brutal, see Eur. *Supp.* 187; Ar. *Ach.* 308; *Pax* 622; *Lys.* 629, 1269–70; Thuc. 2.39.1, 5.105.

In a technique familiar from the Athenian courts, where the behavior of female relatives was regularly used as evidence against men, Peleus indicts Menelaus for his own domestic negligence, citing as examples Helen's elopement with Paris and the general shamelessness of Spartan women. The third agon overturns the mock trials that deprived Andromache of a fair hearing (οὔτε τῷ δίκῃ | κρίναντες, 567–78) and that permitted Menelaus to carry out his lawless plots (ἄκριτα μηχανώμενοι, 549). Justice, effected by persuasion rather than by deceit or force, finally prevails: the child is saved and Andromache rescued from her bonds. Peleus wins this debate and Menelaus retreats, stating his intention neither to do nor to be persuaded of anything base (731). In fact, he vows to confront Neoptolemus openly upon his return, in contrast to his earlier actions, which were portrayed as stealthy and covert (παρὼν δὲ πρὸς παρόντας ἐμφανῶς | γαμβροὺς διδάξω καὶ διδάξομαι λόγους, 738–39).

With Peleus acting as her kurios, Andromache ceases to plead her case; rather, the old man intervenes on her behalf, as her spokesman, and the debate between men takes center stage. Peleus begins with a diatribe against Spartan girls and women, one that echoes the slave woman's earlier denunciation of Laconian men. By attacking Helen, he employs a strategy familiar from the courts by which a speaker uses the lawless behavior of his opponent's female kin to denigrate him. But Peleus begins with the general condition of women in Sparta and then moves to the specific example of Helen to reinforce his claim that their education engenders depravity by inverting gender norms. By means of this argument, he indirectly attacks Spartan men, since their lack of vigilance has directly resulted in the sexual license and immodesty of Spartan females.

> σὺ γὰρ μετ' ἀνδρῶν, ὦ κάκιστε κἀκ κακῶν;
> σοὶ ποῦ μέτεστιν ὡς ἐν ἀνδράσιν λόγου;
> ὅστις πρὸς ἀνδρὸς Φρυγὸς ἀπηλλάγης λέχος,
> ἄκλῃστ' ἄδουλα δώμαθ' ἑστίας λιπών,
> ὡς δὴ γυναῖκα σώφρον' ἐν δόμοις ἔχων
> πασῶν κακίστην.   (590–95)

Are you to be numbered among men, you, the basest of the base?
In what sense can you be counted as a man or esteemed by men?
You who were divorced from your wife by a Phrygian,
having left your household hearth unlocked and unguarded by slaves,
thinking that you had a chaste wife in your house
when she was in fact the basest of them all.

With his contemptuous spate of *anēr* words (590, 591, 592), Peleus impugns Menelaus' manhood, while the words κάκιστος (twice in 590, and note κἀκ as a verbal echo, 595) and λιπών (593, λιποῦσα, 603) equate his abdication of domestic authority with Helen's lack of sexual self-control.[72] The anachronistic use of the technical term for divorce, ἀπαλλάσσεσθαι, contains another implicit criticism: instead of divorcing his wife, as Athenian law would have required, Menelaus accepted her back into his oikos, a point further elaborated later in the speech.[73] The fact that Menelaus was so misled by Helen recalls Semonides' warning at the end of his iambic invective against women, that the wife who appears especially chaste is the one most likely to act outrageously (Semon. fr. 7. 108–9).

This disobedience, Peleus argues, results from the male education received by Spartan women, which required their presence outdoors to compete, half-nude, in masculine athletic activities in an inversion of normal gender roles:

> οὐδ' ἂν εἰ βούλοιτό τις
> σώφρων γένοιτο Σπαρτιατίδων κόρη,
> αἳ ξὺν νέοισιν ἐξερημοῦσαι δόμους
> γυμνοῖσι μηροῖς καὶ πέπλοις ἀνειμένοις
> δρόμους παλαίστρας τ' οὐκ ἀνασχετοὺς ἐμοὶ
> κοινὰς ἔχουσι. κᾆτα θαυμάζειν χρεὼν
> εἰ μὴ γυναῖκας σώφρονας παιδεύετε;
> Ἑλένην ἐρέσθαι χρῆν τάδ', ἥτις ἐκ δόμων
> τὸν σὸν λιποῦσα Φίλιον ἐξεκώμασε
> νεανίου μετ' <u>ἀνδρὸς</u> εἰς ἄλλην χθόνα.   (595–604)

Not even if she wanted to could a Spartan girl be chaste,
since they abandon their houses in the company of young men,
and with bare thighs and loose garments
they occupy the race courses and the public wrestling schools,
things intolerable to me! Is it no wonder, then,
that they do not educate their women to be chaste?
Well might Helen have asked this, when she left the house,
forsaking Zeus *Philios*, and reveled her way to another land
with a young man.

The novel application of παιδεύω to women, a group not normally subject to formal education in the classical world, introduces the idea of education as something subversive and potentially dangerous. Reversing the sentiment expressed by Hippolytus, this passage implies that women may be taught self-control, if instructed properly. According to Peleus, however, the fact that Spartan women receive the wrong type of education com-

---

[72] Storey 1989: 22.

[73] [Dem.] 59.85–88, cf. Aeschin. 1.183. For a discussion of this law, see MacDowell 1978: 88; Cohen 1991: 107, 110, and 124, where he remarks, "The Athenian law of adultery did not aim at regulating adultery as a form of sexual misconduct, but rather as a source of public violence and disorder."

pounds their underlying weaknesses and makes them more licentious, investing them with more power than is prudent. This masculine education undermines traditional gender roles and destroys households; just as girls leave the house, ἐξερημοῦσαι δόμους, in the company of men to engage in athletics, ξὺν νέοισιν, so, too, Helen left her hearth, ἐκ δόμων, in the company of one such young man. This passage might point to a contemporary debate about whether virtue or self-control could be taught, one that used women as a primary example.

Although on one level it is an example of the gender inversion wrought by Spartan education, the allusion to the girls' nudity also points forward to the beauty of Helen's naked breasts, which caused Menelaus to drop his sword (629–30), and the shameful public nudity of Hermione in the subsequent episode.[74] The colloquial reference to Zeus *Philios*, patron of the symposium, in conjunction with ἐξεκώμασε, portrays Helen as a postsympotic reveler who has abandoned the house for the public streets, an image that might even suggest a courtesan.[75] This association is perhaps strengthened by Peleus' sarcastic and comic remark that the Greeks should have paid Helen a wage to stay in Troy (μισθὸν ... | δόντα, 609). And it is hard not to interpret, in the light of Aristophanic sexual metaphors, Peleus' subsequent remark as an obscene innuendo: "You should have reviled her and not moved your spear" (μὴ κινεῖν δόρυ, 607). Such colloquial and comic elements strip away Menelaus' pretensions to reveal him as an absurd caricature of his epic counterpart.

The implicit comedy in this speech further derives from the way in which Peleus assimilates Menelaus to Helen and to women in general, a technique familiar from Attic Old Comedy and literally exemplified by figures such as the Relative in the *Thesmophoriazusae*. Through his figure, military and domestic realms become conflated: attired in gold like his daughter, Menelaus returns from the war with his armor as spotless and lovely as the day he left (κάλλιστα τεύχη δ' ἐν καλοῖσι σάγμασιν, 617). The conflation of martial and erotic pursuits reaches a height of bathos when Peleus describes Menelaus' encounter with Helen after the war:

ἑλὼν δὲ Τροίαν—εἶμι γὰρ κἀνταῦθά σοι—
οὐκ ἔκτανες γυναῖκα χειρίαν λαβών,
ἀλλ', ὡς ἐσεῖδες μαστόν, ἐκβαλὼν ξίφος

---

[74] Aristophanes later makes fun of this passage; see *Lys.* 155. The story of the courtesan Phryne baring her breasts in court probably originated with this mythic allusion; see Ath. 13.590e.

[75] According to Stevens (1971: 169), Nilsson has argued that Zeus *Philios* appears here as the patron of the symposium and that ἐξεκώμασε implies that "Helen abandoned the party to roam about the streets." He points out that the terms κῶμος and κωμάζω can refer "to the sequel to a symposium when drinkers sally out to serenade a mistress," as in Theoc. 3.1. The association of courtesans with the streets and the spaces outside the house is discussed in Chapter 1.

φίλημ' ἐδέξω, προδότιν αἰκάλλων κύνα,
ἥσσων πεφυκὼς Κύπριδος, ὦ κάκιστε σύ.   (627–31)

Having captured Troy—for I will go there with you—
you did not kill your wife once you had taken her in your hands,
but, as soon as you saw her breast, you threw down your sword
and kissed her, fawning over the traitorous bitch,
worsted by Cypris, you scoundrel!

This passage completely collapses the distinction between Menelaus as a
hero and as a lover, portraying him as a coward who puts his own interests
and sexual gratification above everything else.[76] Menelaus' overvaluation
of *erōs*, like that of his daughter, has made him weak and womanish: unable
to control himself, he cannot control his female kin. Thus Peleus turns
Menelaus into a lesson for his audience, one delivered in his extra-dramatic
aside and returned to at the end of the play: "Suitors! Take as your wife
the daughter of a good mother!" (μνηστῆρες, ἐσθλῆς θυγατέρ' ἐκ μητρὸς
λαβεῖν, 623).[77]

As a rhetorical strategy, however, Peleus' diatribe against Spartan women
both reviles Laconian men by demonstrating the profligacy of their women
and critiques a model of education that invests marginal and unscrupulous
figures with power, thus amplifying rather than mitigating their baseness.
The figure of Menelaus, with his clever arguments and disregard for *phusis*,
may in part exemplify the perils involved in the new education promulgated
by the sophists in contemporary Athens, especially given the larger number
of specious arguments in his speeches. In his response to Peleus, he first
establishes a principle of parity between individuals of unequal social status,
in this case, that of husband and wife, as a means of rationalizing his
involvement in his daughter's domestic affairs:

καὶ μὴν ἴσον γ' ἀνήρ τε καὶ γυνὴ στένει
ἀδικουμένη πρὸς ἀνδρός· ὡς δ' αὔτως ἀνὴρ
γυναῖκα μωραίνουσαν ἐν δόμοις ἔχων.[78]   (672–74)

And indeed equally the man and the woman lament
if she be wronged by her husband or likewise
if he holds his wife cheating on him in the house.

---

[76] This cowardice becomes the subject of Peleus' final contemptuous comment when he
lambastes Menelaus for tying up Andromache: "Were you afraid she'd defend herself against
you, taking up a sword?" (ἦ μὴ ξίφος λαβοῦσ' ἀμυνάθοιτό σε | ἔδεισας; 721–22).

[77] The scholion to 623 remarks that this aside was addressed to the audience, πρὸς τὸ
θέατρον. Although this offends the sensibilities of most commentators, including Stevens
(1971: 171), it is dramatically in character for the subsequent advice Peleus delivers about
finding a suitable bride at 1279–83.

[78] Stevens (1971: 176), along with other editors, takes 668–77 to be a histrionic interpola-
tion, remarking that the lines are "weak in argument and confused in expression."

Given the play's repeated emphasis on the dangers posed to the oikos by women left unsupervised in their husbands' absence, Menelaus' claim that female adultery (μωραίνουσαν) has the same weight as any kind of male oversight comes across as exceedingly specious. At the same time, the idea that social positions are relative and individuals thus inherently equal has a parallel in the sophistic treatise, the *Dissoi logoi*. Further, the issue of women's education introduced by the negative example of Sparta may in fact reflect contemporary sophistic debate about the position of women in classical Athens, a point raised in Chapter 1.[79]

Menelaus' abbreviated *apologia* for Helen employs two sophistic arguments familiar from Gorgias' *Helen*: He argues first that the gods, not Helen, were responsible for her flight to Troy ('Ελένη δ' ἐμόχθησ' οὐχ ἑκοῦσ', ἀλλ' ἐκ θεῶν, 680). He then appeals to the irrational and spellbinding power of sight as that which induced him to spare Helen's life (πρόσοψιν, 685). He concludes with a sophistic paradox that returns to the idea of education earlier introduced by Peleus:

ὅπλων γὰρ ὄντες καὶ μάχης ἀίστορες
ἔβησαν εἰς τἀνδρεῖον· ἡ δ' ὁμιλία
πάντων βροτοῖσι γίγνεται διδάσκαλος.   (682–84)

For the Greeks, inexperienced in arms and war,
went into their manhood. Comradeship between
all men becomes a teacher to mortals.

As Stevens notes, the assertion that the Trojan war gave an education in bravery to all Greece may correspond to contemporary rhetorical exercises in defense of Helen.[80] The term διδάσκαλος responds directly to Peleus' allusion to education; but the idea conveyed here, that all men may learn equally in the arena of war, suggests that virtue is not innate but might be taught, as the contemporary sophistic movement maintained. The fact that διδάσκαλος and διδάσκω appear only in the mouths of the play's more contemptible characters, including Hermione and Orestes, reinforces the dangers inherent in a type of education that might provide social mobility for all.[81]

Similarly, Peleus' anachronistic allusions in his response to Menelaus indicate that the debate has indeed shifted to more contemporary political issues. First, he compares the Spartan to a general who takes all the credit for the work his men (δόκησιν, 696), even though he himself has done

---

[79] *Dissoi logoi* 2.17 (= 90 DK). On the sophistic movement and the question of women, see Kerferd 1981: 159–62, and Chapter 1 above.

[80] Stevens (1971: 177) refers to 681–84 as a sophistic paradox that Euripides may have borrowed from Gorgias, or similar rhetorical exercises in defense of Helen.

[81] For διδάσκαλος and διδάσκω in Eur. *Andr.*, cf. 684, 739, 957, 984. See also Kerferd 1981: 37 and 131–38.

nothing, an assertion that echoes Andromache's denunciation of spurious *doxa* at 319–23. The term στρατηγός suggests not only a military post, but also the Athenian elective office, held for fifteen consecutive years by Pericles, but later increasingly assumed by career politicians, as discussed in Chapter 1. He then goes on to critique the democratic officials who snub the masses:

σεμνοὶ δ' ἐν ἀρχαῖς ἥμενοι κατὰ πτόλιν
φρονοῦσι δήμου μεῖζον, ὄντες οὐδένες·
οἱ δ' εἰσὶν αὐτῶν μυρίῳ σοφώτεροι,
εἰ τόλμα προσγένοιτο βούλησίς θ' ἅμα.   (699–702)

The arrogant sitting in public office in the polis
look down on the *dēmos*, even though they are nobodies.
But they are infinitely wiser than them,
if only they also had daring and common purpose.

The words ἀρχαῖς and δήμου further imply a contemporary reference, leading Stevens to conclude that the poet may be alluding to "a growing tendency for generals to take more credit to themselves," or even to the demagogue, Cleon, if the play was produced after 425.[82] It is also possible, given the increasingly important role played by demagogues in the democratic polis after the death of Pericles, that Euripides refers more generally to the dangerous elevation of persons of low social status and great wealth to high political positions by means of the new education and their skillful manipulation of *doxa*. Such a shift in power contributes to the silencing of the wellborn, rendering their eloquent persuasion futile. This silenced *dēmos* is represented first by Andromache and later by Peleus, whose speech Menelaus dismisses as trivial and vain:

τοὺς σοὺς δὲ μύθους ῥᾳδίως ἐγὼ φέρω·
σκιὰ γὰρ ἀντίστοιχος ὡς φωνὴν ἔχεις,
ἀδύνατος, οὐδὲν ἄλλο πλὴν λέγειν μόνον.   (744–46)

Easily do I bear your words.
Like a shadow standing opposite you have a voice,
powerless, nothing else except speech.

Inverting the democratic ideal of speech as that which endows individual men with political power and authority, Menelaus transforms speech into the active sign of marginality. This ineffectual speech recalls the messages earlier sent by Andromache, another marginal figure, and unheeded by all but Peleus; indeed, as the Nurse reminds Hermione in the next scene, the

---

[82] Stevens (1971: 178), who cites in support Dem. 23.198; Aeschin. 3.183, 185, 243; on Cleon, cf. Ar. *Eq.* 392. See also Kovacs 1980a: 69.

testimony of a barbarian slave woman will not count for much in the eyes of Neoptolemus (869–70).

The education of Spartan women condemned by Peleus in this scene provides a parallel for the new education of the sophists in the contemporary Athenian polis, exemplified by the figure of Menelaus in the play. By abolishing traditional, and "natural," gender hierarchies, Spartan education turns women into men, allowing them to leave the house and display their bodies publicly like men, a practice that leads to sexual promiscuity. At the same time, it propagates feminine verbal treachery in men and encourages a dangerous privileging of self-interest over that of the group, as evidenced by Menelaus' womanish pursuit of *erōs*. Such men cannot govern others, either as kurioi in the oikos or as leaders in the city; thus Menelaus, abdicating all domestic responsibility, abandons his daughter, as he had earlier his wife, even though Peleus has ordered him to remove his daughter from his house in a gesture suggestive of a divorce procedure.[83] This second instance of neglect has consequences almost as disastrous as the first, leading ultimately to the destruction of an innocent man.

HERMIONE'S INVECTIVE AGAINST WOMEN

The fourth episode returns to the problem of women inadequately supervised within the house and the opportunities for gossip it engenders. This scene is structured like the initial exchange between Phaedra and the Nurse in the *Hippolytus*. The Nurse informs the audience that Menelaus has abandoned his daughter (ἐρημωθεῖσα, 805; cf. μονάδ' ἔρημον, 855) and admonishes Hermione to cover herself and return to the house. Her allusion to the servants standing guard over Hermione in an attempt to forestall her suicide signals a reversal of Hermione's jealous vigilance over her husband (εἴργουσι φύλακες, 812). Hermione's changed perspective, denoted by her new awareness of the impropriety of her actions (e.g., ἔγνωκε πράξασ' οὐ καλῶς, 815; cf. 823, 894), does not necessarily indicate true remorse, as some critics have argued, but rather demonstrates the lack of self-control, sexual and otherwise, that destabilizes the oikos in the absence of any male authority.[84] Hermione, it seems, can only sustain her contrition until the next man happens along. Her tendency toward

---

[83] Although the phrases ἐκκομίζου παῖδα (639) and φθείρεσθε τῆσδε (715) in reference to the removal of Hermione from her husband's house do not have a technical meaning, I believe that Peleus implies a divorce procedure here. MacDowell (1978: 88) states that a woman's father had right to take her away from her husband, thereby initiating a divorce; cf. Dem. 41.4; Men. *Epit.* 657–58 (= Sandbach 1979: 328–30).

[84] Critics of this scene have gotten sidetracked by the question of whether or not Hermione's remorse is genuine. Burnett (1971: 145) describes her contrition as "real" because "she is so much like us." In contrast, Stevens (1971: 193) argues that she is just putting on an act

excessive emotionalism not only has rendered her vulnerable to the malicious gossip of women, but also makes her easy prey for Orestes' unscrupulous act of persuasion.

This scene relies heavily on the motif of fortune's overturn introduced in the prologue, only now the two women have effectively changed places, with Hermione forced to supplicate in servile fashion as Andromache had earlier (δούλα, 860; ἀγαλμάτων ἱκέτις, 859). Whereas the first agon had concluded with Hermione's promise to force the slave woman off the altar by means of fire, now she melodramatically proposes to immolate herself (847). Similarly, her lyric lament (825–65), lack of resources (ἀμηχανεῖς, 983), and pleas for rescue (ἐπιστολάς, 964) recall the helpless state of Andromache earlier in the play. The similarities between the two women forged by this scene prove the truth of the slave woman's words in the first agon, that the precepts governing women's lives, and the consequences of disobeying them, transcend ethnicity and social status.

Against all tragic convention, Hermione's presence outside the house conveys not agitated *erōs*, but a superficial return to modesty, a reversal that underscores how completely her actions have confused normative gender categories. Throwing her veil to the ground (830–31), she uncovers her breast as a testament to her crime:

τί δέ με δεῖ στέρνα
καλύπτειν πέπλοις; δῆλα καὶ
ἀμφιφανῆ καὶ ἄκρυπτα δε-
δράκαμεν πόσιν.　　　　　　　　　　　　　　　(832–835)

Why should I conceal my chest
with robes? For I have done to my husband
things clear, conspicuous and unhidden.

But this public and almost barbarian display of nudity, because it evokes Helen's naked supplication of Menelaus and the brazenness of Spartan girls (595–600), simultaneously confirms her shameless nature.[85] For this reason, the chorus admonish her to cover herself: "Cover your chest, put on your clothes!" (κάλυπτε στέρνα, σύνδησαι πέπλους, 832). Proving the truth of Peleus' invective against Spartan women, Hermione lacks self-control; instead, excess, τὸ λίαν (866), governs all her actions, causing unrestrained speech and behavior.

Having recognized the seriousness of her crime, Hermione decides that that she can no longer remain in her husband's house (τᾷδ' οὐκέτ' ἐνοικήσω | νυμφιδίῳ στέγᾳ, 857–58), but obdurately remains outside, even when the Nurse exhorts her to return inside:

---

for the sake of Neoptolemus. Similarly, Kovacs (1980a: 74) holds that her grief results from the fact that she has done things she cannot hide (834).

[85] Kovacs 1980a: 71.

ἀλλ' εἴσιθ' εἴσω μηδὲ φαντάζου δόμων
πάροιθε τῶνδε, μή τιν' αἰσχύνην λάβῃς,
πρόσθεν μελάθρων τῶνδ' ὁρωμένη, τέκνον.   (876–78)

But go inside and do not show yourself
before this house, lest you bring disgrace upon yourself
by being seen outside the house, child.

The idea of being seen, conveyed by the participle ὁρωμένη, not only recalls the sight of Helen that caused Menelaus to drop his sword, it also foreshadows the arrival of Orestes, who, upon finding Hermione outside the house, remarks that he sees her clearly (σαφῶς ὁρῶ, 896), an admission that raises the question of what exactly he has seen. Moreover, the word αἰσχύνη, "disgrace," hints at adultery, as it did in Phaedra's great speech. Hermione's visible presence out of doors leads directly and irrevocably to the next domestic disaster, her adulterous liaison with Orestes.

Fresh from the murder of his mother, Orestes' opening words betray his deceitful and dissembling character; stating that he has come to inquire after his cousin (886–89), he defers disclosure of his true purpose, the seduction of Hermione, until 957. The play establishes an equivalency between his own erotic scheming and the feminine domestic treachery of Hermione through the verb ῥάπτω and its cognates, since this word describes both of their plans to eliminate their sexual rivals (εἰς γυναῖκ' ἔρραψας οἷα δὴ γυνή, 911; μηχανορράφος, 1116). The kin terms in his speech ironically echo Hermione's earlier denunciation of barbarians as too inbred (ξυγγενοῦς, 887; φίλη, 890; cf. οἰκείου φίλου, 986). In the same way, the use of patronyms and matronyms in this exchange suggests a genetic continuity in the pattern of their crimes: just as Orestes presents himself as the offspring of Agamemnon and the cunning Clytemnestra, so Hermione appropriately calls herself "the very one whom the Tyndarid woman Helen bore" (ἥπερ μόνην γε Τυνδαρὶς τίκτει γυνὴ | Ἑλένη κατ' οἴκους πατρί, 898–99). Like Menelaus, Orestes intrudes into the female, domestic sphere of another man's house to intervene on behalf of a woman over whom he has no real authority. He, too, has a score to settle over a woman, since Menelaus once promised him Hermione in marriage and then reneged on the agreement (note the marriage language, γυναῖκ' ἐμοί σε δοὺς ὑπέσχετο, 969). The frank acknowledgment of conjugal sex, λέχος (905), as the source of Hermione's troubles, a detail suppressed in all earlier accounts of her situation except that of the first agon, gives the exchange between Orestes and Hermione an unsavory cast. Whereas Andromache had earlier asserted that women ought to conceal their *nosos* from men, an idea frequently reiterated in the *Hippolytus*, Hermione here freely confesses hers to a former suitor and potential seducer (906).

The inappropriate atmosphere of intimacy created by Hermione's sexual confessions, combined with the absence of a kurios, makes Hermione the easy prey of the corrupt Orestes, who opportunistically amplifies the domestic consequences of her betrayal: "For these deeds you fear your husband" (ταρβεῖς τοῖς δεδραμένοις πόσιν, 919). But Hermione defends herself through a scathing invective against women that displaces the blame for her crimes onto other women. She begins by imagining that gossiping women will denounce her to Neoptolemus, who will either kill her or reduce her to slavery, compelling her to serve the bed she formerly ruled (927–28). This thought prompts a lengthy diatribe against women's subversive speech:

κακῶν γυναικῶν εἴσοδοί μ' ἀπώλεσαν,
αἵ μοι λέγουσαι τούσδ' ἐχαύνωσαν λόγους·
Σὺ τὴν κακίστην αἰχμάλωτον ἐν δόμοις
δούλην ἀνέξῃ σοὶ λέχους κοινουμένην;
μὰ τὴν ἄνασσαν, οὐκ ἂν ἔν γ' ἐμοῖς δόμοις
βλέπουσ' ἂν αὐγὰς τἄμ' ἐκαρποῦτ' ἂν λέχη.   (930–35)

The visits of evil women ruined me;
their speech puffed me up with boastful words:
"How can you tolerate that vile spear-prize in your house,
sharing your bed with a mere slave?
By the Queen [Hera], she would not look upon the light
in my house while she reaped the fruit of my bed."

The reference to visits, εἴσοδοι, rather than speech, with its prefix εἰς, connotes the mobility Hippolytus condemns in the women who traffic in speech, whether servants or noblewomen, and the inability of men to control them. Such intercourse renders the oikos vulnerable to encroachment from without and undermines masculine authority within, engendering strife and interfering with male control of the nuptial bed. The women's taunts, realistically portrayed by the feminine oath sworn to Hera, also recall the wordy strife that divided the goddesses in the judgment of Paris and that led not only to domestic discord, but to a massive war. This quoted speech portrays women as exclusively preoccupied with the subject of erōs, while its effect on the listener works as a form of seduction:

κἀγὼ κλύουσα τούσδε Σειρήνων λόγους,
[σοφῶν πανούργων ποικίλων λαλημάτων,]
ἐξηνεμώθην μωρίᾳ. τί γάρ μ' ἐχρῆν
πόσιν φυλάσσειν, ᾗ παρῆν ὅσων ἔδει.   (936–39)

And I, heeding the words of Sirens,
[of clever, evil-doing, crafty chatterings,]
I was swelled up with folly. Why should I have
guarded my husband? I have all that I need.

By comparing women's speech to a Siren song, Hermione shifts the blame in almost Gorgian fashion to speech itself. The line bracketed by Stevens recalls the crooked speech of the Spartans denounced by Andromache at 445–53 and thus equates *dolos* as a feminine form of persuasion with the teachery of Laconian men: both types are depicted as inciting immoral activities in others, leading to a breakdown in civil and domestic order.

Male supervision of women within the household comprises the main theme of the rest of the rhesis, in which Hermione further denounces women and warns of the perils of marriage, thereby recalling Peleus' extra-dramatic advice to suitors (622–23) as well as the two invectives against women uttered by Andromache:

ἀλλ' οὔποτ' οὔποτ'—οὐ γὰρ εἰσάπαξ ἐρῶ—
χρὴ τούς γε νοῦν ἔχοντας, οἷς ἔστιν γυνή,
πρὸς τὴν ἐν οἴκοις ἄλοχον ἐσφοιτᾶν ἐᾶν
γυναῖκας· αὗται γὰρ διδάσκαλοι κακῶν·
ἡ μέν τι κερδαίνουσα συμφθείρει λέχος,
ἡ δ' ἀμπλακοῦσα συννοσεῖν αὐτῇ θέλει,
πολλαὶ δὲ μαργότητι ... κἀντεῦθεν δόμοι
νοσοῦσιν ἀνδρῶν.   (943–50)

Never, never—for I will say it more than once—
should those who have sense and are married
permit women to visit their wives at home.
For they are teachers of evil.
One destroys her marriage bed for gain,
another, having gone astray, wishes company in her sickness,
many out of sheer lust. Thereupon the houses of men
grow diseased.

Hermione here addresses herself not to women, but to men, to whom the job of supervising women within the oikos falls, a responsibility earlier abdicated by Menelaus. Her words thus contain considerable irony, since at this dramatic moment danger lurks not in the cunning speech of women, but in Orestes, whose speech, because duplicitous and erotically motivated, has a feminine coloration. The allusion to gossiping women as διδάσκαλοι κακῶν, "teachers of evil," evokes the sophistic discourse of Menelaus and the dangers of Spartan education enumerated by Peleus. By encouraging adultery, women's speech subverts gender roles within the oikos, just as the new education promoted by the sophists in the democratic polis overturns traditional social hierarchies. The final disease metaphor suggests the impossibility of fully containing this destructive speech because it spreads undetected and without obvious origin.

Hermione's final exhortation, that men guard their houses against these female intruders, contains a palpable irony, since she, who once jealously

guarded her own husband in a reversal of the normal role, is about to
forsake her husband's house for another man:

> πρὸς τάδ' εὖ φυλάσσετε
> κλήθροισι καὶ μοχλοῖσι δωμάτων πύλας·
> ὑγιὲς γὰρ οὐδὲν αἱ θύραθεν εἴσοδοι
> δρῶσιν γυναικῶν, ἀλλὰ πολλὰ καὶ κακά.　　　　(950–53)

In addition, guard well
the door of your houses with bolts and bars.
For the visits of women from outside the house
engender nothing sound, but a great many evils.

The phrase οὐδὲν ... ὑγιές, "nothing healthy" (952), again underscores
the idea of women as a *nosos* while likening their treachery to that of the
Spartans earlier censured by Andromache with the same phrase (448).
Women, who as outsiders imperil stability within the oikos, have as their
correlative in the polis foreigners, whether Spartans or sophists, who
threaten to undermine social and political stability.

Rebuking Hermione for her forthright speech, the chorus point to a
final irony: she who has denounced the speech of women herself speaks
boldly and publicly before a man:

> ἄγαν ἐφῆκας γλῶσσαν εἰς τὸ σύμφυτον.
> συγγνωστὰ μέν νυν σοὶ τάδ', ἀλλ' ὅμως χρεὼν
> κοσμεῖν γυναῖκας τὰς γυναικείας νόσους.　　　　(954–56)

You have let loose your tongue against your own kind.
This sort of thing is pardonable in you, but nonetheless
women must disguise women's sickness.

The fact that Hermione boldly proclaims her *nosos* instead of concealing
it both violates the unspoken pact among women not to inform on one
another and reinforces her lack of self-control.[86] The chorus elide the
"sickness" of women's sexuality with that of their speech: both should be
hidden from men. Although Hermione's invective affiliates her, however
fleetingly, with female propriety, it is undercut by a considerable irony
because it exposes rather than conceals her unrestrained nature, and to a
man, no less.

SLANDER: THE MALE DISEASE

The disease of speech engendered by women's lack of sexual self-control
has its correlative in Orestes, whose initial duplicity sets the standard for

---

[86] The scholion to 954 glosses τὸ σύμφυτον as τὸ γυναικεῖον γένος.

the rest of his speech. Attempting to persuade Hermione to abandon her present marriage and to honor her father's earlier pledge, Orestes sounds remarkably like the sophistic Menelaus, a similarity underscored by the presence of the words σοφόν and διδάξαντος in his opening gnome (957–58). His acknowledgment that he lied about his visit and instead kept a secret watch over Neoptolemus' house further identifies him as a creature of stealth and duplicity (and note the ambiguity of φυλακάς, 961), while a similar combination of secrecy and falsehood will characterize his actions at Delphi. By means of this verbal cunning, he effectively nullifies Hermione's marriage to Neoptolemus, reversing the usual procedure with his promise to restore her to her father: "I will lead you away from this house and I will give you to the hand of your father" (ἄξω σ' ἀπ' οἴκων καὶ πατρὸς δώσω χερί, 984). The role of kurios thus reverts back to Menelaus, from whose house Hermione never fully detached herself: "My father will take concern for my bridals, for it is not mine to make this decision" (νυμφευμάτων μὲν τῶν ἐμῶν πατὴρ ἐμὸς | μέριμναν ἕξει, κοὐκ ἐμὸν κρίνειν τόδε, 987–88). In this sense, her return to her natal oikos reverses the initial bridal procession mentioned at 147–54.[87] And when the chorus inform Peleus that Orestes has led her back to her father's palace, the participle ἄγων echoes the language of the Greek wedding ('Αγαμέμνονός νιν παῖς βέβηκ' ἄγων χθονός, 1061). Like her father and mother before her, Hermione, too, abandons her house (οἴκους μ' ἐξερημοῦσαν, 991; cf. δώματ' ἐκλιποῦσα, 1049).

Like Hermione, Orestes also contrives a means of ensnaring and eliminating his rival, Neoptolemus (μηχανὴ πεπλεγμένη | βρόχοις, 995–96). Operating under stealth, as Hermione had earlier, he refuses to divulge fully his murderous plans (ἣν πάρος μὲν οὐκ ἐρῶ, 997). His stratagem also involves verbal deceit, but instead of a false promise, he uses slander among men, διαβολή, as a means of bringing about Neoptolemus' death (ἀλλ' ἔκ τ' ἐκείνου διαβολαῖς τε ταῖς ἐμαῖς | κακῶς ὀλεῖται, 1005–6). Spreading volatile rumors about the nature of Neoptolemus' visit, he incites the anger of the Delphians against him:

'Αγαμέμνονος δὲ παῖς διαστείχων πόλιν
ἐς οὓς ἑκάστῳ δυσμενεῖς ηὖδα λόγους·
Ὁρᾶτε τοῦτον, ὃς διαστείχει θεοῦ
χρυσοῦ γέμοντα γύαλα, θησαυροὺς βροτῶν,
τὸ δεύτερον παρόντ' ἐφ' οἷσι καὶ πάρος
δεῦρ' ἦλθε, Φοίβου ναὸν ἐκπέρσαι θέλων;   (1090–95)

Once he had arrived at the city, the son of Agamemnon
uttered hostile words in each man's ear:

---

[87] Storey 1989: 21.

"See that man who advances through the hollows of the god
filled with gold, the treasuries of mortals,
who comes a second time to the place where he came before,
wishing to sack the temple of Apollo?"

The quoted speech of the Messenger in this passage, like the quoted speech in Hermione's rhesis, conveys the circulation of slander: disseminated without author or origin, Orestes' rumor recalls the gossip that provoked Hermione to plot the death of her rival.

But Orestes' actions, although also in service of *erōs*, like those of Hermione, have a more civic character. Whereas Hermione's false charges never directly permeate the civic sphere, Orestes' words have an immediate and public effect: his account advances rapidly through the city as a kind of malicious groundswell, a ῥόθιον, amorphous and without author (κἀκ τοῦδ' ἐχώρει ῥόθιον ἐν πόλει κακόν, 1096). Normally used of the sound of waves or a shouting crowd, the term combines the idea of noise and movement, suggesting the susceptibility of the *dēmos* to gossip and rumor.[88] This speech operates as a force uncontrolled by any external power, one that galvanizes the city's leaders to convene a tribunal (ἀρχαί τε, πληροῦντές τε βουλευτήρια, 1097). Though the gossip of women in this play has no direct impact on the male political sphere, as it did in the *Hippolytus*, it nonetheless provides a prototype for the malicious and destructive speech of men recklessly disseminated in the polis.

So persuaded are the citizens of Delphi by this false report that when Neoptolemus truthfully avers a desire to appease Apollo motivated his visit, they refuse to believe him, further corroborating the power of rumor ('Ορέστου μῦθος ἰσχύων μέγα, 1109). Orestes' verbal stratagem inverts the truth by showing Neoptolemus to play the part of a liar (ὡς ψεύδοιτο, 1110). This complex example of verbal treachery unites many of the play's earlier themes: as a μηχανορράφος (1116), Orestes resembles not only Menelaus and the Spartans, denounced by Andromache, but also the female gossipers of Hermione's invective, who devise and circulate false rumors within the house. The means Orestes employs to carry out his crime create an analogy between the circulation of gossip in the oikos, which eludes masculine control, and the difficulty of adequately controlling the spread of slander in the polis. Moreover, the play further correlates male verbal cunning to a corrupt sexuality, that of the seducer and paramour, just as it had earlier portrayed the lack of verbal restraint in women as resulting from their inability to control their sexual impulses.

---

[88] Stevens 1971: 224; the term θόρυβος frequently describes Athenian public gatherings like trials, meetings of the Assembly, and the theater; see Hall 1995: 43; Bers 1985; Pl. *Leg.* 876b1–6; and *Rep.* 6.492b5–c1.

RESCUING MARRIAGE: PELEUS AND THETIS

In the play's final overturn, Peleus is reduced to a status similar to that of Andromache: he has lost his only grandson in addition to his only son.[89] Whereas Peleus had earlier exhorted Hermione to raise herself up (ἔπαιρε σαυτήν, 717; cf. 197), now the chorus must bid him do the same thing (1077; cf. 705). He, too, claims no longer to have a city (οὐκέτ' εἶ, πόλις, πόλις, 1222). And just as Andromache had earlier lamented her own fate and that of her son by means of her *goos* (for the term, 97; cf. 103–16, 501–34), so now Peleus sings a *goos* over the corpse of his grandson returned from Delphi (κατομῶξαι γόοις | κλαῦσαί τε, 1159–60). But by addressing the polis several times in the course of his lyrics, he gives his lament civic implications (1176, 1211, 1222). His apostrophe to marriage shows how the institution of marriage mediates between the two spheres of household and city: "O marriage, o marriage, you who destroyed my house and my city" (ὦ γάμος, ὦ γάμος, ὃς τάδε δώματα | καὶ πόλιν ἀμὰν ὤλεσας, 1186–87). Like his earlier *Hippolytus*, Euripides' *Andromache* represents marriage, and women, its agents, as inherently disruptive of both household and city mainly because women's speech and *erōs* are difficult to control. But although the maidens' song at the end of the *Hippolytus* suggests that the institution of marriage may serve as a means of integrating women into the polis, this play provides no such parting disclaimer, but rather intensifies its atmosphere of invective in the final scene. It first converts Hermione into a kind of Clytemnestra, who has killed her husband, metaphorically cloaking him with death (ἀμφιβαλέσθαι | Ἑρμιόνας Ἀίδαν ἐπὶ σοί, τέκνον, 1191–92), while casting Orestes in the role of the corrupt seducer, Aegisthus, a cowardly stitcher of plots who kills his man unarmed. Such domestic treachery, promoted by women's sexual jealousy and their unchecked speech, leads to wide-ranging social and political upheaval, exemplified by the mythic Trojan war and dramatized in this unlikely domestic dispute between an aging slave woman and her bourgeois mistress.

With the appearance of Thetis from the machine, Peleus finally receives the compensation for which Andromache had earlier prayed (θεοί σοι δοῖεν εὖ καὶ τοῖσι σοῖς, 750). The entrance of the goddess infuses the play with the beneficial aspects of marriage and maternity previously evoked by the suppliant Andromache (χάριν σοι τῶν πάρος νυμφευμάτων, 1231; cf. 20). As benefactor, Thetis rectifies the damage women's speech and *erōs* have wrought by promising domestic harmony and immortality for Peleus. Her phrase "leaving the house of Nereus" (λιποῦσα Νηρέως δόμους, 1232) reverses the betrayals of Hermione and Helen, who earlier abandoned

---

[89] Burnett 1971: 153.

their husbands' houses; here, however, in a marriage gesture, she temporarily leaves her natal oikos to join her husband.

As a *dea ex machina*, Thetis brings to light the hidden crimes of Orestes, guaranteeing their public recognition through the public burial of Neoptolemus' body, which will serve as a lasting rebuke to the Delphians (ὄνειδος, 1241). Andromache in turn will receive commemoration and quasi-immortal status as the mother of the Molossian people through her child with Neoptolemus (1243–47). In this way, the goddess saves the house of Peleus from extinction (1249–50) while conferring immortality upon him (ἀθάνατον ἄφθιτόν τε ποιήσω θεόν, 1256). Even their marriage will become immortal: in another deviation from normative marriage practice, he will permanently abide in Nereus' house as the spouse of Thetis.[90] Achilles also achieves a sort of immortality on the White Island, thus facilitating a reunion of father and son as indicated by the verb ὄψῃ, "you will see" (1259–62). This final speech reverses the destructive action effected by Hermione's accusations in the first part of the play and reestablishes marriage as a form of salvation for mortals, one that provides them with a kind of immortality through offspring.

Whereas Thetis effectively rescues Peleus at the end of the play, accomplishing yet another reversal of fortune, Peleus' last words impart a final lesson to his audience. This advice distills all the play's blame discourse against women into a single message:

κᾆτ' οὐ γαμεῖν δῆτ' ἔκ τε γενναίων χρεὼν
δοῦναί τ' ἐς ἐσθλούς, ὅστις εὖ βουλεύεται,
κακῶν δὲ λέκτρων μὴ 'πιθυμίαν ἔχειν,
μηδ' εἰ ζαπλούτους οἴσεται φερνὰς δόμοις;   (1279–82)

Whoever thinks well must marry from noble houses
and betroth [their daughters] to noble men,
nor should they maintain a desire for union with the base,
not even if one brings a wealthy dowry to the house.

By commanding a large dowry, a wealthy woman could create an economic disparity in her husband's household and continue to maintain strong ties to her natal oikos. Such a woman might potentially undermine her husband's authority, a type of disobedience that takes the form of Hermione's licentious and unrestrained speech in the play. But such a lesson could apply equally well to men in the political sphere: when men of low birth possess sizable wealth, they may rise to power in the democratic polis, particularly by hiring a sophist to teach them the art of persuasion. Although Peleus does not specify this connection in his last speech, the

[90] Storey 1989: 20.

interrelatedness of domestic and political spheres, exemplified in particular by Hermione and Orestes, imply that women's speech in the oikos has broad-scale consequences for the polis.

CONCLUSION

Like the earlier play, Euripides' *Andromache* establishes separate discursive spheres for men and women and then shows how linguistic transgressions of gender boundaries disrupt domestic and political stability. As in the *Hippolytus*, the discourse of matrons not only focuses almost exclusively on erotic concerns, but in fact encourages the adultery of noble women. The pervasive metaphor of disease that assimilates women's speech to their sexuality in the play implies that female gossip operates in stealth and therefore cannot be fully controlled by men. The education of Spartan girls, which provides a metaphor for the new education offered by the sophists in contemporary Athens, leads to an inversion of gender roles, masculinizing its females and predisposing them to adultery while effemi-nizing its males. By portraying Hermione as the product of Spartan gynae-cocracy, Euripides possibly engages with a current debate about the position of women in the democratic polis, an issue taken up by Aristophanes' *Ecclesiazusae* and discussed more fully in the next chapter. Like the *Hippolytus*, the *Andromache* represents its females as possessing a dangerous rhetorical proficiency: the agon between Hermione and Andromache dresses a mundane domestic dispute in sophistic clothing, creating a scene of almost comic bathos and equating feminine seductiveness and sexual license with rhetorical sophistication and verbal guile. Only the invective against women, as an "official" counterdiscourse, can adequately check the potential of their corrupt and deceptive speech practices for undermining social hierarchy within both the household and the city.

Although the play depicts women's speech as directly subverting male social institutions, particularly marriage, the *Andromache* also deploys feminine verbal treachery as a model for the duplicitous speech of men. Whereas the play correlates the deceptive speech practices of women to an overvaluation of *erōs*, it identifies those of men with an aberrant or corrupt sexuality, as exemplified by the cuckold Menelaus and the paramour Orestes. The three agones progressively move away from the domestic sphere to the male political world, suggesting that the discourse that subverts the oikos also undermines the polis: Menelaus, although socially and physically superior to the slave woman, employs cunning persuasion or *dolos* to remove her from the altar, whereas Orestes disseminates false rumors at Delphi as a means of eliminating a sexual rival. By styling both of these characters as sophists, the poet illustrates the dangers of the new education, which afforded politicians a means to move beyond their social stations and to control an unwitting mass with their art of persuasion, an issue taken up more fully in the two Aristophanic plays discussed in the next chapter.

Chapter Six

OBSCENITY, GENDER, AND SOCIAL STATUS IN
ARISTOPHANES' *THESMOPHORIAZUSAE*
AND *ECCLESIAZUSAE*

BECAUSE IT ENGAGES more directly with contemporary political issues than does tragedy, Attic Old Comedy offers an important perspective on the status and function of speech in the democratic polis at the close of the fifth century B.C.E. Through its deployment of tragic poetry and tragic poets, Aristophanic comedy provides a critical discourse on tragedy itself, especially that of Euripides. This chapter examines how Aristophanes uses gendered discourses, particularly obscenity, the defining feature of Attic Old Comedy, to illuminate the threat posed to the city by self-interested demagogues, and even tragic poets, whose arts are portrayed as seducing and deceiving the unwitting mass. As in tragic drama, these deceivers are figured as feminine, whether as women or effeminate men, and their sexual submission is equated with corrupt rhetorical practices. Strongly identified as masculine through the character of the comic buffoon, comic obscenity strips away the illusions conjured by these spurious figures to reaffirm and restore not only gender hierarchy, but also political stability. In order to understand this dynamic more fully, however, it is necessary to examine the nature of comic obscenity and its relation to gender.

The first part of this chapter surveys the evidence for gender-based difference in the deployment of obscenity in the Aristophanic plays that feature speaking female characters, the *Lysistrata, Thesmophoriazusae*, and *Ecclesiazusae*, then speculates that this distinction may have been rooted in ritual *aischrologia* associated with women's fertility cults. The comic buffoon is most closely identified with obscenity in Attic Old Comedy; his language typically contains scatological and pathic or pederastic allusions. In contrast, female obscenity, although it occurs much less frequently, normally has a heterosexual content. But these linguistic practices are not gender-exclusive, since obscenity, like other verbal activities examined in this book, is a flexible genre that may be variously deployed in shaping dramatic character. For example, in the *Thesmophoriazusae*, an effeminate male speaker, Agathon, uses euphemisms as a woman might, rather than more masculine primary obscenities, whereas the speech of older women, like the three crones at the end of the *Ecclesiazusae*, frequently contains male obscenities.

The second part of this chapter explores the political implications of gendered discourses in the two Aristophanic comedies involving gender disguise and transvestism, the *Thesmophoriazusae* and *Ecclesiazusae*. In these plays, several characters employ the words or expressive genres characteristic of the opposite gender, a reversal illustrated by the cross-dressed Relative in the *Thesmophoriazusae* and by the several female characters who invert the traditional speech genres associated with women with their use of masculine political discourse, like the female celebrants of the Thesmophoria in the *Thesmophoriazusae*, Praxagora, and the crones in the *Ecclesiazusae*. As in tragedy, disjunctions between gender and speech in Aristophanic comedy almost always represent a larger social disturbance in the polis. In contrast to the tragedies discussed earlier, however, the comedies of Aristophanes more directly identify as the source of this disorder the seductive and corrupting speech practices of demagogues, embodied by pathics and women; his drama thus provides a framework for understanding Euripides' rhetorical women and verbally cunning men.

Since homosexuality is a modern construction, the term "homosexual" has been avoided as much as possible throughout this chapter; the term "pathic" has been used instead to refer to a sexually submissive male, whereas the word "pederast" has been used of the sexually dominant partner in a male sexual relationship. Dover's dichotomy between penetrator and penetrated, a distinction retained by Foucault, Halperin, Winkler, Cohen, and others who have studied male sexuality in Greco-Roman antiquity, provides an exceptionally useful conceptual framework; however, this model needs to be somewhat modified.[1] As this analysis of Agathon in the *Thesmophoriazusae* shows, a male may be characterized as effeminate not merely because he submits sexually to others, but because he overvalues sex. This explains why Aristophanes represents Agathon both as a pederast interested in young boys at *Thesmophoriazusae* 254 and as a passive sexual partner (βινεῖσθαι, 50, 254). In defining female obscenity, however, the term "heterosexual" has been used to refer to male-female sexual activities, in contrast to those taking place only between men.

GENDER AND COMIC OBSCENITY

Female protagonists seem to have come late to the comic stage, perhaps as late as Aristophanes' *Lysistrata*, a play produced in 411 at the Lenaea.[2] Only two other extant Aristophanic comedies, both of which postdate

---

[1] Foucault 1988; Dover 1989; Halperin 1990a; Winkler 1990a; and Cohen 1991. The Greek passages quoted in this chapter are taken from Hall and Geldart's text (1982) for the *Thesmophoriazusae*, and from Ussher 1973 for the *Ecclesiazusae*.

[2] For the earliest mention of this idea, see Schmid and Stählin 1929–48, 1: 4.418; for later scholars who have echoed this view, see Henderson 1991a: 169–70; 1987b: 107; Taaffe

the *Lysistrata*, feature women in prominent roles: the *Thesmophoriazusae*, produced in Athens in 411, and the *Ecclesiazusae*, performed almost twenty years later. Prior to 411, female characters play only minor roles in Aristophanic comedy, acting mostly as courtesans and flute girls, market women, daughters, and personified abstractions, many of whom do not speak but rather appear as silent objects of male desire.[3] Although scholars have speculated that the comic poet used historical figures, like Lysimache, a priestess of Athena Polias, and Pericles' consort, Aspasia, as models for Lysistrata and Praxagora respectively, the evidence is far from conclusive. It is hard to believe that a female character of Lysistrata's complexity would have suddenly appeared full-blown at the Lenaea without any comic antecedent and that Aristophanes would have then turned around and performed this astonishing feat a second time only a few months later at the city Dionysia. It is more likely that such figures were modeled, at least in part, on the fictional constructs of women in other literary genres, such as tragedy. Whatever their origins, female protagonists, as well as cross-dressed men impersonating women, offered the comic poet an opportunity to render women's speech and to exploit its dramatic potential as a vehicle for conveying political and social issues.

Building on the work of Bain and Adams on Menander and Latin comedy, Sommerstein has argued in a recent essay that certain linguistic elements, such as oaths, pathetic expressions, types of address, particles, and obscene language, differentiate women's language in Aristophanes from that of men.[4] Given the prevalence of obscenity in Attic Old Comedy, it is striking that only Sommerstein, however briefly, has considered the effect of gender on a speaker's use of obscenity.[5] He concludes that female speakers use primary obscenities, a term defined more fully below, far less frequently than men do and, significantly, that they seldom use obscene

---

1993: 48. Dillon (1987: 99–100) links this innovation to the Spartan investment in Deceleia in 413 B.C.E. On women in the other comedies, see Lévy 1976: 99.

[3] Most current scholarship has rejected Wilamowitz's earlier suggestion that these roles were played by naked courtesans, concluding instead that male actors in padded body suits assumed these parts. For a summary of this debate, see Henderson 1987a: 195–96; Pickard-Cambridge 1991: 153; and Dillon 1987: 100–101. Taaffe (1993: 23–47) devotes a whole chapter to the subject, although I do not agree with her conclusion that these mute figures are inherently metatheatrical; see also Zweig 1992.

[4] Sommerstein 1995: 63; Taaffe 1993: passim; on Menander and Latin comedy, see Bain 1984; Adams 1984; Dickey 1995 and 1996.

[5] Henderson (1991a) does not comment specifically on the relation between gender and obscenity. An earlier study of obscenity in Aristophanic comedy by Wit-Tak (1968) incorrectly attributes multiple obscenities to female speakers because it does not distinguish primary obscenity from innuendo; in fact, several instances adduced by Wit-Tak are either highly euphemistic or not obscene at all; for example, ἀποψιλώσομεν (*Thesm.* 538) and διέκυψε καὶ μάλ' εὔχρων (*Thesm.* 644). On women's ritual obscenity at the Demetrian festivals, see Zeitlin 1981; Winkler 1990a: 188–209; Zweig 1992: 81–82.

speech in the presence of men.[6] This finding is consistent with contemporary studies, discussed in Chapter 2, which indicate that this verbal genre is normally prohibited to women and that it tends to occur more often in same-sex groups.[7] In Attic Old Comedy, however, the precise distinction between male and female use of obscenity and how it may be exploited for comic effect has not been fully elaborated.[8] Female obscenity in Aristophanes normally has a heterosexual content and is almost never scatological, whereas male obscenity typically consists of both sexual and scatological terms. This analysis is confined to the *Lysistrata*, *Thesmophoriazusae*, and *Ecclesiazusae*, since women in these plays speak roughly half the lines, in contrast to only about 5 percent of all lines in the other eight extant plays.[9]

The obscenity and sexually explicit gestures found in Attic Old Comedy are unparalleled in ancient literary genres outside of archaic iambic poetry. Henderson distinguishes primary from secondary obscenities by defining primary obscenities as those which refer directly to the "sexual organs, excrement, or the acts which involve them."[10] He includes in this category the terms πέος ("penis"), κύσθος ("cunt"), ψωλός ("all hard-on"), στύομαι ("have a hard-on"), σκῶρ ("shit"), πρωκτός ("asshole"), πέρδομαι ("fart"), βινῶ and βινητιάζω ("fuck"), and δέφομαι ("masturbate"). To this list Sommerstein adds καταπύγων ("pathic"), κινῶ (= βινῶ), προσκίνομαι ("screw"), πυγίζω (but not πυγή, "bugger"), and χέζω

---

[6] Out of seventy-five instances analyzed, men use fifty-five primary obscenities and women twenty; see Sommerstein 1995: 79. Although Taaffe (1993) considers the issue of linguistic gender disguise in her book on women and Aristophanes, she oddly has little to say about gender and obscenity.

[7] Henley (1977: 146–47) makes the following observation about obscenity in contemporary Western culture: "Slang and obscenity are generally taboo to women, and their nonverbal counterparts, such as obscene gestures and what we can call gestural slang, are likewise the prerogatives of male culture." Lakoff (1973: 50) describes obscenity as masculine and argues that women tend to use weaker expletives, such as "oh dear." Similarly, Bornstein (1978: 135) discusses medieval and Renaissance courtesy books that forbid women to curse or joke. It is also worth noting in this context that scatology was especially associated with the speech of second-grade boys in a recent study of conversations between male friends at various life stages; see Tannen 1996: 100. On obscenity as occurring more frequently among same-sex groups, see Coates 1986: 108–9.

[8] Bowie (1993: 258) at one point hints at the distinction: "Male reactions thus seem regularly to be of an excremental nature, with the excrement marking the disturbance of normality."

[9] These estimates are found in Sommerstein 1995: 62n.4: the *Lysistrata* has 768 lines spoken by women, or 58%; the *Thesmophoriazusae* has 708, about 58%, including the lines spoken by the Relative; and the *Ecclesiazusae* has 636, or 54%; in the other eight plays, women speak only about 560 lines, and most of those women are deities.

[10] Henderson 1991a: 35. Bain (1991: 53) observes that many of these terms are slang and thus appear in curse tablets, magical texts, and graffiti, whereas they are "almost entirely absent from the higher prose genres."

("shit").[11] A few other words, although originally nonsexual, also have an improper, crude tone: ληκῶ ("move a limb/fuck"), λαικάζω ("fuck/perform oral sex"), and σπλεκῶ ("fuck").[12] One feature of Attic obscenities was apparently gender-specific: in the case of verbs of sexual congress, female speakers always use the passive form when referring to themselves, whereas males use the active voice.[13] Attic Old Comedy also contains numerous secondary obscenities, including double entendres, medical terminology, euphemisms, and metaphor.[14] Given the absence of primary obscenities in the effeminate Agathon's speech in the *Thesmophoriazusae* and his reliance upon euphemism, innuendo may have been considered more appropriate to women's speech. But because metaphorical usages are so numerous and frequently so difficult to verify in Attic Old Comedy, that topic lies outside the scope of this chapter. A few specific metaphorical or euphemistic terms related to scatological and pathic or pederastic humor will be discussed where relevant in order to place some of my conclusions in a broader context.

As Sommerstein observed, male characters pronounce primary obscenities almost three times more often than their female counterparts do in the *Lysistrata*, *Ecclesiazusae*, and *Thesmophoriazusae*.[15] Breaking down these instances into two types of obscenity, scatological and sexual, we find that most female speakers tend to avoid scatological words, although they do employ sexual slang. Moreover, the amount of primary obscenity used by women varies radically from play to play: more than two-thirds of the primary obscenities uttered by women in Aristophanic comedy appear in the *Lysistrata*,[16] whereas women do not utter a single primary obscenity in the *Thesmophoriazusae*, a point discussed more fully later in this chapter. This variation may be attributed to two causes: first, plot dictates lexical

---

[11] Sommerstein 1995: 79n.52.

[12] On λαικάζω, see Jocelyn 1980.

[13] Bain observes only one instance of a woman *in propria persona* who uses βινῶ; cf. *P Oxy.* 413 verso col. ii 107f.; see Bain 1991: 55. Instead, female speakers employ the desiderative, βινητιῶ, a formulation also standard in love charms. Bain (ibid.: 61) cites βινητιῶμεν (*Lys.* 715) as an example. He further points out that the subject of βινητιῶ is normally a female or a pathic: see ibid.: 61–62; Pl. com. fr. 188. 21 KA; Machon 455 Gow; Lucian *Pseudol.* 27.

[14] Henderson 1991a: 35.

[15] Out the seventy-seven primary obscenities found in the *Lysistrata*, *Ecclesiazusae*, and *Thesmophoriazusae*, fifty-eight are uttered by men and nineteen by women. The discrepancy between my figures and Sommerstein's (see note 6 above) in part results from the fact that I included all of Praxagora's lines as female, even when she is disguised as a man, and all of the Relative's lines as male. Sommerstein, however, counts Praxagora's obscenity at *Eccl.* 228 as an instance of male speech, and the Relative's words at *Thesm.* 493 and 570 as female. As I discuss here, I believe that these usages reveal rather than obscure the true identities of these speakers.

[16] Henderson 1991a: 94.

environment; thus the premise of the *Lysistrata*, a sex strike, necessitates a large number of references to heterosexual behavior. Second, the degree to which men are present in these scenes influences whether women use obscenity.

In the *Lysistrata*, it is Lysistrata who pronounces by far the greatest number of obscenities in the play, all of which occur in the presence of women only (τοῦ πέους, 124; σπλεκοῦν, 152; ἐστυκώς, 214, cf. 152; προσκινήσομαι, 227; παγκατάπυγον, 137; καταπυγωνέστερον, 776; βινητιῶμεν, 715). This usage perhaps reflects her ambiguous gender status as the leader and the only woman who does not succumb to her sexual impulses, a view corroborated by the fact that she is also the only woman to deliver a public oration before men. The crone's comic echoing of her obscenities in the oath-taking scene further contributes to the density (τοῦ πέους, 134; ἐστυκώς, 215; προσκινήσομαι, 228). The Spartan woman, Lampito, also uses a primary obscenity (ψωλᾶς, 143); this usage may suggest Athenian attitudes that viewed foreigners, including Spartans, as uncouth and vulgar. With the exception of καταπύγων a term of general abuse, and its cognates, most of these words refer to conjugal sex and are spoken exclusively in the presence of women.[17]

The primary obscenities uttered by women in the *Lysistrata* begin to dissipate after the oath-taking scene and only appear in the mouths of men during the rest of the play, with the notable exception of ἐπιχεσεῖ (440); even Lysistrata stops using them after 1112, when she returns to the stage to address the assembled men. Critics have cited this linguistic shift to support their argument that Lysistrata's character is modeled on the priestess Lysimache, a figure invested with the authority of public speech.[18] However, I believe that this shift is conditioned by the fact that Lysistrata now addresses a male audience.[19] In a direct quote from Euripides' lost *Melanippe the Wise*, Lysistrata begins by asking her listeners to indulge her, even though she is a woman, a rhetorical device employed by Clytemnestra in the *Agamemnon*, and also by Macaria in Euripides' *Children of Heracles*, as we have seen.[20] She then states that she has learned how to speak publicly from her father and other male elders (1124–27).[21] Because she is speaking to men, Lysistrata adjusts her language accordingly and avoids the obscenity that characterized her earlier speech among women.

The impact of the male internal audience on Lysistrata's self-presentation thus makes Calonice's earlier scatological expletive directed at the male Proboulus all the more remarkable: "By Pandrosus, if you so much as lay

---

[17] On the use of obscenity among women only, see Sommerstein 1995: 79–80.

[18] Zweig 1992: 80; Foley 1982: 8; Henderson 1987a: xxxviii–xxxix.

[19] Henderson 1987a; Zweig 1992: 80.

[20] Eur. *Heracl.* 474–77; Aesch. *Ag.* 855–57; these passages are discussed in detail in Chapter 1 and Chapter 3, respectively.

[21] Lysistrata here parodies Euripides' *Melanippe the Wise*; cf. Eur. fr. 487 *TGF*.

a hand on her [Lysistrata], you will shit all over the place, being trampled under my foot" (εἴ τἄρα νὴ τὴν Πάνδροσον ταύτῃ μόνον | τὴν χεῖρ' ἐπιβαλεῖς, ἐπιχεσεῖ πατούμενος, 439–440). The use of χέζω by a woman is extremely rare in Aristophanes, and quite shocking, as the Proboulus' rejoinder makes clear.[22] But what Sommerstein and others have failed to notice about this exchange is that the speaker is an older woman, a stock figure in Attic Old Comedy typically portrayed as independent, lecherous, and fond of drink.[23] A consistent feature of this character type is coarse and abusive language. The linguistic distinctions evident in the speech of crones, respectable Athenian matrons, and young girls in comedy, and to a lesser extent in tragedy, confirm the importance of considering social status as well as gender in the construction of dramatic character. Older women in Aristophanic comedy enjoy an exceptional status with regard to speech since they more freely utter both scatological and sexual obscenities.[24] Bowie speculates that the comic characterization of crones reflects the greater social freedom enjoyed by older women in many cultures; beyond childbearing, their movements are less restricted, and they are invested with more authority.[25] On both the tragic and the comic stage, then, when men need to be advised or confronted, "it is older women, not young wives, who do the job."[26] Such a portrayal perhaps draws on earlier literary stereotypes, like the figure of Iambe in the *Homeric Hymn to Demeter*.

The rest of the primary obscenities associated with women in Aristophanes occur in the *Ecclesiazusae* and follow a similar pattern: four primary obscenities are spoken by Praxagora, whose role is analogous to that of Lysistrata. Yet Praxagora's use of obscenity is less than straightforward: she uses the passive, feminine form of βινῶ (βινούμεναι, *Eccl.* 228) when rehearsing her speech for the Assembly disguised as a man, in front of women only. Similarly, the verb προσκινήσομαι (256) represents a weakened form of a primary obscenity because it is used as part of an extended sexual double entendre based on the verb ὑποκρούω. In the rehearsal scene, Woman B makes a reference to farting (πέρδεται, 78), dramatically in character with her earlier spate of innuendoes. Sommerstein adduces the three obscenities that occur later in the play as evidence for his

<hr />

[22] Sommerstein (1995: 80) discusses this passage at length.

[23] Calonice upon entering the stage refers to Lysistrata as ὦ τέκνον (Ar. *Lys.* 8), a form of address that implies that she is the elder of the two women. Henderson (1987b: 120) remarks that "forthrightness of speech (including obscenity and abuse) and fearless bellicosity" characterizes older women in Old Comedy, but he does not further elaborate. On the representation of older women in Old Comedy, see Oeri 1948: 30–32; Henderson 1991a: 87, 96–97; Henderson 1987b.

[24] Henderson 1991a: 87; Oeri 1948: 31–32.

[25] Bowie 1993: 266.

[26] Henderson 1996: 26.

hypothesis that the women's use of obscenities, particularly βινῶ (706), δέφομαι (709), and χέζω (1062), represent the "free speech" entailed by the new political regime.[27] However, a closer inspection of the contexts reveals that two of these primary obscenities appear in indirect discourse, when Praxagora quotes the imagined speech of old men: "It has been decreed that the ugly ones get to fuck first (βινεῖν, 706) while the rest of you engage in some hand work (δέφεσθαι, 709) on the porch outside." Crone B utters the third obscenity when she tells the youth with a sudden urge to defecate to "hurry up and shit inside the house" (χεσεῖ, 1062). This particular primary obscenity, as in the case of Calonice, is dramatically in character for old women in Aristophanic comedy and therefore does not reflect changes in the political climate wrought by gynaecocracy.

On the other hand, almost all of the male characters in Aristophanes use primary obscenities regardless of the gender of the internal audience, although they typically appear in the speech of the comic buffoon. In the *Lysistrata*, a play that does not contain such a character, the male chorus, Cinesias, the Proboulus, the male herald, the Athenian, and the Spartan all use primary obscenities, almost all of which, for obvious reasons, pertain to the genitals, sexual arousal, or heterosexual intercourse: βινῶ (934, 954, 966, 1092, 1180) and κινῶ (1166); στύομαι (598, 869, 989, 996, 1178) and ψωλή (979, 1136); πέος (415, 928); and κύσθος (1158). Another term, πρωκτός (1148), has "an exclusively male (and therefore usually homosexual) reference," suggesting pathic behavior, and is used of women only three times in Aristophanic comedy.[28] Although πρωκτός at 1148 refers to a woman, it stereotypically associates the Spartan's sexual proclivities with pederasty; in fact, he later speaks of sexual intercourse as κοπραγω-γῆν (1174), a verb that implies anal penetration, in contrast to the Athenian's more euphemistic plowing metaphor, γεωργεῖν (1173).[29] The Proboulus pronounces the only male scatological reference in the *Lysistrata*, ἐπειχεσεῖ (441), but here the term merely repeats Calonice's earlier use of the word.

The overtly heterosexual connotations of most of the primary obscenities found in the *Lysistrata* starkly contrast with the scatological and pathic obscenity that figures so prominently in the *Thesmophoriazusae* and *Ecclesiazusae*. According to Henderson, "Defecatory jokes and routines are the purest kind of obscene comedy. . . . Sexual jokes can rarely be reduced to such a low level because sex is so important and so complex a part of our

[27] Sommerstein 1995: 80.

[28] Henderson 1991a: 201, 150. For πρωκτός used by men, cf. *Eq.* 364, 368 (Blepyrus); *Thesm.* 1119, 1124 (Archer), and 200, 242, 248 (Relative). The term πρωκτός is used of women in Aristophanes only at *Pax* 876 and *Plut.* 152.

[29] Athenians closely associated institutionalized pederasty with the Spartans; see Jocelyn 1980: 32; Bremmer 1980: 282; Cartledge 1981.

lives; defecation is a remarkably uncomplex process."[30] Most scatological humor revolves around the comic buffoon, usually a lowly, rustic, and elderly male figure in Aristophanes, a role played by Euripides' Relative in the *Thesmophoriazusae* and Blepyrus in the *Ecclesiazusae*.[31] Blepyrus, for example, uses the verb χέζω eight times in the *Ecclesiazusae*, mostly in the defecation scene discussed below. His constipation also presents several opportunities for using the word πρωκτός, a word also associated with pathic behavior. Appropriately, this scene culminates with Blepyrus' assertion that he does not want to become a comic "shitpot," σκωραμίς (*Eccl.* 371); this obscene neologism identifies the language of Attic Old Comedy with excretory humor.[32] The scatological language of Blepyrus is echoed by two other male characters in the *Ecclesiazusae*, Chremes and Man B, who use χέζω (372, 808) and πέρδομαι (464).

In contrast, the speech of Euripides' Relative in *Thesmophoriazusae* focuses on pathic and pederastic rather than scatological humor. In the first part of the play, the Relative makes several pathic jokes involving primary obscenities about the effeminate Agathon: βινῶ (*Thesm.* 50, 206), λαικάζω (57), καταπύγων (200), εὐρύπρωκτος (200), πέος (62, 142), and ἐστυκώς (158). Elsewhere, the Relative similarly exposes Agathon's effeminacy through more euphemistic expressions: for example, he compares Agathon to a famous courtesan, Cyrene (98), and ridicules his transvestism (130–45); at the same time, he exposes his fondness for young boys (ποσθίου, 253).[33] In the scene that follows, when Euripides depilates the Relative's lower body, the term πρωκτός (242 crux, 248) signals a reversal as the Relative, who is told repeatedly to bend over, now assumes the effeminate, pathic position associated with Agathon. Although transformed into a woman, the Relative's speech at the Thesmophoria, particularly the obscenities ληκῶ (493) and χέζω (570), continually undermine his new identity. Similarly, Euripides and Cleisthenes use obscenities, but to a lesser extent than the Relative (notably βινεῖν, 35; and πέος, 643 and 648). The only other character able to match the Relative's vulgarity is the Scythian Archer, who employs pathic terms, albeit in a Scythian dialect, when he voices an intention to bugger the captive Relative (πρωκτό, 1119; πρώκτισον, 1124; πυγίζεις, 1120; πύγισο, 1123).[34] These pathic proclivities are redirected toward the flute girl in the final part of the play (καταβηνῆσι, 1215).

[30] Henderson 1991a: 187.

[31] Henderson (ibid.: 188) notes that sexual humor, in contrast, may appear in noble roles.

[32] The opening scene of Ar. *Ran.* provides another example of the close identification of the comic genre with male scatological humor. For this idea, see especially Edwards 1991.

[33] Although the term ποσθίον is not as obscene as πέος, it never appears in female speech in Aristophanes: cf. *Pax* 1300; *Nub.* 1014; *Thesm.* 1188.

[34] Hall (1989a: 40) describes the Archer's speech as a "linguistic caricature" but does not comment on his use of obscenity.

These examples suggest a gender-based distinction not only in the number of primary obscenities used by male and female characters in Aristophanic comedy, but also in the types of words they use: female speakers almost always employ heterosexual obscenities, whereas male obscenities frequently have a pathic, pederastic, and scatological content. Other euphemistic usages pertaining to defecation, urination, and pathic behavior in the *Thesmophorizusae* and *Ecclesiazusae* support this conclusion. The metaphorical terms for anus and perineum in these plays all refer to men, indicating that the parts of the male body exposed in comedy relate to pathic and pederastic practices, as Henderson observes: "Aside from the phallus and anus, no part of the male anatomy is much referred to in Old and Middle comedy; male heterosexuality and pederasty are the chief subjects of humor and scurrility. The female body, on the other hand, was much exposed, both physically and verbally."[35] Similarly, other words pertaining to defecation, including allusions to constipation, feces, public befouling, privies, and urination, have an exclusively masculine reference in Old Comedy.[36] Out of thirty-three references to the nonsexual functions of the lower body in the *Ecclesiazusae*, *Thesmophoriazusae*, and *Lysistrata*, fully twenty-eight instances are confined to male speech, with only five spoken by women, most of whom are crones.[37] In extant Old Comedy, female speakers avoid the terms πρωκτός, πυγίζειν, and σκῶρ, primary obscenities that may have had both a scatological and a pathic or pederastic reference. On the other hand, pathic humor in which a prominent public figure is ridiculed for his sexual behavior represents a form of invective not confined to the speech of either gender. Male speakers are, however, more likely to allude to the πρωκτός to call attention not only to excretory functions, but also to pathic behavior. For example, Blepyrus' references to well-known pathics in the defecation scene, including Amynon and Antisthenes (*Eccl.* 365–68), show the interchangeability of scatological and

---

[35] Henderson 1991a: 148; in Ar. *Thesm.*, cf. θριγκός (59), ἕδρα (133), ἰσθμός (647), τραμίς (242); in *Eccl.* cf. θύρα (316, 361).

[36] For allusions to constipation, cf. Ar. *Eccl.* 355, 362, 366, 806. The color adjective πυρρός often indicates feces in Aristophanes, cf. *Eccl.* 329, 1061; *Thesm.* 570; for size, cf. *Eccl.* 351; σκωραμίς, *Eccl.* 371. A reference to Cinesias at *Eccl.* 330 relates to his habit of befouling public monuments. Jokes based on urination in comedy usually apply to incontinent old men; cf. *Eq.* 400, 526; *Vesp.* 807ff., 858, 935, 940, 946, 1127f.; *Lys.* 402, 550; in connection with degradation; cf. *Vesp.* 394, a reference to defiling a statue by peeing; *Ran.* 95, impotent poets can only defile lady Tragedy; and *Eccl.* 832, where Carion expresses the fear that the women will urinate on him as part of the female-dominated new regime. Cf. also *Thesm.* 611, 615 (Relative). For outhouses and privies, cf. *Thesm.* 633; κοπρών, cf. *Eccl.* 317, 360, 1059; *Thesm.* 485. The term also has a pathic or pederastic reference, cf. *Eq.* 399. Crepitation: *Thesm.* 484; *Eccl.* 78, 464; *Lys.* 354.

[37] For words relating to defecation and urination spoken by women in Aristophanes, see χέζω (*Lys.* 440; *Eccl.* 1062), βδύλλω (*Lys.* 354), πέρδομαι (*Eccl.* 78), and κατέδει πέλεθον (*Eccl.* 595).

pathic humor. The fact that both Blepyrus and the Relative are theatrically exposed in the same way confirms this: demeaned through depilation and defecation, both show their rumps to the audience.

Both the *Thesmophoriazusae* and the *Ecclesiazusae* deploy pathic and scatological allusions as a means of exposing duplicity and reinforcing prevailing gender ideology, whereas the heterosexual humor of the *Lysistrata* celebrates the restoration of normative social roles made possible by peace. Pathic and pederastic humor have a special place in Aristophanic comedy: the terms *euruprōktos*, "gape-assed," and *katapugōn*, "pathic," are general terms of abuse meant to insult the audience, whereas the comparison of politicians to pathics and even active pederasts is central to the type of raillery encompassed by *onomasti kōmōidein*, "personal ridicule." Even Athens does not escape this type of invective when Aristophanes refers to it as "the city of pathics" (ἡ Κεχηναίων πόλις, *Eq.* 1263). The next section speculates that gender differences in comic obscenity may reflect the separate ritual spheres of men and women. The political aspects of pathic humor may correspond to rituals of scurrilous abuse in the city Dionysia, whereas female obscenity may indirectly evoke the ritual *aischrologia* that was a feature of women's fertility festivals in honor of Demeter.

RITUAL AND THE ORIGINS OF COMIC OBSCENITY

Although women's ritual *aischrologia* has already been discussed at some length in Chapter 2, the subject is worth reviewing because of its relevance for understanding comic obscenity. It has been speculated that comic obscenity derives from the practice of *aischrologia* associated with rituals intended to promote fertility; but this view fails to take into account the fact that ritual *aischrologia* had strong associations with women, whereas Attic Old Comedy was an overwhelmingly masculine genre, or so Aristophanes would have us believe.[38] In particular, *aischrologia* seems to have been a consistent feature of women-only festivals in honor of Demeter. At the Athenian Thesmophoria, for example, women engaged in verbal abuse in imitation of Iambe, the servant who mitigates Demeter's sorrow with obscene jesting in the *Homeric Hymn to Demeter*.[39] Ancient evidence indicates that female *aischrologia* at the Thesmophoria had a sexual content and perhaps accompanied the handling of plastic representations of genitalia.[40] The Haloa also featured abusive mocking (παιδιαὶ πολλαὶ καὶ σκώμματα)

[38] Reckford 1987: 461. See also Deubner 1932: 53 and 57.

[39] Cf. *Hom. Hymn Cer.* 195–205; see also Apollod. 1.5.1; Foley 1994: 45. The Orphic tradition replaced Iambe with Baubo, who apparently cheered up Demeter by lifting her skirts; Fluck 1931: 28; Richardson 1974: 215–16; Olender 1990.

[40] Schol. Lucian *Dial. meret.* 7.4 (= 279.24 Rabe); Cleomedes 2.1 S166.5–7; Deubner 1932: 58; Zeitlin 1982: 144–45.

and possibly involved the participation of hetaeras who indulged in shameful sexual talk.[41] As we have seen, the scholion to Lucian's *Dialogue of the Courtesans* describes the priestesses at the Haloa as advising adultery.[42] At the Stenia, women likewise uttered obscenities.[43] There is also evidence for mocking choruses of men and women in the Syracusan Demeter cult[44] and in the Demetrian festival at Pellene.[45] On Aegina and at Epidaurus, choruses of women hurled obscenities in honor of Damis and Auxesia, no doubt surrogates for Demeter and Kore.[46] Even the private Adonia that celebrated Aphrodite and her mortal consort Adonis, a festival connected with prostitution, may have featured obscene speech.[47] Most of these contexts involved women congregating alone, apart from men. The comic preference for depicting female obscenity as occurring mostly apart from men perhaps imitates the conditions of ritual *aischrologia* at the fertility festivals, and may reflect the gender segregation typical of everyday life.

The scurrilous abuse directed toward individuals that is not necessarily sexual in nature possibly has its origin in rituals associated with both Dionysus and Demeter. According to Henderson, this personal invective was a feature of Dionysian festivals that permitted celebrants "the freedom to say what one wanted."[48] This masculine verbal license functions as a poetic form of the *parrhēsia*, which was the prerogative of adult citizen males in the democratic city. There is evidence to suggest that participants, probably male, jested from wagons as part of the Dionysiac festivals and apparently directed their insults toward specific members of the community who were present.[49] In fact, Heath argues that the comic poets' "special license to abuse" derived from the religious context of the city Dionysia.[50] This type of invective possibly also occurred as part of the Eleusinian mysteries. Adherents may have been subjected to scurrilous attacks by *gephuristai*, veiled men who stood on a bridge over the river Cephesus,

---

[41] Parke 1977: 98; Simon 1983: 98; schol. Lucian *Dial. meret.* 7.4 (= 279.24 Rabe); Deubner 1932: 62.

[42] Schol. Lucian *Dial. meret.* 7.4 (= 279.24 Rabe).

[43] Parke 1977: 88; Simon 1983: 20; Hsch. s.v.; schol. *Thesm.* 834; Eubulus 148 KA.

[44] Diod. Sic. 5.4.7.

[45] Paus. 8.27.9. On insulting choruses of the Anaphaea, see Ap. Rhod. 4.1719ff.; Apollod. 1.9.26; Conon 49. Similarly, Herodotus mentions the verbal abuse of female celebrants of the cult of Isis; cf. Hdt. 2.60.

[46] Hdt. 5.83.

[47] On this festival generally, see Deubner 1932: 222; Winkler 1990a: 189–93. On the sexual content of the Adonia, cf. Ar. *Lys.* 387–96; on the Adonia as inciting promiscuity, see Men. *Sam.* 35–50; Diphilus fr. 50 KA describes an obscene riddle involving τὸ πέος; as a festival for prostitutes, see Diphilus fr. 43 KA.

[48] Henderson 1991a: 15.

[49] Henderson (ibid.: 17–18) remarks that this type of personal invective is a very familiar feature of iambic poetry.

[50] Heath 1987: 27; Ar. *Ran.* 367–68. On the place of *aischrologia* in the polis, cf. Pl. *Rep.* 395e; Arist. *Pol.* 1336b3–23; cf. *Eth. Nic.* 1128a19–30.

as they made their way to Eleusis.[51] Alternatively, Hesychius defines a *gephuris* as a "prostitute on the bridge," indicating that obscene language was appropriate not to respectable wives, but only to prostitutes.[52] Aristophanes implicitly associates these ritual insults with *onomasti kōmōidein* in the *Frogs* (416–30). In this passage, the poet exploits the similarity between comic and ritual abuse by having the chorus play the part of *gephuristai* on the bridge over the Cephisus River who utter comic obscenities (σκώψωμεν, 417).[53] The chorus direct their obscene insults at significant political figures and conflate their rhetorical expertise with their aberrant sexuality: Archedemus, the demagogue (416); Cleisthenes, an effeminate (422); Sebinon, the ἀναφλύστιος (427); and Callias, a womanizer described as having a κύσθος (428–30).

The two types of *aischrologia* involved in male and female fertility cults may reflect a gender-based speech distinction: the scant evidence for the women's festivals suggests that the content of their obscenity was implicitly heterosexual and probably not political, a subject no doubt viewed as appropriate to prostitutes and crones, and to fertility religions in general, whereas the personal invective characteristic of Dionysian rites seems to have had predominantly political overtones, although it made use of sexual language. Still, the evolution of comic obscenity from some sort of ritual abuse associated with fertility cults does not adequately account for the prevalence of scatological and pathic humor in Aristophanes, especially given the fact that scatology in Attic Old Comedy is often linked to impotence and sterility.[54]

To summarize, women's speech contains fewer primary obscenities than that of men, and those obscenities are normally sexual rather than scatological in Aristophanic comedy. Further, women's speech practices in Attic Old Comedy are influenced by the gender of the internal audience, with the result that women use obscenities normally only in the presence of other women. Male obscenity contains additional scatological and pathic or pederastic elements. Finally, I have suggested that these distinctions may reflect the sex-segregated ritual origins of *aischrologia* in ancient

---

[51] Henderson 1991a: 16–17; Parke 1977: 66. On the gender of the *gephuristai*, see Foley 1994: 67, and 45, where Foley argues that although these figures seem to have been male, there may have been a female tradition of mockers who sat on wagons nearby: see schol. Ar. *Plut.* 1014. It is not clear whether the *pannuchis* involved ritual obscenity: in favor of this view, see Richardson 1974: 215; Foley 1994: 67; *contra* Deubner 1932: 73ff.

[52] Hsch. γ 469. Dover (1993: 247) follows Hesychius in asserting that the *gephuris* may have been a man disguised as a woman, or at least veiled.

[53] Muecke 1977: 53; Richardson 1974: 214.

[54] On the Blepyrus scene as an example of this view, see Foley 1982; Rothwell 1990: 56–57; Bowie 1993: 258. The fact that scatological references often have a pathic association further confirms this interpretation. However, Edwards (1991) argues for positive associations with excrement in Old Comedy, pointing out that dung serves as food for the comic Pegasus, who enables Trygaeus to save Greece; cf. Ar. *Pax* 137–39.

Greece. They may also point to a preference for assigning euphemistic speech to women; scatology, because of its shocking coarseness, might not have been considered appropriate for female characters. The following section examines several key scenes in the *Thesmophoriazusae* and *Ecclesiazusae* that confirm these differences and reveal how the comic poet manipulates gendered speech practices in order to expose the dangers posed by the art of persuasion to the democratic city-state.

COMIC MASCULINITY: THE RELATIVE IN THE *THESMOPHORIAZUSAE*

Produced at the city Dionysia in 411, just a few months after the *Lysistrata*, the *Thesmophoriazusae* illustrates the role of obscenity in representing gender and its permutations in Aristophanic comedy. In this play, Euripides calls upon his relative by marriage to sneak into the women's celebration of the Thesmophoria, where the tragic poet is to be prosecuted for slandering women in the theater. The Relative eventually agrees to this scheme and subsequently allows himself to be depilated and dressed as a woman. He then infiltrates the Thesmophoria, where he delivers a speech in defense of Euripides. A linguistic slip eventually reveals his true identity, at which point the Relative enacts several escape scenes from Euripidean drama. The play concludes with Euripides' stratagem for securing his kinsman's release: the poet disguises himself as a procuress and then successfully distracts the slow-witted Scythian Archer with a young girl as the Relative escapes. Much of the comedy derives from the incongruity of genres and genders, as Zeitlin has argued in her treatment of gender issues in the play.[55] Building on her work, I argue that the play problematizes the role of speech in the democratic polis by associating tragic mimesis, and tragic poets generally, with the seductive and corrupting rhetorical practices of the sophists, practices that the comic poet correlates with aberrant sexuality. Euripides' kinsman provides a comic antidote to this social and political problem: his coarse, comic masculinity repeatedly disrupts the world of theatrical illusion and signals the restoration of a normal sexual and social order. Through his use of obscenity, the Relative's masculinity is never completely compromised.

Whitman's remark that even in the scene at the Thesmophoria, the Relative's "rough, comic masculinity keeps tearing through the texture, leaving the tragic scheme in tatters" has generally been accepted, although scholars disagree as to how, exactly, he exposes himself.[56] Sommerstein

---

[55] Zeitlin 1981.
[56] Whitman 1964: 223; Taaffe 1993: 78.

argues that his language does not betray him, as it does the women rehearsing for the Assembly in the *Ecclesiazusae*.[57] Taaffe, on the other hand, comments: "The Relative displays the same trouble maintaining his new linguistic gender identity that other Aristophanic characters in some gender disguise do."[58] Although Taaffe does not deal explicitly with the Relative's obscenity, she argues that the misogynistic content of the Relative's speech at the Thesmophoria divulges his masculine identity.[59] What none of these scholars fully considers is how obscenity first helps to construct the Relative's masculine character, and then, once he is disguised, how it repeatedly jeopardizes his feminine identity; in fact, it is an obscene linguistic slip that results in his ultimate discovery. In this sense, the Relative's inability to maintain the illusion of female speech contrasts with Praxagora's success in representing a male speaker in the Assembly in both language and demeanor, with little intrusion of her feminine identity. Further, the Relative's inability to impersonate women's language successfully reveals the importance of speech in constructing masculine political and sexual identity in the theater as in the polis. The comic poet thus closely correlates a character's speech with his sexual practices: because primary obscenity represents a type of violation, the Relative's coarse speech establishes him as the sexual aggressor in relation to the effeminate Agathon, whose rhetorical cleverness and tragic innuendo reflect his status as a pathic and a pederast.

The Relative is established early in the play as strictly masculine both in physical appearance and in speech: he is described as hairy (215–16) and rustic (ἀγροιώτης, 58), and as an old man (γέρων, 63; cf. 146, 585, 941, 1006). Whitman compares his comic masculinity to the character of the uncouth Scythian Archer, who appears at the end of the play;[60] in fact, the Relative and the Archer are the only two male characters to wear the comic phallus in the *Thesmophoriazusae*.[61] They are also distinguished by their exceedingly vulgar language, as Henderson remarks: "Though not the hero, the buffoonish Relation, like the heroes of earlier comedies, holds a virtual monopoly on obscenity and general outspokenness, of which there is a great abundance in this play."[62] The effeminate tragic poet Agathon serves as a foil for the Relative's blunt and sexually aggressive speech. Much of the Relative's masculinity, therefore, consists of making pathic jokes at Agathon's expense. There are several remarks on the tragic

[57] Sommerstein 1995: 63; *pace* Henderson (1991a: 191), who argues that it is an obscene linguistic slip that reveals the Relative's identity.

[58] Taaffe 1993: 87.

[59] Ibid.: 90.

[60] Whitman 1964: 224.

[61] The Relative's comic phallus is mentioned at Ar. *Thesm.* 239, 643ff., 1114; the Archer's is indicated by Ar. *Thesm.* 1188. See *Stone* 1981: 89–90 and 100.

[62] Henderson 1991a: 87.

poet's effeminate appearance, from his paleness (31) and lack of hair (33) to his questionable sexual practices; in fact, Agathon is depicted not only as effeminate but as a male prostitute.

The dialectic between comic and tragic speech begins as soon as Agathon's Servant addresses Euripides and his kinsman. This scene initiates a pattern that recurs throughout the first part of the play, in which the Relative recasts the Servant's unwitting and grandiloquent remarks as obscene comments mostly concerned with Agathon's pathic sexual practices. Thus when the Servant announces Agathon's imminent appearance, "For Agathon of the lovely words, our leader (πρόμος, 50), is about to—," the Relative replies, "Be fucked?" (βινεῖσθαι, 50). The Relative takes πρόμος to refer to someone who takes the forward sexual position,[63] thus substituting a comic obscenity for the Servant's high-flown rhetoric. The Servant then describes the poetic activity of Agathon with a series of craft metaphors that invite another obscene interruption:

Θε.　μέλλει γὰρ ὁ καλλιεπὴς ᾿Αγάθων,
　　　πρόμος ἡμέτερος—. . . .
　　　δρυόχους τιθέναι δράματος ἀρχάς.
　　　κάμπτει δὲ νέας ἁψῖδας ἐπῶν,
　　　τὰ δὲ τορνεύει, τὰ δὲ κολλομελεῖ,
　　　καὶ γνωμοτυπεῖ κἀντονομάζει
　　　καὶ κηροχυτεῖ καὶ γογγύλλει
　　　καὶ χοανεύευ.

Μυ　　　　　καὶ λαικάζει.　　　　　　　(49–57)

Servant:　Agathon of the lovely words, our leader
　　　　　is about to . . . lay the timbers of a new play.
　　　　　He is bending new knots of words,
　　　　　he chisels some and glues others,
　　　　　he hammers out maxims and creates antitheses,
　　　　　he melts wax and rounds it out,
　　　　　and he pours it into a mold—

Relative:　　　　　　　　　　　　And sucks cock.

Embedded in the craft metaphors are two references to fancy rhetorical techniques associated with the sophists: first, the verb χοανεύω recalls the χοάνη of Euripides' sophistic speech at 13–18; similarly, ἀντονομάζω suggests the rhetorical figure of substitution.[64] The Relative correlates

---

[63] See Jocelyn (1980: 37 and 62n.280), who retains the original πρᾱμος, a word not attested elsewhere. Most editors of the manuscript have substituted πρόμος, an epic contracted from πρόμαχος.

[64] Thuc. 6.4.6; see Sommerstein 1994: 161.

corrupt political practices to sexual behavior since the verb λαικάζω, related to ληκῶ, implies "an act which in the view of the speaker degrades the addressee."[65] In this particular instance, the Relative compares the poet's love of crafting unusual phrases to fellatio, a debasing sexual act in the eyes of Athenians, normally performed only by women and prostitutes.[66] In fact, Aristophanes repeatedly associates verbal manipulation and corruption, whether in the theater or in the Assembly, with deviant sexual behavior: "The orators whom the comedians constantly accused of deceiving the *dēmos* and of being given to unmanly sexual practices promoted their deceptions by movements of the lips and tongue as well as of the lower trunk."[67] Not surprisingly, therefore, Euripides specifies as one of Agathon's most salient characteristics his sophistic rhetorical ability (187).

The pattern of substituting comic obscenity for tragic grandiosity continues when the Servant first addresses the Relative directly: "What Rustic approaches these corniced walls?" (τίς ἀγροιώτας πελάθει θριγκοῖς; 58). The Relative responds by giving the craft metaphors an obscene twist:

ὃς ἕτοιμος σοῦ τοῦ τε ποιητοῦ
τοῦ καλλιεποῦς ⟨κατὰ⟩ τοῦ θριγκοῦ
συγγογγύλας καὶ συστρέψας
   τουτὶ τὸ πέος χοανεῦσαι.   (59–62)

One who is ready to take you and your poet of the lovely words,
rounding you up and turning you over,
to pour my prick up your cornice.

By loading the innocuous terms καλλιεποῦς, θριγκοῦ, συγγογγύλας, and χοανεῦσαι with obscene meanings, the Relative implicitly assimilates Agathon's poetic craft to his sexual status as a pathic.[68] Similarly, the Relative's use of τὸ πέος reinforces his own masculine linguistic and theatrical identity by distancing him both politically and sexually from the effeminate Agathon; presumably some phallic stage business, indicated by τουτί, accompanied these lines as well.[69] The Servant's subsequent remark that Euripides'

[65] Jocelyn 1980: 15. On the degradation implied by oral sex, see also Henderson 1991a: 153; Halperin 1990a: 97; Dover 1989: 101–2; for other instances, cf. Ar. *Ach.* 79, 529, 537; *Eq.* 167; *Thesm.* 493.

[66] For the noun, cf. Ar. *Ach.* 529, 537; see Jocelyn (1980: 38), who comments, "There can be no doubt that penetration of the mouth constituted a standard form of physical insult in Greek as in Latin communities."

[67] Jocelyn 1980: 26. On questionable sexual practices, see Ar. *Eq.* 878–80; *Nub.* 1093–94; *Vesp.* 686–95; *Eccl.* 112–13; on deceptive orators, *Ach.* 370–74, 633–42; *Vesp.* 283, 666–68, 1007.

[68] Austin (1990: 13–14) argues that the Relative describes anal, not oral, rape in this scene; see also Sommerstein 1994: 161.

[69] Stone 1981: 88 and n. 64.

kinsman must have been ὑβριστής as a young man again defines him as the sexual aggressor, for the male prostitute was spoken of as hiring himself out for *hubris*, for other people to treat as they pleased.[70] The person who hired the prostitute was therefore someone who paid for the right to violate his body.

As Agathon finally enters, wheeled out on the *eccyclēma*, the Relative claims to see not a man but Cyrene, a courtesan celebrated for her "twelve positions," a remark that further associates the tragic poet with prostitution.[71] Dressed in effeminate, perhaps Ionian, finery, Agathon's speech is remarkably free of obscenities.[72] This feature is obviously conditioned in part by genre: as the mouthpiece of tragic poetry, Agathon must speak tragically, a symbol of "the emasculated art of contemporary tragedy, invented by Euripides."[73] But the fact that Euripides, who is similarly characterized as sophistic, employs obscenities like the Relative does (βεβίνηκας, 35, and κέρκος, 239) suggests that Agathon is being singled out as womanish. His use of lyric speech strongly associates him with women, since the tragedians rarely gave lyric verses to men in their plays. In his opening prayer, he identifies himself as the female leader of a chorus of young girls (κοῦραι, 102), who perform a cult song like that at the end of Euripides' *Hippolytus*, and then maintains a feminine persona throughout the song by referring to himself with feminine participial endings, δεξάμεναι (101), κλῇζουσα (117), and ὀλβίζουσα (118). Even his music reflects this incongruity of gender and speech: his feminine lyre, described as the "mother of hymns," has a masculine shout (κίθαρίν τε ματέρ' ὕμνων | ἄρσενι βοᾷ δόκιμον, 124–25). Agathon concludes his song with another feature of female speech, the *ololugē*, a feminine ritual cry of celebration discussed in Chapters 2 and 3.[74]

---

[70] Halperin 1990a: 96; Dover 1989: 34–39. For the use of *hubris* in the sense of sexual degradation, cf. Aeschin. 1.55, 108, 116, 188. Sommerstein (1994: 162) seems to miss the sexual connotations of this term.

[71] Ar. *Ran.* 1327–28; the scholia to this passage mention that the name appeared several times in Aristophanes' other comedies. I find Henry's suggestion that the Relative actually addresses Cyrene in the audience intriguing, but it seems more likely that he refers instead to Agathon, who has just entered: see Henry 1985: 13, 24.

[72] Henderson 1991a: 87. Wit-Tak (1968: 363) notes that Agathon does not react to the Relative with obscenity, even though he has "every inducement" to do so. Snyder (1974) argues that Agathon's unusual dress, the flowing *krokōtos* and accessories, identify him with the depictions of Anacreon found on vases during the first half of the fifth century.

[73] Henderson 1991a: 88; on tragedy and effeminacy, see Zeitlin 1981; on the link between comedy and obscenity, see Edwards 1991.

[74] Although ancient commentators attributed this stage direction to the Relative, who supposedly mocks Agathon's effeminate song, I follow van Leeuwen's suggestion that it should be attributed to Agathon and his chorus, who are imitating women; see Sommerstein 1994: 166.

Analyzing the meter of Agathon's song as predominantly Ionic, critics have argued that it conveys a seductive, feminine tone, since Ionia was a region the Greeks associated with sexual promiscuity and decadence. However, Parker has recently argued that Aristophanes modeled this lyric passage on cult songs, specifically comparing it to a fragment of Sappho in ionics concerning the cult of Adonis.[75] This erotic song has the effect of arousing the Relative in much the same way a prostitute might:[76]

ὡς ἡδὺ τὸ μέλος ὦ πότνιαι Γενετυλλίδες
καὶ θηλυδριῶδες καὶ κατεγλωττισμένον
καὶ μανδαλωτόν, ὥστ' ἐμοῦ γ' ἀκροωμένου
ὑπὸ τὴν ἕδραν αὐτὴν ὑπῆλθε γάργαλος.   (130–34)

Queenly Genetyllides, how sweet is his song,
how effeminate, how french-kissed with the tongue out,
so that as I listened a tickle crept under my very seat.

The Relative first invokes the Genetyllides, deities closely connected with Aphrodite and therefore with female sexuality; a women's festival in their honor was held at Colias near Phalerum.[77] The rest of his response contributes to the thematic portrayal of Agathon as a prostitute, since tongue-kissing was apparently the specialty of prostitutes and other sexually experienced women (and men).[78] As in the case of λαικάζω, to stimulate someone orally was considered inherently degrading. The effect of Agathon's words on the Relative further suggests that he is being implicitly compared to a pathic. Although not in a context of degradation, Plato's *Phaedrus* describes the same tickling sensation aroused in the charioteer by the sight of his *erōmenos* or beloved.[79]

In the rest of his speech (135–45), the Relative focuses on Agathon's physical appearance, parodying a passage from Aeschylus' lost *Edonoi* about the effeminate Dionysus. The subject is the gender confusion created by the cross-dressed Agathon, who probably wears at least some of the feminine garments listed.[80] The Relative begins by calling the tragic poet a womanish

---

[75] Parker (1997: 403) remarks: "The song takes the form of a cult hymn in dialogue between a celebrant and a chorus of female worshippers. A fragment of such a song, generally attributed to Sappho (*PLF* 140), is in ionics, and belongs to the oriental cult of Adonis."

[76] Muecke 1982a: 48–49; on the luxury and decadence conveyed by Ionic meter, see Dale 1948: 119; and Hall 1989b: 82–84. Note that the crone decked out as a prostitute at *Eccl.* 883 also sings an Ionian ditty.

[77] Sommerstein 1994: 166; cf. Ar. *Nub.* 52; *Lys.* 2; Paus. 1.1.5; Plut. *Sol.* 8.4. The scholion also associates the Genetyllides with Artemis and childbirth.

[78] Ar. *Ach.* 1201; *Nub.* 51; Henderson 1991a: 182.

[79] Pl. *Phdr.* 253e6; Muecke 1982a; Dover 1989: 163.

[80] Muecke (1982a: 49) points out that since the Relative's words parody Aeschylus, they may not realistically describe Agathon's dress.

man, a γύννις (136), and then dwells on the incongruous elements of his costume: "What does a *barbitos* chatter to a saffron gown? What a lyre to a hair net? What is a *lēkuthos* doing with a breast-band?" (τί βάρβιτος | λαλεῖ κροκωτῷ; τί δὲ λύρα κεκρυφάλῳ; | τί λήκυθος καὶ στρόφιον; 137–39). The term *krokōtos* refers to a woman's most attractive garment, usually reserved for special occasions like religious festivals and possibly associated with prostitutes, since it was considered seductive.[81] Further, the verb λαλέω, which describes the sound of the *barbitos*, denotes the uneducated, garrulous speech of women in Aristophanes, as we saw in Chapter 2.[82] The Relative then moves from clothing to Agathon's physical features:

πότερον ὡς ἀνὴρ τρέφει;
καὶ ποῦ πέος; ποῦ χλαῖνα; ποῦ Λακωνικαί;
ἀλλ' ὡς γυνὴ δῆτ'· εἶτα ποῦ τὰ τιτθία;   (141–43)

Were you raised as a man? Then where's your penis?
Where's your cloak? Your Laconian shoes?
Or were you raised as a woman? In that case, where are your breasts?

Agathon obviously lacks both the comic phallus worn by the Relative and the padded breasts typically used by male actors playing women in both tragedy and comedy.[83] The emphasis on costume and the inability to detect the body beneath the clothes suggest that this whole speech can be read as a metatheatrical comment on the compromised gender status of the cross-dressed tragic actor,[84] later derided by Socrates for his emasculating performance (Pl. *Rep.* 395d5–e2).

In response, Agathon tenders a theory of poetic mimesis, one that confuses physical reality with dramatic appearance:

ἐγὼ δὲ τὴν ἐσθῆθ' ἅμα γνώμῃ φορῶ.
χρὴ γὰρ ποιητὴν ἄνδρα πρὸς τὰ δράματα

---

[81] Stone 1981: 174–75; Saïd 1987: 226; cf. Ar. *Lys.* 44–51, 219–20, 645. Note that the heavily made-up crone in the *Ecclesiazusae* wears a *krokōtos* in an attempt to seduce a passerby much as a prostitute might; on the scene, see Ussher 1973: 195. Cf. *Lys.* 258, where the adverb νύκτωρ possibly implies that Agathon walks the streets at night like a prostitute; see Sommerstein 1994: 174.

[82] In the plays of Aristophanes containing women with speaking parts: *Thesm.* 138, 267, 393 (Euripides' slander), 578 (men gossiping in the agora), 717, 1082 (Echo, who is characterized as a woman), 1087 (Echo), 1097, 1109, 1110; *Lys.* 356 (female chorus), 442, 627; *Eccl.* 119, 120, 129, 230, 1058. For a discussion of this term and relevant bibliography, see also Taaffe 1993: 86n.36, and 116n.22; cf. also Men. *Sam.* 241; Men. fr. 66. 3; Lucian *Rhetorum praeceptor* 23. For λαλέω used of male gossip in the agora, cf. Ar. *Thesm.* 578 and *Eccl.* 302.

[83] Halperin (1990a: 97) describes the male prostitute in similar terms: "To be a prostitute meant, in effect, to surrender one's phallus—to discard the marker of one's socio-sexual precedence—and so it was, next to enslavement, the worst degradation a citizen could suffer, equivalent to voluntary effeminization."

[84] On the metatheatrical implications of this scene, see Taaffe 1993: 82.

ἃ δεῖ ποιεῖν πρὸς ταῦτα τοὺς τρόπους ἔχειν.
αὐτίκα γυναικεῖ' ἢν ποιῇ τις δράματα,
μετουσίαν δεῖ τῶν τρόπων τὸ σῶμ' ἔχειν.   (148–52)

I put on clothing to match my frame of mind.
For a man who is a poet must adopt manners
appropriate to the plays he composes.
For example, if he creates a play about women,
he must make his body adopt their mannerisms.

Consistent with the pattern established earlier in the exchange with the
Servant, only the sexual consequences of Agathon's aesthetic theory interest the Relative: "Then do you sit on top (κελητίζεις) when you do a
Phaedra?" (153). The Relative's question refers not only to Euripides'
Hippolytus, but also to prostitution, because the sexual position of sitting
astride a partner was considered a specialty of courtesans,[85] further associating Agathon with pathic or womanish sexual behavior. The tragic poet
further elaborates on his theory of mimesis: "If he wishes to write a play
about men, he already has what he needs in his body. But mimesis must
capture that which we do not possess" (154–56). As before, the Relative
reduces this theory to a sexual scenario in which he supplies the effeminate
Agathon with the part of the body he lacks: "Then just give me a call the
next time you're writing a satyr play and I will collaborate with you, long
and hard, from behind" (157–58).

The Relative's scurrilous attacks on Agathon's sexual status accelerate
when the tragic poet refuses to comply with Euripides' request. Agathon's
allusion to Euripides' trouble as a πάθημα (199) provokes yet another
pathic joke from the Relative: "Just as you, you pathic, are gape-assed not
by words but by sufferings!" (καὶ μὴν σύ γ' ὦ κατάπυγον εὐρύπρωκτος εἶ
| οὐ τοῖς λόγοισιν ἀλλὰ τοῖς παθήμασιν, 200–201). The crude masculine
obscenities κατάπυγων and εὐρύπρωκτος once again simultaneously expose the tragic poet as effeminate and reinforce the Relative's role as
sexually and linguistically dominant. A final instance of comic obscenity
substituted for tragic innuendo completes the pattern of exchange between
Agathon and the Relative. Agathon euphemistically asserts that he cannot
attend the Thesmophoria without provoking the wrath of the women,
because they consider him a rival: "They think I steal their nocturnal tricks
and deprive women of sex" (δοκῶν γυναικῶν ἔργα νυκτερείσια | κλέπτειν
ὑφαρπάζειν τε θήλειαν Κύπριν, 204–5). The Relative, true to form, substitutes a primary obscenity for Agathon's sexual innuendoes: "What do you
mean 'steal' (κλέπτειν)? By Zeus, 'be fucked' is more like it" (βινεῖσθαι,
206). The interaction between Agathon and the Relative in the *Thesmophoriazusae* strongly correlates linguistic practices to a character's sexuality

[85] Sommerstein 1994: 168–69; on Phaedra as a whore, cf. Ar. *Ran.* 1043; on the sexual
position, *Vesp.* 500–501; Men. *Pk.* 484.

and inherently critiques sophistic speech as seductive and corrupting. The consistent use of primary obscenity by the Relative establishes him as purely masculine and therefore sexually dominant. Agathon's avoidance of any type of obscenity, whether primary or secondary, his use of sexual innuendo, and his rhetorical facility betray his compromised gender status as an effeminate, sexually submissive, and yet oversexed male. Finally, the opening scene of the *Thesmophoriazusae* forges a link between tragic poets and politicians: both use costume and rhetoric to deceive their audiences, in contrast to the comic poet, who, by continually revealing the mechanics of the play, illuminates the truth.[86] In the same way, the comic buffoon strips away the pretenses embedded in the deceptive, euphemistic, and paratragic speech of his interlocutors.

RENDERING THE FEMALE: THE RELATIVE'S FLAWED PERFORMANCE

At the dramatic level, the pathic humor that colors the dialogue between the Relative and Agathon prepares the spectators for a role reversal: the Relative, by submitting to Euripides, will now play the part of the feminized male and himself become the object of pathic jokes: "Take me and use me in whatever way you wish" (ἐμοὶ δ' ὅ τι βούλει χρῶ λαβών, 212). For an adult citizen male in classical Athens to allow another person absolute authority over his body implied a complete loss of social status.[87] Euripides thus takes Agathon's aesthetic theory at face value by subjecting the Relative to several procedures geared to make him appear more like a woman, including the shaving of his beard and the depilation of his pubic hair.[88] Indeed, the verb κύπτω serves as a thematic reminder that the Relative, in baring his rump, now assumes the position of the passive sexual partner, while Euripides assumes the dominant position.[89]

And yet the Relative never completely succumbs to his effeminate role. Although he himself appears like a woman or effeminate male, cleanshaven and comely (εὐπρεπής, 233) in his *krokōtos* (253), depilated and potentially vulnerable to sexual attack like Agathon, he still retains his masculine identity by continuing to use obscenity and to make pathic jokes. Once shaven, the Relative jests that he looks like Cleisthenes, a well-

---

[86] Foley 1988b: 44. On the tragic art as a source of deception, cf. Gorg. (82.23 DK).

[87] Halperin (1990a: 97), citing Dover, observes that the male prostitute, by submitting his body to another, became no better than a slave.

[88] Depilation was associated not only with female prostitutes, but also possibly with pathics, who may have practiced anal depilation, since hair on an *eromenos* was considered unattractive; see Hansen 1976: 174–75 and n. 46; Halperin 1990a: 88; cf. Ar. *Ach.* 119: ὦ θερμόβουλον πρωκτὸν ἐξυρημένε.

[89] On κύπτω, cf. Ar. *Thesm.* 236, 239; and the scholion to *Lys.* 231, which associates κύπτω with prostitutes; see also Henderson 1991a: 180.

known political figure and a frequent target of pathic humor in Aristophanes (235), and further asserts that singeing will turn him into a δελφάκιον,
slang for the genitals of a woman (237). His obscene references to his
perineum, τραμίς (246), to his anus, πρωκτός (248), and to the penis,
πόσθιον (254), expose his speech as typically masculine. The presence of
the comic phallus serves a similar function: when Euripides exhorts him
to watch the tip of his κέρκος ("tail," 239), a euphemism for the comic
phallus, which obstructs the singeing process, he further calls attention to
Relative's physical masculinity. Even though the Relative twice swears by
female deities in this scene, these oaths actually serve to emphasize his
masculinity further: he expresses his refusal to have his face completely
shaven with an ironic oath to Demeter (225), while his oath to Aphrodite
mocks Agathon's tragic effeminacy (254).

Once the Relative's physical transformation is complete, Euripides enjoins him to speak like a woman:

ἀνὴρ μὲν ἡμῖν οὑτοσὶ καὶ δὴ γυνή
τό γ' εἶδος· ἢν λαλῇς δ', ὅπως τῷ φθέγματι
γυναικιεῖς εὖ καὶ πιθανῶς.   (266–68)

This man really now appears to be a woman.
Only, if you talk, try to do to a good and persuasive job
of making your voice like a woman's.

Presumably he refers not to the pitch of the voice, but to the oaths, case
endings, and other linguistic features appropriate to female speech. This
interpretation is confirmed by the Relative's impudent reply: "Not by
Apollo, unless you swear to . . ." (269). In swearing by a deity strongly
associated with men, the Relative immediately undermines Euripides' injunction.[90] But once Euripides agrees to rescue him should their plan go
awry, the Relative adopts the appropriate markers of female speech, referring to himself with feminine participles (λαβοῦσα, 285; ἔχουσαν, 288).
And yet several obscenities and sexual euphemisms threaten to subvert his
feminine disguise, revealing that his masculinity is never far from the
surface. For example, his "prayer" to Demeter and Persephone contains
two obscene puns: "And may my daughter, Little Piggy (χοῖρον), meet
a wealthy man . . . and may my son, Little Prick (ποσθαλίσκον), have
intelligence and good sense" (289–91). Because only male speakers use
πόσθη in extant Aristophanic comedy, the term ποσθαλίσκον potentially
undermines the Relative's feminine persona; indeed, he has just used
the diminutive in reference to Agathon's clothing.[91] In contrast to the

---

[90] Sommerstein 1995: 65; cf. Ar. *Eccl.* 158–60, and the exceptional example, *Lys.* 917.

[91] Taaffe (1993: 87) enumerates a couple of other instances in this speech that give away
the Relative's identity: his prayer for good luck and a safe return (283–84), and his prayer
for escape (288). However, she misinterprets the sexual joke at 289–91 as evidence for his

effeminate Agathon, the Relative never fully realizes his transformation into a woman; rather, we are reminded at several critical junctures that Euripides' kinsman merely plays the part of a woman, and does a rather poor job, at that.

RHETORIC AND OBSCENITY AT THE THESMOPHORIA

The women of the Thesmophoria represent a further inversion of gender roles and speech practices exemplified by the effeminate Agathon and the cross-dressed Relative. Whereas Agathon looks and speaks like a woman, the women use the language of the male orators in the Assembly. The poet thus makes use of a dramatic convention also found in tragedy: he first establishes male and female discursive spheres as separate, and then shows how these different speech communities permeate and infiltrate each other through the transgressive speech of individuals. Only the Relative, now disguised as a woman, succeeds in retaining his masculine identity through his persistent use of obscenity. Scholars have interpreted this reversal in various ways, with Taaffe placing emphasis on its metatheatrical implications, and others focusing on the theme of "woman on top" and the comic possibilities engendered by the incongruity of women using male political language.[92] I argue, however, that Aristophanes, by assigning male political speech to women, identifies the rhetorical practices of the Assembly with lower-class and morally suspect individuals, like Agathon, demagogues, and their teachers, and thus implicitly critiques the whole process of political debate at Athens.

He begins by establishing a dialectical relation between the exclusively female realm of the Thesmophoria and the male civic institutions of the courts and the Assembly. We learn from the play that the public business transacted in the Assembly and law courts ceased during the three-day period of the Festival (78–80) and that the Relative enters on the second day, the Nesteia, a day devoted to fasting and lamenting in ritual observance of the sorrows of Demeter (80, 376–77). In place of the suspended activity of male civic institutions, the women at the Athenian Thesmophoria established their own government, complete with female officials, *archousai*, who corresponded to the male *archontes*.[93] In the play, the women refer to their meeting as an "Assembly" (376), calling themselves the *dēmos* or the *boulē* of the women (335, 353, 1145). Since the word *dēmos* had

---

female characterization on the grounds that it shows feminine guile. In light of the Relative's consistent use of obscenity elsewhere in the play and the women's complete lack of obscenity, I do not see how this view can be accurate.

[92] Taaffe 1993: 87–94; Bowie 1993: 206–7; Zeitlin 1981: 173.

[93] Isac. 8.19; Burkert 1985: 242; Detienne 1989: 138; Bowie 1993: 207.

become increasingly associated with the lower classes by the last quarter of the fifth century, as discussed in Chapter 1, it potentially affiliates the women with this sector of the Athenian polis. Their speech is described as masculine and political by means of the terms *agoreuein* (305, 379) and *ekklēsiazein* (330); the women also swear an oath (359) before discussing their proposals and decrees (ψηφίσματα καὶ νόμον, 361). Designated as *rhētores* or orators (382), the women don the traditional speaker's garland before stepping forward to address the crowd (380). The dialectical relation between the masculine political sphere and the women's Thesmophoria is further underscored by the location of the festival: in contrast to most Greek cities, which held the festival outside their walls, Athens held its Thesmophoria near the Pnyx.

In a detailed treatment of the scene, Haldane has shown how closely the opening ceremony of the Thesmophoria (295–371) imitates and parodies elements of the Athenian Assembly.[94] The Heraldess begins with a prose prayer (295–311) in which the appropriate gods are invoked, states the subject of her prayer, and concludes with a paean call, a regular procedure in a public ritual.[95] The chorus' response, a choral hymn (312–30), possibly further echoes the state prayer in the deities addressed. A second prayer (331–51) follows and contains a curse similar to the herald's ritual curse that convened the meeting.[96] The final formulation, "May that person perish miserably, himself and his household" (κακῶς ἀπολέσθαι τοῦτον αὐτὸν κᾠκίαν, 349), closely approximates the end of the judicial or heliastic oath sworn annually by jurors in the courts.[97] Finally, the presence of the Scythian Archer at the end of the scene further suggests the Athenian Assembly, since one of the Archer's primary tasks was removing people from the podium under the instructions of the *prutaneis*.[98]

Although the formal aspects of the scene recall aspects of the democratic process at Athens, the concerns expressed by the women are stereotypically feminine. The Heraldess's account of the crimes normally punishable by Athenian law, such as collaborating with the enemy or fostering tyranny, quickly deteriorate into a series of private, feminine offenses, such as passing off someone else's baby as one's own, tattling on the sexual misadventures of one's mistress, and conveying false information from a lover. Cited as particularly heinous in carrying out crimes against women are adulterers who deceive their mistresses and break their promises, crones who give presents to their lovers, courtesans who cheat on their boyfriends, and tavern keepers who deny women their full measure of wine (339–48).

---

[94] Haldane 1965a.
[95] Thuc. 6.32; Ar. *Vesp.* 863–90; *Ran.* 864–88; *Pax* 431–58.
[96] Haldane 1965a: 42; cf. Dem. 8.130, 23.97; Isoc. 4.157.
[97] Haldane 1965a; cf. Dem. 24.151; Isoc. 4.157; and Andoc. *De mysteriis* 96–97.
[98] Hall 1989a: 44.

By linking the formal structure of the Thesmophoria to democratic procedures in the polis, this scene invites the spectators to view the women's rhetorical skill from a political perspective.[99] Like demagogues who manipulate the *dēmos* for personal ambition, women are depicted as skillful and crafty speakers. The female chorus applaud Woman A's polished speech, which adheres to conventional rhetorical models of the time,[100] calling her a clever speaker (δεινότερον λέγουσης, 436) with an intricate mind (πολυπλοκωτέρας, 434). Her words are deemed ποικίλοι, "tricky" (438), a term elsewhere associated with deceptive speech.[101] The chorus conclude by comparing her to Xenocles, son of Carcinus (440–42), a writer of tragedies with political ambitions, an allusion that raises the specter of the sophistic tragic poet Agathon and again makes patent the link between politicians and tragic poets. Described by weaving metaphors, this clever speech also has erotic implications, suggesting the garlands woven by the anonymous, lovesick girl in Woman A's speech (400–401). Appropriately, the chorus also praise the Garland Seller's speech in similar terms, describing her mind, like her craft, as entangling or intricate (πολύπλοκον, 463).[102] These terms not only signify women's work, but quite possibly hark back to the craft metaphors describing Agathon's poetic activity, thereby connecting the women's speech to the corrupt rhetorical practices wielded by the socially inferior in the Assembly and in the courts. Finally, from a broader perspective, the women, in putting Euripides on trial, prove themselves to be worthy of the invective they seek to punish. They confirm the commonplace that women are innately deceptive, acting one way in the presence of men and another when alone. The debate scene in the *Thesmophoriazusae* makes a mockery of the democratic process enacted in the Athenian Assembly and in the law courts: the issues debated by the women are portrayed as trivial and their rhetorical techniques, like those of the Athenian politicians, as deceptive and subversive.

Of considerable importance to our discussion is the fact that the female celebrants do not utter any primary obscenities, in striking contrast to the *aischrologia* that formed a central component of the ritual practices at the Thesmophoria.[103] Puzzling, in this light, are the frequent attempts on the part of scholars to assimilate the women's speech in this part of the play to ritual *aischrologia*; Wit-Tak, for example, concludes: "The nature and frequency of obscenity in *Thesmophoriazusae* is undoubtedly influenced by

[99] Bergren 1983.

[100] Murphy (1938: 108) delineates a proemium (383–88), prosthesis (389–94), proofs (395–428), and epilogue (428–32).

[101] Johnston 1995: 189.

[102] For other weaving images, cf. Ar. *Thesm.* 447, 458, 566, 738.

[103] Only Henderson (1991a: 87) perceptively observes that the women do not "utter a single obscenity in their opening of the meeting (295–330) or in their description of Euripides' slanders (331–465)."

the actual occurrence of obscene practices and language at the feast itself."[104] Only Woman A, an older woman, utters mild secondary obscenities with her threat to depilate the crotch of the disguised Relative (ἀποψιλώσομεν τὸν χοῖρον, 538), her allusion to "breast" (τιτθούς, 640, 691), and the suggestive, although not inherently obscene, remark on the Relative's errant phallus: "It's peeking out, and has an extremely good color" (διέκυψε καὶ μάλ' εὔχρων, 644). These obscenities are, as we have noted already, dramatically in character for the comic old woman. Woman B employs only a very bland euphemism, "She was deflowered" (ἐξεκόρησε, 760). In the same class are the playful sexual allusions of the female chorus in the parabasis (785–845), suggested by καταδάρθωμεν, "sleep," παίζουσαι, "playing around" (795), and ἀπέδωκεν, "give out" (813). In fact, the women make only the most polite references to their sexual liaisons: the Heraldess, in her opening prayer, refers to several infractions of the female code, most of which involve betraying other women's sexual secrets (339–51). Further, the Garland Seller's speech may possibly contain a double entendre that links her craft to prostitution (cf. 446–52).[105] One of the great ironies of the play, therefore, is that it contains no female *aischrologia*, even though its action takes place on the second day of the festival, the day on which scholars have speculated this ritual speech occurred.[106] The poet may have avoided any representation of primary female obscenity, along with other details about the women's rituals, because it would have bordered too closely on sacrilege. The absence of primary obscenities from the women's speech markedly contrasts with the presence of those spoken by the Relative and Cleisthenes, who, even though portrayed as an effeminate in the mold of Agathon, twice utters a primary obscenity at the Thesmophoria (πέος, 643, 648; cf. the pun on ἰσθμός, 647).

Although the Relative accurately impersonates women's speech at the level of grammar, using feminine case endings when referring to himself and swearing by female deities,[107] the content of his speech and his persistent obscenity continually identify him as male. His invective against women

---

[104] Wit-Tak 1968: 365n.1, Haldane (1965a: 44) identifies the content of Ar. *Thesm.* 339–48 as a form of "erotic jesting," although it contains no obscenities. Finnegan (1990: 101) asserts that speaking female characters in Aristophanes' plays contribute to the obscenity just as much as men do. On the absence of obscenity in this play, see Henderson 1991a: 87.

[105] For this suggestion, see Ruck 1975: 17; see also Bowie (1993: 211), who similarly sees *aischrologia* in the speech of the female Herald.

[106] I believe this theory derives from a passage in Callimachus that links the practice of *aischrologia* to fasting at a festival of Demeter; cf. Callim. fr. 21.8ff. See Parke 1977: 82–83. Bowie (1993: 208), without explanation, assigns *aischrologia* to the first day of the festival.

[107] For feminine pronouns and endings used by the Relative in Ar. *Thesm.*, cf. αὐταὶ γάρ ἐσμεν (473), ἔχουσαι (473), αὐτῇ (476), ἐμαυτῇ (477), οὖσαν (480), καταχέσασα (487), ἐχομένη (489), ὅσαι πάρεσμεν (541), διδοῦσαι . . . | . . . φάμεν (558–59); ἀσθενοῦσαν (617). He also swears by female deities, including Artemis (517, 569); and the Twain (594).

recalls the literary antecedents discussed earlier, and found in Hesiod's *Theogony* (585–616) and Euripides' *Hippolytus* (616–68), and perhaps sets him apart from the other speakers, although we have seen that female characters may employ this genre against their wayward peers.[108] The female chorus later critique this type of male speech in the parabasis, mocking it with their ironic allusion to the Hesiodic idea of women as a *kakon*.[109] Certainly part of the joke is that the Relative utters a discourse notoriously associated with Euripides in the tragic poet's defense. Whether or not this invective jeopardizes the Relative's feminine disguise, he certainly flaunts his masculinity through his use of obscene language.[110] A closer look at the language of this scene (466–633) illustrates how the Relative's preoccupation with obscenity, both sexual and scatological, finally undermines his disguise once and for all.

In his defense of his kinsman, the Relative argues that the women are guilty of crimes far worse than those dramatized by Euripides. Using himself as an example, the Relative states that "she" lost "her" virginity at age seven and that "she" cheated on "her" husband after only three days of marriage. Then "she" admits to copulating at an altar of Apollo and to sleeping with male slaves. The speech begins with a degree of euphemism probably intended as feminine in tone: "she" designates sexual intercourse as "sleep" (καθηῦδεν, 479) and the loss of "her" virginity as διεκόρησεν (480), a term also used by Woman B later in the scene. Although "she" properly uses the passive voice to refer to "her" sexual role as a woman, the modest and indirect tone immediately begins to degenerate: using the rather violent slang term for sexual intercourse, ἠρειδόμην (488), the Relative describes bending forward over Apollo's shrine, κύβδα (489), a sexual position earlier mentioned in connection with him during the depilation scene (cf. 230, 236, 239). The verb σποδούμεθα, "pound, crush" (492), although not a primary obscenity, also conveys an extremely coarse tone. The sexual vocabulary culminates in a primary obscenity, ληκώμεθα (493), related to λαικάζω, which the Relative had earlier used in reference to Agathon (257). Similarly, the Relative employs the word πόσθιον (515) at the end of his speech, a word that has a double reference: as the quoted speech of an old woman (γραῦς, 505), it is consistent with the dramatic characterization of the comic crone, and yet it also evokes the Relative's previous uses of the term (cf. 253, 291). Finally, the speech concludes with a double entendre on παθοῦσαι: "Why

---

[108] I am hesitant to identify the content of this speech as strictly masculine, as do Taaffe (1993: 90) and Saïd (1987: 232). For the rhetorical structure of the speech, see Murphy 1938: 108–9.

[109] Ar. *Thesm.* 787, 789 (twice), 791, 794, 796, 797, 799.

[110] Henderson (1991a: 89) comments that the Relative "tactlessly uses a large number of obscene expressions, in pointed contrast to the speakers for the women, who used none"; cf. Bowie 1993: 211.

are we angry at Euripides, when we women have suffered (παθοῦσαι) nothing worse than we have done?" (518–19); the verb possibly has a sexual meaning, recalling the Relative's pathic joke on πάθημα at 201.

Even more noteworthy, however, are the repeated scatological terms in the Relative's speech: indeed, as Henderson has pointed out, the Relative's identity is finally revealed by his incorrect reference to a male chamber pot. The term κοπρών (485), used to describe a trip to the outhouse as a pretext for a wife's secret tryst with her lover, first hints at the masculinity of the speaker. This term, although not strongly obscene, suggests κόπρος and all its comic associations with pathic behavior.[111] The fact that κοπρών appears in conjunction with στρόφος (484), a term normally applied to crepitation in comedy, further strengthens the scatological tone of the passage. When Woman A threatens to depilate the Relative a second time, as a punishment for his insolent speech (566; cf. 538), the Relative continues the scatological motif with the verb χέζω, "to ease one's self," later in the scene when he threatens Woman A: "I will make you shit that sesame cake you ate" (τὸν σησαμοῦνθ' ὃν κατέφαγες, τοῦτον χεσεῖν ποιήσω, 570). As pointed out earlier, the verb χέζω, like most scatological terms, rarely appears in women's speech in Aristophanes.

The Relative then turns to urination, an activity mentioned only infrequently in Old Comedy and always in connection with men. Anxious to escape detection by his male interlocutor, Cleisthenes, the Relative fakes an urgent need to urinate ("Let me pee," ἔασον οὐρῆσαί με, 611), a strategy similar to the one used by the youth in the *Ecclesiazusae* to evade the lecherous old woman (*Eccl.* 1059ff.). Later, he employs the technical term from medicine, στραγγουριῶ, "strangury," to explain his delay. The references to defecation and urination play against the Relative's feminine disguise and prepare the spectators for the final linguistic slip that will reveal his masculine identity once and for all. Pressed by Cleisthenes to describe the rituals of last year's Thesmophoria, the Relative claims that a certain Xenylla, after drinking a lot of wine, called for a σκάφιον, a chamber pot for women; but he makes a mistake, when he asserts there was no ἀμίς, "male chamber pot," available (633). As Henderson explains, the ἀμίς, a type of funnel-shaped urinal, was typically used at banquets or meetings where one could not easily leave the premises, whereas σκάφιον is a euphemistic term used of its female equivalent.[112] Similarly, the comic

---

[111] According to Henderson (1991a: 193), the term is almost always used of dung in connection with buggery. At Ar. *Eq.* 295, the Sausage Seller uses the word κοπροφορήσωσε when he threatens Cleon with anal rape; but the Spartan ambassador in the *Lysistrata* uses a similar term, κοπραγωγῆν (*Lys.* 1174), of male/female intercourse.

[112] Henderson 1991a: 191; for a σκάφιον, see the Berlin vase that depicts a naked woman urinating into a shallow basin; Berlin, Staatliche Museen, no. 3757, from Orvieto, ARV² 404, 11; *CVA* pl. 24, 2; cf. also Louvre Hydria, G51, by the Dikaios Painter, ARV² 32, 1; *CVA* 53, 1 and 4; discussed in Kilmer 1982.

urinal, σκωραμίς, a neologism coined by Blepyrus in the *Ecclesiazusae*, caps a scene of extreme scatological and masculine vulgarity. The intrusion of masculine comic speech, especially scatology, into the female space of the Thesmophoria reinforces gender norms by exposing the Relative as male in gender and speech.

The Relative undermines his feminine persona in other ways relating to his speech practices. Dressed down by Woman A for his insulting defense of Euripides, the Relative claims that he has license to speak according to the terms of *parrhēsia*, guaranteed to *female citizens* (ὅσαι πάρεσμεν ἀσταί, 541); in actual practice, *parrhēsia* was the right of adult citizen males in classical Athens, as discussed in Chapter 1. Similarly, when his true identity is about to be discovered, he utters a comic exclamation typically associated with men in Aristophanes, κακοδαίμων ἐγώ (604, 650). This utterance denotes comic distress both in the depilation scene and in his later trouble with the Archer.[113] A similar play of gendered terms dogs the Relative's attempts to render famous tragic women in his parodies of Euripidean rescue scenes: although he refers to himself by the feminine gender, as does Euripides, when he plays Helen,[114] Woman C refuses to be taken in and pointedly uses the male gender in designating him.[115] But just as before, the Relative cannot completely suppress his masculine identity: when he says, "I am ashamed before you with my outraged cheeks" (αἰσχύνομαί σε τὰς γνάθους ὑβρισμένη, 903), his words have a double meaning. He both expresses a sentiment appropriate to a modest girl and calls attention to his masculine identity, since γνάθος serves as a verbal reminder of his clean-shaven state (221; cf. 575, 583).[116] The feminine participle, ὑβρισμένη, also points back to ὑβριστής (63), with its connotations of sexual violence. The Relative further reveals himself with an obscene pun, substituting ἐσχάρα, a slang term for labia, for the original Euripidean phrase, ἐς χέρας: "O you who approach your wife's *eskhara* after a long absence" (912).[117] When his performance fails to achieve the desired effect, he reverts to the masculine expression ὁ κακοδαίμων (925). His version of the tragic character Andromeda is even less polished. Several times he uses the wrong grammatical gender, referring to himself with male case endings; he even goes so far as to incongruously juxtapose κημός, the funnel-shaped voting urn used by jurors in the courts (1031), with a

[113] Ar. *Thesm.* 229, 232, 237, 925, 1004 (Relative); 1006, 1225 (Archer); 892 (Woman addressing Relative); cf. *Eccl.* 323 (Blepyrus); 746, 760 (Man B); 1093, 1102 (Youth); *Lys.* 449 (Proboulus); 845 (Cinesias).

[114] Ar. *Thesm.* 850, 861, 890, 896, 901, 902, 903, 905, 907, 909, 918.

[115] Ar. *Thesm.* 875, 879, 887, 892, 893, 898, 920. See also Hall (1989a: 49), who remarks that only Euripides manages to use "the correct gender for each actor in accordance with the mythical roles he has conjured up."

[116] Sommerstein 1994: 215.

[117] Ibid.: 215–16; Henderson 1991a: 143; cf. schol. *Eq.* 1286.

feminine participle (ἔχουσα, 1031).[118] And the fact that throughout the scene he engages in lament, a speech genre strongly, although not exclusively, associated with women in Attic tragedy, further contributes to the humorous gender disjunctions.[119]

THE SCYTHIAN ARCHER AND THE RECOVERY OF MASCULINITY

The Relative's female costume and inverted theatrical role lead to his final indignity: clamped to a board and transformed into a pathic for the Archer's pleasure, he becomes in body, but not in speech, a thing of use, like the despised male prostitute. Although foreign, the Scythian Archer reinvests the play with pathic humor, restoring comic masculinity and normative gender roles. Two of the main ethno-linguistic features of the Scythian Archer in the *Thesmophoriazusae* are his gender blunders and his use of obscenity. The Archer has a grammatical problem with just about every aspect of Greek grammar, including tense, case, and gender; his adjectives and nouns seldom agree as in, for example, καλὴ τὸ σκῆμα, "fair is the form" (1188).[120] Another obvious characteristic of his speech is obscenity: like the Relative at the beginning of the play, the Archer is preoccupied with pathic sex, a theme absent from the women's speech at the Thesmophoria. As the sexual prey of the Archer, the immobilized Relative thus provides several opportunities for pathic joking. The fact that he repeats, in dialect form, some of the pathic verbal abuse earlier employed by the Relative against Agathon shows just how much their roles have become inverted (πρωκτός, 1119, 1124; τὸ πόσθιον, 1188; cf. 253, 291, 515). The Archer also employs πυγή in the same way (1120, 1123), although the term can have a heterosexual application, as at 1187. These obscenities play against Euripides' tragic and effeminate euphemism for sexual intercourse, "to fall into the bed and nuptial couch" (πεσεῖν ἐς εὐνὴν καὶ γαμήλιον λέχος, 1122).

---

[118] For other instances of the male gender used by the Relative in Ar. *Thesm.*, cf. με ... τὸν | πολυστονώτατον (1022–23), ὀλοόν (1027), μέλεος (1037), ὦ τάλας ἐγὼ τάλας (1038), κροκόεντα (1044). For feminine usages, cf. ἐμπεπλεγμένη (1032), λιτομένα (1040).

[119] On lamentation in this part of Ar. *Thesm.*, cf. γοᾶσθε (1036), γόον (1041), ἰώ μοι μοίρας (1047), κλάειν ἐλεινῶς (1063), παναθλίου (1107).

[120] Hall 1989a: 39. Hall (ibid.: 41; 1997: 96) identifies the slave's response to the Relative as a characteristic gender blunder (ἀποτανουμένη λαλῇς, 1109). But this slip suggests that the Archer momentarily enters into Euripides' dramatic ruse by identifying the Relative with Andromeda, the female dramatic character he represents. His character is thus consistent with those of the duped barbarian kings found in Euripides' escape plays, namely the *Helen* and *Iphigenia in Tauris*. See Hall 1989a: 41. Bobrick (1991) argues that the end of the *Thesmophoriazusae* is in fact modeled on the *Iphigenia in Tauris*, although she does not mention Hall's thesis, which would have strengthened her point.

Finally released from his shackles, the Relative resumes his proper masculine role as head of his oikos, and, presumably, as a citizen of Athens:[121]

σὺ δ' ὅπως ἀνδρικῶς
ὅταν λυθῇς τάχιστα φεύξει καὶ τενεῖς
ὡς τὴν γυναῖκα καὶ τὰ παιδί' οἴκαδε.   (1204–6)

And you, as soon as you are released,
flee as quickly as possible, like a man,
and make for your wife and children at home.

In returning home, the Relative will become a man again (ἀνδρικῶς), engaged not in the risible sexual practices mocked throughout the play, but rather in a heterosexual union that, through the production of children, ensures the perpetuation of the family and the city. But his escape is brought about by another theatrical device: transformed into the procuress Artemesia, Euripides dupes the Archer with a sexual trick while the old man escapes. His art, like that of his tragic compatriot, Agathon, embodies the capacity for speech to corrupt and deceive through questionable, erotic means, like those employed by prostitutes and sophists who "taught the art of enticing the favor (εὔνοια) of one's hearers by skillful flattery."[122] To this category also belong the female celebrants of the Thesmophoria, whose speeches reveal how they regularly deceive men in their own homes. The part of the gull, now taken by the Archer, corresponds to that of the dramatic spectator, as well as to the juror in the courts, who is easily taken in by the illusory tableaux placed before him. Only the comic buffoon, by continually asserting masculinity through his obscene speech, defiantly resists the effeminizing effects of such deception. Although the Relative becomes like a woman in physical appearance, and even to some extent in speech, he cannot maintain the illusion for long, either in this scene or at the Thesmophoria. Aristophanes' treatment of the Relative in the *Thesmophoriazusae* demonstrates that masculine identity, once compromised on the comic stage, must eventually be restored.[123]

A FEMALE RHĒTŌR: PRAXAGORA IN THE *ECCLESIAZUSAE*

The *Ecclesiazusae*, produced around 393/92, raises many of the same issues of speech and gender explored in the *Thesmophoriazusae*; like the earlier play, the *Ecclesiazusae* features a scene of cross-dressing and assigns

---

[121] Several scholars have related the freeing of the Relative to the practice of releasing prisoners at Athens on the third day of the Thesmophoria; see Hansen 1976: 184–85n.96; Bowie 1993: 208.

[122] Murphy 1938: 72–73.

[123] Rothwell (1990: 53) argues that "men in women's clothes are a mockery of femininity and are symbolically stripped of their public power. The only way for a cross-dressed actor, on stage or in real life, to restore his integrity and his identity is by exposing his masculinity

a central role to comic obscenity. In the *Thesmophoriazusae*, it was an elderly man who played the part of a woman at a women-only festival; in this play, Athenian matrons disguise themselves as men in order to infiltrate a masculine civic space, the Athenian Assembly, where they put forward their proposal to take control of the government. In the first part of the play the women gather in their husbands' rustic clothes in order to rehearse their assigned parts as rural members of the Assembly. Their leader, Praxagora, guides their rehearsal, correcting inappropriate female language and behavior and pronouncing a rhetorically polished speech of her own. The crude scene in which Blepyrus, Praxagora's husband, defecates outside their house dressed in his wife's clothes follows this rehearsal and introduces his subsequent exchange with his wife, who relates the principles of her new regime. The play concludes with a comic demonstration of the consequences of the gynaecocracy, as three crones descend upon a powerless youth, each laying claim to him according to the new laws of the state.

Henderson comments on what is probably the most distinguishing feature of this comedy, its relentless use of obscenity: "The smuttiness of the sexual vocabulary of the whole play—there is more coarse slang from hitting and piercing, for example, than in any other play—constantly emphasizes an unadorned and unlovely view of copulation."[124] This aspect of the play prompted Strauss to conclude: "It is not sufficient to say that the *Assembly of Women* is the ugliest comedy; it is *the* ugly comedy."[125] Dismissed for its crudeness, the *Ecclesiazusae* has not received the critical attention devoted to the other Aristophanic comedies until recent years, when interest in the representation of women in fifth-century Athenian drama and their role in the Athenian polis has prompted scholars to look more closely at the play.[126] Like the *Thesmophoriazusae*, this play critiques the role of speech in the polis by creating a disjunction between gender and linguistic practices. In particular, the female speakers at the Assembly embody the potential of deceptive rhetoric to seduce and corrupt Athenian citizens, who are portrayed as easily deceived and more interested in gratifying their own physical needs than in politics. Finally, the fact that Blepyrus never fully recovers a normative gender identity in speech emphasizes the irreversible process of social disintegration brought about by Praxagora's democratic government.

---

under his disguise." It should be pointed out that although this model obtains to the comic buffoon, it does not seem to apply to figures like Agathon, whose compromised gender status never changes in the course of the play.

[124] Henderson 1991a: 102.

[125] Strauss 1966: 279.

[126] Foley 1982 remains one of the most important articles to grapple with the role of women in the *Ecclesiazusae* and *Lysistrata*; see also Saïd 1979; Rothwell 1990; and Taaffe 1993: 103–33.

Those scholars who have embraced the idea of political reform and even gynaecocracy as the central message of the play accordingly view Praxagora's use of rhetoric as ameliorative and beneficial to the city.[127] As Saïd and Foley have both argued, Praxagora models her government on the oikos, a value system that privileges the interests of the individual over those of the group and that therefore would not have been viewed as a viable political alternative by the spectators.[128] Similarly, I argue that Aristophanes used his portrayal of gynaecocracy as a means of urging his audience to consider the negative consequences of free speech in a radical democracy through a reductio ad absurdum: by extending the principle of equality upon which Athenian democracy was founded to women, the poet shows the dangers of widening the circle of participation in the contemporary polis. Rather than eliminating the self-interest that characterized the city governed by men, the women's reforms are shown to be even more self-serving than those of the men because they are preoccupied with securing the sexual gratification of female citizens, an idea comically conveyed by the three haggling crones at the end of the play.[129] The depiction of gynaecocracy attributed to Sparta and represented by the character of Hermione in the *Andromache* also draws the same conclusion: if women have the political and economic power, they will use it to gain control of the bedroom.

Aristophanes' representation of the women's speech in the Assembly conjoins the archaic stereotype of female deceptiveness in service of *erōs* to the contemporary issue of sophism and demagogues in the Athenian polis. The women's seductive rhetoric therefore serves as a vehicle for demonstrating the corrupting potential of words, especially those spoken by demagogues, to sway the mass in the Assembly and the courts. Thus Praxagora's persuasive rhetoric, like the speech of Agathon and Euripides in the *Thesmophoriazusae*, becomes a means of empowering the socially and sexually subordinate and therefore of undermining the normative political order. Moreover, just as the *Thesmophoriazusae* correlated speech practices to sexuality in the sophistic and paratragic language of the effeminate Agathon and the obscene remarks of the manly Relative, so, too, the

---

[127] For the suggestion that Aristophanes seriously entertained the idea of *gunaikokratia*, see Sommerstein 1984: 333 and n. 94. Rothwell (1990) rejects this view and argues for a positive assessment of Praxagora's rhetorical skills. Much ink has been spilled on the similarities between Praxagora's regime and that proposed by Plato in his *Republic*, a debate that has diverted attention away from the more important issues of the play: for detailed summaries, see Adam 1963: 350ff.; Ussher 1973: 157ff.; David 1984: 20–24.

[128] Saïd 1979: 55; Foley 1982: 16–19.

[129] By far the majority of scholars have understood the social changes proposed by Praxagora and her friends as negative: see in particular Saïd 1979 and Foley 1981. For the play as a critique of Athenian political self-interest, see Ober and Strauss 1990: 265–66. They show how the play erases and then redraws boundaries between mass and elite as part of its central focus on egalitarianism and its limits.

Ecclesiazusae in the final scene equates women's license to speak publicly with prostitution.

Whereas the *Thesmophoriazusae* draws a parallel between the women's religious festival and male political institutions at Athens, the *Ecclesiasuzae* continually emphasizes the correspondence between the theater of Dionysus and the Pnyx, a relation that provides many opportunities for metatheatrical humor based on these two types of public performance, an association already strongly implanted in the Athenian imagination by the mid-fifth century, as discussed in Chapter 1. Within the play, the rehearsal scene creates a direct link between the two discursive spheres: its allusions to "rehearsing parts, going over lines, avoiding mistakes in delivery, and learning to make effective use of costumes, masks and props, all serve to portray the Assembly debate as a special kind of performance."[130] At one point, Praxagora directly addresses the spectators as though they are members of the Assembly (165–68).[131] Even Praxagora's name, "one who is active in the agora,"[132] reinforces this similarity. As a fusion of both male and female characteristics and speech practices, Praxagora, like Lysistrata, mediates between the two realms, first as an exemplar of the tragic actor who rehearses his part and accurately renders the speech of the opposite gender, and later as an accomplished public speaker in the Assembly who seduces "his" audience with "his" deceptive speech.

In her apostrophe to the oil lamp that begins the prologue, Praxagora shows the interrelation between women's deceptiveness and their pursuit of *erōs*:

σοὶ γὰρ μόνῳ δηλοῦμεν εἰκότως, ἐπεὶ
κἂν τοῖσι δωματίοισιν Ἀφροδίτης τρόπων
πειρωμέναισι πλησίον παραστατεῖς,
λορδουμένων τε σωμάτων ἐπιστάτην
ὀφθαλμὸν οὐδεὶς τὸν σὸν ἐξείργει δόμων.
μόνος δὲ μηρῶν εἰς ἀπορρήτους μυχοὺς
λάμπεις ἀφεύων τὴν ἐπανθοῦσαν τρίχα.   (7–13)

We are revealed to you alone, and with good reason,
since you stand near our trials in the turns of love
in our chambers, and no one excludes your eye,
custodian of our sexual positions, from the house.
You alone cast your light into the secret depths
of our thighs, singeing off the luxurious hair.

Praxagora invokes the lamp because of its special role as an accomplice in women's nocturnal escapades. She portrays women as doubly deceitful:

---

[130] Reckford 1987: 345.
[131] Taaffe 1993: 118n.26.
[132] Rothwell 1990: 83.

not only are their misdeeds secret, but even their appearance, improved by cosmetic depilation, is misleading, a point reinforced by the crone's heaving use of cosmetics at the end of the play. The prologue's paratragic and euphemistic elements further signify the deceptive potential of women's speech by recalling the grandiose, tragic rhetoric of Agathon and his servant in the *Thesmophoriazusae*.[133] The repeated occurrence of the verb λανθάνω (23, 26, 35, 77, 98, 103, 337) in the subsequent scene further identifies women with subterfuge, an affinity that Praxagora later argues uniquely qualifies them for civic leadership: adept at deceiving others (ἐξαπατᾶν εἰθισμέναι, 238), a female ruler would never be deceived. The prologue also equates feminine duplicity and secrecy with female complicity: the lamp does not betray the women's sexual secrets (οὐ λαλεῖς, 16) in the same way that the women do not reveal their own religious secrets in observance of the Thesmophoria (443). Not surprisingly, therefore, does Aristophanes represent the women as having formulated their plan at another women-only festival in honor of Demeter, the Skira, a festival similar to the Thesmophoria, in which the women formed their own government and performed secret rites (18, 59).[134] The prologue foreshadows the explicitly sexual agenda that will characterize Praxagora's legislation and suggests that the women's reforms will lead not to improving conditions within the polis, but only to protecting their access to sex.

The separate and secretive women's sphere described by the prologue takes shape dramatically as the women gather to rehearse their parts. The way they name each other underscores the fact that they are among women only: rather than addressing each other by their husbands' names, as men would do (cf. *Thesm.* 605–20), the women interchangeably use both their husband's names and their own names in addressing one other.[135] The first scene (14–284), with its many obscene double entendres, also identifies sex as the major preoccupation of women and their primary topic of conversation. Praxagora, who speaks almost all of the obscenities in the first scene,[136] initiates the series of sexual innuendoes with her pun on seats and hetaeras: "Now we, companions, must take our seats" (καταλαβεῖν δ' ἡμᾶς ἕδρας [21] | δεῖ τὰς ἑταίρας [23]). According to Ussher, the joke refers to a tragic actor, Phyromachus, derided for inadvertently aspirating a vowel, saying ἕδρας instead of ἕδρας.[137] Moreover, this allusion has a double significance for the play: first, it precedes the rehearsal scene in which Praxa-

---

[133] Henderson 1991a: 101–2.

[134] Deubner 1932: 40–50; Burkert 1985: 230–31; Simon 1983: 22–24.

[135] On the conventions of naming women in comedy, see Sommerstein (1980: 394), who notes that out of 104 references to women's names in Aristophanes, 62 are spoken by women. Skinner (1987) has also speculated that the practice of using the metronymic may have been a feature of women's speech among other women, a point discussed in Chapter 2.

[136] Henderson 1991a: 101.

[137] Ussher 1973: 75–76.

gora's companions will make many linguistic mistakes as they attempt to render male speech. Second, the word ἑταίρα and the obscene pun on ἕδρας, "seats," in the sense of chair or buttocks, foreshadows the abrogation of prostitution from the city under the new government and its symbolic reappearance at the end of the play in the form of the three comic crones.

Although the women use few primary obscenities in this scene, Henderson concludes that their speech "would have sounded discordantly violent and almost dirty" in comparison with the women's speech featured in the earlier two plays.[138] Woman A and Woman B, with their sexual joking correspond to the crone Calonice in the *Lysistrata*, although neither is explicitly characterized in that role.[139] Woman B announces her presence with a double entendre about her Salaminian husband's sexual prowess: "He rode me the whole night in bed" (39–40; cf. *Lys.* 59ff.). Although Woman B does not use any primary obscenities in this scene, her remark contains a "crude and explicit reference to intercourse rather than mere innuendo."[140] Her anomalous reference to farting, πέρδεται (78), a scatological term not normally found in women's speech, confirms the outrageousness of her speech.

Much of this sexual innuendo conflates the political procedures of the Athenian Assembly with sexual practices, reflecting the women's inability to separate sexual and domestic concerns from civic business, as well as the close association in Aristophanic comedy between sex and politics. For instance, Praxagora's nautical double entendres play upon the association of sailing with sexual intercourse and governance (106–9). Praxagora employs an obscene pun on ὑποκρούω, a verb meaning both to interrupt and to assault sexually, in response to Woman A's query about what she will do if someone interrupts her in the Assembly (τί δ' ἢν ὑποκρούωσίν σε; 256): "I will not be backward since I am not inexperienced in interruptions" (προσκινήσομαι | ἅτ' οὐκ ἄπειρος οὖσα πολλῶν κρουμάτων, 256–57). The term ὑποκρούω, in its coarse, obscene sense, will later figure prominently in the speech of the crones. The women's lack of familiarity with voting procedures in the Assembly prompts Woman A's obscene joke on sexual positions: "How will we remember to raise our hands there, since we are accustomed only to raising our legs?" (263–65; cf. *Lys.* 229).[141] Although the matrons use few primary obscenities in the *Ecclesiazusae*'s first scene, their speech repeatedly strays to sexual topics unsuitable to public oration, disclosing their chronic preoccupation with *erōs*.

Just as the linguistic incompetence of the transvestite Relative ultimately reinforces Athenian gender ideology in the *Thesmophoriazusae*, so in the

---

[138] Henderson 1991a: 102.

[139] Ibid.: 101.

[140] Ibid.: 102.

[141] On the juxtaposition of sexual and political concerns in this scene, see Rothwell 1990: 50.

Ecclesiazusae the fact that the women do not manage to render male speech accurately in the rehearsal scene confirms at the conceptual level women's inexperience in rhetoric and their unfitness for public speaking. Although dressed like men, with their Laconian shoes, their walking sticks, their fake beards, and their cloaks, the women cannot be fully masculine unless they speak like men. Praxagora, in a manner reminiscent of Euripides in the *Thesmophoriazusae*, thus exhorts them to adopt masculine verbal habits: "Come now, and speak well and in a manly fashion, propping yourself up with your staffs" (ἄγε νυν ὅπως ἀνδριστὶ καὶ καλῶς ἐρεῖς | διερεισαμένη τὸ σχῆμα τῇ βακτηρίᾳ, 149–50). She refers not merely to the appropriate markers of male speech, such as case endings, forms of address, and oaths, but also to the male declamatory practices of the Assembly that would have accompanied the holding of the staff and the wearing of the speaker's garland.[142] And yet no matter how many times Praxagora prompts the women, they repeatedly commit linguistic blunders, like the tragic actor Phyromachus invoked in the prologue.

The inaccuracies revealed in the women's impersonation of male speech are instructive because they indicate what linguistic markers the spectators might have associated with women. Woman B, a particularly poor performer, immediately blunders when she states that she intends to comb wool while waiting for the Assembly to commence. Then, during the rehearsal proper, she swears by Demeter and Persephone (155), deities normally invoked only by women. Praxagora upbraids her with an ambiguous reference to her gender, using both a feminine and a masculine participle in reference to her: "You swore by the Twain being a man (ἀνὴρ ὤν, 158), although you did say (εἰποῦσα, 159) some very clever things." Woman B corrects herself and swears a masculine oath by Apollo (160). She again botches her lines when she addresses the "Assembly" as "O seated women" (ὦ γυναῖκες αἱ καθήμεναι, 165). When Praxagora chastises her for this error ("Are you saying women again, you idiot, when you mean men?" γυναῖκας αὖ, δύστηνε, τοὺς ἄνδρας λέγεις; 166), Woman B cleverly recovers with a pathic joke directed at the audience: "I meant Epigonus there. For in looking at the audience I thought I was talking to women" (167–68). Woman A then starts making mistakes, invoking Aphrodite instead of a masculine deity (189). The fact that Praxagora so easily slips in and out of linguistic character throughout this scene demonstrates her intellectual superiority, while the mistakes of the other women stereotypically reveal their incompetence. Like Lysistrata, who appears unmoved by the sexual appetites that weaken the resolve of her peers, Praxagora possesses self-control, which earns her the title of *stratēgos*, general.

---

[142] On the staff, cf. Ar. *Eccl.* 150, 276–77, 546; see Rothwell 1990: 83n.20. On the speaker's wreath, cf. *Eccl.* 131, 148, 163.

The women not only must adopt those linguistic elements which identify masculine speech, they also must familiarize themselves with the speech practices of the Assembly and even the country tunes characteristic of old men: "And sing an old man's song as you go, imitating the ways of country folk" (ἄδουσαι μέλος | πρεσβυτικόν τι, τὸν τρόπον μιμούμεναι | τὸν τῶν ἀγροίκων, 277–79). Once they have outfitted themselves and practiced their lines, the women follow the conventions of male speech, using the appropriate case endings (ὅς, 291a; κεκονιμένος, 291b; στέργων, 292a; βλέπων, 292b; κατεπείγων, 294; σαυτῷ, 295a; λαβόντες, 297; πλησίοι, 297), addressing themselves as men (ἄνδρες, 285), and calling themselves by common male names (Χαριτιμίδη, Σμίκυθε, Δράκης, 293a–b). And yet their performance humorously plays with the incongruities of their speech and gender: as they congratulate themselves for remembering to use the male form of address, they immediately commit another linguistic blunder by referring to themselves with a feminine participle, ἐνδυόμεναι (288), and with the phrase τὰς ἡμετέρας φίλας (299), which they quickly correct to φίλους (300). In contrast to Praxagora's, their speech confirms that they are never fully in control of their masculine impersonations.

Although the prologue identifies Praxagora as typically female in her concern with sexual matters, the rest of the play foregrounds her rhetorical skills; she maintains the illusion of a male speaker where her companions fail.[143] For example, she consistently uses the appropriate case endings in her rehearsal speech (παραδόντες, 229; σκεψάμενοι, 232; εὐδαιμονοῦντες, 240), and she employs rhetorical formulations characteristic of public speaking, like τίς ἀγορεύειν βούλεται (130), while her question "Is there anyone else who wishes to speak? (ἔσθ' ἥτις ἑτέρα βούλεται λέγειν, 147) playfully mocks the standard Athenian phrase with its feminine pronouns. In contrast to the other women, Praxagora knows how to make a public oration (δημηγορήσων, 429; cf. 400) and deploys a version of the invective against women in the speech she intends to deliver at the Assembly:

τοὺς ἄνδρας ἐπιτρίβουσιν ὥσπερ καὶ πρὸ τοῦ.
μοιχοὺς ἔχουσιν ἔνδον ὥσπερ καὶ πρὸ τοῦ.
αὑταῖς παροψωνοῦσιν ὥσπερ καὶ πρὸ τοῦ.
οἶνον φιλοῦσ' εὔζωρον ὥσπερ καὶ πρὸ τοῦ.
βινούμεναι χαίρουσιν ὥσπερ καὶ πρὸ τοῦ.   (224–28)

They grind away their men in sex, as they always have.
They have lovers in their houses, as they always have.
They buy a dainty side dish, as they always have.
They love unmixed wine, as they always have.
And they like a good fuck, too, as they always have.

---

[143] Byl (1982) connects Praxagora with feminine mimesis and craftiness.

This speech strongly resembles the Relative's misogynistic harangue at the Thesmophoria in that it alludes to "the more shocking . . . deceits of women" and culminates with a primary obscenity, βινούμεναι (228), characteristic of male speech, while feminine in both voice and gender.[144] The fact that only male speakers in Aristophanic comedy (as elsewhere) employ the verb βινῶ illustrates its shock value when uttered by a woman. The comic humor in this scene derives not only from the idea of a woman impersonating a man, but also from the fact that Praxagora adduces in support of her claim that women are capable of running the city the very peccadilloes that provoke the most suspicion in men. Her premise, that although women may be capable of many petty, domestic crimes, they are by nature conservative and predictable, comically approximates Hippolytus' invective about woman's permanently flawed nature.

Praxagora's rhetorical expertise calls attention to another incongruity in this scene: women had no formal training in rhetoric in Athens and could not speak in public.[145] Thus Praxagora, like Lysistrata, claims that she acquired this art from men whom she heard declaiming in the Assembly when, as a refugee from the country, she lived near the Pnyx (243–44). The women remark several times on her cleverness and rhetorical mastery (δεινοτέρα, 516; cf. 571, 573), and even refer to her at one point as a man. Woman A applauds her speaking ability by calling her an intelligent man (ὡς ξυνετὸς ἀνήρ, 204), in much the same way we saw the chorus of Argive elders praise Clytemnestra; her exceptional rhetorical ability also stamps Praxagora as masculine in the eyes of Woman B, who refers to her as ὦγαθέ, "my good man" (213). The women repeatedly refer to her as the General, a word normally masculine in gender but made feminine in this instance by means of its article (ἡ στρατηγός, 491, 500; cf. 246).

Although Praxagora receives approbation from the women for her clever speech, Aristophanes casts quite another light on her rhetorical skills by obliquely comparing her to an *erōmenos*. In reporting the events of the Assembly to Blepyrus, Chremes describes Praxagora as a pathic in language reminiscent of Agathon: "A very handsome young man, pale-skinned, you know, like Nicias" (εὐπρεπὴς νεανίας | λευκός . . . ὅμοιος Νικίᾳ, 427–28; cf. *Thesm.* 191). Praxagora thus embodies the suspect rhetorical practices of the new demagogues who are undermining and corrupting the political system and who are often depicted as pathics in Aristophanic comedy.[146] In fact, Praxagora herself several times reminds the spectators of this correspondence, beginning with her allusion to Agyrrhius, the radical democrat credited with introducing the three-obol wage for attending the Assembly:

---

[144] Henderson 1991a: 102.

[145] A passage in pseudo-Plutarch asserts that the courtesan Aspasia might have spoken in public if she had been allowed to do so; see Ehlers 1966: 77; Rothwell 1990: 36; and the discussion in Chapter 1.

[146] Ar. *Ach.* 702–12; Murphy 1938: 72; Rothwell 1990: 77–78.

Ἀγύρριος γοῦν τὸν Προνόμου πώγων' ἔχων
λέληθε· καίτοι πρότερον ἦν οὗτος γυνή.
νῦνι δ', ὁρᾷς, πράττει τὰ μέγιστ' ἐν τῇ πόλει.   (102–4)

No one ever noticed Agyrrhius when he had the beard of Pronomus.
For indeed he used to be a woman, once.
But now he manages the most important affairs in the city.

The scholiast identifies Agyrrhius as an *euruprōktos*, an effeminate in his
sexual practices, a fact that he has disguised by wearing a beard (presumably
he was clean shaven, like other pathics). The joke on Agyrrhius represents
an Aristophanic commonplace that the best politicians are those who are
the most sexually aberrant.[147] The passage further invites a comparison
between Praxagora and Agyrrhius, since she, too, wears an artificial beard
and will soon run the city.

Praxagora makes explicit the link between pathics, rhetoric, and women
a few lines later when she answers Woman A's question, "And how shall
this female-minded consortium of women make public orations?" (καὶ
πῶς γυναικῶν θηλύφρων ξυνουσία | δημηγορήσει; 110–11). By comparing
the women to pathics well-versed in rhetoric, Praxagora reassures them
that although they are inexperienced, they have the natural ability to
speak well:

λέγουσι γὰρ καὶ τῶν νεανίσκων ὅσοι
πλεῖστα σποδοῦνται, δεινοτάτους εἶναι λέγειν.
ἡμῖν δ' ὑπάρχει τοῦτο κατὰ τύχην τινά.   (112–14)

For they say that the young men who are banged the most
are also the cleverest speakers.
And luckily this ability belongs to us by nature.

This persuasive power derives from not only from women's passivity, but
also from the seductiveness normally attributed to the passive sexual partner, whether a female or a pathic. Because seductive and cunning at the
same time, the art of rhetoric equips the sexually and socially subordinate
with a tool for prevailing over their superiors. Thus Chremes, upon returning from the Assembly, describes the women as cobblers (σκυτοτόμοι,
385, 432), one of the lowest social classes at Athens; the pallor of their
faces, a result of plying their craft indoors (λευκοπληθής, 387), assimilates
them to women. These lower-class craftsmen are portrayed as easily swayed
by rhetoric; indeed, they are the first to approve Praxagora's plan (432),
in contrast to the recalcitrant farmers, who jeer (ἐκ τῶν ἀγρῶν, 432). And
yet these "cobblers" successfully dupe the male members of the Assembly,
who do not suspect that the crowd thronging the Pnyx consists of anything

---

[147] Rothwell 1990: 78.

but men (383). Not surprisingly, therefore, Woman A uses a stock sophistic phrase, δεινὴ καὶ σοφή (245), in admiring approval of Praxagora's oration.[148] The fact that Praxagora is associated with the dangerous potential of rhetoric to erode social boundaries in classical Athens clearly militates against the view that Aristophanes represents her use of *peithō* as a positive means of achieving stability for the polis.[149]

BLEPYRUS' SCATOLOGICAL OBSCENITY

The crudely explicit scene between Blepyrus and his neighbor, with its abundant scatological language, provides an ironic and shocking contrast to the women's rehearsal in the first part of the play. Although the defecation scene in the *Ecclesiazusae* probably ranks as one of the most offensive dramatic moments in extant Old Comedy, Aristophanes apparently was more restrained than his counterparts in this respect. Triclinus, commenting on the scatology of *Clouds* 295–97, mentions that other comic poets frequently depicted men defecating and engaged in other vulgar acts on stage.[150] As I have shown above, Aristophanic comedy associates this type of obscenity with comic masculinity, but in contrast to the Relative's predominantly pathic humor in the *Thesmophoriazusae*, which is aggressively directed toward an effeminate male and represents a positive affirmation of masculinity in a world of inverted gender roles, Blepyrus' scatology discloses the degrading consequences of Praxagora's ascent to power even as it posits masculine self-interest as its cause. In Henderson's words, "While his wife has risen to the highest position possible in the city, Blepyrus has sunk to the lowest."[151] A more precise glance at the scatological terms found in this scene confirms that this reversal also has a sexual component: by identifying him with pathic behavior, Blepyrus' constipation embodies his compromised social and sexual status. Just as the Relative's use of obscenity establishes his character as sexually dominant, so Blepyrus' scatology reflects his passive and sexually subordinate role as husband of a powerful political figure.

Whereas the women's masculine attire invests them with at least a veneer of public authority, the elderly Blepyrus (γέρων, 323), husband of Praxagora, has been reduced to the opposite position by his feminine clothing. He appears outside his house in order to relieve himself, in full view of his neighbors and the spectators, having unwillingly thrown on his wife's

---

[148] Ibid.: 87.
[149] This positive interpretation of Praxagora's rhetoric normally goes hand-in-hand with a utopian reading of the play; see ibid.: 75.
[150] Edwards 1991: 163.
[151] Henderson 1991a: 102.

little *krokōtos* (332), her shawl, and her Persian slippers (317–19), a humiliating publicity that further contributes to his debasement. The degradation of Blepyrus entailed by Praxagora's public position is also underscored by the repeated allusions to excrement and elimination in this scene: the verb χέζω occurs eight times (313, 320, 322, 345, 347, 368, 372, 640), along with several other more euphemistic terms relating to excrement and elimination (ἀποπατέω, 351, 354; κόπρος, 317, 360; τὸ πυρρόν, 329; Cinesias, the "befouler," 330; ἀχράς, the prickly pear blocking his excretion, 355).

Although scatological, many of these terms also have a sexual allusion; in particular, Blepyrus personifies his excrement as a pathic penetration: "This Coprean man keeps banging at my gate" (ὁ δ' ἤδη τὴν θύραν | ἐπεῖχε κρούων ὁ κοπρεαῖος, 316–17). The term θύρα, like the other terms for the anus discussed above, almost always has an association with pathic behavior in Aristophanic comedy,[152] whereas the verb κρούω, used earlier by Woman B in her obscene double entendre, is slang for sexual intercourse. In a pun on a deme name, Blepyrus similarly imagines his excrement as a form of buggery: "But as it is, this man from Achras, whoever he is, has put a bolt up my ass" (νῦν μὲν γὰρ οὗτος βεβαλάνωκε τὴν θύραν | ὅστις ποτ' ἔσθ' ἄνθρωπος ἀχραδούσιος, 361–62). According to Henderson, the verb βαλανόω, because it means to slide a bolt into a lock, implies penetration, especially given that βάλανος is slang for penis.[153] Finally, Blepyrus' plea for a doctor leads to a pathic reference to Amynon, "an expert in proctology" (τίς τῶν καταπρώκτων δεινός ἐστι τὴν τέχνην; 364), and to Antisthenes, a figure apparently known for his chronic constipation, "whose anus knows the meaning of wanting to shit" (οἶδεν τί πρωκτὸς βούλεται χεζητιῶν, 368).[154]

His final address to Eileithyia, the goddess of childbirth invoked by women in labor, further reinforces the idea of Blepyrus' compromised sexual and political status. On one level it recalls the Relative's mock-tragic apostrophe to the Genetyllides (*Thesm.* 130), an invocation that highlighted Agathon's effeminacy. These allusions to female fertility deities perhaps reflect the infertility and impotence of the masculine polis, whose strength has been sapped by unmanly men.[155] The birth metaphor recurs

---

[152] Ibid.: 199.

[153] Ibid.: 119.

[154] Henderson (ibid.: 231) cites Antisthenes as a pathic, taking ἕνεκά γε στεναγμάτων (367) to refer to the narrow passage of the anus. Ussher (1973: 127) translates the phrase "as far as groans go" and makes no mention of Antisthenes' sexual proclivities. The later allusion to him in the context of constipation (808) indicates that this was the primary association; however, as I have shown, pathic behavior and scatology are often conflated in Aristophanes.

[155] Bowie 1993: 258. Rothwell (1990: 56–57) interprets Blepyrus' comment at *Eccl.* 468 as an expression of impotence, whereas Foley (1982: 14) understands Blepyrus' oath as a metaphor "for the barrenness of the men's political leadership." I cannot agree, however,

later in the play when Praxagora falsely asserts that she left the house, borrowing her husband's clothes, to help a friend in the throes of childbirth (ὠδίνουσα, 528–29). When Blepyrus complains that he has missed the Assembly and a day's wage on her account, she replies that a boy was delivered (ἄρρεν γὰρ ἔτεκε παιδίον, 549). Blepyrus mistakes her meaning in his response: "To the Assembly?" (550). Instead of assisting in childbirth, Praxagora has produced a new state, while Blepyrus, rather than engaging in the business of the city, has delivered a stool. He has become a laughing-stock, a "comic shitpot" (σκωραμὶς κωμῳδική, 371).[156] In contrast to his wife, who exerts a measure of self-control uncharacteristic of women in Athenian drama, Blepyrus has even lost control over his own body.

Whereas the earlier sexual obscenities of the women revealed them to be motivated by self-interest, Blepyrus' constipation not only underscores his self-absorption, it also symbolizes his "individualistic hoarding of material possessions."[157] Blepyrus embodies the self-interest of Athenian citizens, who participate in government only for financial gain; indeed, he regrets only the loss of his three-obol wage (380, 547–48). At first glance, Blepyrus' scatological obscenity merely serves to identify him with comic masculinity, as the Relative's speech did in the *Thesmophoriazusae*. Upon closer inspection, however, we see that the obscenity in this scene subverts rather than affirms his masculinity: by equating defecation with sexual and social submission, Blepyrus' scatology vividly illustrates the negative implications of Praxagora's legislation for the citizens while exposing masculine self-interest as its cause.

SPEECH IN THE GYNAECOCRACY

The subsequent exchange between Praxagora and Blepyrus superficially reinstates normative gender roles, a return signified by their speech practices; but this standard is gradually eroded as the scene progresses. At first, Praxagora reconstructs herself as a traditional Athenian wife rather than a political leader, using a strategy similar to that of Clytemnestra in her speech to the Messenger (Aesch. *Ag.* 587–614). By portraying herself as a traditional Athenian wife in the presence of her husband, Praxagora

---

with Rothwell's insistence on the "rejuvenation" of Blepyrus, because the overriding metaphor here is not impotence but infertility.

[156] Edwards (1991: 164) maintains that Blepyrus' σκωραμὶς becomes "a virtual emblem for comedy as a whole," although I think he exaggerates the positive associations of excrement in Old Comedy. For other comic heroes and scatology, cf. Ar. *Eq.* 997–98, 1057; *Pax* 1235–37; *Vesp.* 625–26; *Av.* 1116–17; *Ran.* 1074–76; 1089–98; *Plut.* 313

[157] Rothwell 1990: 53; Reckford (1987: 346) simply states, "The Athenians, like Blepyrus, need relief."

temporarily deflects attention away from her new role as *stratēgos*. She begins by stating that a friend in labor called her away from their house during the night (ὠδίνουσα, 528–29), a justifiable absence for women. A shift in speech practice accompanies this transition from political to domestic topics: in defending herself against charges of adultery, she utters a typically female exclamation (οὐ δῆτα τάλαν ἔγωγε, 526). She asserts the veracity of her account by swearing a female oath to Demeter and Kore (532) and avoids obscenities or sexual innuendo, in contrast to Blepyrus, who utters several, beginning with βινεῖται (525). Praxagora portrays herself as physically weak and delicate (λεπτὴ κἀσθενής, 539), in contrast to her masculine persona in the rehearsal scene. When told that the city has been handed over to the women, her response betrays a female point of view: "To do what? Weave?" (ὑφαίνειν, 556).[158] Finally, Praxagora repeatedly flaunts her falseness in this scene, much like the tragic Clytemnestra: she feigns surprise first that the Assembly has already met and that the new decree has been passed, although the spectators, and the chorus, already know the role she has played in the new legislation (450–52). She expresses her amazement by invoking Aphrodite (558), an oath that both reinforces her feminine self-presentation and ironically alludes to the place of this particular goddess, as a deity associated with female sexuality and prostitutes, in the new government.

Praxagora's lack of obscenity also reinforces her feminine self-presentation. Instead, she adopts in her husband's presence the paratragic euphemisms characteristic of women, euphemisms that the prologue linked to feminine subterfuge. She refers to sexual intercourse as sleeping or lying with (ξυγκαταδάρθειν, 612, 622, 628; ξυγκατακεῖσθαι, 613; καθευδούσθαι, 617), as making children (παιδοποεῖν, 615), as granting favors (χαρίζεσθαι, 629), and as stealing away Aphrodite, a tragic parody also employed by Agathon in the *Thesmophoriazusae* (ὑφαρπάζειν Κύπριν; cf. *Thesm.* 205). Her speech contains a few more explicit terms, including ὑποκρούω in the sexual sense (617); the euphemistic hapax δευτεριάζειν, "to make a second pressing" (634); and a familiar, possibly feminine, reference to genital depilation (τὸν χοῖρον ἀποτετιλμένας, 724; cf. ἀποψιλώσομεν τὸν χοῖρον, Woman A, *Thesm.* 538). Moreover, Praxagora adheres to gendered verbal conventions in representing the speech of others: she portrays a young girl as using the euphemism "to sleep with" (καθεύδειν, 700), in contrast to the old men's primary obscenities for sexual intercourse (βινεῖν, 706) and their reference to masturbation (δέφεσθαι, 709). Blepyrus' scatological and sexual obscenities partially erode Praxagora's feminine self-presentation by stripping away the euphemistic and grandiose terms with

---

[158] With the verb ὑφαίνειν, Praxagora substitutes a feminine activity for a masculine one, following Woman B, who earlier stated her intention to comb wool during the Assembly (*Eccl.* 89).

which she cloaks her meanings, as evidenced by his use of the primary obscenity βινεῖται (525), in an attempt to unmask the true reason for her absence. This technique of comic exposure in which a coarse male character uses obscenity to reveal the feminine duplicities of his interlocutor is also found in the scene between Agathon and Euripides in the *Thesmophoria-zusae*.

But Praxagora's feminine persona soon falls away, and her role as *rhētōr*, so carefully constructed in the first scene, takes center stage: she retains her right to speak (τὴν γυναῖκ' ἔα λέγειν, 564) and then enumerates the political consequences of her plan. By eliminating greed and self-interest, her government will effectively banish false witnesses, sycophants, stealing, jealousy, poverty, slander, and repossession from the city (561–67). Casting aside her feminine posture, she begins her speech on a rhetorical note: "I will prove it (ἀποφανῶ) to you so that you will side (μαρτυρεῖν) with me and that man will not speak against (ἀντειπεῖν) me" (569–70). As before, the chorus praise her intelligence (571–72) and her inventive power of speech (γλώττης ἐπίνοια, 574). Further, they refer to her stratagem as σοφός (577), a term that recalls Woman A's sophistic formulation in praise of Praxagora at 245. She introduces her idea with a typical rhetorical formula, διδάξω (583; cf. 215), and even uses a male participle, τοῦ φράζοντος (588), in referring to herself. The authority conveyed by these rhetorical markers is reinforced by her scatophagous comment addressed to Blepyrus: "You will eat excrement before I do" (κατέδει πέλεθον πρό-τερός μου, 595). Although πέλεθος is not a primary obscenity, the scatolog-ical content of her remark identifies it as implicitly masculine and specifically evokes the earlier speech of Blepyrus; only here it produces the opposite effect by identifying Praxagora as verbally and sexually dominant.[159] More-over, the fact that the word for interrupt, ὑποκρούω (588), also has sexual connotations, as we earlier saw, compounds the role reversal. Praxagora's right to speak publicly as the city's leader results in Blepyrus' silent subordi-nation. And yet his masculine obscenities continually deflate this role inversion; he undermines his wife's authority not only by interrupting, but also by a familiar means of comic paraphrase: "Then will our shit be held in common, too?" (596). Blepyrus substitutes a more literal and obscene term for his wife's high-flown rhetoric and thus exposes the absurdity of the new system.

As in the defecation scene, Blepyrus' obscenities here call attention to his greed and self-interest even as they attempt to reaffirm gender norms. When Praxagora states that the citizens will hold everything in common and details the economic merits of the plan (597–610), Blepyrus again

---

[159] The meaning of this remark is not clear: Henderson (1991a: 192–93), citing Ussher, takes it to be a popular joke or fable not necessarily insulting in meaning. However, it is hard to imagine a scatophagous remark that is not intended to be abusive.

reduces this proposition to its most crudely literal and self-interested terms: "You mean if someone sees a pretty girl and wants to poke her (σκαλα-θῦραι, 611), he will give her a gift from his own stores, but of the things in common, he will have his share when he goes to bed with her?" (ξυγκα-ταδαρθών, 613). Praxagora replies that since sex will also be publicly held, he will be able to sleep with the girl for free. Although not a primary obscenity, the term σκαλαθῦραι introduces the vulgar sexual tone that consistently characterizes Blepyrus' opportunist reactions to Praxagora's new policies. Pondering the problem of the sexual availability of the most attractive women, he asks: "Won't everyone then go to the house of the prettiest girl and attempt to bang her?" (ἐρείδειν, 615). Praxagora modifies her original proposal with an important corollary: "If a man wants to sleep with the prettiest girl, he'll have to sleep with a homely one first" (618). Responding that the policy will foster impotence in old men, Blepyrus again asserts his self-interest with a primary obscenity, τὸ πέος (620). Blepyrus' obscenities, which continually lay bare his conspicuous greed, simultaneously unveil the self-interested motives of the women, whose "oarlock[s]" (τρύπημα, 624) will never be empty as the result of the new legislation. More significantly, comic obscenity in this scene underscores the paradox that democracy, by espousing a principle of equality, actually promotes self-interest among its citizens. Invoking Apollo in a manly fashion (631), Praxagora confirms that her plan is inherently democratic (δημοτική γ' ἡ γνώμη, 631). Her ironic masculine oath, like her previous oath to Aphrodite, reflects at the level of language the complete inversion of social norms wrought by the new regime.

As Blepyrus further contemplates the consequences of the new regime, his blunt speech, like that of the Relative in the *Thesmophoriazusae*, further exposes the dangerous consequences of Praxagora's coup d' état. By promoting radical equality among its members, the democratic form of government taken to its extreme abolishes natural and social hierarchies. For example, when Blepyrus raises the problem of determining the parents of offspring born in the new state, he speculates that sons will be more likely to disrespect their fathers: "Won't they be even more likely to shit on them (ἐπιχεσοῦνται) when they don't even know who they are?" (638–40). Here Blepyrus' use of a scatological obscenity captures the degradation brought about by the collapse of the normative social order. The ramifications of unknown parentage for pederastic relationships are even more alarming, as Praxagora points out:

Πρ. πολὺ μέντοι δεινότερον τούτου τοῦ πράγματός ἐστι—
Βλ.   τὸ ποῖον;
Πρ. εἴ σε φιλήσειεν Ἀρίστυλλος φάσκων αὑτοῦ πατέρ' εἶναι.
Βλ. οἰμώζοι γ' ἂν καὶ κωκύοι.
Πρ. σὺ δέ γ' ὄζοις ἂν καλαμίνθης.   (646–48)

Praxagora: I know something even more terrible than this—
Blepyrus: What?
Praxagora: If Aristyllus should kiss you, alleging you to be his father!
Blepyrus: He would regret it, lamenting.
Praxagora: Then you would smell of mint.

Praxagora's pun on καλαμίνθη, which suggests both "mint" and "human excrement" (μίνθος), hints at Aristyllus' coprophilia, also alluded to in *Wealth* (*Plut.* 314). Because normally associated with women, as discussed in Chapter 2, the term κωκύοι (648) implies an effeminate male like Agyrrhius or Epigonus. By identifying pathic sexual practices with excrement, as Blepyrus does, this exchange further elucidates the repellent consequences of the new laws.

We witness a similar process at work in the obscenity of Man B, who staunchly refuses to contribute his property to the common stores (769–70, 832, 873). Like Blepyrus, Man B uses scatological obscenity, but his crude speech conveys his self-interested reticence in submitting to the new regime: appalled at the willingness of Chremes and his other neighbors to contribute their goods to the city, he cites Antisthenes, previously mentioned by Blepyrus at 366, whose inability to eliminate (χέσαι, 808) translates into a reluctance to contribute to the city. More significantly, he reinforces his refusal to comply with Praxagora's decree with a further obscenity: he will take care that the women do not piss on him (κατουρῆσαι, 832), an act inherently degrading, especially if performed by a socially inferior person. Man B is a holdout: by refusing to recognize the new government, he represents uncompromised masculinity, and his use of obscenity reflects this status. Although Blepyrus exposes the weaknesses of Praxagora's proposal through his use of masculine obscenity, he nonetheless assumes a subordinate role: in his parting words, he refers to himself not by his own name but in typically feminine terms as "the husband of the general" (τὸν τῆς στρατηγοῦ τοῦτον, 727).

Praxagora's proposal results in another benefit for women: prostitution is banned from the city (πόρνας, 717), thereby eliminating sexual competition among women. This corollary reveals Praxagora's whole plan to be in service of female sexual gratification and thus confirms the self-interested motives of the women already alluded to in the opening scene. But her decree is implicitly ironic, for although prostitution will be abolished, it has the effect of converting all free-born women into courtesans or procuresses who freely and publicly offer their services, or those of others:

αἱ δὲ γυναῖκες κατὰ τὰς διόδους
προσπίπτουσαι τοῖς ἀπὸ δείπνου
τάδε λέξουσιν· 'δεῦρο παρ' ἡμᾶς·
ἐνθάδε μεῖράξ ἐσθ' ὡραία.'

(693–96)

> The women in the thoroughfares
> will fall on the men coming from dinner
> and say: "Come over to me.
> There is a pretty young girl over here."

As a result of Praxagora's decree, women may appear outside and speak freely to men, in a reversal of their usual role; in achieving sovereignty over their bodies, they simultaneously gain the prerogative of speech. In contrast, the bodies of adult male citizens, once inviolate under the city's laws, may now be used for the pleasure of women. This equation between free speech and sexual promiscuity prefigures the final scene in the *Ecclesiazusae*, in which three crones vie over a young man, each citing the new law in support of her claim, in an incongruous juxtaposition of legal jargon and sexual obscenity.

THE SPEECH OF OLDER WOMEN

The older women depicted in the final part of the *Ecclesiazusae* resemble courtesans both in their speech and in their physical appearance.[160] Crone A has applied white lead to her face and wears the seductive *krokōtos*, or saffron robe, associated with prostitutes (878–79).[161] Her seductive song (883), like that of Agathon, connotes "effeminacy and even lasciviousness,"[162] and her playful demeanor (παίζουσα, 881) further suggests an erotic context. Indeed, the Youth at one point bluntly refers to two of the crones as prostitutes (τοῖν κασαλβάδοιν, 1106) in his sailing metaphor. Finally, the chorus' metatheatrical comment that the spectators resemble courtesans "who remember only their last lovers" (*Eccl.* 1161) perhaps gains more force if we understand the previous scene as one of prostitution.[163] Although the staging of this scene is disputed, Crone A apparently

---

[160] Webster (1950: 23) refers to them as "merciless caricatures of the aged hetaera." Henry (1985: 25) argues against this interpretation, citing as evidence the passages in which Praxagora states prostitution will be eliminated; cf. *Eccl.* 689–709, 718–24. For another aging hetaera, cf. Ar. *Plut.* 959–1006.

[161] Slater (1989: 47) argues that the references to *lēkuthoi* in this scene represent a "self-conscious allusion to the theatrical mask" because the white ground of these vases is similar to the crone's mask covered with white lead, or ψιμύθιον. The reference at *Eccl.* 1101 is particularly interesting, since the *lēkuthos* is described as held against the face; the term γναθοῖς implies a male face and thus strengthens Slater's point about the inherent metatheatricality of this motif. See also Stone (1981: 26–27), who suggests the women wear white round masks with makeup painted on them.

[162] Muecke 1982a: 48; Dale (1948: 119) identifies this song as Ionian, but Parker (1997: 536) argues against this view, with his observation that "rhythmically at least, there is nothing perceptibly 'Ionian' about the song when it comes. The metre is pure trochaic, except for a single choriamb at 898."

[163] Webster 1950: 23.

occupies the doorway and eventually the outside of the house (θύρασι, 993), where she flagrantly parades her body, behavior associated earlier in the play with sexual availability, in contrast to the Girl's modest peeping from the window (παρακύπτω, 884, 924).[164] An alternative theory holds that the crones actually stand on the rooftops as if courtesans celebrating the Adonia, with the Youth playing the part of the god.[165] Indeed, the pervasive sexual obscenities spoken by the old women in this scene are suggestive not only of the prostitutes they resemble but of this festival generally.[166]

It is therefore peculiar that McLeish attributes to the crones an almost Victorian modesty in their use of language.[167] On the contrary, their speech confirms the hypothesis set forth at the beginning of this chapter that older women in Attic Old Comedy have an exceptional status regarding speech: they use obscenities freely, even in the presence of men. The fact that the girl completely avoids obscenities, substituting euphemisms instead, lends further support to this view.[168] For instance, the Girl refers to Crone A's sexual ambitions as "stripping off the unwatched vines" (ἐρήμας ... | ... τρυγήσειν, 885–86) and insults her with an oblique allusion to a dildo, personified as Orthagoras (916). At one point she states an intention to avoid any type of obscenity or innuendo by remaining silent (914). In the presence of the Youth, she also scrupulously shuns obscenity, using instead the mildest of euphemisms: she alludes to him as her bedmate (ξύνευνος, 953); she attributes her troubles to the god Eros (Ἔρως με δονεῖ, 954b); she speaks of her πόθος (957) and uses similarly euphemistic language for sexual intercourse, "to come into my bed" (ἐς εὐνὴν | τὴν ἐμὴν ἱκέσθαι, 959a–b) and "to sleep" (καθεύδειν, 1039). The duet sung by the pair possibly represents a version of the *paraclausithuron*, the lover's complaint sung at his mistress's door. In this burlesque of a popular song, however, the Girl appears to take the male part and the youth that of the waiting girl, a gender-role confusion that perhaps reflects the chaos entailed by Praxagora's legislation.[169] In contrast to the Girl,

[164] Mastronarde 1990: 257–58.

[165] Bowie 1993: 266–67; Fraenkel 1936: 265; cf. Pollux 4.129, whom Bowie quotes as saying, "In comedy, pimps, old women and women look down from the roof."

[166] Rothwell 1990: 8n.37.

[167] McLeish (1980: 99) inexplicably asserts that the youth is the one who employs most of the obscenity in this scene: "It is the young man who utters most of the bawdy: the old women are his butts, and preserve the dignity of their language almost intact. Their use of coy euphemisms (for example, καθεύδειν, 'to sleep with,' 1051) or words of whose sexual meaning they seem unaware (for example, κόπτειν, 'to knock,' 976) supports the view that they are trying to be as ladylike as possible."

[168] Wit-Tak 1968: 364.

[169] For this interpretation, see Olson (1988), who argues against Bowra (1958) that the duet enacts a type of popular sung by young men with courtesans. For further discussion, see Parker 1997: 546.

Crone A utters multiple secondary obscenities: her sexual allusion to τϱῆμα, "oarlock" (906), recalls the coarse language of Blepyrus, while her use of the verb σποδεῖσθαι, "to bang" (908, 942, 1016; cf. 113), perpetuates the violent analogy between striking and sexual intercourse established in the rehearsal scene. Crone A also hints at fellatio with her reference to λάβδα, the first letter of λεσβιάζειν (920).

Nor does the Crone adopt a different tone with the Youth; if anything, the obscenities intensify in his presence. When he refuses to go to bed with her, preferring the Girl instead (διασποδῆσαι, 939), the Crone immediately invokes the new law, comically juxtaposing the vulgar verb σποδῶ with various legal terms:

> οἰμώζων ἄϱα, νὴ Δία, σποδήσεις.
> οὐ γὰϱ τἀπὶ Χαϱιξένης τάδ' ἐστίν.
> κατὰ τὸν νόμον ταῦτα ποιεῖν
> ἔστι δίκαιον, εἰ <u>δημοκϱατούμεθα</u>. (942–45)

> Then you'll cry while you bang.
> We're no longer in the time of Charixena, you know.
> But according to the law, it is right to do this,
> if we are really a democracy.

Praxagora's absurd decree conveys the frightening consequences of a democracy that extends its membership to all individuals and that protects and encourages self-interest. And it is noteworthy in this regard that the law court in contemporary Athens was the civic institution most likely to have been populated by the lower classes. Forced against his will, the Youth loses the most important privilege of Athenian citizenship, mastery over his own body. At the level of speech, the women's sexual obscenities, like those of Blepyrus, call attention to their opportunism while investing them with the authority normally associated with comic men. Moreover, the disjunction between speech and gender created by their excessive legalisms reflects the profound disturbance of normative gender roles brought about by the new government. These pervasive linguistic transgressions travesty male political institutions and ultimately expose the flaws implicit in the contemporary democratic process. In the world of the *Ecclesiazusae*, the democracy that guarantees free speech to all engenders inversions of sexual and political hierarchy.

After the love duet between the Youth and the Girl, the crone reappears to claim her would-be lover with a series of double entendres on knocking and sexual intercourse (976–77); these coarse sexual references, like those of Blepyrus in his exchange with Praxagora, establish the crone as the sexual aggressor. The Youth attempts to elude her by identifying himself with men who derive their pleasure from sources other than women:

Anaphlustius, the masturbator (979), and Sebinos, the pederast, two characters linked at *Frogs* 428.[170] In a similar strategy, he pretends to be an *eisagōgeus*, "an official who set limits in the monetary value of cases to be heard in court,"[171] only his legal rhetoric has a decidedly sexual cast:

> ἀλλ' οὐχὶ νυνὶ τὰς ὑπερεξηκοντέτεις
> εἰσάγομεν, ἀλλ' εἰσαῦθις ἀναβεβλήμεθα.
> τὰς ἐντὸς εἴκοσιν γὰρ ἐκδικάζομεν. (982–84)

We're not handling any cases over sixty at the moment;
we have dismissed those until a later date.
We're currently judging only those under twenty.

In their struggle for domination, both the Youth and the old woman alternate obscenity and legal language, speech practices associated with authority in the theater and in the Assembly. Imputing a sexual meaning to a judicial term, since the verb εἰσάγω also means to take a woman in marriage (see below), the old woman responds to the Youth's claim: "That was under the old rule, my pretty; but now you must handle our case first" (εἰσάγω, 986). The banter continues with more obscene puns on knocking (κρούω, 989–91) and other types of innuendo until she restates the decree (ψήφισμα, 1013) in full:

> ἔδοξε ταῖς γυναιξίν, ἢν ἀνὴρ νέος
> νέας ἐπιθυμῇ, μὴ σποδεῖν αὐτὴν πρὶν ἂν
> τὴν γραῦν προκρούσῃ πρῶτον. ἢν δὲ μὴ 'θέλῃ
> πρότερον προκρούειν, ἀλλ' ἐπιθυμῇ τῆς νέας,
> ταῖς πρεσβυτέραις γυναιξὶν ἔστω τὸν νέον
> ἕλκειν ἀνατεὶ λαβομένας τοῦ παττάλου. (1015–20)

It has been decreed by the women, that if a young man
desires a young girl, he is not permitted to bang her
before he bangs an old woman first. And if he does not wish
to bang her first but wants only the young girl,
then let it be permitted for the older women to drag him away,
with impunity, taking him by his peg.

Although Rothwell has proposed that the crones, like the Furies in Aeschylus' *Eumenides*, represent the force behind the law, I think that their exaggerated legalisms betray their impotence rather than their power: unable to overcome the youth by means of sheer physical force, they must

---

[170] Citing Ar. *Lys.* 1092 and 1113, Henderson (1991a: 221) notes that masturbation and pederasty were perhaps related because they were considered the last resort for men deprived of women.

[171] Rothwell 1990: 68.

resort to the law and verbal cunning instead (1022).[172] In this parody of
the legal system, the law provides a person of low birth with a means of
rectifying wrongs, thus contributing to excessive litigiousness among the
Athenians and to the overall degeneration of the polis. When the Youth
suggests that he go free on bail (ἀφαιρῆται, 1023), the Crone replies:
"No man has the legal authority to enter into contracts in excess of one
medimnos" (1024–25).[173] As a reversal of the Athenian law regarding
financial transactions of women, this decree in particular illustrates the
reduced social position of men in the new city because they have lost their
sexual, financial, and judicial power. Finally, when Crone A employs the
technical term εἰσάγειν (1037; cf. 986) for bringing the Youth into her
house, she inverts normal Athenian wedding ritual in which the man led
his bride to his natal oikos. The new laws have converted the Youth into
a bride just as they made Blepyrus occupy the position of a wife.

A second old woman then descends on the youth and spars with Crone
A over who retains the legal right to sleep with him first. Crone B, in a
manner even more legalistic than that of Crone A, recites the letter of
the law:

αὕτη σύ, ποῖ παραβᾶσα τόνδε τὸν νόμον
ἕλκεις, παρ' ἐμοὶ τῶν γραμμάτων εἰρηκότων
πρότερον καθεύδειν αὐτόν;   (1049–51)

You there, where do you think you're dragging him,
when you yourself have broken the law?
For isn't he supposed to sleep with me first
according to the law as written?

She then employs a rhetorical technique familiar from the courts, asserting
the primacy of the law over individual agency: "It is not I, but the law
that is dragging you" (ἀλλ' οὐκ ἐγώ, | ἀλλ' ὁ νόμος ἕλκει σε, 1055).[174] A
third old woman enters and quibbles with the second crone over the youth:
"According to the law (κατὰ τὸν νόμον), he ought to follow me" (1077).
The capricious reinterpretation of the law according to personal interest
quickly degenerates into a shouting match between the crones. As embodi-
ments of the law, they illustrate how the courts and the Assembly serve
as vehicles for the weak and the self-interested to redress their wrongs and
attain power over their rivals.

Like Euripides' kinsman in the *Thesmophoriazusae*, the Youth then alleges a need to defecate as a means of evading the crone:

---

[172] For Rothwell (ibid.: 74), the crones embody "the destructive *peitho* that uses . . . force."

[173] On the law limiting the financial transactions of women and children, cf. Isae. 10.10.2;
see also Ussher 1973: 217.

[174] Ussher 1973: 221; cf. Arist. *Rh. Al.* 1442b8; Lys. 1.26.

ἴθι νυν ἔασον εἰς ἄφοδον πρώτιστά με
ἐλθόντα θαρρῆσαι πρὸς ἐμαυτόν· εἰ δὲ μή,
αὐτοῦ τι δρῶντα πυρρὸν ὄψει μ' αὐτίκα
ὑπὸ τοῦ δέους.   (1059–62)

Come now, let me pluck up my courage
once I have gone to the bathroom. If I don't,
you will see me do something yellow
right here on the spot out of fear.

But the Crone quickly establishes dominance over him by means of a crude
scatological obscenity: "Come on and hurry up—you can shit inside"
(ἔνδον χεσεῖ, 1062). Like Calonice in the *Lysistrata*, whose use of χέζω
affords her the upper hand with the Proboulus, the old woman with her
crude obscenity signifies the complete role inversion entailed by the new
laws. But in contrast to the obscenity of men in Attic Old Comedy,
which repeatedly exposes the deceptions of their interlocutors, the crones'
vulgarities only serve to assert and maintain their hegemony; thus the third
old woman's scatological allusion has no other purpose than to force the
youth's compliance. In the *Ecclesiazusae*, comic obscenity signifies both
degradation and authority: In the case of Blepyrus, whose obscenity joins
pathic behavior to scatology, it expresses the subordination of men to
women in a gynaecocracy. At other points, it serves a function similar to
that of the obscenity of the Relative in the *Thesmophoriazusae*: it continually
strips away the deceptions of the other characters. And yet in the final
scene, the sexual and scatological humor of the crones serves to establish
their power over the reluctant youth. These uses of obscenity reveal a
chaotic social structure vulnerable to change and marked by unstable
gender roles, a world in which Blepyrus' compromised masculinity can
never be fully restored.

CONCLUSION

In the *Thesmophoriazusae* and the *Ecclesiazusae*, transvestite characters
allow us a glimpse into the dramatic construction of gender by exposing
conventions of speech and costume. Case endings, forms of address, oaths,
and types of obscenity comprise the most obvious markers of male and
female speech, although, as we have seen, content may also reveal a character's gender. By exploiting incongruities between gender and speech, Old
Comedy explores the larger issue of the place of speech in the democratic
polis. On the one hand, it links the speech of sexually subordinate and
lower-class figures to suspect rhetorical practices, practices that invest the
speaker with an inappropriate, even dangerous, access to power. On the

other hand, Attic Old Comedy employs obscenity, which it explicitly identifies as masculine through its association with the comic buffoon, as a tool for unmasking these deceptions and reinforcing social norms. In the *Thesmophoriazusae*, for example, the Relative thwarts the rhetorical and dramatic chicaneries of his interlocutors, particularly Agathon and the women, through his use of comic obscenity. Moreover, his recourse to obscenity repeatedly affirms that his compromised status is only temporary; the women's control is restricted to the religious sphere, and normative masculinity is fully restored to the polis at the end of the play.

This positive view of masculinity disappears in the *Ecclesiazusae*, perhaps reflecting the comic poet's increasing disillusionment with political life after Athens' defeat in the Peloponnesian war.[175] Nonetheless, comic obscenity is still deployed as a means of illuminating the city's vulnerability to the spurious rhetoric of charlatans: the scatological representation of Blepyrus discloses the impotence and ineffectiveness of a citizenship corrupted by self-interest, while Praxagora wins an easy victory over the male citizens through her demagogic sleight-of-hand. As a tool of the crones, obscenity becomes a means of enforcing the hollow authority of a corrupt political system. Indeed, the compromised speech practices of all the characters in the *Ecclesiazusae* illustrate the complete fragmentation of social identity brought about by Praxagora's regime in a savage burlesque of the democratic process. As the defining verbal genre of Attic Old Comedy, obscenity, whether scatological, pathic, pederastic, or heterosexual, equips the comic poet with a flexible and incisive tool for exposing the illusions of the theater and the Assembly.

[175] David (1984: 3) stresses the economic consequences of early fourth-century democracy at Athens.

Chapter Seven

CONCLUSION

BY IDENTIFYING some of the discursive practices and verbal contexts identified with women in fifth-century Athenian drama, this book has attempted to shed light on how the dramatic poets exploited these conventions as a means of constructing character and of conveying larger social and political issues. These plays largely rely on a conception of male and female discursive spheres as distinct: the women are confined to the domestic circle of the household, where they speak mostly to servants and other women; male speech, in contrast, typically occurs among men in a public and political context. As a consequence of this ideological segregation, women are frequently portrayed as speaking differently when alone than they do in the presence of men. The plays also depict the relative verbal isolation of women as the source of their solidarity and complicity; this collective verbal presence invests them with a subversive power that leads to adultery, betrayal of the household, and erosion of gender and class lines. Although figured as separate, these gendered discursive spheres continually intersect and overlap in the plays examined in this book, whether women's speech assumes a masculine form and permeates the world of men, or whether male speech, tainted by feminine, erotic concerns, corrupts both the oikos and the polis.

Because the fifth-century democratic polis equated free speech with adult citizen males, just as it did the inviolability of the body, women's appropriation of male verbal strategies depicted in these plays enacts a kind of gynaecocracy, both in the house and in the city, a state of affairs literally dramatized in the *Ecclesiazusae*, in which women dominate and marginalize men. In several cases, female characters are depicted as deviating from normal feminine verbal practices and appropriating masculine public genres: Clytemnestra and Hermione boast a prerogative of speech akin to that of men, whereas the female characters in the *Thesmophoriazusae* and *Ecclesiazusae* imitate male orators and civil procedure. In assigning Clytemnestra masculine verbal activities and presenting her as engaging almost exclusively with male interlocutors, Aeschylus elucidates and reinforces his characterization of a masculinized and indomitable female figure. Even Phaedra, whose struggle to remain silent identifies her as obeying feminine verbal norms, appropriates a male discursive form, the new technology of writing associated with the administration of democracy in the classical Athenian polis, in order to preserve her good name while bringing disaster on her house. And yet the disruptive and eroticized discourse of figures like Phaedra and Andromache arises from a complicit, feminine speech community whose insidious schemes result from a lack of supervision in the oikos. Conversely, by assigning feminine verbal genres to male characters, particularly seductive or cunning persuasion, the dramatic poets transform them into risible or despicable characters: Agathon's deployment of women's speech practices and genres, including euphemistic and tragic language, female cult song, and seductiveness, makes him the target of the Relative's pathic, masculine humor, whereas the unscrupulous Orestes' use of seductive persuasion and slander in the *Andromache* underscores his overvaluation of private, erotic concerns.

Recent critics have remarked that women's speech and presence outside the house in Athenian drama, as well as in the democratic polis, always entail a profound disturbance of the social order: "There is no public position from which a woman can speak and not be out of place."[1] Although this view applies to many tragedies and comedies, this book has suggested that it needs modification. First, social status plays an important role in determining the type of verbal genre adopted by a speaker and its domestic and civic ramifications. For example, the plays discussed in this book present the speech of matrons as particularly dangerous; their inability to control their sexual impulses and their complicity with one another incite adultery in the *Hippolytus* and the *Andromache*. In the *Thesmophoriazusae* and the *Ecclesiazusae*, on the other hand, women's adulterous proclivities generate strategies for circumventing masculine surveillance, even leading to a new form of government in which women, not men, will control access to sex. The identification of matrons' speech with adultery reflects prevailing male concerns about controlling sexuality and thereby the legitimacy of offspring, especially in the absence of the male kurios, an issue probably uppermost in the minds of Athenian men, who were frequently away at war during this period. Because sexually inexperienced, virgins are represented as lacking the verbal guile of their married counterparts; for this reason, Artemis entrusts the chorus of maidens with the official, didactic version of Phaedra's story at the end of the *Hippolytus*. In comedy, older women, freed of some of the restrictions placed on younger women because they are past the age of childbearing and beyond the need for guardianship, speak more crudely and with more authority, as we saw in the *Thesmophorizusae* and the *Ecclesiazusae*. Social class also appears to have an impact on the construction of dramatic character: in the *Hippolytus*, Phaedra's semantic ambiguities contribute to the portrayal

---

[1] Goldhill 1992: 41. Loraux (1986: 323) similarly states, "If silence is as necessary and natural to woman as logos is to man, a woman cannot deliver a speech without profoundly disturbing the order of things." Compare also the remark of Segal (1993: 124), "A woman's relation to the public discourse of the city, even in the realm of Aphrodite, must remain problematical."

of a wellborn and discreet matron who speaks euphemistically about sexual matters, in contrast to the coarse and blunt speech of the servile Nurse. Attic drama makes cultural distinctions in depicting the verbal habits of its characters as well; thus Hermione embodies Athenian stereotypes about verbally dominating and deprecating Spartan women and their lack of sexual self-control.

This book has also suggested that the ancient Greek literary tradition singles out one form of women's discourse as benefiting rather than harming the city and the households of men: religious speech, or speech that accompanies a ritual action or defends a ritual activity, especially that of virgins. In Euripides' scenes of voluntary sacrifice, for example, unmarried girls deliver speeches in which they publicly proclaim their willingness to die, either on behalf of a political cause, like Greek victory over Troy, as exemplified by Iphigenia in *Iphigenia in Aulis* (1368–1401), or on behalf of the preservation of the family, as in the case of Macaria in *Children of Heracles* (500–535). Similarly, Antigone's public disobedience in defense of the unwritten laws regarding burial shows the importance of female ritual roles to the city and the authority invested in them. The fact that Attic drama could deploy virgins in service of a political or religious ideal points also to the pervasive association of virgins with truthful discourse; so, too, we find the respected priestess as a stock figure of feminine authority in Athenian drama, including Theonoe in Euripides' *Helen*, the priestesses of Apollo at Delphi represented in Aeschylus' *Eumenides* and in Euripides' *Ion*, and Lysistrata, whose character is perhaps modeled on that of a historical priestess of Athena and who claims the prerogative of public speech in Aristophanes' play. A fragment from Euripides' lost *Melanippe Captive* underscores the important role played by women's mantic utterance in the polis:

> Men's criticism of women is the worthless twanging of a bowstring and evil talk. Women are better than men, as I will show. . . . They manage the household and preserve within the things carried by sea; nor in the absence of the wife is a house tidy or prosperous. Consider their role in religion, for that, in my opinion, comes first. We women play the most important part, because women prophesy the will of Zeus in the oracles of Phoebus. And at the holy site of Dodona near the sacred oak, females convey the will of Zeus to inquirers from Greece. As for the sacred rituals for the Fates and the Nameless Ones [i.e., the Erinyes], all these would not be holy if performed by men, but prosper in women's hands. In this way women have a rightful share in the service of the gods. Why is it, then, that women must have a bad reputation?[2]

Embedded in a play that seems to have contained numerous examples of the *psogos* against women,[3] this speech functions as a defense of women's

---

[2] Translation from Fant and Lefkowitz 1992: 13–14. For the passage, see Page 1942: 113–15, no. 13; for the first three lines, see Eur. fr. 499 *TGF*.

[3] On invective in Euripides' *Melanippe Captive*, cf. frs. 493, 494, 497, 498, and 502 N².

role within the household and city; in particular, the fragment identifies their official religious service as priestesses and as ritual participants as the only valid activity that should draw them outside the house.

Even matrons, particularly widowed mothers, may speak with authority to save rather than disrupt the polis in Attic drama; their speech, like that of the virgins discussed above, also has a basis in ritual. The figure of Aethra in Euripides' *Suppliants* provides a good example of the moral, maternal authority of women and their power to work good for the city.[4] Like Antigone, she acts on behalf of religious law to allow the mourning Argive mothers to bury their slain sons. But in contrast to Clytemnestra or Hermione, Aethra works through men rather than taking matters into her own hands. She expressly states that women should act through men: "It is seemly for women, whoever are wise, to do everything through men" (πάντα γὰρ δι' ἀρσένων | γυναιξὶ πράσσειν εἰκὸς, αἵτινες σοφαί, Eur. *Supp.* 40–41). When asked to inform Theseus of the situation, she defers to a man, Adrastus, the Argive king, asking him to speak on behalf of herself and the rest of the women (109, 1013–14). Finally, although addressed to the king of Athens, her speech is not really public since she addresses her son, a person over whom she was likely to exert the most authority.[5] Furthermore, Aethra approaches him as a suppliant (102–3). In this context, Theseus can acknowledge the wisdom of women:

Αι. εἴπω τι, τέκνον, σοί τε καὶ πόλει καλόν;
Θη. ὡς πολλά γ' ἐστὶ κἀπὸ θηλειῶν σοφά.   (293–94)

Aethra: May I say something beneficial both to you and to the city?
Theseus: Yes, since women do say many wise things.

Theseus validates his mother's public speech because she acts in a ritual context, as a suppliant and advocate of maternal mourning; their exchange implies that the democratic polis recognized the validity of women's public speech when it pertained to religious matters.[6] By the fourth century B.C.E., the religious authority of women is a rhetorical trope in Attic oratory, as evidenced by the end of *Against Neaera*, where Apollodorus summons as

[4] Goff (1995: 71) argues that Aethra's authority stems from her maternity, a point reinforced by the claim of mothers in Aristophanic comedy; they assert their right to air opinions about civic business because they produce male heirs; see Chapter 1, note 83 above. This authority may also relate to the role of mothers in conferring *parrhēsia* on their male children.

[5] As Foxhall observes in Attic oratory, "The *kurios* over whom a mother is likely to have had most influence and thus control was an adult son." Foxhall 1996: 150; cf. Cleoboule in Dem. 39, who urged her son to bring a case on her behalf.

[6] Goff (1995: 74) argues that Aethra's involvement in a specific ritual, the proerosia, about which not much is known, sanctions her speech. This allows her to "move beyond maternal imperatives and equips her with a powerful discourse of Athenian identity and mission." However, the fact that she acts in defense of unwritten laws and in a context of supplication already fully identifies her with ritual activities.

a group the wives and daughters of the Athenian polis in unanimous condemnation of the hetaera and her activities, perhaps in evocation of the collective ritual activity of the Thesmophoria ([Dem.] 59.110–11).[7] Both tragic and comic plays represent female characters as deploying ritual language and activities, whether ritual lament, voluntary sacrifice, or mantic utterance, in service of the city. Moreover, the Adonia provides a ritual paradigm for the sex strike that brings about an end to the Peloponnesian war in the *Lysistrata*, whereas the women hatch their plot for gynaecocracy at the Skira in the *Ecclesiazusae*.[8] Just as the silence and seclusion of historical Athenian women cannot be understood as monolithic or absolute, so fifth-century drama does not always portray women's public speech as transgressive.

Nonetheless, Athenian drama frequently depicts women's speech as subversive, particularly when it approximates male discursive forms. The disturbance of social and political hierarchy entailed by women's appropriation of men's speech functions not simply as a morality tale intended to teach the male spectators to be more vigilant about their wives, a lesson the female celebrants of the Thesmophoria allege their men have learned in the theater in Aristophanes' *Thesmophoriazusae*. Given the restricted role played by women in Athenian public life, and their veritable absence from the political spheres in which male civic identity was constructed, particularly the theater, it seems that tragic and comic women imparted a different type of warning to their male audience. Viewed through the lens of Aristophanic comedy, a genre that engages quite directly with contemporary political issues, the plays discussed in this book can be understood as employing gendered discourses as a medium for commenting on the status of male speech in the polis. Although they dramatize feminine verbal license and duplicity through gossip, or through more public, authoritative genres like oratory, these plays do not suggest that such an appropriation might actually take place. Nor can one imagine that women's speech posed any kind of real danger to the polis in the minds of the male spectators; if it did, it would not have been the subject of comic parody. Rather, the threat of subversion within the political sphere was found among the spectator's own ranks, among men of uncertain birth and unscrupulous intent, who learned the art of persuasion as a means of promoting themselves in the Assembly and the courts. Women, traditionally viewed as political outsiders, with ambiguous domestic loyalties, duplicitous and tireless in their pursuit of *erōs*, provided the dramatic poets with a vehicle for illustrating the disastrous consequences of political power placed in the wrong hands.

---

[7] For this idea, see Goff 1997; Gagarin (forthcoming); on the moral authority of women in Attic oratory, see Lys. 32.12–17 and Dem. 47.57.

[8] Goff 1995: 77.

BIBLIOGRAPHY

EDITIONS

Adam, J. 1963. *The Republic of Plato.* Vol. 1. 2d ed. Cambridge.
Allen, T. W., W. R. Halliday, and E. E. Sikes. 1980. *The Homeric Hymns.* 2d ed. Amsterdam.
Audollent, A. 1967. *Defixionum tabellae.* Frankfurt.
Austin, C. 1968. *Nova Fragmenta Euripidea in papyris reperta.* Berlin.
———. 1969. *Menandri Aspis et Samia.* Berlin.
Barrett, W. S. 1964. *Euripides, Hippolytos.* Oxford.
Campell, D. A. 1967. *Greek Lyric Poetry.* London.
Dale, A. M. 1984. *Euripides' Alcestis.* New York.
Denniston, J. D. 1959. *The Greek Particles.* Oxford.
Denniston, J. D., and D. Page. 1972. *Aeschylus, Agamemnon.* Oxford.
Diels, H., and W. Kranz, eds. 1960. *Die Fragmente der Vorsokratiker.* 3 vols. Berlin.
Diggle, J. 1984–94. *Euripides, Fabulae.* 3 vols. London.
Dover, K. J. 1993. *Aristophanes, Frogs.* Oxford.
Edmonds, J. ed. 1946. *The Characters of Theophrastus.* Cambridge, Mass.
Fraenkel, E. 1950. *Aeschylus, Agamemnon.* 3 vols. Oxford.
Garvie, A. F. 1988. *Aeschylus, Choephori.* Oxford.
Hall, F., and W. Geldart, eds. 1982. *Aristophanis Comoediae.* Vol. 2. Oxford.
Halleran, M. 1995. *Euripides, Hippolytus.* Warminister.
Henderson, J. 1987a. *Aristophanes, Lysistrata.* Oxford.
Hornblower, S. 1991. *A Commentary on Thucydides.* 2 vols. Oxford.
How, W., and J. Wells. 1967. *A Commentary on Herodotus with Introduction and Appendixes,* Vol. 1. Oxford.
Innes, D., ed. and trans. 1995. *Demetrius' On Style.* Cambridge, Mass.
Kassel, A., and C. Austin. 1991. *Poetae comici graecae.* Vol. 5. Berlin.
Kirk, G. S. 1990. *The Iliad: A Commentary.* Vol. 2. Cambridge.
Lagarde, P. de. 1967. *Analecta Syriaca.* Osnabrück.
Page, D. 1942. *Sappho and Alcaeus: An Introduction to the Study of Ancient Lesbian Poetry.* Oxford.
Preisendanz, K. 1973. *Papyri graecae magicae: Die griechischen Zauberpapyri.* Vol. 1. Stuttgart.
Rabe, H. 1971. *Scholia in Lucianum.* Stuttgart.
Radt, S., and B. Snell. 1977–86. *Tragicorum graecorum fragmenta.* Vols. 1–4. Göttingen.
Richardson, N. J. 1974. *The Homeric Hymn to Demeter.* Oxford.
Sandbach, F. H. 1979. *Menandri reliquiae selectae.* Oxford.
Snell, B. 1961. *Bacchylides.* Leipzig.
Sommerstein, A. 1989. *Aeschylus, Eumenides.* Cambridge.
———. 1994. *Aristophanes' Thesmophoriazusae.* Warminster.
Stevens, P. T. 1971. *Euripides, Andromache.* Oxford.

Thesleff, H. 1965. *The Pythagorean Texts of the Hellenistic Period*. Abo.

Ussher, R. G. 1973. *Aristophanes, Ecclesiazusae*. Oxford.

Voigt, E.-M. 1971. *Sappho et Alcaeus: Fragmenta*. Amsterdam.

West, M. L. 1980. *Hesiod Works and Days*. Oxford.

————. 1989. *Iambi et elegi graeci*. Vol. 1. Oxford.

————. 1992. *Iambi et elegi graeci*. Vol. 2. Oxford.

Wünsch, R. 1897. *Inscriptiones graecae*. Vol. 3, part 3. Berlin.

STUDIES, COMMENTARIES, DICTIONARIES

Adams, J. N. 1984. "Female Speech in Latin Comedy." *Antichthon* 18: 43–77.

Albini, U. 1974. "Un dramma d'avanguardia: L'Andromaca di Euripide." *Maia* 26: 83–95.

Aldrich, K. 1961. *The Andromache of Euripides*. University of Nebraska Studies 25. Lincoln.

Alexiou, M. 1974. *The Ritual Lament in Greek Tradition*. Cambridge.

Allen, J. T., and G. Italie. 1954. *A Concordance to Euripides*. Berkeley and Los Angeles.

Ambrose, P. 1994. "Did Women Sing in the *Thesmophoriazusae*?" In *Didaskalia* Supplement 1. Proceedings from the Conference "How Is It Played? Genre, Performance, Meaning," Texas A & M University, October 1994.

Ardener, E. 1975. "Belief and the Problem of Women." In S. Ardener 1975: 1–17.

Ardener, S., ed. 1975. *Perceiving Women*. London.

Armstrong, D., and A. E. Hanson. 1986. "The Virgin's Voice and Neck: Aeschylus' *Agamemnon* 245 and Other Texts." *BICS* 33: 97–100.

Armstrong, D., and E. Ratchford. 1985. "Iphigeneia's Veil: Aeschylus, *Agamemnon* 228–248." *BICS* 32: 1–12.

Arnott, P. 1989. *Public and Performance in the Greek Theatre*. London and New York.

————. 1994. "Separatism and the Alleged Conversation of Women." *C & M* 45: 27–50.

Assaël, J. 1985. "Misogynie et féminisme chez Aristophane et chez Euripide." *Pallas* 32: 91–103.

Austin, C. 1967. "De nouveaux fragments de L'Erechthée d' Euripide." *Recherches de papyrologie* 4: 11–67.

————. 1990. "Observations critiques sur les Thesmophories d' Aristophane." *Dodone* 19: 9–29.

Avery, H. C. 1968. "My Tongue Swore, But My Mind Is Unsworn." *TAPA* 99: 19–35.

Bacon, H. 1964. "The Shield of Eteocles." *Arion* 3: 27–38.

Bailey, F. G. 1971. "Gifts and Poison." In *Gifts and Poison*, edited by F. G. Bailey, 1–25. Oxford.

Bain, D. M. 1984. "Female Speech in Menander." *Antichthon* 18: 24–42.

————. 1991. "Six Greek Verbs of Sexual Congress." *CQ* 41: 51–77.

Bakhtin, M. 1986. "The Problem of Speech Genres." In *Speech Genres and Other Late Essays*, translated by V. McGee, 60–102. Austin, Tex.

Barlow, S. 1971. *The Imagery of Euripides*. London.

Baron, D. 1986. *Grammar and Gender*. New Haven and London.

Bassi, K. 1989. "The Actor as Actress in Euripides' *Alcestis*." In *Women in Theatre*, edited by J. Redmond, 19–30. Cambridge.

———. 1995. "Male Nudity and Disguise in the Discourse of Greek Histrionics." *Helios* 22: 3–22.

Bergren, A. 1983. "Language and the Female in Early Greek Thought." *Arethusa* 16: 69–95.

Berns, G. 1973. "Nomos and Physis: An Interpretation of Euripides' *Hippolytos*." *Hermes* 101: 165–87.

Bers, V. 1985. "Dikastic *thorubos*." In *Crux: Essays in Greek History Presented to G.E.M. de Ste. Croix*, edited by P. Cartledge and D. Harvey, 1–15. London.

———. 1994. "Tragedy and Rhetoric." In *Persuasion: Greek Rhetoric in Action*, edited by I. Worthington, 176–95. London and New York.

Betensky, A. 1977. "Aeschylus' *Oresteia*: The Power of Clytemnestra." *Ramus* 6: 11–25.

Bierl, A. 1990. "Dionysus, Wine, and Tragic Poetry: A Metatheatrical Reading of P.*Köln* VI 242A=*TrGF* II F646a." *GRBS* 31: 353–91.

Blok, J. 1987. "Sexual Asymmetry: A Historiographical Essay." In *Sexual Asymmetry: Studies in Ancient Society*, edited by J. Blok and P. Mason, 1–57, Amsterdam.

Bobrick, E. 1991. "Iphigeneia Revisited: *Thesmophoriazusae* 1160–1225." *Arethusa* 24: 67–75.

Bollack, J. 1981. "Le Thrène de Cassandre *Agamemnon*, 1322–1330." *Rev. Ét. Grec.* 94: 1–13.

Bonnafé, A. 1989. "Clytemnestre et ses batailles: Éris et Peitho." In *Architecture et poésie dans le mond grec: Hommages à Georges Roux*, edited by E. Étienne, M.-T. Le Dinahet, and M. Yon, 149–57. Lyon and Paris.

Bornstein, D. 1978. "As Meek as a Maid: A Historical Perspective on Language for Women in Courtesy Books from the Middle Ages to *Seventeen* Magazine." In Butturff and Epstein 1978: 132–38.

Boulay, Julia du. 1974. "Gossip, Friendship, and Quarrels." In *Portrait of a Greek Mountain Village*, 201–29. Oxford.

Boulter, P. 1966. "*Sophia* and *Sophrosyne* in Euripides' *Andromache*." *Phoenix* 20: 51–58.

Bowie, A. M. 1993. *Aristophanes: Myth, Ritual and Comedy*. Cambridge.

Bowra, C. M. 1958. "A Love-Duet." *AJPhil.* 79: 376–91.

Brashear, W. M. 1979. "Ein Berliner Zauberpapyrus." *ZPE* 33: 261–78.

Braund, D. C. 1980. "Artemis Eukleia and Euripides' *Hippolytus*." *JHS* 100: 184–85.

Bremer, J. M. 1975. "The Meadow of Love and Two Passages in Euripides' *Hippolytus*." *Mnemos.* 28: 268–80.

———. 1980. "An Enigmatic Indo-European Rite: Paederasty." *Arethusa* 13: 279–89.

Bruns, I. 1901. *Frauenemancipation in Athen: Ein Beitrag zur attischen Kulturgeschichte des funften und vierten Jahrhunderts*. Kiel. [Reprinted in *Die Verfassungsdebatte bei Herodot; Polistisches Denken bei Herodot; and Frauenempanciaption in Athen*. New York, 1979.]

Bucholtz, M., and K. Hall, eds. 1995. *Gender Articulated: Language and the Socially Constructed Self*. New York and London.

Burian, P. 1985. *New Directions in Euripidean Criticism.* Durham, N.C.

Burkert, W. 1985. *Greek Religion.* Translated by J. Raffan. Cambridge, Mass.

Burnett, A. P. 1971. *Catastrophe Survived: Euripides' Plays of Mixed Reversal.* Cambridge, Mass.

———. 1983. *Three Archaic Poets: Archilochus, Alcaeus, Sappho.* Cambridge, Mass.

———. 1986. "Hearth and Hunt in Euripides' *Hippolytus.*" In *Greek Tragedy and Its Legacy,* edited by M. Cropp, E. Fantham, and S. E. Scully, 167–85. Calgary.

Bushala, E. W. 1969. "Συζύγιαι Χάριτες, *Hippolytus* 1147." *TAPA* 100: 23–29.

Butler, J. 1990. *Gender Trouble.* New York and London.

Butturff, D., and E. Epstein, eds. 1978. *Women's Language and Style.* Akron, Ohio.

Buxton, R.G.A. 1982. *Persuasion in Greek Tragedy: A Study of Peitho.* Cambridge.

———. 1994. *Imaginary Greece: The Contexts of Mythology.* Cambridge.

Byl, S. 1982. "La Mètis des femmes dans l'Assemblée des femmes d'Aristophane." *Revue belge de philologie et d'histoire* 60: 33–40.

Calame, C. 1977. *Les Choeurs de jeunes filles en Grèce archaïque.* 2 vols. Rome.

———. 1994–96. "From Choral Poetry to Tragic Stasimon: The Enactment of Women's Song." *Arion* 3: 136–54.

———. 1997. *Choruses of Young Women in Ancient Greece: Their Morphology, Religious Role, and Social Functions.* Translated by D. Collins and J. Orion. Boston and London.

Calder, W., III. 1979. "The Riddle of Wilamowitz's *Phaidrabild.*" *GRBS* 20: 219–36.

Cameron, A. 1939. "Sappho's Prayer to Aphrodite." *Harv. Theol. Rev.* 32: 1–17.

Cameron, D. 1985. *Feminism and Linguistic Theory.* London.

———. 1995. "Rethinking Language and Gender Studies: Some Issues for the 1990s." In Mills 1995: 31–44.

———. 1997. "Performing Gender Identity: Young Men's Talk and the Construction of Heterosexual Masculinity." In Johnson and Meinhof 1997: 47–64.

Caraveli, A. 1980. "Bridge between Worlds: The Greek Women's Lament as Communicative Event." *Journal of American Folklore* 93: 129–57.

———. 1986. "The Bitter Wounding: The Lament as Social Protest in Rural Greece." In *Gender and Power in Rural Greece,* edited by J. Dubisch, 169–94. Princeton.

Cartledge, P. 1981. "Spartan Wives: Liberation or Licence?" *CQ* 31: 84–105.

Case, S.-E. 1985. "Classic Drag: The Greek Creation of Female Parts." In *Feminism and Theatre,* 317–27. London.

Caven, B. 1990. *Dionysius I: War-lord of Sicily.* New Haven.

Chantraine, P. 1956. *Études sur la vocabulaire grec.* Paris.

———. 1968. *Dictionnaire étymologique de la langue grecque.* 5 vols. Paris.

Chapman, G. A. 1983. "Some Notes on Dramatic Illusion in Aristophanes." *AJPhil.* 104: 1–23.

Christ, M. 1992. "Ostracism, Sycophancy, and the Deception of the Demos: [Arist.] Ath. *Pol.* 43. 5." *CQ* 42: 336–46.

Clark, C. 1996. "The Gendering of the Body in Alcman's *Partheneion* 1: Narrative, Sex, and Social Order in Archaic Sparta." *Helios* 23: 143–72.

Claus, D. 1972. "Phaedra and Socratic Paradox." *YClS* 22: 223–38.

Coates, J. 1986. *Women, Men and Language.* London and New York.

———. 1995. "Language, Gender and Career." In Mills 1995: 13–30.

Cohen, D. 1989. "Seclusion, Separation and the Status of Women in Classical Athens." *G&R* 36: 3–15.

———. 1991. *Law, Sexuality, and Society: The Enforcement of Morals in Classical Athens.* Cambridge.

———. 1992. "Article Review: Sex, Gender and Sexuality in Ancient Greece." *C Phil.* 87: 145–60.

Cole, S. G. 1981. "Could Greek Women Read and Write?" In Foley 1981a: 219–45.

Collard, C. 1971. *Supplement to the Allen and Italie Concordance to Euripides.* Groningen.

———. 1975. "Formal Debates in Euripides' Drama." *G&R* 22: 58–71.

Conacher, D. J. 1961. "A Problem in Euripides' *Hippolytus.*" *TAPA* 92: 37–44.

———. 1967. *Euripidean Drama: Myth, Theme and Structure.* Toronto.

———. 1981. "Rhetoric and Relevance in Euripidean Drama." *AJPhil.* 102: 3–25.

Connor, W. R. 1971. *The New Politicians of Fifth-Century Athens.* Princeton.

Coulon, V. 1957. "Aristophanes, *Thesmophoriazusen* 1015–1055." *Rh. Mus.* 100: 186–98.

Craik, E. 1987. "Euripides' First *Hippolytos.*" *Mnemos.* 40: 137–39.

———. 1993. "ΑΙΔΩΣ in Euripides' *Hippolytos* 373–430: Review and Reinterpretation." *JHS* 113: 45–59.

Crane, G. 1993. "Politics of Consumption and Generosity in the Carpet Scene of the *Agamemnon*," *C Phil.* 88: 117–36.

Crocker, L. 1957. "On Interpreting *Hippolytus.*" *Philologus* 101: 238–46.

Csapo, E., and W. Slater. 1995. *The Context of Ancient Drama.* Ann Arbor.

Dale, A. M. 1948. *The Lyric Meters of Greek Drama.* Cambridge.

———. 1969. *Collected Papers.* Cambridge.

Danek, G. 1992. "Zur Prologrede der Aphrodite und Hippolytos des Euripides." *Wien Stud.* 105: 19–37.

Danforth, L. 1982. *The Death Rituals of Rural Greece.* Princeton.

David, E. 1984. *Aristophanes and Athenian Society of the Early Fourth Century B.C.* Leiden.

Davis, N. Z. 1978. "Woman on Top: Symbolic Sexual Inversion and Political Disorder in Early Modern Europe." In *The Reversible World: Symbolic Inversion in Art and Society,* edited by B. Babcock, 147–90. Ithaca.

Dean-Jones, L. 1991. "The Cultural Construct of the Female Body in Classical Greek Science." In Pomeroy 1991: 111–37.

———. 1994. *Women's Bodies in Classical Greek Science.* Oxford.

Detienne, M. 1989. "The Violence of Well born Ladies: Women in the *Thesmophoria.*" In *The Cuisine of Sacrifice among the Greeks,* edited by M. Detienne and J.-P. Vernant, translated by P. Wissing, 129–47. Chicago.

Deubner, L. 1932. *Attische Feste.* 2d ed. Berlin.

———. 1941. "*Ololygê* und *Verwandtes.*" *Abhandlungen Preussischen Akadamie der Wissenschaft Phil.-Hist. Kl.* 1: 3–28.

Dickey, E. 1995. "Forms of Address and Conversational Language in Aristophanes and Menander." *Mnemos.* 48: 257–71.

Dickey, E. 1996. *Greek Forms of Address from Herodotus to Lucian.* Oxford.

Dillon, M. 1987. "The *Lysistrata* as a Post-Dekeleian Peace Play." *TAPA* 117: 97–104.

Dimock, G. E., Jr. 1977. "Euripides' *Hippolytus*, or Virtue Rewarded." *TClS* 25: 239–58.

Dingels, J. 1967. "Das Requisit in der griechischen Tragödie." Diss., Tübingen.

Dodds, E. R. 1925. "The ΑΙΔΩΣ of Phaedra and the Meaning of the *Hippolytus*." *CR* 39: 102–10.

Dolan, J. 1985. "Gender Impersonation Onstage: Destroying or Maintaining the Mirror of Gender Roles?" *Women and Performance* 2: 5–12.

Dover, K. J. 1970. "Lo stile di Aristofane." *Quaderni urbinati di cultura classica* 9: 7–23.

———. 1972. *Aristophanic Comedy.* Berkeley and Los Angeles.

———. 1974. *Greek Popular Morality in the Time of Plato and Aristotle.* Oxford.

———. 1988. "Anecdotes, Gossip and Scandal." In *The Greeks and Their Legacy*, 45–52. Oxford.

———. 1989. *Greek Homosexuality: Updated and with a New Postscript.* Cambridge, Mass.

Easterling, P. E. 1973. "Presentation of Character in Aeschylus." *G&R* 20: 3–19.

———. 1985. "Anachronism in Greek Tragedy." *JHS* 105: 1–10.

———. 1987. "Women in Tragic Space." *BICS* 34: 15–26.

———. 1993. "The End of an Era? Tragedy in the Early Fourth Century." In Sommerstein et al. 1993: 559–70.

———, ed. 1997. *The Cambridge Companion to Greek Tragedy.* Cambridge.

Eden, K. 1986. *Poetic and Legal Fiction in the Aristotelian Tradition.* Princeton.

Edwards, A. 1991. "Aristophanes' Comic Poetics: ΤΡΥΞ, Scatology, ΣΚΩΜΜΑ." *TAPA* 121: 157–79.

Ehlers, B. 1966. *Eine vorplatonische Deutung des sokratischen Eros: Der Dialog Aspasia des Sokratikers Aeschines.* Munich.

Ehrenberg, V. 1951. *The People of Aristophanes: A Sociology of Old Comedy.* 2d ed. Oxford.

Eitrem, S. 1944. "Les Thesmophoria, les Skirophoria et les Arrhétophoria." *Symb. Osl.* 23: 36–53.

Ellendt, F. 1872. *Lexicon Sophocleum.* Berlin.

Erbse, H. 1966. "Euripides' *Andromache*." *Hermes* 94: 276–97.

Euben, J. P., ed. 1986. *Greek Tragedy and Political Theory.* Berkeley and Los Angeles.

Fant, M., and M. Lefkowitz. 1992. *Women's Life in Greece and Rome.* 2d ed. Baltimore.

Faraone, C. A. 1985. "Aeschylus' ὕμνος δέσμιος (*Eum.* 306) and Attic Judicial Curse Tablets." *JHS* 105: 151–54.

———. 1990. "Aphrodite's ΚΕΣΤΟΣ and Apples for Atalanta: Aphrodisiacs in Early Greek Myth and Ritual." *Phoenix* 44: 219–43.

———. 1991. "The Agonistic Context of Early Greek Binding Spells." In *Magika Hiera*, edited by C. Faraone and D. Obbink, 3–32. Oxford.

———. 1992a. "Aristophanes, *Amphiaraus*, fr. 29 Kassel-Austin: Oracular Response or Erotic Incantation?" *CQ* 42: 320–27.

————. 1992b. "Sex and Power: Male-Targetting Aphrodisiacs in the Greek Magical Tradition." *Helios* 19: 92–103.

————. 1993. "The Wheel, the Whip and Other Implements of Torture: Erotic Magic in Pindar *Pythian* 4.213–19." *CJ* 89: 1–19.

————. 1994. "Deianira's Mistake and the Demise of Heracles: Erotic Magic in Sophocles' *Trachiniae*." *Helios* 21: 115–35.

Farrar, C. 1988. *The Origins of Democratic Thinking: The Invention of Politics in Classical Athens*. Cambridge.

Feld, S. 1982. *Sound and Sentiment: Birds, Weeping, Poetics, and Song in Kaluli Expression*. Philadelphia.

Ferrari, G. 1997. "Figures in the Text: Metaphors and Riddles in the *Agamemnon*." *C Phil.* 92: 1–45.

Finnegan, R. 1990. "Women in Aristophanic Comedy." *Platon* 42: 100–106.

Fishman, P. 1983. "Interaction: The Work Women Do." In Henley, Kramarae and Thorne 1983: 89–101

Fitton, J. 1967. Review of Barrett 1964. *Pegasus* 8: 17–43.

Fitzgerald, G. J. 1973. "Misconception, Hypocrisy and the Structure of Euripides' *Hippolytus*." *Ramus* 2: 20–40.

Flintoff, E. 1987. "The Treading of the Cloth." *Quaderni urbinati de cultura classica* 54: 119–30.

Fluck, H. 1931. *Skurrile Riten in griechischen Kulten*. Endingen.

Foley, H. P., ed. 1981a. *Reflections of Women in Antiquity*. New York.

————. 1981b. "The Concept of Women in Athenian Drama." In Foley 1981a: 127–68.

————. 1982. "The 'Female Intruder' Reconsidered: Women in Aristophanes' *Lysistrata* and *Ecclesiazusae*." *C Phil.* 77: 1–22.

————. 1988a. "Women in Greece." In *Civilization of the Ancient Mediterranean: Greece and Rome*, edited by M. Grant and R. Kitzinger, 1301–17. New York.

————. 1988b. "Tragedy and Politics in Aristophanes' *Acharnians*." *JHS* 1988: 33–47.

————. 1993. "The Politics of Tragic Lamentation." In Sommerstein et al. 1993: 101–43.

————, ed. 1994. *The Homeric Hymn to Demeter: Translation, Commentary, and Interpretive Essays*. Princeton.

Foucault, M. 1988. *The Use of Pleasure: The History of Sexuality*. Vol. 2. Translated by R. Hurley. New York.

Fowler, B. H. 1978. "Lyric Structures in Three Euripidean Plays." *Dioniso* 49: 15–51.

Foxhall, L. 1989. "Household, Gender and Property in Classical Athens." *CQ* 39: 22–44.

————. 1994. "Pandora Unbound: A Feminist Critique of Foucault's *History of Sexuality*." In *Dislocating Masculinity*, edited by A. Cornwall and N. Lindisfarne, 133–46. New York and London.

————. 1996. "The Law and the Lady: Women and Legal Proceedings in Classical Athens." In *Greek Law in Its Political Setting: Justifications Not Justice*, edited by L. Foxhall and A.D.E. Lewis, 133–52. Oxford.

Fraenkel, E. 1936. "Dramaturgical Problems in the *Ecclesiazusae*." In *Greek Poetry and Life*, edited by C. Bailey, E. A. Barker, C. M. Bowra, J. D. Denniston, and D. L. Page, 257–76. Oxford.

———. 1964. *Kleine Beiträge zur klassichen Philologie*. Vol. 1. Rome.

Frischer, B. D. 1978. "*Concordia Discors* and Characterization in Euripides' *Hippolytos*." *GRBS* 11: 85–100.

Funghi. 1984. *The Oxyrhynchus Papyri* 52: 1–5.

Gagarin, M. 1976. *Aeschylean Drama*. Berkeley and Los Angeles.

———. 1990. "The Nature of Proofs in Antiphon." *C Phil*. 85: 22–32.

———. 1994. "Probability and Persuasion: Plato and Early Greek Rhetoric." In Worthington 1994: 46–68.

———. Forthcoming. "Women's Voices in Attic Oratory." In *Making Silence Speak*, edited by L. McClure and A. Lardinois. Princeton.

Gager, J. 1992. *Curse Tablets and Binding Spells from the Ancient World*. Oxford and New York.

Gal, S. 1991. "Between Speech and Silence: The Problematics of Research on Language and Gender." In *Gender at the Crossroads of Knowledge*, edited by M. di Leonardo, 175–203. Berkeley and Los Angeles.

———. 1995. "Language, Gender and Power: An Anthropological Review." In Bucholtz and Hall 1995: 169–82.

Garber, M. 1992. *Vested Interests: Cross-Dressing and Cultural Anxiety*. London and New York.

Gardner, J. F. 1989. "Aristophanes and Male Anxiety: The Defence of the *Oikos*." *G&R* 36: 51–62.

Garner, R. 1987. *Law and Society in Classical Athens*. New York.

Garzya, A. 1952. "Interpretazione dell' 'Andromaca' di Euripide." *Dioniso* 14: 109–38.

Geltzer, R. 1975. "Tradition und Neuschöpfung in der Dramaturgie des Aristophanes." In Newiger 1975: 283–316.

Gernet, L. 1981. " 'Value' in Greek Myth." In *Myth, Religion and Society*, edited by R. L. Gordon, 111–46. Cambridge.

Gill, C. 1990. "The Articulation of the Self in Euripides' *Hippolytus*." In *Euripides, Women, and Sexuality*, edited by A. Powell, 76–107. London and New York.

Gilleland, M. 1980. "Female Speech in Greek and Latin." *AJPhil*. 101: 180–83.

Gilula, D. 1981. "A Consideration of Phaedra's εὔκλεια." *Sileno* 7: 121–33.

Gluckman, M. 1963. "Gossip and Scandal." *Current Anthropology* 4: 307–16.

Goebel, G. 1989. "*Andromache* 192–204: The Pattern of Argument." *C Phil*. 84: 32–35.

Goff, B. 1990. *The Noose of Words: Readings of Desire, Violence and Language in Euripides' Hippolytos*. Cambridge.

———. 1995. "Aithra at Eleusis." *Helios* 22: 65–78.

———. 1997. "Apollodorus's Imaginary Citizens." Paper delivered at the annual meeting of the American Philological Association in Chicago.

Goffmann, E. 1976. "Gender Display." *Studies in the Anthropology of Visual Communication* 3: 69–77.

Goheen, R. 1955. "Aspects of Dramatic Symbolism: Three Studies in the *Oresteia*." *AJPhil*. 76: 113–37.

Golden, M. 1985. " 'Donatus' and Athenian Phratries." *CQ* 35: 9–13.

Golder, H. 1983. "The Mute Andromache." *TAPA* 113: 123–133.

Goldhill, S. 1984a. "Two Notes on τέλος and Related Words in the *Oresteia*." *JHS* 104: 169–76.

———. 1984b. *Language, Sexuality, Narrative: The Oresteia*. Cambridge.

———. 1986. *Reading Greek Tragedy*. Cambridge.

———. 1990. "The Great Dionysia and Civic Ideology." In Winkler and Zeitlin 1990: 97–129.

———. 1991. "Comic Inversion and Inverted Commas: Aristophanes and Parody." In *The Poet's Voice*, 167–222. Cambridge.

———. 1992. *The Oresteia*. Cambridge.

———. 1994. "Representing Democracy: Women at the Great Dionysia." In *Ritual, Finance, Politics*, edited by R. Osborne and S. Hornblower, 347–69. Oxford.

———. 1997a. "The Audience of Athenian Tragedy." In Easterling 1997: 54–68.

———. 1997b. "The Language of Tragedy: Rhetoric and Communication." In Easterling 1997: 127–50.

Gould, J. 1980. "Law, Custom, and Myth: Aspects of the Social Position of Women in Classical Athens." *JHS* 100: 38–59.

Graf, F. 1974. *Eleusis und die orphische Dichtung Athens in vorhellenistischer Zeit*. Berlin.

Graham, H. F. 1947. "The Escape-Ode in *Hippolytus*." *CJ* 42: 275–76.

Greene, E. 1994. "Apostrophe and Women's Erotics in the Poetry of Sappho." *TAPA* 124: 41–56.

Greene, W. C. 1951. "The Spoken and the Written Word." *Harv. Stud.* 60: 23–59.

Gregory, J. 1990. *Euripides and the Instruction of the Athenians*. Ann Arbor.

Grene, D. 1939. "The Interpretation of the *Hippolytus* of Euripides." *C Phil.* 34: 45–58.

Griffith, M. 1995. "Brilliant Dynasts: Power and Politics in the *Oresteia*." *Classical Antiquity* 14: 62–129.

Griffith, R. D. 1988. "Disrobing in the *Oresteia*." *CQ* 82: 552–54.

Gruber, W. E. 1983. "Systematized Delerium: The Craft, Form and Meaning of Aristophanic Comedy." *Helios* 10: 97–111.

Guthrie, W.K.C. 1971. *The Sophists*. Cambridge.

Haldane, J. A. 1965a. "A Scene in the *Thesmophoriazusae* 295–371." *Philol.* 109: 39–46.

———. 1965b. "Musical Themes and Imagery in Aeschylus." *JHS* 75: 37–38.

Hall, E. 1989a. "The Archer Scene in Aristophanes' *Thesmophoriazusae*." *Philol.* 133: 38–54.

———. 1989b. *Inventing the Barbarian: Greek Self-Definition through Tragedy*. Oxford.

———. 1995. "Lawcourt Dramas: The Power of Performance in Greek Forensic Oratory." *BICS* 40: 39–58.

———. 1996. *Aeschylus Persians*. Warminster.

———. 1997. "The Sociology of Athenian Tragedy." In Easterling 1997: 93–126.

———. 1998. "Ithyphallic Males Behaving Badly; or, Satyr Drama as Gendered Tragic Ending." In *Parchments of Gender: Deciphering the Bodies of Antiquity*, edited by M. Wyke, 13–37. Oxford.

Hall, E. 1999. "Actor's Song in Tragedy." In *Performance Culture and Athenian Democracy*, edited by S. Goldhill and R. Osborne.

Halperin, D. 1990a. "The Democratic Body: Prostitution and Citizenship in Classical Athens." In *One Hundred Years of Homosexuality*, 88–112. London and New York.

———. 1990b. "Why Is Diotima a Woman?" In Halperin, Winkler, and Zeitlin 1990: 257–308.

Halperin, D., J. Winkler, and F. Zeitlin, eds. 1990. *Before Sexuality*. Princeton.

Hamilton, R. 1978. "Prologue, Prophecy and Plot in Four Plays of Euripides." *AJPhil.* 99: 277–302.

Hammond, N.G.L. 1965. "Personal Freedom and Its Limitations in the *Oresteia*." *JHS* 85: 42–43.

Hansen, H. 1976. "Aristophanes' *Thesmophoriazusae*: Theme, Structure, and Production." *Philol.* 120: 165–85.

Hansen, P. A. 1977. "The Robe Episode of the *Choephori*." *CQ* 72: 239–40.

Hanson, A. E. 1990. "The Medical Writer's Woman." In Halperin et al. 1990: 309–38.

Hardwick, L. 1993. "Philomel and Pericles: Silence in the Funeral Speech." *G&R* 40: 147–62.

Harriot, R. 1986. *Aristophanes: Poet and Dramatist*. Baltimore.

Harris, W. 1989. *Ancient Literacy*. Cambridge, Mass.

Harvey, F. D. 1966. "Literacy in the Athenian Democracy." *Rev. Ét. Grec.* 79: 585–635.

Hathorn, R. Y. 1956–57. "Rationalism and Irrationalism in Euripides' *Hippolytus*." *CJ* 52: 211–18.

Heath, M. 1987. *Political Comedy in Aristophanes*. Göttingen.

Henderson, J. 1977. "Aristophanes and the Events of 411." *JHS* 97: 112–26.

———. 1987b. "Older Women in Attic Old Comedy." *TAPA* 117: 105–29.

———. 1990. "The *Demos* and Comic Competition." In Winkler and Zeitlin 1990: 271–313.

———. 1991a. *The Maculate Muse: Obscene Language in Attic Comedy*. 2d ed. Oxford.

———. 1991b. "Women and the Athenian Dramatic Festivals." *TAPA* 121: 133–47.

———, ed. and trans. 1996. *Three Plays by Aristophanes: Staging Women*. New York and London.

Henley, N. 1977. *Body Politics: Power, Sex and Nonverbal Communication*. Englewood Cliffs, N.J.

Henley, N., and B. Thorne, eds. 1975. *Language and Sex: Difference and Dominance*. Rowley, Mass.

Henley, N., C. Kramarae, and B. Thorne, eds. 1983. *Language, Gender and Society*. Rowley, Mass.

Henry, M. 1985. *Menander's Courtesans and the Greek Comic Tradition*. Frankfurt and New York.

———. 1995. *Prisoner of History: Aspasia of Miletus and Her Biographical Tradition*. Oxford.

Herzfeld, M. 1985. *The Poetics of Manhood: Contest and Identity in a Cretan Mountain Village*. Princeton.

———. 1991. "Silence, Submission, and Subversion: Toward a Poetics of Womanhood." In *Contested Identities: Gender and Kinship in Modern Greece*, 79–97. Princeton.

Hirschon, R. 1978. "Open Body/Closed Space: The Transformation of Female Sexuality." In *Defining Females: The Nature of Women in Society*, edited by S. Ardener, 66–68. New York.

Holst-Warhaft, G. 1992. *Dangerous Voices*. London and New York.

Hulley, K. 1953. "The Prologue of the *Ecclesiazusae*," *Classical World* 46: 129–31.

Humphreys, S. 1983. *The Family, Women and Death*. London and New York.

Hunter, V. 1994. *Policing Athens: Social Control in the Attic Lawsuits, 420–320 B.C.* Princeton.

Italie, G. 1955. *Index Aeschyleus*. Leiden.

Jameson, M. 1990a. "Domestic Space in the Greek City-State." In *Domestic Architecture and the Use of Space*, edited by S. Kent, 92–113. Cambridge.

———. 1990b. "Private Space and the Greek City." In *The Greek City*, edited by O. Murray and S. Price, 171–95. Oxford.

Janko, R. 1988. "Berlin Magical Papyri 21243: A Conjecture." *ZPE* 72: 293.

Jenkins, I. D. 1985. "The Ambiguity of Greek Textiles." *Arethusa* 18: 109–54.

Jeske, J., and K. Overman. 1984. "Gender and the Official Language." *International Journal of Women's Studies* 7, 4: 322–35.

Jesperson, O. 1922. *Language, Its Nature, Development and Origin*. London.

Jocelyn, H. D. 1980. "A Greek Indecency and Its Students: ΛΑΙΚΑΖΕΙΝ." *PCPS* 26: 12–66.

Johnson, S., and U. Meinhof, eds. 1997. *Language and Masculinity*. Oxford and Cambridge, Mass.

Johnston, S. I. 1995. "The Song of the *Iynx*: Magic and Rhetoric in *Pythian* 4." *TAPA* 189: 177–206.

Jones, D. 1980. "Gossip: Notes on Women's Oral Culture." *Women's Studies International Quarterly* 3: 193–98.

Jones, J. 1962. *On Aristotle and Greek Tragedy*. Oxford.

Jordan, D. R. 1985. "A Survey of Greek Defixiones Not Included in the Special Corpora." *GRBS* 26: 151–97.

———. 1992. "The Inscribed Lead Tablet from Phalasarna." *ZPE* 94: 191–94.

Jouan, F. 1984. "Euripide et la rhétorique." *LEC* 52: 3–13.

Just, R. 1989. *Women in Athenian Law and Life*. London and New York.

Kagarow, E. 1929. *Griechische Fluchtafeln*. Leopoli.

Kaimio, M. 1977. *Characterization of Sound in Early Greek Literature*. Helsinki.

Kakridis, I. T. 1928. "Der Fluch des Theseus im *Hippolytos*." *Rh. Mus.* 77: 21–33.

Kamerbeek, J. C. 1943. "L'Andromaque d'Euripide." *Mnemos.* 11: 47–67.

Katz, M. 1994a. "The Character of Tragedy: Women and the Greek Imagination." *Arethusa* 27: 81–103.

———. 1994b. "Politics and Pomegranates Revisited." In Foley 1994: 212–42.

Kawashima, S. 1986. "ΑΙΔΩΣ and ΕΥΚΛΕΙΑ: Another Interpretation of Phaedra's Long Speech in the *Hippolytus*." *SIFC* 4: 183–94.

Keenan, E. 1974. "Norm-Makers, Norm-Breakers: Uses of Speech by Men and Women in a Malagasy Community." In *Explorations in the Ethnography of Speaking*, edited by Ed. R. Bauman and J. Sherzer, 125–43. Cambridge.

Kennedy, G. 1963. *The Art of Persuasion in Greece*. Princeton.

Kerferd, G. B. 1981. *The Sophistic Movement.* Cambridge.

Kilmer, M. 1982. "Genital Phobia and Depilation." *JHS* 102: 104–12.

Klerk, V. de. 1997. "The Role of Expletives in the Construction of Masculinity." In Johnson and Meinhof 1997: 144–58.

Knox, B.M.W. 1952. "The *Hippolytus* of Euripides." *YClS* 13: 3–31. (= Knox 1979: 205–30.)

———. 1979. *Word and Action: Essays on the Ancient Theater.* Baltimore.

Komornicka, A. 1981. "Sur le langage érotique de l'ancienne comédie attique." *Quaderni urbinati di cultura classica* 38: 35–83.

Kovacs, D. 1980a. *The Andromache of Euripides.* Chico, Calif.

———. 1980b. "Euripides' *Hippolytus* 100 and the Meaning of the Prologue." *C Phil.* 75: 130–37.

———. 1980c. "Shame, Pleasure and Honor in Phaedra's Great Speech (Euripides, *Hippolytus* 375–87)." *AJPhil.* 101: 287–303.

———. 1987. *The Heroic Muse: Studies in the* Hippolytus *and* Hecuba *of Euripides.* Baltimore.

Kramarae, C. 1981. *Women and Men Speaking.* Rowley, Mass.

Kuhns, R. 1962. *The House, the City and the Judge: The Growth of Moral Awareness in the Oresteia.* Indianapolis.

Kunstler, B. 1987. "Family Dynamics and Female Power in Ancient Sparta." *Helios* 13: 31–48.

Kurke, L. 1995. "Herodotus and the Language of Metals." *Helios* 22: 36–64.

Lacey, W. K. 1964. "Thucydides II.45.2." *PCPS* 10: 47–49.

Lakoff, R. 1973. "Language and Woman's Place." *Language in Society* 2: 45–80.

———. 1975. *Language and Woman's Place.* New York.

———. 1978. "Women's Language." In Butturff and Epstein 1978: 139–58.

Lardinois, A. 1994. "Subject and Circumstance in Sappho's Poetry." *TAPA* 124: 57–84.

Lebeck, A. 1971. *The Oresteia: A Study in Language and Structure.* Cambridge, Mass.

Leclerc, M.-C. 1993. *La parole chez Hésiode.* Paris: Belles Lettres.

Lee, K. 1975. "Euripides' *Andromache*: Observations on Form and Meaning." *Antichthon* 9: 4–16.

Lefkowitz, M. 1984. "Aristophanes and Other Historians of the Fifth-Century Theater." *Hermes* 112: 143–53.

Leitao, D. 1995. "The Perils of Leukippos: Initiatory Transvestism and Male Gender Ideology in the Ekdusia at Phaistos." *Classical Antiquity* 26: 130–63.

Lévy, E. 1976. "Les femmes chez Aristophane." *Ktéma* 1: 99–112.

Lewis, D. M. 1955. "Notes on Attic Inscriptions II, XXIII: Who Was Lysistrata?" *Annals of the British School in Athens* 1: 1–13.

Lloyd, M. 1992. *The Agon in Euripides.* Oxford.

Lloyd-Jones, H. 1970. *The Agamemnon by Aeschylus.* Englewood Cliffs, N.J.

———. 1975. *Females of the Species.* London.

Longo, O. 1990. "The Theater of the Polis." In Winkler and Zeitlin 1990: 12–19.

Loraux, N. 1978. "Sur la race des femmes et quelques-unes des ses tribus." *Arethusa* 11: 43–87.

———. 1981. "Le lit, la guerre." *L'Homme* 21: 37–67.

———. 1985. "La cité, l' historien, les femmes." *Pallas* 32: 7–39.

——. 1986. *The Invention of Athens.* Translated by A. Sheridan. Cambridge, Mass.

——. 1987. *Tragic Ways of Killing a Woman.* Translated by A. Forster. Cambridge, Mass.

——. 1993. *The Children of Athena.* Translated by C. Levine. Princeton.

Luschnig, C.A.E. 1980. "Men and Gods in Euripides' *Hippolytus.*" *Ramus* 9: 89–100.

——. 1983. "The Value of Ignorance in *Hippolytus.*" *AJPhil.* 104: 115–23.

——. 1988. *Time Holds a Mirror: A Study of Knowledge in Euripides'* Hippolytus. Leiden.

Maas, P. 1944. "ΕΠΕΝΙΚΤΟΣ." *Hesperia* 13: 36–37.

——. 1962. *Greek Meter.* Translated by H. Lloyd-Jones. Oxford.

MacDowell, D. M. 1978. *The Law in Classical Athens.* Ithaca, N.Y.

Macleod, C. W. 1975. "Clothing in the *Oresteia* I." *Maia* 27: 201–3.

Maltomini, F. 1988. "*P.berol.* 21243 formulario magico: Due nuove letture." *ZPE* 74: 247–48.

Martin, R. 1989. *The Language of Heroes.* Ithaca, N.Y.

Martino, F. de, and A. Sommerstein, eds. 1995. *Lo spettacolo delle voci.* Bari.

Mastronarde, D. 1990. "Actors on High." *Classical Antiquity* 9: 247–94.

McClure, L. 1995. "Female Speech and Characterization in Euripides." In de Martino and Sommerstein 1995: 35–60.

——. 1997a. "Clytemnestra's Binding Song: A. *Ag.* 958–974." *CJ* 92: 123–40.

——. 1997b. "*Gunaikos Logos:* Speech, Gender and Spectatorship in Aeschylus' *Oresteia.*" *Helios* 24: 112–35.

McLeish, K. 1980. *The Theatre of Aristophanes.* New York.

Meltzer, G. 1996. "The 'Just Voice' as Paradigmatic Metaphor in Euripides' *Hippolytus.*" *Helios* 23: 173–90.

Michelini, A. 1987. *Euripides and the Tragic Tradition.* Madison, Wis.

Miller, A. P. 1973. "Studies in Sicilian Epigraphy: An Opisthographic Lead Tablet." Diss., Chapel Hill.

Mills, S., ed. 1995. *Language and Gender: Interdisciplinary Perspectives.* New York.

Mitchell, R. 1991. "Miasma, Mimesis and Scapegoating in Euripides' *Hippolytus.*" *Classical Antiquity* 10: 97–122.

Momigliano, A. 1971. "La libertà di parola nel mondo antico." *Rivista storica Italiana* 83: 499–524.

Monsacré, H. 1984. *Les Larmes d' Achille: Les héros, la femme et la suffrance dans la poésie d' Homère.* Paris.

Moreau, A. 1976–77. "L'Oeil maléfique dans l'oeuvre d' Eschyle." *Rev. Ét. Anc.* 78–79: 56–57.

Moritz, H. 1979. "Refrain in Aeschylus: Literary Adaptation of Traditional Form." *C Phil.* 74: 187–213.

Mossé, C. 1991. "Women in the Spartan Revolutions of the Third Century B.C." In Pomeroy 1991: 138–53.

Mossman, J. M. 1996. "Waiting for Neoptolemus: The Unity of Euripides' *Andromache.*" *G&R* 93: 143–56.

Muecke, F. 1977. "Playing with the Play: Theatrical Self-consciousness in Aristophanes." *Antichthon* 11: 52–67.

——. 1982a. "A Portrait of the Artist as a Young Woman." *CQ* 32: 41–55.

Muecke, F. 1982b. " 'I Know You—By Your Rags': Costume and Disguise in Fifth-Century Drama." *Antichthon* 16: 17–34.

Muellner, L. 1976. *The Meaning of Homeric EYCHOMAI through Its Formulas.* Institut für Sprachwissenschaft des Universität. Innsbruck.

Murnaghan, S. 1988a. "Body and Voice in Greek Tragedy." *Yale Journal of Criticism* 1: 23–43.

———. 1988b. "How a Woman Can Be More Like a Man: The Dialogue between Ischomachus and His Wife in Xenophon's *Oeconomicus.*" *Helios* 15: 9–22.

Murphy, C. T. 1938. "Aristophanes and the Art of Rhetoric." *HSCP* 49: 69–113.

Musarillo, H. 1974. "The Problem of Lying and Deceit and the Two Voices of Euripides' *Hippolytus* 925–931." *TAPA* 104: 231–38.

Nancy, C. 1984. "Euripide et le partie des femmes." *Quaderni urbinati di cultura classica* 46: 111–36.

Nestle, W. 1901. *Euripides: Der Dichter der griechischen Aufklärung.* Stuttgart.

Neustadt, E. 1929. "Wort und Geschehen in Aischylos *Agamemnon.*" *Hermes* 64: 243–65.

Newiger, H. J., ed. 1975. *Aristophanes und die alte Komödie.* Darmstadt.

———. 1980. "War and Peace in the Comedies of Aristophanes." *YCIS* 26: 219–37.

Nilsson, M. 1955. *Geschichte der griechischen Religion.* 2 vols. Munich.

Norsa, M. 1927. "Frammenti di un inno di Philokos." *SIFC* 5: 87–92

North, H. 1977. "The Mare, the Vixen, and the Bee: *Sophrosyne* as the Virtue of Women in Antiquity." *ICS* 2: 35–48.

Ober, J. 1989. *Mass and Elite in Democratic Athens.* Princeton.

Ober, J., and B. Strauss. 1990. "Drama, Political Rhetoric, and the Discourse of Athenian Democracy." In Winkler and Zeitlin 1990: 237–70.

Oeri, H. 1948. *Der Typ der komischen in der griechischen Komödie.* Basel.

Olender, M. 1990. "Aspects of Baubo: Ancient Texts and Contexts." In Halperin et al. 1990: 83–113.

Olson, S. D. 1987. "The Identity of the Δεσπότης at *Ecclesiazusae* 1128f." *GRBS* 28: 161–66.

———. 1988. "The 'Love Duet' in Aristophanes' *Ecclesiazusae.*" *CQ* 38: 328–30.

Orban, M. 1981a. "*Hippolyte:* Palinode ou revanche?" *LEC* 49: 3–17.

———. 1981b. "*Hippolyte:* Souffrir pour comprendre." *LEC* 49: 193–212.

Østerud, S. 1970. "Who Sings the Monody 669–79 in Euripides' *Hippolytus?*" *GRBS* 11: 307–20.

Ostwald, M. 1986. *From Popular Sovereignty to the Sovereignty of Law: Law, Society, and Politics in Fifth Century Athens.* Berkeley and Los Angeles.

———. 1990. "*Nomos* and *Phusis* in Antiphon's Περὶ Ἀληθείας." In *Cabinet of the Muses: Essays on Classical and Comparative Literature in Honor of Thomas G. Rosenmeyer,* edited by M. Griffith and D. Mastronarde, 293–306. Atlanta.

Padel, R. 1993. "Women: Model for Possession by Daemons." In *Images of Women in Antiquity,* edited by A. Cameron and A. Kuhrt, 3–19. Detroit.

Page, D. 1936. "The Elegiacs in Euripides' *Andromache.*" In *Greek Poetry and Life,* edited by C. Bailey, E. A. Barber, C. M. Bowra, J. D. Denniston, and D. L. Page, 206–30. Oxford.

———. 1942. *Select Papyri.* Vol. 3. Cambridge, Mass.

Parke, H. W. 1977. *Festivals of the Athenians*. Ithaca, N.Y.

Parker, L.P.E. 1997. *The Songs of Aristophanes*. Oxford.

Parker, R. 1983. *Miasma: Pollution and Purification in Early Greek Religion*. Oxford.

Parry, A. 1956. "The Language of Achilles." *TAPA* 87: 1–7.

Parry, H. 1966. "The Second Stasimon of Euripides' *Hippolytus*." *TAPA* 97: 320–26.

Patterson, C. 1987. "*Hai Attikai:* The Other Athenians." *Helios* 13: 49–67.

Peradotto, J. 1964. "Some Patterns of Nature Imagery in the *Oresteia*." *AJPhil.* 85: 378–93.

———. 1969. "Cledonomancy in the *Oresteia*." *AJPhil.* 90: 1–21.

Philips, S., and A. Reynolds. 1987. "The Interaction of Variable Syntax and Discourse Structure in Women's and Men's Speech." In Philips, Steele, and Tanz 1987: 71–94.

Philips, S., S. Steele, and C. Tanz, eds. 1987. *Language, Gender and Sex in Comparative Perspective*. Cambridge.

Phillippo, S. 1995. "Family Ties: Significant Patronymics in Euripides' *Andromache*." *CQ* 45: 355–71.

Pickard-Cambridge, Sir A. 1962. *Dithyramb, Tragedy and Comedy*. Oxford.

———. 1991. *The Dramatic Festivals of Athens*. 2d ed. Oxford.

Pigeaud, J. 1976. "Euripide et la connaissance de soi: Quelques réflexions sur *Hippolyte* 73 à 82 et 373 à 430." *LEC* 44: 3–24.

Pintacuda, M. 1978. *La musica nella tragedia greca*. Maggio.

Podlecki, A. 1966. "The Power of the Word in Sophocles' *Philoctetes*." *GRBS* 7: 233–50.

———. 1990. "Could Women Attend the Theater in Ancient Athens? A Collection of Testimonia." *Ancient World* 21: 27–43.

Pollitt, J. J. 1972. *Art and Experience in Classical Athens*. Cambridge.

Pomeroy, S., ed. 1991. *Women's History and Ancient History*. Chapel Hill.

Prins, Y. 1991. "The Power of the Speech Act: Aeschylus' Furies and Their Binding Song." *Arethusa* 24: 177–95.

Pucci, P. 1977a. *Hesiod and the Language of Poetry*. Baltimore.

———. 1977b. "Euripides: The Monument and the Sacrifice." *Arethusa* 10: 165–95.

Putnam, M. 1960. "*Throna* and Sappho 1.1." *CJ* 56: 79–83.

Rabinowitz, N. S. 1984. "Proliferating Triangles: Euripides' *Andromache* and the Traffic in Women." *Mosaic* 17: 111–25.

———. 1986. "Aphrodite and the Audience: Engendering the Reader." *Arethusa* 19: 171–85.

———. 1987. "Female Speech and Female Sexuality: Euripides' *Hippolytos* as Model." *Helios* 13: 127–40.

———. 1993. *Anxiety Veiled: Euripides and the Traffic in Women*. Ithaca, N.Y.

———. 1994. "The Male Actor of Greek Tragedy: Evidence of Misogyny or Gender-Bending?" *Didaskalia* suppl. 1. Proceedings from the Conference "How Is It Played? Genre, Performance, Meaning," Texas A & M University, October 1994.

Raheja, G. 1996. "The Limits of Patriliny: Kinship, Gender and Women's Speech

Practices in Rural North India." In *Gender, Kinship, Power: A Comparative and Interdisciplinary History*, edited by M. J. Maynes, A. Waltner, B. Soland, and U. Strasser, 149–74. New York and London.

Rau, P. 1967. *Paratragoedia: Untersuchung einer komischen Form des Aristophanes*. Munich.

Rayor, D. 1993. "Korinna: Gender and the Narrative Tradition." *Arethusa* 26: 219–31.

Reckford, K. 1972. "Phaëthon, Hippolytus and Aphrodite." *TAPA* 103: 405–32.

———. 1973. "Phaedra and Pasiphaë: The Pull Backward." *TAPA* 104: 307–28.

———. 1987. *Aristophanes' Old-and-New Comedy*. Chapel Hill.

Redfield, J. 1977–78. "The Women of Sparta." *CJ* 73: 146–61.

Reinhardt, K. 1960. "Die Sinneskrise bei Euripides." In *Tradition und Geist*, 227–56. Göttingen.

Reisman, K. 1974. "Contrapuntal Conversation in an Antiguan Village." In *Explorations in the Ethnography of Speaking*, edited by R. Bauman and J. Sherzer, 110–24. Cambridge.

Richlin, A. 1991. "Zeus and Metis: Foucault, Feminism, Classics." *Helios* 18: 160–79.

Rivier, A. 1958. "Euripide et Pasiphaé." In *Lettres d' Occident: Études et essais offerts à André Bonnard*, edited by G. Anex and A. Rivier, 51–74. Neuchâtel.

Robertson, D. 1923. "Euripides and Tharyps." *CR* 37: 58–60.

Robertson, H. G. 1939. "Legal Expressions and Ideas of Justice in Aeschylus." *C Phil.* 34: 209–19.

Romilly, J. de. 1975. *Magic and Rhetoric in Ancient Greece*. Cambridge, Mass.

Rosellini, M. 1979. "*Lysistrata*: Une Mise en scène de la féminité." *Les Cahiers de Fontenay* 17: 11–32.

Rosenmeyer, P. 1991. "Simonides' Danaë Fragment Reconsidered." *Arethusa* 24: 5–29.

———. 1996. "Love Letters in Callimachus, Ovid and Aristaenetus, or the Sad Fate of a Mailorder Bride." *MD* 36: 9–31.

Rosivach, V. J. 1994. *The System of Public Sacrifice in Fourth-Century Athens*. Atlanta.

Rothwell, K. S. 1990. *Politics and Persuasion in Aristophanes'* Ecclesiazusae. Leiden.

Ruck, Carl P. 1975. "Euripides' Mother: Vegetables and the Phallos in Aristophanes." *Arion*, n.s. 2: 13–57.

Saïd, S. 1979. "L'Assemblée des femmes: Les Femmes, l' économie et la politique." *Les Cahiers de Fontenay* 17: 33–69.

———. 1987. "Travestis et travestissements dans les comédies d' Aristophane." *Cahiers du group interdisciplinaire du théâtre antique* 3: 217–47.

Saxonhouse, Arlene. 1992. *Fear of Diversity: The Birth of Political Science in Ancient Greek Thought*. Chicago.

Scarpi, P. 1976. *Letture sulla religione classica: L'Inno Omerico a Demeter*. Florence.

Schaps, D. 1977. "The Woman Least Mentioned: Etiquette and Women's Names." *CQ* 27: 323–30.

Schein, S. 1982. "The Cassandra Scene in Aeschylus' *Agamemnon*." *G&R* 29: 11–16.

Schmid, W., and O. Stählin. 1929–48. *Geschichte der griechischen Literatur*. Vols. 1–5. Munich.

Schwabl, H. 1966. *Hesiods Theogonie: Eine unitarische Analyse*. Vienna.

Scott, W. 1984. *Musical Design in Aeschylean Theater*. Hanover and London.

Seager, R. 1983. "Aristophanes' *Thes*. 493–496 and the Comic Possibilities of Garlic." *Philol*. 77: 138–42.

Séchan, L. 1911. "La Légende d'Hippolyte dans l'antiquité." *Rev. Ét. Grec*. 24: 105–51.

Segal, C. 1962. "Gorgias and the Psychology of the Logos." *HSCP* 66: 99–155.

———. 1965. "The Tragedy of the *Hippolytus*: The Waters of Ocean and the Untouched Meadow." *HSCP* 70: 117–69.

———. 1969. "Euripides' *Hippolytos* 108–112, Tragic Irony and Tragic Justice." *Hermes* 97: 297–305.

———. 1970. "Shame and Purity in Euripides' *Hippolytus*." *Hermes* 98: 278–99.

———. 1972. "Curse and Oath in *Hippolytus*." *Ramus* 1: 165–80.

———. 1974. "Eros and Incantation: Sappho and Oral Poetry." *Arethusa* 7: 139–60.

———. 1979. "Solar Imagery and Tragic Heroism in Euripides' *Hippolytos*." In *Arkturos: Hellenic Studies Presented to B.M.W. Knox*, edited by G. M. Bowerstock, W. Burkert, and M. Putnam, 151–82. Berlin and New York.

———. 1988a. "Theatre, Ritual and Commemoration in Euripides' *Hippolytus*." *Ramus* 17: 52–74.

———. 1988b. "Confusion and Concealment in Euripides' *Hippolytus*: Vision, Hope and Tragic Knowledge." *Métis* 3: 263–82.

———. 1992. "Signs, Magic, and Letters in Euripides' *Hippolytus*." In *Innovations of Antiquity*, edited by R. Hexter and D. Selden, 420–56. London and New York.

———. 1993. *Euripides and the Poetics of Sorrow*. Durham, N.C.

———. 1995. *Sophocles' Tragic World*. Cambridge, Mass.

Seremetakis, C. N. 1991. *The Last Word: Women, Death and Divination in Inner Mani*. Chicago.

Sevieri, R. 1991. "Linguaggio consapevole e coscienza individuale di Clitennestra nell' Agamennone di Eschilo." *Dioniso* 61: 13–31.

Shaw, M. 1975. "The Female Intruder: Women in Fifth-Century Drama." *C Phil*. 70: 255–66.

Sherzer, J. 1987. "A Diversity of Voices: Men's and Women's Speech in Ethnographic Perspective." In Philips, Steele, and Tanz 1987: 95–120.

Simon, E. 1983. *Festivals of Attica: An Archaeological Commentary*. Madison, Wis.

Sinclair, R. 1988. *Democracy and Participation in Athens*. Cambridge.

Skinner, M. A. 1987. "Greek Women and the Mêtronymic: A Note on an Epigram by Nossis." *Ancient History Bulletin* 19: 39–42.

———. 1991. "Nossis Thêlyglôssos: The Private Text and the Public Book." In Pomeroy 1991: 20–47.

———. 1993. "Woman and Language in Archaic Greece, or, Why Is Sappho a Woman?" In *Feminist Theory and the Classics*, edited by N. Rabinowitz and A. Richlin, 125–44. London and New York.

———. 1996. "Zeus and Leda: The Sexuality Wars in Contemporary Classical Scholarship." *Thamyris* 3: 103–23.

Slater, N. 1985. "Vanished Players: Two Classical Reliefs and Theatre History." *GRBS* 26: 333–44.

———. 1989. "Lekythoi in Aristophanes' *Ecclesiazusae.*" *Lexis* 3: 43–51.

———. 1990. "The Idea of the Actor." In Winkler and Zeitlin 1990: 385–96.

———. 1997. "Waiting in the Wings: Aristophanes' *Ecclesiazusae.*" *Arion* 5: 97–129.

Smith, W. D. 1960. "Staging the Central Scene of the *Hippolytus.*" *TAPA* 91: 162–77.

Snyder, J. M. 1974. "Aristophanes' Agathon as Anacreon." *Hermes* 102: 244–46.

Solmsen, F. 1973. "Bad Shame and Related Problems in Phaedra's Speech (Eur. Hipp. 380–388)." *Hermes* 101: 420–25.

Sommerstein, A. 1980. "The Naming of Women in Greek and Roman Comedy." *Quaderni di storia* 11: 393–418.

———. 1984. "Aristophanes and the Demon Poverty." *CQ* 34: 314–33.

———. 1995. "The Language of Athenian Women." In de Martino and Sommerstein 1995: 61–85.

Sommerstein, A., S. Halliwell, J. Henderson, and B. Zimmerman, eds. 1993. *Tragedy, Comedy and the Polis.* Bari.

Sörbon, G. 1966. *Mimesis and Art, Studies in the Origin and Early Development of an Aesthetic Vocabulary.* Stockholm.

Sorum, C. 1995. "Euripides' Judgment: Literary Creation in *Andromache.*" *AJPhil.* 116: 371–88.

Spacks, P. M. 1985. *Gossip.* New York.

Stallybrass, P. 1986. "Patriarchal Territories: The Body Enclosed." In *Rewriting the Renaissance: The Discourses of Sexual Difference in Early Modern Europe,* edited by M. Ferguson, M. Quilligan, and N. Vickers, 123–42. Chicago.

Stanford, W. B. 1937. "Γυναικὸς ἀνδρόβουλον ἐλπίζον κέαρ." *CQ* 31: 92–93.

———. 1942. *Aeschylus in His Style.* Dublin.

———. 1967. *The Sound of Greek: Studies in the Greek Theory and Practice of Euphony.* Berkeley and Los Angeles.

Stehle, E. [Stigers.] 1981. "Sappho's Private World." In Foley 1981a: 45–61.

———. 1990. "Sappho's Gaze." *Differences* 2: 88–125.

———. 1997. *Performance and Gender in Ancient Greece.* Princeton.

Steidle, W. 1968. *Studien zum antiken Drama unter besonderer Berücksichtigung des Bühnenspiels.* Studia et Testimonia Antiqua 4. Munich.

Stone, L. 1981. *Costume in Aristophanic Comedy.* New York.

Storey, I. 1989. "Domestic Disharmony in Euripides' *Andromache.*" *G&R* 36: 16–27.

Strauss, L. 1966. *Socrates and Aristophanes.* Chicago.

Sultan, N. 1993. "Private Speech, Public Pain: The Power of Women's Laments in Ancient Greek Poetry and Tragedy." In *Rediscovering the Muses,* edited by K. Marshall, 92–110. Boston.

Sutton, D. F. 1989. "A Handlist of Satyr Plays." In *Satyrspiel,* edited by B. von Seidensticker, 287–331. Darmstadt.

Taaffe, L. 1993. *Aristophanes and Women.* London and New York.

Taillardat, J. 1965. *Les Images d'Aristophane.* Paris.

Tambiah, S. J. 1968. "The Magical Power of Words." *Man* 3: 175–208.

Tannen, D. 1996. *Gender and Discourse.* Oxford.

Taplin, O. 1977. *The Stagecraft of Aeschylus: The Dramatic Use of Exits and Entrances in Greek Tragedy*. Oxford.

———. 1978. *Greek Tragedy in Action*. Berkeley and Los Angeles.

———. 1980. "The Shield of Achilles within the *Iliad*." *G&R* 27: 1–21.

———. 1986. "Fifth-Century Tragedy and Comedy: A *Synkrisis*." *JHS* 106: 163–74.

Thalmann, W. 1985a. "Speech and Silence in the *Oresteia* 1: *Agamemnon* 1025–1029." *Phoenix* 39: 99–117.

———. 1985b. "Speech and Silence in the *Oresteia* 2." *Phoenix* 39: 221–37

Thomas, R. 1989. *Oral Tradition and Written Record in Classical Athens*. Cambridge.

Thompson, D'Arcy. 1936. *A Glossary of Greek Birds*. Oxford.

Thomson, G. 1966. *The Oresteia of Aeschylus*. Vol. 1. Amsterdam.

Turato, F. 1976. "Seduzione della parola e dramma dei segni nell' Ippolito di Eurpide." *Bollettino dell' Istituto filogia greca* 3: 159–83.

Turner, V. 1995. *The Ritual Process: Structure and Anti-Structure*. New York.

Ussher, R. G. 1969. "The Staging of the *Ecclesiazusae*." *Hermes* 97: 22–37.

Vellacott, P. 1976. *Ironic Drama: A Study of Euripides' Method and Meaning*. Cambridge.

Vermeule, E. 1974. *Aspects of Death in Early Greek Art and Poetry*. Berkeley and Los Angeles.

Vernant, J.-P. 1988. "Tensions and Ambiguities in Greek Tragedy." In Vernant and P. Vidal-Naquet 1988: 29–48.

Vernant, J.-P., and P. Vidal-Naquet. 1972. *Mythe et tragédie en Grèce ancienne*. Paris.

———. 1988. *Myth and Tragedy in Ancient Greece*. Translated by J. Lloyd. New York.

Versnel, H. 1993. "The Roman Festival for Bona Dea and the Greek Thesmophoria." In *Inconsistencies in Greek and Roman Religion*, vol. 2, *Transition and Reversal in Myth and Ritual*, 228–88. Leiden.

Vickers, M. 1989. "Alcibiades on Stage: *Thesmophoriazousae* and *Helen*." *Historia* 38: 41–65.

Waern, I. 1960. "Greek Lullabies." *Eranos* 58: 1–8.

Walker, S. 1993. "Women and Housing in Classical Greece: The Archaeological Evidence." In *Images of Women in Antiquity*, edited by A. Cameron and A. Kuhrt, 2d ed., 81–91. Detroit.

Walsh, G. B. 1984. *The Varieties of Enchantment*. Chapel Hill, N.C.

Webster, T.B.L. 1950. *Studies in Later Greek Comedy*. Manchester.

———. 1967. *The Tragedies of Euripides*. London.

Weedon, C. 1987. *Feminist Practice and Poststructuralist Theory*. Oxford.

Weill, N. 1966. "Adôniazousai ou les femmes sur le toit." *BCH* 90: 664–98.

West, C., and D. Zimmerman. 1983. "Small Insults: A Study of Interruptions in Cross-Sex Conversations between Unacquainted Persons." In Henley, Kramarae, and Thorne 1983: 102–17.

West, M. L. 1974. *Studies in Greek Elegy and Iambus*. Berlin and New York.

Whallon, W. 1980. *Problem and Spectacle: Studies in the Oresteia*. Heidelberg.

White, R. 1975. *The Interpretation of Dreams: The Oneirocritica of Artemidorus*. Park Ridge, N.J.

Whitman, C. 1964. *Aristophanes and the Comic Hero*. Cambridge, Mass.

Wilamowitz-Moellendorff, Ulrich von, ed. 1891. *Euripides' Hippolytos*. Berlin.

———. 1893. *Aristoteles und Athen*. Vol. 2. Berlin.

———. 1925. "Lesefrüchte." *Hermes* 60: 280–316. (= *Kleine Schriften* 4: 368–403.)

———. 1927. "Lesefrüchte." *Hermes* 62: 276–98. (= *Kleine Schriften* 4: 431–453.)

Williamson, M. 1995. "Sappho and the Other Woman." In Mills 1995: 76–94.

Willink, C. W. 1968. "Some Problems of Text and Interpretation in the *Hippolytus*." *CQ* 18: 11–43.

Winkler, J. J. 1990a. *The Constraints of Desire: The Anthropology of Sex and Gender in Ancient Greece*. London and New York.

———. 1990b. "The Ephebe's Song." In Winkler and Zeitlin 1990: 20–62.

Winkler, J. J., and F. Zeitlin, eds. 1990. *Nothing to Do with Dionysos?* Princeton.

Winnington-Ingram, R. P. 1948. "Clytemnestra and the Vote of Athena." *JHS* 68: 130–47.

———. 1960. "*Hippolytus*: A Study in Causation." In *Euripide*, edited by O. Réverdin, *Entretiens*, Fondation Hardt, 169–97. Zurich.

———. 1969. "Poiētēs Sophos." *Arethusa* 2: 127–42.

Wit-Tak, Thalien. 1968. "The Function of Obscenity in Aristophanes' *Thesmophoriazusae* and *Ecclesiazusae*." *Mnemos.* 21: 357–65.

Worthington, I., ed. 1994. *Persuasion: Greek Rhetoric in Action*. London and New York.

Wünsch, R. 1897. *Defixionum tabellae Atticae*. Appendix to *Inscriptiones Graecae*, Vol. 3. Berlin.

Zeitlin, F. 1965. "The Motif of the Corrupted Sacrifice in Aeschylus' *Oresteia*." *TAPA* 96: 463–508.

———. 1966 "Postscript." *TAPA* 97: 645–53.

———. 1981. "Travesties of Gender and Genre in Aristophanes' *Thesmophoriazusae*." In Foley 1981a: 169–217.

———. 1982. "Cultic Models of the Female: Rites of Dionysus and Demeter." *Arethusa* 15: 129–57.

———. 1984. "The Dynamics of Misogyny in the *Oresteia*." In *Women in the Ancient World: The Arethusa Papers*, edited by J. Peradotto and J. P. Sullivan, 159–91. Buffalo, N.Y.

———. 1985a. "Playing the Other: Theater, Theatricality, and the Feminine in Greek Drama." *Representations* 11: 63–94.

———. 1985b. "The Power of Aphrodite: Eros and the Boundaries of the Self in the *Hippolytus*." In *Directions in Euripidean Criticism*, edited by P. Burian, 52–111. Durham, NC.

———. 1990. "Playing the Other: Theater, Theatricality, and the Feminine in Greek Drama." In Winkler and Zeitlin 1990: 63–96.

———. 1996. *Playing the Other: Gender and Society in Classical Greek Literature*. Chicago.

Zweig, Bella. 1992. "The Mute Nude Female Characters in Aristophanes' Plays." In *Pornography and Representation in Greece and Rome*, edited by A. Richlin, 73–89. Oxford and New York.

INDEX